WORLD HUNGER

A Reference Handbook

WORLD HUNGER

A Reference Handbook

Patricia L. Kutzner

Executive Director,
World Hunger Education Service

CONTEMPORARY WORLD ISSUES

ABC-CLIO

Santa Barbara, California
Oxford, England

Library of Congress Cataloging-in-Publication Data

Kutzner, Patricia L.
    World hunger: a reference handbook / Patricia L. Kutzner.
        p. cm. — (Contemporary world issues)
    Includes bibliographical references and index.
    Summary: Gives a broad overview of the many dimensions of world
    hunger, focusing specifically on the context of economic, social,
    political, and scientific constraints that affect global food security.
        1. Food supply. 2. Poor—Nutrition. 3. Malnutrition. 4. Hunger.
    5. Starvation. 6. Famines. 7. Food relief. 8. Agricultural assistance.
    [1. Hunger. 2. Food supply.]   I. Title. II. Series.
        HD9000.5.K883 1991   363.8—dc20   90-25185

ISBN 0-87436-558-9 (alk. paper)

98 97 96 95 94 93 92 91   10 9 8 7 6 5 4 3 2 1

ABC-CLIO, Inc.
130 Cremona Drive, P.O. Box 1911
Santa Barbara, California 93116-1911

This book is printed on acid-free paper ∞ .
Manufactured in the United States of America

Contents

Preface

WITH MORE THAN ENOUGH FOOD in the world to feed everyone, hundreds of millions of men, women, and children still go hungry. Surely we can make the world work better than this.

That challenge is the subject of *World Hunger:* how the task of ending world hunger is currently understood, how such understanding has evolved in recent decades, how key events and people contributed to this evolution, and what now is the thrust of expert consensus on future action.

The book's threefold message is simple. First, world hunger *can* be ended and therefore it must be ended; to allow it to continue would be unconscionable. Second, although the goal is now within reach for the first time in history, achieving it will require complex and difficult choices at many levels of human action and organization. Finally, to succeed at all, we must see the obstacles and options clearly and know what we're doing. None of this is as easy as it may sound.

Humanity has not always had abundant food. The scourge of hunger has plagued human existence throughout history. No era has passed without starvation and famine, and until rather recently, societies blessed with well-fed populations and long periods of plenty have been exceptional.

Since the mid-1970s, international dialogue on the world hunger issue has named food security as the goal. In the language of that dialogue, food security has a specific meaning: "access by everyone at all times to enough food to sustain an active life." At the beginning of this century, few thoughtful students of political economy within and among nations dared imagine that such all-encompassing food security could become a reasonable demand to make of public policy. Most observers of history would have viewed the availability of food for all people at all times as little short of miraculous and therefore an absurd expectation. Today, however, that very objective is advocated in sober seriousness to governments and the international development community by practical men and women the world over. In recent decades a few developing societies, in fact, have accomplished or come very close to accomplishing that remarkable feat, proving that it can be done despite meager wealth.

Even in the presence of adequate natural resources, however, knowledge and technology cannot end hunger without the power and freedom to apply their potential to that purpose. The exercise of power and freedom to apply knowledge, technology, and natural resources in ways that end hunger is, in turn, a political, economic, and social question, while determination to so act is a question of value judgments and belief systems. In the end, sufficient political will must be forged out of power, freedom, and determination if food security for all people is to become an effective priority, nationally and internationally.

These and other questions at the heart of the problem of world hunger, as it has been viewed since the 1960s, are explored in the opening chapter. The overview of the issue is divided into two parts, "Seeing the Problem" and "Seeking Solutions." Throughout the chapter and those that follow, the kind of perspective is sought that combines the viewpoints of hunger's victims with expertise and experience from many different professional disciplines. Only with such a perspective, the author is convinced, can we hope to grasp the hunger problem and its solutions clearly in all their complex reality.

Chapter 2 presents a chronology of significant events from 1940 through 1989. The world food crisis of 1972–1974 and the United Nations World Food Conference of 1974 are pivotal in current global understanding and response to hunger, but the roots of the problem and efforts to address it go back much earlier in time, earlier than 1940, although that is where this account starts. Events related to the Second World War gave birth to the Food and Agriculture Organization of the United Nations, instigated the overwhelming majority of private voluntary institutions still involved in the hunger issue, and gave unprecedented impetus to nutrition research, including the landmark Minnesota study of starvation in which American conscientious objectors to military service served as guinea pigs. The massive international relief effort to prevent starvation in Europe in the late 1940s under the aegis of the United Nations—unprecedented in scope—prefigures global cooperation to end food crises in Asia and Africa in the 1960s, 1970s, and 1980s. Bilateral assistance agencies now active in the hunger picture all arose during the Cold War decades of the 1950s and 1960s when political and economic dialogue added "international development," "the third world," "development strategies," "development assistance," "trickle down," and many other terms to the vocabulary of the hunger issue, while mass media made "population explosion" and "Green Revolution" household words. The chronology shows that consensus on the implications of these new concepts continued to change during the 1970s and 1980s, as yet newer concepts replaced or joined older ones in the evolving dialogue on hunger.

Chapter 3 sketches some of the most significant actors in that evolving dialogue, men and women who approach hunger from many different directions and work in diverse arenas. For reasons of space, the selection here is limited to people actively influencing policy and public understanding of the issues within the past two decades.

Chapter 4 presents additional facts and data related to significant topics identified by the first chapter's overview. Chapter 5 describes those agencies within the United Nations system directly involved with matters of food security and the principal governmental and nongovernmental organizations in the United States engaged in research, problem analysis, and policy advocacy concerned specifically with hunger. Chapter 6 provides an annotated bibliography of books and periodicals of particular value for further study and research, and Chapter 7 offers a similar guide to electronic references, educational films, and other audiovisual resources. The book concludes with a glossary of acronyms and major terms.

The author thanks the Food and Agriculture Organization of the United Nations, the United Nations Children's Fund, the United Nations Population Fund, the World Bank, the Population Reference Bureau, and the Economic Research Service of the U.S. Department of Agriculture for permission to reprint the charts and figures appearing in chapter 4.

Principal funding for research came from the Presiding Bishop's Fund for World Relief of the Episcopal Church, the Anna H. and Elizabeth M. Chase Fund of Philadelphia Yearly Meeting of the Society of Friends, the Division of World Hunger of the Iowa Board of Global Ministries of the United Methodist Church, and the board of directors of World Hunger Education Service.

Many individuals who made this book possible deserve acknowledgment: Heather Cameron, who insisted that it be written, and Judyl Mudfoot, who painstakingly labored to be sure it was done right; Nancy Marvel, James and Margery Akins, Julie Burland, Kithe Durand, Bartlett Harvey, Anne Hollingshead, Evelyn and Albert Moorman, Andrew Rice, and Irene Tinker, all of whom provided early support and encouragement without which the first steps on the long journey might never have been taken; Sandra Amis, Emayeneme Etta, and Robbyn Swan, who volunteered help at critical junctures; and Preston and Ann Browning, Billie Day, Kathlin Smith, and especially Phillip Hesser, providers of extraordinary support in the most difficult part of the project who ensured the journey's completion.

Finally, recognition is due to a host of unnamed associates in the work of World Hunger Education Service over the course of the past fourteen years. Every page here owes a debt to the resources for research and interpretation that their efforts made possible: the reference library; the network of contacts on the front lines of policy research and advocacy; and the priceless exposure to ideas and information that came as the chief perquisite of the author's office as executive director. In the deepest sense, this is their book.

1

Overview of the World Hunger Problem

Seeing the Problem

Men and women on the farms of Asia, Africa, and Latin America produced more than half of all the grain harvested in the world in the 1989/90 crop year: 95 percent of the rice, 42 percent of the wheat, and 34 percent of grains such as maize, sorghum, and millet, called "coarse grains" in the language of the international grain trade.[1] At the same time, despite ample world food supplies, at least half a billion people in those regions, about 10 percent of the earth's population, lacked enough food to eat, while another half billion lived at constant risk of hunger.

The food missing in the daily lives of these millions comes to a very small part of the world's annual harvest. A calculation for the 1987/88 crop year, for example, estimated that merely 15 to 20 million tons of grain that year would have eliminated the hunger of 750 million underfed people.[2] This quantity amounted to only 2 percent of the world's grain harvest in 1987/88 and very slightly more than 10 percent of the unsold wheat and rice stocks carried over to the next year by the international grain trade.[3]

The great majority of the hungry live in rural areas—from 60 percent of hungry Latin Americans to 80 percent or even 90 percent of the hungry people in countries of Africa and Asia. Most of the world's underfed teenagers and most of the underfed mothers and fathers of hungry children help to grow and harvest the world's food. Nevertheless, they go hungry day after day, year after year. The greater part of the circumstances of their hunger is beyond their control and will remain beyond their control until the underlying causes of those circumstances change. Meanwhile, their lives wither away under hunger's relentless attack with scant attention from news media, policy makers, or the world in general. The tragedy of chronic hunger unfolds too slowly for the television camera, and it lacks the drama of famine.

As this is being written, news headlines warn of impending starvation for up to 8 million people in southern Sudan unless food reaches them quickly. Hostages to a long civil war, their agriculture has been destroyed by warring factions that also block trade and emergency relief coming from other countries. Warfare, directly and indirectly, accounts for much of the suffering of hunger today, as it has throughout history.

Headlines do not speak, however, of the 40 thousand young children who will die hunger-related deaths today and tomorrow and every day this year. They are dying in the Sudan, yes, but also in India, Pakistan, Bangladesh, the Philippines, Mozambique, Zaire, Uganda, Haiti, Bolivia, Honduras, and many other countries across the globe. Every year some 14 million children under the age of five, according to UNICEF and the World Health Organization, die from a combination of malnutrition and common illnesses, most of which can be prevented by relatively simple, low-cost methods.[4]

Famine from the effects of war or other causes remains part of the world hunger problem. The lives blighted and brought to early death by chronic hunger, however, number not 8 million—monstrous as that figure is—but hundreds of millions. Judging from the Fifth World Food Survey (1985) of the United Nations Food and Agriculture Organization (FAO) and from trends of rising poverty in most developing countries during the deep economic recession and debt crisis of the 1980s, the World Food Council estimates that at least 550 million people now suffer from a chronic lack of food.[5]

Recent poverty research by the World Bank finds 1.1 billion people (approximately one-third of the population in developing countries) too poor to meet all of their basic needs for food, shelter, fuel for cooking and warmth, health care, and other essential goods and services. Among this population are 630 million whom the World Bank calls "extremely poor," people with annual incomes of less than $275. While all hungry people are poor, it does not follow necessarily, of course, that all poor people are hungry. People as extremely poor as these, however, are doubtless hungry most of the time. The World Bank's researchers are careful to point out that poverty research, alone, gives no evidence of the nutritional status of individuals or groups. Nevertheless, many discussions of world hunger cite the World Bank's poverty estimates as hunger statistics.[6]

Meanwhile, agricultural surpluses from North America and Europe depress the prices farmers the world over receive for their crops. This, too, is the world food problem: the sad paradox of many farmers being driven into debt (and eventually out of farming) by incomes that fail to cover even their farming costs, while millions of people go hungry for lack of the food these same farmers produce. The problem of debt afflicts farmers in developing countries no less than farmers in the United States.

Hunger in a world of agricultural surplus makes no sense. World production of staple food is adequate to cover every person's basic caloric needs.[7] Clearly, something is terribly awry in the way the world is feeding (or not feeding) itself. That much everyone agrees. The solutions proposed, however, vary greatly from one expert to another. This happens because every analysis arises from some particular way of looking at the problem; and there are many, many different ways of approaching world hunger. Seeing the hunger issue accurately and clearly is a complex challenge. The task is much more complex than political leaders or the public expected back in 1974, when the United Nations General Assembly convened a World Food Conference to turn the tide of a growing, worldwide crisis.

Is the hunger problem getting better or growing worse? Both answers can be correct, depending on which statistic is used. In terms of the absolute number of chronically undernourished people, the answer is "worse." There were at least 115 million more people growing hungry in 1990 than at the time of the 1974 World Food Conference.

In terms of the percent of world population that lacks food, however, the trend is encouraging. Total population increased more than a billion during the fifteen year period from 1974 to 1990. So it is also true that more people than ever before are not hungry and that the percent of the chronically undernourished in the world's population has declined. Perhaps the World Food Council summarizes the situation best:

> Although the world is now feeding one billion more people than at the time of the 1974 World Food Conference, the objective of assuring food security for all people has been moving further away.[8]

Conventional wisdom in the 1990s knows that specialists from any one field of expertise need to listen carefully to the expertise of specialists also from other fields. Nutritionists, economists, anthropologists, political scientists, sociologists, public health workers, heads of state, community organizers, farmers, and agricultural scientists—all need to learn from one another, for no one profession and no one perspective has all of the tools or all of the answers needed to deal with hunger. More than ever before, the effort to end hunger is a cooperative venture among many different professions and institutions. In the 1990s conventional wisdom is coming also to recognize what people working at the grassroots long have known: that it is crucial to find out what the hungry themselves know about the causes and cures for their situation.

Africa is the region where hunger is growing most rapidly, but Asia is still home to 57 percent of the world's chronically hungry people and 83 percent of its malnourished children, concentrated especially in the seven countries of South Asia, that is, on the Indian subcontinent and the island nations of Sri Lanka and the Maldives.

Most victims of hunger in any region will be found in households dependent for their income on micro-enterprises or casual day-labor, households with poor land to farm or none at all, and especially households headed by women, which tend everywhere to be the poorest of all. The percent of women-headed households is growing rapidly as men migrate to cities in search of higher income. Women manage alone in 40 percent of the households now in some parts of rural Africa. In other regions, the percent of women-headed households ranges from 10 percent to 30 percent.[9]

Even in the same household, the extent of hunger often differs from one person to another. For example, nutritional ignorance commonly leads to neglect of the extra needs of small children and of women who are pregnant or breast feeding. In many poor households, survival for everyone dictates a strategy that protects the strength and energy of male income earners.

Men and older boys eat, therefore, even when others go hungry. In a situation where a culture traditionally grants low status to the female gender (as in India, Bangladesh, or Pakistan, for example), women and girls typically suffer much more severe malnutrition than men and male children, a fact reflected in far higher female death rates.

Wherever hunger persists and whatever the circumstances, there can be no adequate substitute for the wisdom of direct experience. Without the view from below, no perspective on the hunger problem can be complete.

Even as specialists continue to seek better knowledge and more workable solutions in each specific situation of hunger, nearly everyone agrees that what is known could eliminate most hunger already if only national governments put that knowledge into practice. Political will to rank the end of hunger high among national priorities is the most essential and the most sorely missing ingredient for solution of the world hunger problem—a will expressed in national budgets, policy decisions, and action, not just in rhetoric. In this sense, the persistence of hunger in a country like the United States greatly resembles the persistence of hunger in a country like India, Ethiopia, or Brazil.

None of India's severely undernourished will be found in the state of Kerala, despite the fact that Kerala's per capita GNP ($182) is even lower than the very low Indian average ($290). By giving public health and nutrition high priority in government policy, Kerala, like China, Chile, Cuba, and Costa Rica, has achieved longer life expectancy and lower infant mortality than many places with far greater financial resources. Hunger's worst aspects can be conquered long before economic development ends poverty.

Working on Empty Stomachs

Each year, as already noted, about 14 or 15 million of the world's chronically hungry people do not survive their fifth birthdays. Most of those who do survive early childhood eventually establish their own households and care for their families as well as they can. In rural areas, they are families of landless day laborers and subsistence farmers, along with poorer sharecroppers, tenant farmers, herdsmen, and nomads. In urban areas, they are families without steady income or those that earn very little at the most menial tasks or working in many kinds of micro-enterprises, from cottage industry to street vending. Despite poverty, their lives are often rich in human dimensions of caring, loyalty, hope, dreams, worship, and celebration that give life meaning.

The hunger that is their daily companion is not only the physical and psychological discomfort the well-fed call hunger. This hunger means having too little to eat to obtain the minimum food energy (calories) and protein needed for an active life. When eaten in sufficient quantity, rice, wheat, and other staple foods will supply not only enough energy and protein but also many essential vitamins and minerals, especially if eaten together with beans, nuts, or vegetables. Underfed people, by definition, do not get that quantity. They are literally undernourished. Lacking food enough for calories and proteins, they almost always lack also critical vitamins and minerals. Anemia is very common. Vitamin A deficiency is also common, damaging vision and lowering resistance to every kind of infection and infectious disease. The chronically undernourished sicken often, age early, and die too soon.

Despite hunger's pains and fatigue, however, the world's half a billion or more underfed people labor. Men, women, and children all labor. They have to labor slowly, of course, because of their weakened condition; productivity is low. Exertion that a well-fed person scarcely notices will cause an undernourished one to tremble, feel dizzy, and break out into a cold sweat. They must rest often. Thoughts move sluggishly, too, and it is hard to concentrate or to learn something new. Without enough food to supply the energy active bodies and minds require, people are unlikely to perceive and act upon new possibilities. It takes energy to analyze, to innovate, to plan, and to organize. The underfed often have barely enough energy to perform the routine tasks of daily existence.

All of them, rural or urban, labor at survival, they labor to "get ahead," they labor to find wage-labor, they labor for every morsel they eat. They have no choice. Even the conspicuous beggars in urban centers—actually a minuscule fraction of the world's hungry—are laboring in a distorted form of micro-enterprise: their parents' beggary or their own. Typically, hungry people in developing countries labor from the age of five or six until forced to stop by the infirmity of age, which comes early as a result of undernourishment's constant stress. Women carry a double burden, responsible for most of the household's daily subsistence while also trying to increase the household's food supply and income. Women's labor commonly starts before sunup and continues until well after dark. But no matter what they do, male or female, hunger is never far away.

Official economic statistics call many of the hungry "unemployed," but that is a misnomer based on an industrial system's notions of employment. So inadequate a term is this for describing the reality of people's lives, to cite just one example, that none of the nonwage work a woman or other family member does to sustain the household can be called "employment." In reality, the developing world's hungry never have the luxury of not being employed in the struggle to survive. (Ironically, many famine victims who reach a refugee camp have easier lives and more food there than they experience at home when there is no famine.)

Official statistics also speak of the hungry being "underemployed," a term that seems to say hungry people could be working harder than they do. However, if underemployed is understood to mean that they are under-rewarded for their labor or working in situations that neither fully utilize nor fully reward their skills and potential, then the term comes close to the mark.

When we talk about the world hunger problem, we have to ask why so much arduous effort meets with so little success.

Seeing the Obstacles

What are the obstacles to greater rewards for that labor? That is one way of trying to see the causes of and possible solutions for hunger. This is a fundamental question for anyone concerned about helping the poor. It is also a central policy question for social and economic development progress generally. Economists, sociologists, political scientists, specialists on women in development, health and education specialists, agricultural scientists, engineers, and technicians within various fields—all have different ways of examining this question. Important insights can come from many different directions.

Behind hunger stands poverty, and behind poverty stands powerlessness to bring about change. Powerlessness, in turn, has many roots: the absence of resources or assets to invest in change; the absence of knowledge to produce change; the absence of sufficient health, energy, and vitality to apply even the knowledge and resources already at hand or to seek what is missing; and the absence of organization among the powerless to obtain collectively what they cannot do individually.

Another obstacle is the way those with relatively greater power use that power to keep their privileged status. Sometimes this abuse of power takes the form of violence or threats of violence to prevent the poor from organizing effectively or from acquiring resources and knowledge. More often it happens subtly. Interference with efforts by the poor to improve their situation is more flagrant, more violent, and more commonly tolerated or encouraged by officials in some societies than in others. To one degree or another, however, the operation of this obstacle should be suspected in any society with significant gaps between rich and poor.

Seeing a Food System

The many different processes and relationships through which people obtain food is a food system. A well-functioning food system protects the food security of everyone. Then everyone, at all times, can eat enough to sustain a healthy, active life. In a poorly functioning food system, some people go hungry.

Our understanding of hunger cannot be complete until the picture includes three dynamic patterns that make up a modern food system. One set of patterns operates at the macro level. It includes the roles played by governments and intergovernmental organizations, the roles played by multinational corporations, and the influence on the world prices of food and other commodities wielded by speculators and investors who buy and sell on the commodities exchange. This macro level is the national and international context of food production, food trade, food utilization, and food distribution. A second set of patterns operates at the micro level. This is the level where individuals and households experience what happens as they produce, buy, sell, and consume food in their communities.

The third set of dynamics we must grasp in order to see the hunger problem clearly is how macro and micro interact. For example, with new knowledge and perhaps improved seeds and fertilizer provided at the community level by an official or private voluntary agency, national or international, poor farmers may succeed in reaping large harvests of a crop they expect to improve household income and purchasing power: a positive macro-micro interaction. Their production success may not turn into greater family welfare, however, if a government marketing board or multinational corporation monopolizes the opportunity those farmers have to market that crop and pays them too little for it: a negative macro-micro interaction. With no other outlet, the farmers must either sell the harvest for whatever they can get or let it rot. The net result is that these farm families remain as poor and hungry as before they received the technical training and improved seeds or fertilizers that increased the productivity of their land and labor—even hungrier than before, if they invested most of their land and labor into producing the cash crop and grew less food than usual for household consumption. If farmers can count on a fair price, of course (a very big "if"), shifting their investment of land and labor into new crops for the market can put more food onto their tables than before, providing also that the food they need is ample in the local markets and priced within their range.

As another example, a landless family's ability to purchase a subsistence diet may be wiped out by inflation when a national government in the South—deeply in debt to foreign banks and development financing agencies and with export earnings shrinking from declining global markets for its commodities—devaluates its currency, cuts food subsidies, and allows prices of consumer goods to rise in order to meet preconditions for financial assistance from the World Bank and International Monetary Fund in the country's macroeconomic crisis. Increased hunger and poverty at the microeconomic level (especially but not only in urban areas) is the tragic and unfair price paid in the 1980s and 1990s by millions of poor people victimized by structural adjustment policies prescribed by conventional economists as the best medicine for the South's debt crisis.

In another example of the interaction between macro and micro, the ability of consumers to obtain adequate food in local markets (the micro level) is affected by the quantity of food stocks available nationally (the macro level). National supplies need not be inadequate in any absolute physical sense to be inadequate pragmatically, because of the way a supply quantity influences the prices consumers must pay. This is acutely important in the matter of hunger, since an increase in the cost of food affects the poor far more severely than others. This is demonstrated by a study in India. Changes in the quantity of staple foods available in the market were correlated over several years with changes in the price of food to find out the typical price increase that occurred when market supplies dropped 10 percent below average. The study then examined how such a price change affected the consumption of staple foods by people in the poorest fifth of the population compared with consumers in the richest fifth. The difference was striking. With a 10 percent drop in the quantity of food in the market, the richest fifth reduced their purchase of food staples by 8 percent. The poorest fifth of consumers, in contrast, purchased 40 percent less food than usual! The impact on food consumption was 500 percent more severe on the poor than on the rich from an identical change in food prices. Considering the poor nutritional level of even the normal diets among India's poor, such an impact is truly alarming.[10]

For yet another example, rural laborers whose income depends on the production and export of jute (as in Bangladesh) may find their livelihood destroyed when synthetic fibers replace jute in global manufacturing processes. Corporately funded research and development in the North continually creates new products that undercut global market demand for fibers, minerals, and other primary commodities from the South upon which millions of jobs and much of the revenue of national governments depend. All of this, and more, is part of the intricate dynamics of a food system.

Attempting to see a food system as a whole, then, means to grasp its whole range of actors, from the molecules and nutrients in a clump of soil to the boardrooms of powerful banks and multinational corporations that control more wealth than many of the countries where hunger abounds. When John Donne wrote, "No man is an island," it was not the world's food system he had in mind. If he were writing those words today, however, he might as well mean that, too. He could have said equally well that no woman or child is an island, no family is an island, no village, not even the remotest community, is an island. Teilhard de Chardin, scientist–contemplative philosopher, reminds us, "It is no longer the simple field, however big, but the whole world which is required to nourish each one of us."

From this perspective, to "see" the world hunger problem is to penetrate the complex workings of the systems within systems within systems that make up the world in which we live. It is an ecological perspective in the largest possible sense—physical ecology, social ecology, political ecology, and economic ecology all wrapped up into one big ecology of present-day human life. Then the study of hunger becomes a powerful lens illuminating in a special way the vast, intricate web of history past and present—for the purpose of creating a different future.

In 1974, then Secretary of State Henry Kissinger said in his address to the World Food Conference:

> The profound promise of our era is that for the first time we may have the technical capacity to free mankind from the scourge of hunger. Therefore, today we must proclaim a bold objective—that within a decade no child will go to bed hungry, no family will fear for its next day's bread, and that no human being's future and capacities will be stunted by malnutrition.[11]

That bold objective is still the goal, but it has become transparently obvious that technical capacity, while important, is not enough. Technology is devised and applied by human beings to specific, value-laden ends within human social systems. No technology is "systems-neutral."[12]

Social science research now leaves little room for doubt that many of the roots of Africa's food crisis are traceable to harm done by Western innovations to workable African food systems and hence to African food security. Some of these innovations disrupted traditional technological adaptations to fragile environments and severely, perhaps permanently, damaged soil and water resources. Other innovations in the name of modernization and progress upset traditional social structures that protected the food security of communities and their individual members. Both technological and social disruptions, time and again, rendered a large percentage of Africa's women agriculturalists less able to produce food.

Insights from research about the hunger of particular groups of actual human beings will vary from context to context. Hungry people struggle within many, many different cultural, social, and physical environments throughout the world, each context with its own operating rules.

Generalizations from preconceived theories can be dangerously blinding, if the objective is to see hunger accurately. Amartya Sen's research, for example, strongly suggests that the three million lives lost in the Bengal famine of 1943–1944 were lost because of just such a blindness on the part of governmental authorities. Because the authorities were certain that the cause

of the famine had to be a sudden drop in food supplies, they
didn't notice that, instead, the cause was a sudden drop in
income among specific groups of people that snowballed into
horrifying proportions.[13]

Malthusian Anxiety

For almost two centuries, until less than two decades ago, conventional wisdom said that hunger was the consequence of
overpopulation and that famine resulted from an extreme
imbalance between the food available and the number of people
to be fed. Thomas Robert Malthus, a British cleric, appears to be
the first modern thinker to attempt reasoned analysis of the
social and economic consequences of population growth. In
1798, Malthus predicted that—human reproduction being as it
was (growing geometrically) and agricultural production being
as it was (growing only arithmetically)—periodic famine would
be inevitable unless some other death-dealing calamity like war
or plague limited the natural growth of populations.[14] Malthus,
knowingly or not, echoed Ben Jonson, a contemporary of
Shakespeare. "Famine cures famine," Jonson had said approximately 200 years before Malthus. When enough people have
died, the balance between food and people is restored and
famine stops by itself.

Neither Malthus nor Jonson were advocating that famine is
a good thing. They merely reported what they saw as a tragic and
inevitable law of nature. For a long, long time, few inquiries
seriously challenged this assumption by examining the actual
details of historical experience more closely. It simply seemed
logical that where there is great hunger, there must be too little
food available for the number of people. From such a perspective, the most obvious avenues for prevention of food crises
would be, on the one hand, to prevent excess population and, on
the other hand, to increase food production. These two approaches have, in fact, dominated both official and unofficial
thinking about world hunger for most of the twentieth century.

Before looking at the research-based growth in wheat and
rice production popularly called the Green Revolution, or at the
questions raised by the population explosion, it may be useful to
bring into focus some alternative viewpoints on the nature of the
hunger problem. These less conventional views evolved simultaneously with contemporary concern about food supply and

population but with much less fanfare until after the World Food Conference of 1974. When these socioeconomic perspectives finally did burst into the spotlight, they drove the analytical pendulum to the other extreme, discrediting Malthusian anxiety. In the 1990s, however, most serious discussions of the world hunger problem take the whole range of perspectives into account. That was not true 20 or 30 years ago.

Protecting the Vulnerable

Pediatricians, nurses, nutritionists, and social workers who deal with poor people in developing countries as individuals, year in and year out, see the world hunger problem differently from agricultural scientists and also from economists, demographers, or anyone else accustomed to working at the macro level of analysis. The advocacy of family planning ("birth spacing") by those with a microview, for example, is not from fear that the world will run out of food. Rather, they know the terrible toll too many births take on the health and welfare of mother and child. As to the world food problem, they see up close the consequences of chronic hunger among women who bear underweight infants doomed before they are born—hungry women who often die in the agony of giving birth. They witness the consequences of undernourishment on the brains and bodies of infants and small children. They observe over and over again, in anger and sorrow, how quickly and easily the little improvement they accomplish today in a family's health and welfare is overwhelmed tomorrow by economic and social forces beyond their control.

Until the 1970s, these health and nutrition professionals reported their findings to one another in journals, at professional meetings, and in U.N. committees and advisory groups of nutrition experts. Then, however, a concerted effort began to widen the discussion to include development economists and macrodevelopment planners. In 1972, the International Conference on Nutrition, National Development and Planning took place at the Massachusetts Institute of Technology and was attended by officials from 75 countries. One of the event's planners was Alan Berg, former USAID food aid director during the Bihar famine threat in India (1966–1967) who had become deputy director for nutrition in the World Bank's Department of Population and Nutrition Projects. The other planner was Nevin Scrimshaw, M.I.T. professor, renowned authority on nutrition in developing countries, and chairman of the U.N. Protein-Calorie Advisory Group. The following year saw publication of the papers from that conference and also of Berg's book, *The Nutrition Factor: Its Role in National Development* (Brookings Institution, Washington, D.C.). Nutrition planning to promote national objectives in economic and social development emerged as a new professional specialty. Nutrition planners (or food policy specialists) addressed development economists and policy planners not accustomed to thinking of food and agriculture either in terms of discrete groups of individuals most vulnerable to malnutrition or in terms of the economic benefits to be gained by protecting a country's human resources.

The nutrition planners explained that undernutrition occurs among the poor in most countries even when food is plentiful but that the situation gets much worse when food prices rise. They explained that malnutrition's most serious impact occurs among women of child-bearing age and among infants and small children. They explained that hunger also reduces the productivity of adults and the benefit children gain from time spent in school. The planners argued that nutrition interventions targeted to reach the most vulnerable groups can reduce hunger's most severe human toll long before general gains are made in reducing poverty. They suggested that the numbers are not beyond reach and the costs would be modest (for example, the smallest shift of financial resources from weaponry to nutrition programs could make such efforts possible).

The priorities of nutrition planners have not been adopted widely into national policies or given high priority in the majority of countries, but these insights are now present in national food policy discussions (as distinct from merely agricultural policy) wherever such discussions occur. The fifth resolution passed by the World Food Conference urges all nations to "formulate and integrate food and nutritional plans . . . aiming at improved consumption patterns in their socioeconomic and agricultural planning."[15]

A new consensus at the World Food Conference recognized that the formation of policy to prevent hunger and food crises includes but exceeds the portfolios of ministers of agriculture. At the Food and Agriculture Organization of the U.N., however, national governments are represented typically by their agricultural ministries. Therefore, following the World Food Conference, a new entity called the World Food Council was established by the General Assembly, with rotating national representation "at the ministerial or plenipotentiary level." The World Food Council's task is to monitor and encourage national and international action on World Food Conference resolutions and to make recommendations to other United Nations bodies regarding food production, nutrition, food security, food trade, and food aid. The World Food Council held its first annual meeting in June 1975.

Rich-Poor: The Growing Gap

Attention to the political economy of hunger and poverty grew sharply as the progress expected from the first United Nations Development Decade, the decade of the 1960s, failed to materialize. At this time, the development strategies advocated almost universally by mainstream Western economists followed views articulated by W. W. Rostow, professor of economic history at M.I.T. These views assumed that societies achieve broad-based prosperity through a generalized pattern of succeeding stages of economic growth and modernization. "Development," by this assumption, consists in transforming traditional societies with little or no economic growth into ever-expanding modern societies with high rates of growth and high consumption patterns. The most critical stage in this progression is the take-off, "the great watershed in the life of modern societies," as Rostow called it. Take-off occurs, Rostow theorized, when investments in a relatively narrow complex of industry and technology produce a certain critical mass of economic activity:

> The take-off is the interval when the old blocks and resistances to steady growth are finally overcome. The forces making for economic progress, which yielded limited bursts and enclaves of modern activity, expand and come to dominate the society. Growth becomes its normal condition.[16]

World Bank loans, U.S. economic foreign aid, and, indeed, most economic development assistance going to non-Communist developing countries in the 1960s aimed to create the conditions presumed for take-off in the recipient countries. Social analysis after social analysis, however, revealed that the rich elite were getting ever richer and more powerful while the poor were growing still poorer and becoming more numerous. The benefits of growth were not "trickling down" from the top to ever wider groups within these countries as the planners had expected or, if they were, the trickle-down stopped before it reached a very large, unbenefitted population at the bottom. With national emphasis (as advised by the development experts) on investment in infrastructure for a modern industrial society and on state-of-the-art, capital-intensive industry, more and more people were becoming "marginalized" from the entire development process. The groups pushed out to the margins of the economy had neither productive assets, nor political influence, nor a productive workplace in the capital-intensive growth strategies. They were ignored in national development planning as surplus labor and left to their own devices to avoid starvation.

By the early 1970s, the World Bank's new president, Robert McNamara, acknowledged the failure of the bank's development lending to help the poor and began to beat the drum for "basic human needs" strategies to alleviate the condition of people living in poverty so "absolute"

> that it prevents realization of the potential of the genes with which one is born; a condition of life so degrading as to insult human dignity—and yet a condition of life so common as to be the lot of some 40 percent of the peoples of the developing countries.[17]

McNamara continued to press the bank's governors to support special consideration for the poor rather than looking only at the "bottom line" of bank lending. At the board of governors' meeting in 1979 in Belgrade, he repeated:

> Growth is absolutely essential, and every effort must be made to increase it in the developing societies. But while a necessary condition for reducing poverty, growth is not in itself a sufficient condition. It is naive to assume in any society that absolute poverty will automatically melt away simply because the gross national product is rising.[18]

Long before the World Food Conference, ethical consciences were aroused widely by the glaring contrast between lifestyles of wasteful overconsumption among the elites in "poor countries" (and in rich countries, generally) and the lives of underconsumption endured by millions of hungry people. Highly inequitable relationships of power and wealth between the industrialized nations of Western Europe and North America and the struggling economies of newly independent nations just emerging from colonial status also aroused arguments for a "new international economic order" in which Britain's Lady Barbara

Ward Jackson was a prominent voice for "justice to the developing nations."

Well-publicized statements condemning exploitation of the poor and calling for greater equity in sharing the world's resources had come during the 1960s from the Catholic Church's historic Vatican II consultation (the Second Ecumenical Vatican Council, 1962–1965) and from religious leaders such as Pope John XXIII, Pope Paul VI, and Dom Helder Camara, Archbishop of Recife in northeastern Brazil, an area that became the classic illustration of growing poverty in a "high-growth" developing country that had experienced take-off. The seeds of these influences took root and continued to grow stronger during the 1970s.

Challenging the Conventional Wisdom

Moral indignation about hunger, poverty, inequitable development, and inequitably shared power was running at high tide by the time of the World Food Conference. Conference delegates who read as far as paragraph 181 in the U.N. Economic and Social Council's *Assessment of the World Food Situation, Present and Future* found this blunt statement:

> The causes of inadequate nutrition are many and closely interrelated including ecological, sanitary and cultural constraints, but the principal cause is poverty. This in turn results from socioeconomic development patterns which in most of the poorer countries have been characterized by a high degree of concentration of power, wealth and incomes in the hands of relatively small elites of national or foreign individuals or groups.[19]

In preparation for the conference, a few researchers and public policy advocates from North American and European nonprofit, nongovernmental organizations (NGOs)—notably Susan George, Frances Moore Lappé, and Joseph Collins—began to ask unconventional questions. What did those plaguey North American grain surpluses imply when millions were on the verge of starvation? What was actually happening to the food produced in the world? Was it really impossible for "hungry countries" to feed their own people? Did people really have to be hungry? They asked these questions with passionate interest and indignation. They undertook, literally, a radical reexamination of facts and statistics, determined to get to the roots of the matter and to take no prior explanation for granted. The global marketplace came under close scrutiny.

Not surprisingly, the process of asking why the emperor has no clothes on, with total irreverence toward established powers and experts, produced new theories. Common to all of these new theories is the conviction that hungry people and hungry nations can meet their food needs through self-reliance. For example, through widely read books and public speaking, Lappé and Collins began in 1977 to convert thousands of U.S. Malthusians to completely non-Malthusian assumptions about hunger. In essence, their message is that every country in the world has the resources necessary for its people to free themselves from hunger; that the root causes of both hunger and high birth rates are the insecurity and poverty of the majority that result from the control over basic national resources by a few; that hunger is only made worse when approached as a technical problem; that political and economic inequalities are the greatest stumbling block to development; that safeguarding the world's agricultural environment and people freeing themselves from hunger are complementary goals; and that agriculture must become, first and foremost, a way for people to produce the food they need and only secondarily a possible source of foreign exchange.[20]

Hunger in the Marketplace

"Food is more than a trade commodity," pleaded Sir John Boyd-Orr in 1946. "It is an essential of life." The first director-general of the new Food and Agriculture Organization of the United Nations, Boyd-Orr fruitlessly proposed plans for a World Food Board to protect nations and people from hunger in the world market system. That market system does not distribute food on the basis of nutritional need. This is one of the most troubling and complex realities of the world hunger problem.

World hunger analysts, of whatever ideological bent, know now that in the second half of the twentieth century, neither chronic hunger nor famine can be explained by a lack of enough food on the planet to feed the people who are hungry. Whether or not overpopulation in particular locations explains severe and extensive hunger in those locations in earlier eras is a different question. And whether or not hunger will be caused at some point in a future age by population exceeding the earth's productive capacity is a different question still. In our era, whenever people have starved or gone hungry, it has been because they could not obtain food that was available—available either from local production and the stocks held by local merchants or from merchants or governments importing food from other areas.

Not even during the 1972–1974 world food crisis did the world run out of grain. This is not to deny that grain supplies did drop to a record low level or that there was a severe food crisis in Asia and Africa. People were starving or on the verge of starvation in several countries and were very hungry in larger than usual numbers in other countries, while the governments of the most seriously affected countries found themselves unable to import enough food. The causes of that hunger, however, have to be sought in explanations other than overpopulation in relationship to available food. Explanations must include an examination of the background of skyrocketing world grain prices. The world price for a ton of wheat in 1972 was $60; by 1974 it was $210. Inflation in the price of rice was even worse: from $129 in January 1971 to an all-time high of $630 in April 1974.[21]

Only five very secretive businesses controlled the world grain trade at that time: Cargill, Cook, Continental, Dreyfus, and Bunge. Cook, the only one with publicly traded stock, has since vanished. The others are family dynasties, as mysterious as ever. The only one to originate in North America, Cargill, is considered the largest and richest of them and one of the most powerful multinational corporations in existence. What do these grain corporations mean to the world hunger problem? Expert views range from "not much" to "everything." Because of the privacy of the companies' operations, it is hard to know.[22]

During recent famines in Ethiopia, in another example of the workings of the marketplace, foreign food aid being trucked to famine areas from ships at the docks passed food leaving the famine areas on other vehicles. Merchants were taking food from famine areas to parts of the country where there was no famine.[23] Why? Because famine victims, by definition, are destitute, while people in nonfamine areas have money to buy food. What else were the merchants to do? If they gave away much of the food they had purchased to sell for their own livelihood, they, too, risked destitution. If a society is to cope with its hunger problems in an equitable way, it must do that as the whole system. Exchanging one set of victims for another is a poor answer.

The economic laws of supply and demand that move food

(and all other commodities) throughout the global marketplace imply "demand" in one particular sense: the demand of a consumer who not only desires something but can pay for the thing desired. Only such demand is "effective demand" in the market. It is economic demand, not nutritional demand in the sense of a requirement for health. The hungry must remain hungry in the market if they lack effective demand. However, a market system will soon break down and be unable to distribute any food at all if it defies the market's rules of exchange.

The slogan "food for people, not for profit" that was popular with hunger activists in the 1970s has a good ring, but it ignores an important fact: It is not only unfair to people who produce food but it is counterproductive for the hungry. Without some profit for the producers of food, there will soon be no food to distribute. Outside of semi-slavery or other violent exploitation, no men or women will labor to produce a surplus for others to eat, year after year, while their own reward merely sustains the ability to repeat the same arduous labor again for the next harvest. Subsistence farming is less arduous, and subsistence farming is what farmers do when greater effort goes unrewarded. But subsistence farming produces no surplus for anyone outside the farming household.

Food beyond a farm household's own needs—food available for others to consume—will be produced most willingly and most efficiently only when the producers have a reasonable expectation of gaining a profit with which they can improve the quality of their existence in a way of their own choosing. China, the Soviet Union, and most other centrally planned economies, where private profit among food producers was previously considered a capitalist evil, have given up on "food for people, not for profit." Their experience has convinced them that profit is an essential component of an effective food system. In several African countries, too, governments have discovered in recent years that when they allow their farmers to get fair prices for their crops national food shortages begin to disappear—especially if fertilizers, seeds, credit, and marketing infrastructure appropriate to small farmers are available as needed.

The way the global marketplace functions at present is rife with social and economic inequity, foolish distortions of resource use that sacrifice long-range necessity (even survival) for immediate profit, and skillful, high-powered manipulation of consumer choice toward unhealthy and uneconomic products. A classic illustration is the infant formula debacle in developing countries, where formula marketing schemes convince poor women that their babies will be healthier on formula when, in fact, formula use endangers infants because of unavoidable misuse of the product in circumstances of poverty and poor sanitation.

Despite these and other flaws operating in the global marketplace, no one has yet developed a more effective way to move food from producers to consumers on a global scale than a market system driven to a large extent by product supply and economic demand. More food is now available to more people on the planet than at any previous period of history, thanks in part to the global food trade. If approximately 10 percent to 15 percent of the world's people are going hungry, the converse is that approximately 85 percent to 90 percent are not. Generally speaking, a market economy in an interdependent world seems to work fairly well in meeting the needs of that 85 percent to 90 percent who can participate in the market.

Another way to look at the world hunger problem, then, is to see it as the inability of 10 percent to 15 percent of the world population to participate adequately in the market. From that vantage point, the search for solutions to hunger moves in two different directions. One train of thought seeks alternatives to the market for distributing food to the relatively small percent who have been marginalized. The other line of inquiry seeks ways to enable the hungry to join the much larger group who meet their needs effectively through the market as it presently exists.

The most commonly proposed alternatives to the market as a means of ensuring enough food for the disadvantaged 10 percent to 15 percent are a dole (food aid); management of collective food supplies by a local or national government, pursuing the socialist ideal of "from each according to his ability, to each according to his need"; or food self-reliance ("grow your own") that is detached from market forces. Efforts to help the hungry meet needs through the marketplace focus on increasing their incomes through a variety of schemes, depending on apparent opportunities and options.

Despite progress in famine prevention achieved by international cooperation since the great world food crisis of 1972–1974, the problem of the world's chronically hungry remains very much as Boyd-Orr saw it 45 years ago and as Susan George describes it today:

> [T]hose 15 million children and those 800 million "absolute poor" are of precious little interest to a world system that regards food not as a basic human right but as a commodity to be bought and sold. People who are unable to become Consumers with a capital "C" have no influence whatever on a system that is programmed to understand the language of money.[24]

Entitlement to Food

Boyd-Orr failed to persuade the international community in 1946 to establish a world system of food reserves for emergencies and to regulate price fluctuations in the world's grain trade in such a way that everyone could be assured of enough to eat at all times. However, Boyd-Orr's goal, if not his method, has become accepted internationally as the legitimate meaning of food security.

This acceptance has come about partly through the World Food Conference, partly through the activities of the World Food Council established by that watershed conference, and partly through the work of food policy analysts in other agencies of the United Nations system. "The term 'food security'," says a 1986 World Bank study, "[means] access by all people at all times to enough food for an active, healthy life."[25] In official discussions now, the goal of solving the world hunger problem is expressed most commonly as "establishing food security."

Food security involves supplies from a country's own production augmented by food produced elsewhere and access to those supplies by everyone. The assumption that access to food follows automatically from the availability of food is the central flaw in views of the hunger problem that see only numbers of people and quantities of food. Access and availability are not the same condition.

Where there is hunger, the path to a workable solution starts by asking what normally entitles people to a share of food in the particular social context in which they are living. What are the "rules of the game" when it comes to food in that context within that society?

Is money (purchasing power) the key to entitlement? Can entitlement occur through barter of something other than money? Does entitlement come by virtue of the labor and other resources invested in growing food? Can it come by virtue of owning land on which food is grown even without the owner's own labor to grow it? How does family social position affect entitlement to food in the community? And what about entitlement differences among different members of the same household? Who has priority in entitlement to food within the household, community, or national policy: the very young? the very old? adult wage-earners? boys in preference to girls? men in preference to women? Each one of these differences in entitlement can be found operating somewhere in the world today. The particular training, perspective, and research methods of anthropology can throw important light on entitlement questions.

The entitlement question recognizes two very basic facts about the world hunger problem. First, not everyone goes hungry in so-called hungry countries, not even in instances of famine. Second, poverty is not a sufficient explanation for hunger. While all hungry people in the world today are probably also poor, the reverse is not true: Not all poor people in the world today are also hungry. We have already noted that some very poor countries such as China and Cuba, and one of India's poorest states, Kerala, have succeeded in eliminating or nearly eliminating serious undernutrition among their populations by means of public policies that positively affect entitlement to food.

In each instance where hunger is a chronic problem, we must understand the rules of entitlement to food that operate in that instance in order to see the problem accurately. The second step is to probe for the reasons that some people are not able to participate adequately in the existing food system. Only when we know those two things can we begin to think clearly about possible solutions to the problem.

Triage and Lifeboat Ethics

In the 1960s, population anxiety reached a peak. Fear of the consequences of the population explosion added *triage* and *lifeboat ethics* to the language of ethical discussion about appropriate response to the world hunger problem. Both triage policy and lifeboat ethics are diametrically opposed to religious and humanitarian views on the subject.

"The battle to feed all of humanity is over," wrote the prominent Stanford University biologist Paul Ehrlich in his prologue to *The Population Bomb* in 1968. Ehrlich, a neo-Malthusian, was convinced that the battle was lost. According to Ehrlich, because of the number of people who were already born and growing up to produce more people, the world would not be able to feed everyone alive during the 1970s.

The year before *The Population Bomb* was published, the brothers William and Paul Paddock—one a foreign service officer, the other an agricultural scientist, both with experience in developing countries—published their own very specific prediction of doom, *Famine—1975!* In the imminent and inevitable cataclysm of massive famine, the Paddocks warned, not even the agricultural abundance of the United States would suffice to feed all of the starving. They argued that, therefore, the United States should have a "triage" policy in readiness for choosing which hungry developing countries to rescue and which to allow to starve.

Triage is a practice followed by doctors under conditions in which the possibility of treatment is too restricted to cover all of the wounded, such as on a battlefield. The wounded are diagnosed into three groups: those likely to recover on their own, those likely to die no matter what is done for them, and those who are likely to recover if they receive help. Medical attention is reserved for this last group. The first two are left for nature to take its course. Similarly, said the Paddocks, the United States should assist only those countries willing and able, with U.S. help, to do what is necessary to reduce their populations and gradually overcome their food scarcity. Some countries could muddle through the coming crisis without help. As for the rest, they would be such "basket cases" that food aid would only prolong their misery and merely postpone the inevitable calamity. Aid to such countries (Bangladesh and India were among the countries the Paddocks had in mind) ultimately would be wasted.

Instead of triage, Garrett Hardin, a biologist like Ehrlich and equally pessimistic about the earth's future under the burgeoning human population, proposed the "ethics of the lifeboat." Imagine a lifeboat full of survivors afloat in the sea and surrounded by people who are about to drown. The people facing certain death are desperate to get aboard the lifeboat. What should the people on the lifeboat do? The boat is already full. If more people come on board, the boat will surely capsize and everyone will be lost.

The logic of Hardin's parable is clear, but the moral implications are murky. The right of the lifeboat passengers (primarily Americans and Western Europeans) to their privileged position, according to Hardin, is by virtue of greater wisdom and self-discipline in having fewer children. However, Hardin's ethic ignores the stress these privileged few place upon the earth's carrying capacity for human life by their destructive technology and wasteful, overconsumptive lifestyles. In terms of consumption of the planet's resources, the earth can afford a second Bangladesh more easily than a second United States! Lifeboat ethics also overlooks the extent to which the lifeboat minority's privileges derive from military conquests and colonialism in the past and from present uses (or abuses) of political, military, and economic power that greatly help to explain why the people struggling not to drown lack their own lifeboats.

Triage and lifeboat ethics are anathema to non-Malthusians and to most neo-Malthusians also. Ethical debates aside, however, what about the role of population in the world hunger problem? Is it really a bogus issue?

The Population Problem

The rate of world population growth peaked in the early 1960s at slightly more than 2 percent a year and has been declining ever since. Annual growth is currently estimated to be about 1.6 percent and is still going down. Global agricultural production (food and nonfood) grew steadily from 1961 through 1985 at an average annual rate of 2.6 percent—faster in developing countries, slower in North America, Europe, Australia, and New Zealand. Food production globally (with Africa the big exception) kept ahead of population growth, contrary to expectations in the early 1960s.[26]

Neo-Malthusian expectations of the 1950s and 1960s have been confounded thus far regarding Asia, which is home to more than half the world's people and 57 percent of the chronically undernourished. Asia's enormous population did indeed grow another 55 percent from 1960 to 1980, but rice production grew even faster, by 60 percent, with average yields per hectare increasing 40 percent. In the late 1960s, new high-yielding rice and wheat varieties began to spread rapidly, along with government supported irrigation, fertilizer, and agricultural extension services. During the 1950s and 1960s, for example, India depended repeatedly on foreign aid to check serious famines and was the largest recipient of U.S. food aid. By the 1970s, however, India had become self-reliant in rice and wheat, with reserve stocks to cover typical year-to-year harvest fluctuations due to weather conditions.[27] Now India is a world exporter of grain in years of normal harvest (although it is still home to about one-third of the world's chronically undernourished). The other major factor in Asia's surprising record was the demographic success of China's draconian family planning policies; the unprecedentedly rapid decline in China's rate of population growth held Asia's overall population within limits lower than anyone could have predicted.

The implication of current population growth projections remains alarming, nevertheless. Despite a slower annual rate of increase, the world is adding more than 85 million people each year during the 1990s, equivalent to one-third of the U.S. population. When Malthus wrote his essay in 1798, the world had fewer than one billion people (about the number being added now each year) and the rate of growth was about one-half of 1 percent annually. Two centuries later there are more than five times as many people and the rate of growth is almost four times faster. There were 2 billion people on the planet in 1930. Somewhere during 1987, the 5 billionth person was born. A 6 billionth is expected to arrive by the year 2000.

When population finally stops growing, there are expected to be 14 billion people instead of the 10 billion estimated previously, the United Nations Population Fund (UNFPA) announced in May 1989.

The reason for the higher estimate is that family planning campaigns in developing countries have not been as effective as expected.[28] This is hardly surprising where the status of women has improved little or not at all. Women who have little education, little or no power to make fertility decisions for themselves, and few options for either social respect or economic survival aside from child-bearing make poor clients for family planning programs. Changes in attitudes and patriarchal social traditions affecting women are the neglected keys to reduced population growth.

If these estimates come close to the mark, it will be necessary to feed almost three times as many people within 50 years. Furthermore, because of environmental degradation and urban growth, this feat will have to be accomplished in all likelihood on less land and less arable land and with less irrigation.[29] Meanwhile, per capita agricultural production has plateaued in both developed and developing regions. The Economic Research Service of the U.S. Department of Agriculture finds that the overall rate of growth in agricultural production has been slowing since the 1970s. There is no way to predict when or if new successes in agricultural research will match the productivity gains of the 1960–1980 period.

The total world food supply is not yet in jeopardy, and, as we have seen, hunger is not yet explained by a worldwide food shortage. The immediate hunger consequences of population growth lie in its influence on those things that entitle people in most societies to claim an adequate share of the food that is available: access to the means of production and access to paid employment.

Landlessness and Unemployment

FAO reports a very serious decline in the amount of arable land farmed per farm worker. As rural populations increase, small farmers subdivide their land among their heirs (almost universally male heirs only), who divide it among their sons in turn, and so on. With each passing generation, farm sizes become smaller and smaller. Eventually plots are too small and too fragmented to be economically viable at all. Then the owner, usually deeply in debt to the village money lender, either forfeits the land as debt payment or sells out to a larger farmer in desperation. Either way, the household is soon poorer than ever and is totally dependent thenceforth on sporadic daily wage-labor to survive.

The vast majority of farm households in developing countries must make do on farms of two hectares (approximately five acres) or less. In Asia and the island nations of the Pacific, the ratio of arable land farmed per farm worker in the early 1960s was about one hectare; by the year 2000, FAO estimates the ratio will be barely three-quarters of a hectare per farm worker. In Africa, the 1961–1965 ratio of 2.37 hectares per farm worker is expected to drop to 2.04 hectares by 2000, and in North Africa and the Middle East the ratio is predicted to fall from 2.89 hectares in the early 1960s to 2.21 by the end of the century.[30]

Only in Latin America is the amount of land in cultivation increasing, but this pattern does little for the poor. Most of the increase is a result of wealthy landowners farming previously underutilized land, and doing so with capital-intensive (highly mechanized) methods rather than with labor-intensive methods that would create more employment for the rural poor. The rate of rural-to-urban migration in Latin America is the highest in the world. Still worse, many thousands of hectares of heavily forested land are being cleared for agriculture, especially in Brazil and Central America. Profits from agricultural production on fragile tropical forest soils last usually only three or four years before the land's ability to support green plants is wholly devastated, perhaps permanently. Additional long-range environmental costs of expanding "arable" land in this manner include disruption of regional rainfall patterns, destruction of wildlife habitat, loss of invaluable genetic species, increased downslope erosion and pollution, and so on.

The nutrition problem in many parts of the developing world can be improved more by an increase in person-years of employment than by an increase of grain production, advises noted Green Revolution scientist M. S. Swaminathan, former director of the International Rice Research Institute. Fighting the "famine of jobs" will be as essential as maintaining adequate food production for the rest of the twentieth century.[31]

The International Labour Organization (ILO) reports a widespread rural employment crisis in the developing world. In Bangladesh, where 86 percent of the rural population live in poverty, an estimated 26 percent of the total rural labor force in 1977 were landless and another 11 percent owned so little land that they were almost wholly dependent on wage-labor.[32] This picture has surely worsened since then. In 1987, the World Food Council found evidence of dramatic increases in the number of unemployed people in many countries. Records for India showed an increase of 10 million unemployed between 1980 and 1985. In Indonesia and Thailand, unemployment increased at a rate of 6 percent to 7 percent annually in the 1970s, a trend that continued into the 1980s. In Brazil, the number of unemployed more than doubled between the early 1970s and early 1980s. At the same time, poor people were forced to bear the brunt of the suffering caused by inflation and other structural adjustment policies adopted to cope with Brazil's debt crisis. In nearly all African countries, wage employment has declined significantly during the deepening economic crisis there.[33]

Official employment statistics, of course, account for only those workers and job seekers who come to the attention of official record keepers. Employment statistics are likely to omit large numbers of the poor, who either fear officialdom and avoid its attention or pass their lives, in any case, in places and circumstances remote from the data gatherers. Furthermore, as noted before, most official employment research ignores workers who do not receive a wage—such as women and youth working in household subsistence tasks and in the household's farm or non-farm enterprises.

An average of 47 million new paying jobs must be created each year from now to the end of the century just to keep pace with population growth, according to the ILO. The youth population (ages 15 to 24) is expected to increase from 775 million to 1.117 billion between 1985 and 2025. In 1985, only 5 percent to 15 percent of that age group held employment in well-established industries, a situation expected to grow worse. Most young people in developing countries have to seek a livelihood either in the rural sector or in low-paying jobs in the urban informal sector—typically as street vendors or laborers in undercapitalized "here today, gone tomorrow" micro-enterprises.[34]

Seeking Solutions

Since the overwhelming majority of the world's chronically undernourished people live in rural areas and since poverty is the major cause of hunger, the search for solutions to the world hunger problem must start with the rural poor. Enabling this segment of society to improve food security for their households greatly reduces the world hunger problem. This task is both fundamental and immense.

Battling Rural Poverty

The proportion of the rural population living below the national poverty line in 1987 was 86 percent in Bangladesh, 61 percent in Nepal, 50 percent in India, 47 percent in Indonesia, and 41 percent in the Philippines.[35] Per capita GNP, despite its inadequacy to explain the level of welfare of a country's population, gives at least a rough indication of national ability to apply economic resources toward improving the general standard of living. A number of countries with lower GNP than the Philippines ($590) meet their populations' basic nutritional needs more adequately than does that highly inegalitarian society. However, it is significant that, of the 20 African and Asian countries singled out by the World Food Council for special concern, only the Philippines had a GNP in 1987 exceeding

Indonesia's $450. In India GNP was $300; in China, $290; in Ethiopia, $130; in Bangladesh and Nepal, $160.[36]

"So immense is the worldwide extent of rural poverty," said IFAD's president, Idriss Jazairy, in 1989, "that it is only by releasing an internal dynamism of self-reliance that the poor can hope to attain durable food security for themselves."[37] IFAD, the International Fund for Agricultural Development, is the first international financial institution created exclusively for the benefit of poor men and women in rural areas. Like the World Food Council, IFAD was mandated by the World Food Conference of 1974 as part of the new international resolve to end hunger.

IFAD targets the most backward regions of those countries that are already extremely poor, where roads are often nonexistent, communications are inadequate, and many people have been left out of the mainstream of economic development. It attempts to serve as a catalyst for bottom-up development in which the skills, traditions, and creativity of the poor within their own communities are mobilized. Prior to IFAD, a number of nongovernmental organizations (NGOs)—such as Trickle-Up (a U.S. voluntary agency), the Self-Employed Women's Association of India, the Grameen Bank of Bangladesh, and the Sarvodaya Shramadana movement in Sri Lanka—had found this to be the best route to immediate and sustainable progress among the poor. IFAD draws on the experience of such NGOs and on the technical expertise of its fellow U.N. agencies, especially FAO.

While working within existing social traditions as much as possible, IFAD does not hesitate to require the communities it assists to include women fully in the planning, decision making, and benefit sharing. It does this not only out of a sense of fair play but also out of conviction gained from experience regarding sound economic development. No society, in IFAD's view, can afford to waste the potential of half of its members.

Women's Roles

Women were invisible in economic policy deliberations until quite recently. Research and policy initiatives generated by the United Nations Decade for Women (1975–1985) are changing that. As the economic significance of women in national food systems becomes better known, women's crucial role in workable solutions to world hunger is also better understood. Women's labor produces almost half of the world's total food. In Africa, three-fourths of the agricultural labor is done by women, who produce up to 90 percent of the food consumed in some rural areas.

Africa's declining food security, it is now seen, has been due in no small measure to modernization schemes that assign land title only to individual "heads of household" (and assume this means the husband); that provide credit thereafter only to land-owners (now male, by definition); that introduce mechanization to which only men have access; and that stress production of commercial export crops that compete with women's labor, time, and land for domestic crops, without compensating women who have to work on their husbands' crops for the productivity that has been taken away from women's cropping. All such male-biased, gender-blind forms of "agricultural progress" have eroded the productivity of Africa's women farmers. In Malawi, for example, it has been found that women do twice as much work as men on maize, the country's staple food crop, an equal amount of work on cotton, the chief export crop, and still have their domestic chores to do at home. Another study in Zambia found that the size of the harvest depended less on what the land could yield potentially than on the number of daylight hours women could spend on farming.[38]

The dynamics of women's productivity and the obstacles to productivity women face in Asia, Latin America, and the Near East are less understood as yet, but new research is slowly correcting planners' ignorance of women's roles in those food systems, too. Generally speaking, United Nations research estimates that women perform almost two-thirds of all the hours worked in the world, receive one-tenth of world income, and own less than 1 percent of world property.[39]

If concern for justice and human rights were not enough motivation for trying to understand women's special economic and social obstacles, women's importance in national economic production alone could account for the new professional specialty called Women in Development, often shortened to WID. WID studies and WID policy now form an important part of the work of all international development agencies. National governments, on the whole, have been slower to grasp women's full significance for development progress.

Micro-Enterprise

Employment in very small industrial enterprises has been found by ILO to range from about 50 percent to 90 percent of the total manufacturing employment in many countries, and the share of manufacturing employment located in rural areas is often more than half the national total. For example, this figure is about 87 percent in Indonesia, 86 percent in Sierra Leone, 75 percent in Sri Lanka, 70 percent in Bangladesh, 63 percent in Malaysia, 57 percent in India, and 50 percent in Pakistan.[40] The projects IFAD funds often center on credit schemes for micro- or small-scale enterprises, including but not limited to farming. A large percentage of the micro-entrepreneurs are women, sometimes even the majority.

The role of micro-enterprise in alleviating poverty and also in building broad-based economic growth in developing countries has attracted increasing interest over the past decade. The U.S. Agency for International Development (A.I.D., or USAID) led the way in research on micro-enterprise with its Program for Investment in the Small Capital Enterprise Sector (PISCES) project from 1978 to 1985. So effective was this initial program that USAID has followed it with two more programs covering the period from 1985 to 1994: ARIES, or Assistance to Resource Institutions for Enterprise Support, and MEDS, or Micro-Enterprise Development Support.

The U.S. House of Representatives Select Committee on Hunger conducted hearings on micro-enterprise development as a means of reducing hunger in 1987. One of the expert witnesses was David Richards, director of the NGO Development Program in the International Institute for Environment and Development. From his extensive experience in Africa and Asia, Richards provided several insights worth quoting at length:

> Loaning money to the poor cannot be taken lightly. The poor are engaged in a survival strategy and asking them to go into debt for . . . a venture that may or may not succeed is a weighty responsibility. . . . The problem with micro-enterprise and small enterprise is that it operates at the margin. The surplus, the profit generated, just barely covers the cost of operating. . . . How can you get a $10-enterprise to become a $12-enterprise? [That is the challenge.] Because no enterprise . . . is going to be able to continue providing income sufficient to meet the needs of the owner through time [if] it operates at the margin. . . .

Among the many reasons that people are poor is that they do not own or have control over productive assets. Productive assets are land, machinery, buildings, equipment, and knowledge of techniques about how to add value to resources, crops, or raw materials. Simply put, these are the tools of increased productivity. The fundamental challenge of development is getting ownership or control of productive assets into the hands of the poor. [But] ownership . . . is not enough. The crucial element is control. . . . some degree of influence backward to raw materials and forward to markets is needed if the benefits of increased productivity are not to be [withheld from the micro-entrepreneurs and] appropriated to others.[41]

Under the right circumstances, however, the Grameen Bank in Bangladesh has discovered that a loan as small as $1, used wisely by the previously destitute recipient (in this case a beggar woman who bought ribbons to sell door to door), can begin to lift a person out of poverty. By 1986, the Grameen Bank had 226 branches operating in about 3,600 villages throughout Bangladesh. It had lent out more than $30 million in loans to entrepreneurs organized in groups of five persons with no collateral. The average loan was $60; the largest was $200. The repayment rate after 10 years of operating this program was nearly 99 percent.[42]

IFAD's president, Jazairy, may well be right: "The poor are not a problem; they are a largely untapped asset for development."[43]

Focus on Farmers

Advancing the prosperity of small farmers is the key to broad-based rural economic growth in most developing countries. The linkages between agricultural growth and the rest of the economy are many and varied. Agriculture supplies the raw materials for employment-intensive micro- and small-scale industries in rural areas. Agricultural growth requires additional purchases by farmers of fertilizer and equipment, and this in turn creates income for merchants and manufacturers, large and small. To produce more food, farmers need more energy, which can be provided by animal labor, human labor, or petrol. To the extent that the additional energy is paid for, new jobs are created and incomes rise for someone besides the farmer.

Research in Malaysia, Bangladesh, and India indicates that as the income of male farmers rises, from 40 percent to 80 percent of the increase is spent on materials and construction to improve housing, and also on entertainment and other local goods and services.[44] In Malaysia and Nigeria, IFPRI researchers found male farmers spending typically 40 percent of their additional income on locally produced, labor-intensive, non-agricultural goods and services and another 20 percent on livestock products, fruits, and vegetables for household consumption.[45] (Neither of these studies examined the use of increased income by women, although a few studies in some African cultures have noted significant differences in the spending priorities of women and men.)

Better communications infrastructure both follows and supports agricultural growth. The transport of farm and nonfarm enterprise materials and products to and from markets generates further employment. Obviously, such commerce requires improved communications between the village and neighboring villages and towns. All-weather roads—lacking in a great many of the villages where poor farmers live—must be constructed and maintained, creating still more employment. Gradually electricity and telecommunications are added. Better communication systems and related technologies reduce the intellectual and comfort gaps between city and village. This, in turn, makes more people with professional training—teachers, doctors, scientists, engineers, and administrators—willing to live in the village and apply their skills and knowledge there instead of clinging to urban areas. The entire socioeconomic infrastructure of the village improves steadily. Those youths of the village who manage to obtain higher education are more willing to return, so the "brain drain" away from the village is checked.

In villages with good communications infrastructure, IFPRI researchers have found agricultural employment per hectare of arable land to be 4 percent higher than in villages lacking this infrastructure. In nonagricultural enterprises, employment was 30 percent higher, and wage rates were 12 percent higher.[46] In villages with good roads in Bangladesh, only 12 percent of the population fell below the absolute poverty line, compared with 21 percent below the poverty line in villages without good roads.[47]

A very high proportion of the income of the poor in developing countries is spent on food, and most of any additional income received goes first of all to buying food. Studies in India show that the poor will spend 60 percent of increased income on grain and almost 80 percent of the increase on food products generally.[48] Obviously, whatever increases the income of a country's poor (whether farmers or not) will also increase the prosperity of the country's farmers. The more successful a country's farmers are in producing food, the more stable will be both the supply and the price of food available in the markets.

The poor benefit all around when agricultural growth is based on prosperity among small farmers. They benefit as small farmers themselves, they benefit as rural workers whose employment depends directly or indirectly on the prosperity of local farmers, and they benefit as consumers buying food in the market. When agricultural growth bypasses small farmers, however, the same dynamics do not apply. On the contrary, when the small-farm sector is marginalized by economic change the gap between rich and poor widens, a smaller percentage of the local population is able to buy goods and services in the rural community, rural employment declines, and the community itself withers and dries on the vine.

Science and Small Farmers

Helping small farmers to prosper requires, among other things, helping them to reap larger harvests from their land and to get higher returns from the amount of labor, fertilizer, and other inputs they invest in their crops. Farmers in developing countries achieve impressive results with traditional technology. Often there is agronomic and ecological wisdom in that technology that must not be lost. But everywhere, traditional technology seems to have reached the limits of its productivity while ever more people need sustenance and employment. Technical innovations are needed. That means science.

In order to benefit small farmers and the rural poor, however, the design of technological innovation and the way the new technology is made available should fit the actual circumstances of these population groups, meaning their economic and social circumstances as well as the scientific circumstances of soil and climate. For example, the risk of crop failure and the need to borrow capital should be at least no greater, and preferably less, for the small farmer using the new technology than with traditional technology. The new technology should preserve and, if possible, increase employment in rural areas rather than force more people to migrate to urban slums. The new technology should enhance, rather than diminish, the productivity, status, and economic opportunity of women. Finally, the new technology should be readily sustainable in the local situation, ecologically and socially.

Through indifference to the circumstances of poorer households, smaller farmers, and rural women, agricultural science and technology too often have served to increase the relative advantages of the already advantaged members of rural societies and to widen the gap between rich and poor. This charge often has been made of the Green Revolution that swept Asia and parts of Latin America after the mid-1960s. By the 1990s, fortunately, the total situation of small-farmer households was receiving more attention in scientific research on food production in developing countries. The risk of inequitable benefits from such research, however, remains high.

The application of modern science to food production in developing countries is fairly recent. During the European colonial period, agricultural science was applied almost exclusively to the tropical export crops favored by European markets. These crops did not include rice, cassava, sorghum, teff, beans, or other staple foods of the poor. Nor did these applications include wheat cultivation in Asia or Africa, because wheat for European consumption was amply available from elsewhere. Japanese and Indian agricultural scientists had long conducted their own research on rice, but the scientific revolution in agricultural research addressed to the problems of small farmers and hunger in developing countries came with the founding of the International Rice Research Institute (IRRI) in the Philippines, the first of the international agricultural research centers (IARCs).

There are now 13 IARCs doing research to improve the production in developing countries of barley, field beans, cassava, chickpeas, cowpeas, maize, pasture grasses, pearl millet, pigeonpeas, rice, sorghum, sweet potatoes, triticale, bread wheat, and durum wheat. One IARC promotes and coordinates a global network of seed banks to preserve the genetic diversity of wild and domesticated plants related to the world's food supply. Another IARC specializes in helping developing countries improve their own research capacity. A third, IFPRI, specializes in social science research on issues of food security and the socio-economic implications of technological innovation.

Several IARCs are doing research on farming systems to discover how different crops (for example, field crops interspersed with tree crops or corn and beans grown simultaneously in the same field), low-cost farming technology, small animal production, and other household needs and priorities can be combined for the most satisfying overall result for the farming household. Such micro-level interdisciplinary research that combines agricultural science with anthropology and other social sciences is a far cry from the conventional research of modern monocropping agriculture, where the objective is to maximize the yield of one commercial crop upon which a farmer is expected to concentrate his or her entire investment.

The most famous IARC event is still IRRI's release of new high-yielding varieties (HYVs) of rice in the late 1960s. Rice HYVs yield up to five tons per hectare where only two grew before, and their relative indifference to seasonal changes in day length and temperature permits farmers to obtain two or three crops of rice annually from fields where only one rice crop could be grown before. HYVs respond more favorably to fertilizer application than traditional varieties, and the newer rice varieties do better than traditional varieties even without fertilizer. It is this tremendous expansion of the productive capacity of rice farmers (and, later, of wheat farmers) without any expansion of land area that was called the Green Revolution by the excited news media of the Malthusian 1960s.

Asia is a continent of small-scale farmers where more than 75 percent farm less than two hectares of land. Nevertheless, Asia produces more than twice as much wheat as the United States and Canada combined and 90 percent or more of the world's rice. Asians export less than 2 percent of their rice and less than 3 percent of their wheat. They are their own best customers.[49] Rice alone is the main source of calories and protein for more than 1.5 billion low-income Asians. The HYVs of the Green Revolution enabled Asian rice production to keep ahead of explosive population growth, but not very far ahead. Unfortunately, the HYVs presently available are not suitable to the climates, rainfall, and soils of large areas of India and other developing nations. Even so, much more can be done with existing technology to enable small farmers to expand their food production and their incomes than has already occurred. Where much of the arable land is owned by small elites, of course, agricultural research is a very poor answer to hunger.

The first benefits of Green Revolution technology went to the more prosperous farmers who were willing and able to invest in the irrigation, fertilizers, and pesticides the early HYVs required. Recent HYVs, however, have been bred for high resistance to disease and insects and give higher yields than traditional varieties even without fertilizer. Moreover, with better government support of small farmers through credit schemes and extension, the adoption of HYV rice appears to depend more on local suitability than on farm size in India, the Philippines, and Bangladesh, for example. In China, HYVs are used on 95 percent of all rice land.

There is great need for continuing research adapted to the needs of the developing world's small farmers. As the architect of India's Green Revolution and one of the world's most eminent agricultural scientists, M. S. Swaminathan's assessment of the situation is worth citing at length:

> [A]lthough the new technologies have in many cases been used economically by all farmers, regardless of their farm size, the technologies themselves are not "resource neutral." Farmers need cash inputs to enhance agricultural output. Modernization of agriculture involves the increased use of purchased inputs and a greater dependence on marketing opportunities. . . . Inadequate attention to small farm management has increased production costs and risk. Agricultural scientists must find more ways to enhance the resource neutrality of technology by substituting non-monetary or inexpensive inputs for high-cost inputs and by minimizing yield fluctuations caused by weather aberrations and pest epidemics. New technologies must ensure that labour demand increases faster than its supply [so there will be jobs for more people at higher wages] and that food supply increases faster than demand [so rising food prices do not hurt the poor]. These objectives require that social, biological and physical scientists work as teams.[50]

Agrarian Reform

Agrarian reform is a recurrent theme in discussions of policies and strategies to end hunger in developing countries. Agrarian reform often includes land reform, but it attempts much more. Agrarian reform seeks to help poorer and disadvantaged households obtain access to all of the basic resources needed to make a farm prosper—water, fertilizer, improved seeds, credit, and markets, in addition to land. Agrarian reform seeks to bring about more equitable sharing of the benefits of rural development rather than to add to the prosperity merely of those groups in rural society who are already the more prosperous. Just as important—or even more so—agrarian reform can rebalance inequitable scales of power so that the previously disadvantaged have a stronger voice in deciding what kind of changes are to be made, who is to bear the costs, and how the benefits are to be distributed.

As with so much else that could correct conditions causing hunger, political will and political power are the keys to agrarian reform. The most successful large-scale agrarian reform in recent times was carried out in Japan during the U.S. military occupation following World War II. South Korea, Taiwan, and the Indian state of Kerala have also implemented significant agrarian reforms. In many countries where hunger and poverty abound, governments have formal agrarian reform policies on the law books. Because of the unpopularity of agrarian reform among politically powerful groups who would have to share their power with people over whom they now have an advantage, such policy statements and legislation are widely circumvented or ignored.

In the Philippines, for example, 10 percent of the population owned 90 percent of the land at the time of the 1971 Constitutional Convention. Land reform provisions were written into the new national constitution and a government program was instituted to redistribute land titles (patents) in rice- and corn-growing areas. By 1986, according to the Philippine Ministry of Agrarian Reform's statistics, less than 4 percent of the tenants and very small farmers who qualified to receive land from these reforms had actually been granted patents. Most Philippine farmers were still sharecropping tenants, often having to pay as much as 50 percent of their crop to the landlord in addition to high charges for access to irrigation and usurious interest for credit—paid also to the landlord. Land reform has moved no faster under President Corazón Aquino. In January 1987, unarmed tenant farmers demonstrating outside the president's official residence for accelerated reforms were fired on by army troops without warning, killing 19, according to reports in the Philippine press. Fifteen days later, a committee of the Aquino Cabinet appointed to study the demonstrators' petition agreed with most of the proposals. Implementation remains the tougher hurdle.

It is encouraging to see the World Food Council beginning to emphasize the significance of land reform in strategies to end hunger. In a report to the Sixteenth Ministerial Session meeting in Bangkok, 21–24 May 1990, the council's executive director noted:

> Farmers' incomes depend critically on the land-tenure system. Disparity in size of land holdings creates inequity, and insecure and exploitive tenurial arrangements inhibit investment. A number of countries have taken steps toward agrarian reform. . . . However, much still needs to be done to address the question of equitable distribution of production resources. Comprehensive land reform, particularly in high-potential agricultural areas, has been difficult in most countries and will require clear and strong political commitment. . . . Such efforts need to be accompanied by effective measures (credit, infrastructure, marketing, etc.) to enable small farmers to substantially increase their productivity and incomes. [51]

Environment and Hunger

One of the bitter ironies of the world hunger problem is that half of the chronically hungry rural poor live on land that could greatly increase their incomes and produce much more food, given appropriate technology and investment, according to IFPRI's director, John Mellor. Furthermore, this could be done without harming the environment. Instead, as economic development raises the prosperity of the general population, rural poverty becomes more and more concentrated in areas where land is highly vulnerable to degradation and very unsuitable for cultivation. That is precisely why the poor live there: no one else wants that land. As they struggle to meet their needs in such inhospitable environments, inevitably and helplessly they make matters still worse.

The case of Nepal is an object lesson in the links between poverty, environmental degradation, and the worsening nutritional status of households. Without advances in agricultural technology to increase productivity on Nepal's lowland soils, farmers cannot sustain their incomes there as rising population results in farms becoming smaller. Farmers are forced to clear and crop the hillsides, increasing erosion and flood risks. The forested area of Nepal's hills dropped by 55 percent to 60 percent between the late 1960s and early 1980s.

The forested areas have been pushed so far from settlements to create space for crops that it now takes women more than an hour longer each day to collect fuelwood and fodder for farm animals than it did ten years ago. This time is taken partly from women's time for working on the family's crops, reducing total farm labor for crops by about 24 percent and lowering agricultural productivity. In addition, women's time for food preparation and child care are reduced. IFPRI estimates that these combined effects of deforestation have reduced food consumption in Nepalese farm households about 100 calories per capita each day. The nutritional content of Nepalese diets is also declining, because hillside cropping patterns shift away from rice and other high-calorie foods. In addition to severe erosion and floods that affect both Nepal and vast areas of neighboring India and Bangladesh, the overall result is a downward spiral of poor health and malnutrition, further weakening the ability of Nepalese households to cope with their urgent need for change.[52]

The key to reversing this decline, according to Mellor, is to increase farmer productivity for rice and other high-calorie crops on the good land. This would feed more people on less land and increase farm incomes at the same time. Perennial woodlots for fuelwood and fodder could be cultivated on the hillsides to reduce women's burden and restore time for other essentials. With increased incomes (if the experience of other countries holds true), lowland rice-producing farm households would become consumers for the luxury of fruit from perennial orchards, making it economically possible to plant the hillsides with trees that halt environmental destruction. The consumer market for nonfarm, labor-intensive products and services would also increase with higher incomes from increased farm productivity, generating off-farm employment. Finally, overall poverty reduction would create a social environment in which measures to reduce population growth have more chance of succeeding. To expect population growth to decline before poverty declines is to whistle in the wind. The key to such a chain of events, however, is increased productivity for staple food crops such as rice on lowland acreage under Nepal's agronomic conditions—either through new HYVs for these conditions or new agronomic systems, both of which are awaiting discovery by agricultural science.

Food Aid

It may seem strange to end, rather than begin, a discussion of solutions for the world hunger problem with the topic of food aid. But that is where food aid belongs in the picture: as the last resort when a country lacks any other means to supply food to its population.

Where a genuine shortage of food is the case, food aid can save lives and prevent serious undernutrition in the short run. In the long run, however, it can lead to even greater hunger. Food aid is simply grain or other commodities imported, either at no cost to the receiving country or at a lower cost than the world market price. But increased productivity and prosperity among small farmers is clearly a crucial element in the solution to hunger and rural poverty in a developing country. Unfair competition from food aid can be devastating to the development of the economic and social foundations of self-reliant food security.

Some critics of food aid note also that such aid can be used to prop up undemocratic, corrupt, and unpopular governments, delaying the reforms needed to end the poverty and powerlessness at the root of most hunger. Examples enough can be found to support such criticism.

Still, the short-run dilemma remains: What, if not food aid, is to keep people from starving until other measures solve the food problem in a country where shortages mean excessively high prices for consumers and no food at all for many and where the government lacks the means to import food at normal market prices?

Supporters of the U.S. P.L. 480 food aid program point to countries like India and South Korea, which once relied heavily on food aid but then "graduated" from such dependence. Food aid, they claim, helped make that advance possible. This is a difficult argument to prove or disprove, because the economic and agricultural progress that enables countries to move beyond food aid depends on a whole complex of policies, programs, and economic trends. Determining what weight among all of these factors should be credited to food aid is probably impossible. Food aid administrators and advocates continually seek ways for food aid to be used constructively.

The present lack of food security in many developing countries is due in considerable degree to neglect of the small-farm sector in the development strategies of the 1950s and 1960s (continuing into the 1970s and 1980s, although less so). Small farmers practicing traditional agriculture were viewed as backward peasants who obstructed modern progress. Their labor was exploited by central governments instead of respected and helped to become more productive and more profitable as a cornerstone for that progress. There is wide agreement among world hunger specialists now that when imported food aid competes with the crops of local farmers, permanent food security is undermined.

A more subtle risk to genuine development that lies in food aid is psychological. People are the agents of progress, after all, and people with hope and self-confidence are much better agents than those who feel hopeless and helpless. Hungry individuals sometimes want and need self-respect even more than food. Self-respect and self-confidence, however, are closely related to coping and meeting challenges and to being producers and contributors, not just receivers. People who have lost confidence and self-esteem have lost a fundamental driving force for development progress. In the matter of power and empowerment, who experiences the greater sense of both: the person or nation able to donate food to another, or the one who feels dependent on that gift?

From that perspective, alone, it becomes less surprising to learn that many developing countries are donors to IFAD, to the IARCs, to UNICEF and FAO, and to the United Nations World Food Programme, which distributes food aid. In 1989, four developing countries contributed to the International Emergency Food Reserve created by the U.N. General Assembly in 1975 and managed by the World Food Programme: India (per capita GNP $300), Lesotho ($370), Mauritius ($1,490), and Sri Lanka ($400).[53] Their financial contributions are small compared with those of the usual donor nations—for example, the United States with per capita GNP $18,530 or Japan, $15,760—but they are very large in proportion to relative economic strength. A number of developing countries exchange roles as food aid donors and food aid recipients from year to year, depending on their circumstances.

The World Food Conference of 1974 established an annual minimum target of 10 million tons of pledged food aid to be available to low-income, food-deficit countries from donor nations. That target has been met for most of the years since 1974. Usually the target of 500,000 tons of grain for the International

Emergency Food Reserve is met also.

Furthermore, as a result of the 1972–1974 world food crisis, FAO created a Global Information and Early Warning System on Food and Agriculture (GIEWS). The purpose of this system is to prevent crises from one year to the next by facilitating planning and action in time to save lives. FAO's findings are reported monthly to national and international officials in *Food Outlook*. This, however, is crisis prevention in the narrow, most immediate sense; it does not address the root causes of such crises. Droughts, floods, and bad weather cause crop failures in North America and Europe, too, that do not result in hunger crises in these regions. Nevertheless, as long as countries still lack the economic and political capacity to prevent extensive suffering and loss of life in emergencies through their own planning and resources, the international food aid planning implied by FAO's Global Information and Early Warning System is necessary.

By itself, food aid can never eliminate the world hunger problem. The perspective is too narrow and too short-range. Information such as these highlights from FAO's March 1990 GIEWS report, however, can nip food emergencies in the bud:

> Even assuming normal weather, 1990 production is unlikely to be large enough to meet trend consumption in 1990/91. . . . With stocks at their lowest level for many years, adverse weather would have serious consequences. . . . Conditions for winter grains are favourable in North America, Europe, U.S.S.R. and India but prospects are mixed in north and southern Africa. . . . Global consumption of cereals is forecast to increase by 2 percent in 1989/90, but per capita consumption in developing countries may decline. World cereal stocks are expected to decline further in 1989/90. The low wheat stocks of major exporters [the United States, Canada, EEC, Australia, and Argentina] give cause for particular concern. Cereal food aid shipments will increase this year to 11.6 million tons, reflecting the allocation of over 2 million tons to eastern Europe. Shipments to low-income, food-deficit countries are expected to be only slightly higher than last year. A cause of particular concern is the substantial unmet food aid requirement of Angola, Ethiopia, Mozambique and Sudan [all areas where warfare or other armed violence is the major cause of hunger]. The global refugee situation has deteriorated further, with the refugee population now estimated at 15 million [mainly in sub-Saharan Africa and Afghanis in Pakistan]. Their 1990 food aid requirements are estimated at 1.3 million tons.

The dependence on food aid by less developed countries as a group has been decreasing. To the extent that this indicates higher levels of national food self-reliance—increased agricultural production and increased ability to pay normal prices for imported food—the decline is very good news. In 1970/71, food aid accounted for 35 percent of all cereal imports in the less developed countries. In 1987/88, only 15 percent of their imported cereals came from food aid, on average.[54] The figure rises much higher for the worst cases, particularly in sub-Saharan Africa. India, however, the largest recipient of food aid until the early 1970s, is now food self-reliant.

Part of the reason for the declining share of food aid in developing-country imports is that, by policy decision, U.S. food aid is much less easily available than it was before grain stocks were nearly depleted in the 1972–1974 world food crisis. The shock of scarcer U.S. food aid was a salutary warning to national planners in developing countries who had neglected their own farmers. More than 20 percent of all U.S. cereal exports in the 1960s were food aid, primarily sold on concessionary terms (credit for long periods at low interest). From 1980 through 1987, however, food aid accounted for just slightly more than 4 percent of U.S. cereal exports.[55]

Food aid supports U.S. foreign policy now as it has since the beginning of P.L. 480 in 1954. The major allocations go for political reasons to countries considered strategically important. To ensure that enough food is available for humanitarian relief, Congress in 1980 created a minimum 4 million–ton Food Security Wheat Reserve that backstops the amount of food provided by P.L. 480 funding levels from year to year. Even so, U.S. humanitarian food aid cannot go to countries on the State Department's political embargo list, such as Nicaragua under the Sandinista government or Vietnam still. Ethiopia was on the embargo list, too, until public outcry about the famine of 1984 overwhelmed—or altered—the administration's view of political expediency. Private voluntary organizations such as CARE and Catholic Relief Services are the major channels for administering grants of U.S. humanitarian food aid. This aid supports primarily special programs for refugees or maternal and child nutrition.

The United States contributes about half of the food distributed by the U.N./FAO World Food Programme. The rest comes from other food surplus producers and by purchase on the world market with funds contributed by nonagricultural donors. The World Food Programme is apolitical and provides food on a grant basis to support social and economic development projects or for emergency purposes. Currently, the U.N./FAO World Food Programme supplies about two-thirds of all food aid for refugees. The quantity of food aid supplied to people uprooted by drought or violence increased between 1977 and 1988 from 42,000 tons to 570,000 tons. In 1988 and 1989, more than 70 percent of the grain distributed from the 500,000–metric ton International Emergency Food Reserve went to refugees.

Food aid as a solution to hunger comes up in discussions of assistance to the hungry again and again mainly because the food is "there." The governments who control food surpluses are more willing to donate food that is costing them money to store than they are to donate an equivalent value in money and go on storing surplus food. The citizens of surplus countries also are more ready to support donations of food than of tax dollars, so food aid is politically easier to do.

When food aid can meet the marketing needs of food producers in developing countries at the same time that it meets the needs of people short of food, then food aid builds food security on many fronts simultaneously. This can be done when aid consists of cash to buy food rather than donations of imported food.

An experiment by UNICEF in Ethiopia in 1984 demonstrated the multiple advantages of "cash aid" instead of food aid. UNICEF provided cash to an Ethiopian village in a drought-stricken area equal to the cost of bringing in foreign food aid for the 2,000 farming families of the area. In return, those who were physically able contributed labor to a range of local employment schemes, building roads and small-scale irrigation facilities. Each family received cash according to the family's size. Since the villagers had money with which to buy food, merchants sold them food from other regions where there was no drought. The final outcome, UNICEF discovered, was better fed children than before the drought, adults who retained everything they needed to resume farming as soon as the rains returned (including their health, which is at great risk in crowded refugee camps), and a village in better condition for development progress than before. All of this was accomplished without donated food and at less cost than imported food aid.[56]

From a development perspective, the most beneficial of all food aid is a triangular transaction in which a donor buys surplus food produced by developing-country farmers with a surplus for shipment as aid to a food-deficit country or region. In 1989, the European Economic Community planned to deliver one-fourth of its food aid pledge for sub-Saharan Africa through triangular transactions instead of donating its own agricultural products. This method gives the donor seeking to promote food security double value for the donated dollar. Harvest surpluses and short-falls fluctuate from country to country and year to year. FAO's Global Information and Early Warning System attempts to pro-mote South-South food trade, food swaps (maize for rice or wheat, for example), and triangular food aid transactions. For example, the February 1990 *Food Outlook* advised the inter-national community:

> According to FAO's latest estimates, 12 developing countries of sub-Saharan Africa hold exportable surpluses of about 1.2 million tons, mostly in coarse grains [maize and sorghum]. While much of this will be exported through normal commercial channels, special donor assistance will be required. The aggregate import require-ments in coarse grains of the deficit countries total 2.3 million tons. . . . In 1989/90 donor support is also needed by 16 countries for the purchase and internal movement to deficit areas [of the producing country] of exceptional local surpluses of 0.5 million tons; so far donors have reported plans for the purchase and internal distribu-tion of around 0.1 million tons. . . . Thus, further donor assistance is urgently required for unutilized exportable surpluses totalling 1.2 million tons in 12 countries and for the local purchase and internal distribution of a further 0.4 million tons in 11 countries.[57]

Is Food a Human Right?

In 1941, U.S. President Franklin Roosevelt named "freedom from want" as one of the four "essential freedoms" for which World War II was being fought. In 1966, the United Nations General Assembly approved an International Covenant on Economic, Social, and Cultural Rights. Nations that signed the covenant thereby recognized "the fundamental right of everyone to be free from hunger" and agreed to take steps to secure that right for their citizens. In 1974, FAO Director-General Addeke H. Boerma spoke for basic common sense when he observed, "If human beings have a right to life at all, they have a right to food." In 1976, the U.S. Congress passed a Right to Food Resolution, which declared the sense of Congress to be "that all people have a right to a nutritionally adequate diet." Still today, however, the right to food exists more in the realm of rhetoric than of law.

Only very recently have the international human rights movement and the legal profession given serious attention to the question of a right to food. In 1982, the U.N. Subcommittee for the Prevention of Discrimination and the Protection of Minorities authorized a study on the right to food under the direction of Asbjorn Eide of Norway. In 1984, the United Nations University published an international bibliography on the subject prepared by Eide's project, and the same year the Netherlands Institute of Human Rights (SIM) sponsored an international conference titled "The Right to Food: From Soft to Hard Law." One outcome of these events is the Right to Food Committee within the International Law Association. The committee's mandate is to investigate possibilities to make the right to food "hard law" instead of, as at present, only "soft law."

Gandhi is reputed to have said, "If I keep for myself more than I need of something that another lacks, I am a thief."

Following Vatican II, Pope Paul VI reached very similar conclusions from Catholic moral theology:

> [P]rivate property does not constitute for anyone an absolute and unconditional right. No one is justified in keeping for his exclusive use what he does not need, when others lack necessities. . . . the right to property must never be exercised to the detriment of the common good.[58]

As yet, however, the right to food does not carry the same force of law as the right to hold property for one's own exclusive use. No matter how hungry someone may be, taking food "owned" by someone else will still be treated as theft, not the exercise of a right, under most systems of law. Despite common approval of moral exhortations about the right to food, the implications of institutionalizing such a right are still enveloped in ambiguity and conflicting values.

The problems of human greed, human need, authentic community, and the relationship between humankind and the rest of nature are prominent in ethical, theological, and psychological discussions of the hunger issue. For the religious person, one's response to the presence of hunger in the world also involves questions of the believer's right relationship to God and to God's Creation.[59]

What is it, ultimately, that justifies "need"? What justifies conversion of the earth's resources to human ends? When is a claim to "need" actually an expression of greed? By what measure is one person's claim justly weighed against the claim of another? When is individual surplus socially positive, when negative? Is community among persons possible without mutual trust? Are either community or trust possible where some hunger while others eat? Where does an individual's responsibility for meeting needs end and the community's responsibility begin? Are the claims of justice different in circumstances of abundance than in circumstances of scarcity? When does a "need" become a "right"?

Assumptions about the ethics of distributive justice are central to the choice of response to the world hunger problem. This is a topic, however, that has received relatively scant professional treatment outside of the Church. Among current American philosophers, Henry Shue is well-known for his work on distributive justice and food policy.[60] In 1987, the first of the colloquia on the world food problem, now conducted annually by the Smithsonian Institution, examined "Science, Ethics, and Food," but subsequent colloquia have omitted the topic of ethics, leaving only science and food.[61]

Conclusion

Progress among the hungry rarely captures headlines. It makes a much less dramatic photograph than famine victims. Nevertheless, we have seen that the world is feeding 1 billion more people than it did in 1974. We note that developing countries as a group depend far less on food aid to meet their needs than 20 years ago. There is also considerable evidence that the extent of poverty worldwide was declining in the 1950s, 1960s, and 1970s. The major cause of the population explosion, in fact, was not higher birth rates but longer life expectancy due to improved health and nutrition.

Until the sharp reduction of government health and nutrition programs during the debt crisis of the 1980s and the similarly caused drop in household income and purchasing power for food and other essentials during that decade, the health and nutrition of infants and children had enjoyed 30 years of steady improvement in nearly every country. During the six years of 1980 through 1985, the World Food Council estimates that the number of undernourished people increased by 50 million, compared with an increase of only 15 million during the entire decade of the 1970s. The council attributes that extraordinary deterioration primarily to structural adjustment programs and the economic crisis.[62] If the present economic crisis and the harsher aspects of structural adjustment in debt-burdened countries can be overcome, it is highly probable that developing countries will resume their slow but steady improvement in meeting basic needs.

Advocates of sustainable systems of food security accept ultimate limits to the world's food supply as a given, but they claim the neo-Malthusians are unduly pessimistic. Under the influence of the twentieth century's environmental ecology and population movements, few deny that the earth is a finite planet with a limited carrying capacity for the human species. Many believe, however, that very good lives can be lived within those limits by many more people than are here already—but not without changing current patterns of technology and resource consumption.

By changing the way we use and distribute access to the earth's resources, an additional nine billion people can be accommodated in good health and reasonable comfort. The Buckminster Fullers and E. F. Schumachers of our time confidently predict this—but they also speak urgently of change because positive change needs to come soon. Agriculture, for example, must regenerate the soil's fertility, protect limited water resources, and produce crops by ecologically benign and sustainable means. Diets will need to obtain most of their calories and protein from grain directly instead of by feeding the grain first to animals where grain is converted into nutrients much less efficiently. Technology must rely on renewable resources with better technology found for recycling old products into new. Finally, broadly based economic growth and distributive equity must become higher social priorities than they are now in most countries. Values receive greater support from public policy and economic and social institutions. Gandhi may be right: "The earth has enough for everyone's need but not enough for everyone's greed."

If hunger ever ceases to be a major world problem, the primary agents of change will be people who have known intimately its gnawing pain and weakness and its threat to their children. They have the most at stake. They are demonstrating even now in their multitude of local organizations and enterprises the greatest dynamism for such change. In the 12 years since IFAD began to carry out its World Food Conference mandate to help small farmers and the rural poor, the experience of working with these neglected populations has been highly encouraging. Promoting self-reliant progress among the poor is what IFAD and many other organizations are doing, slowly but surely, taking care that women as well as men participate in the design and management of change and share the benefits. Most important of all, the poor themselves—women, especially—are casting off hopelessness, fear, and ignorance to demand change.

The World Commission on Environment and Development (also known as the Brundtland Commission) asked an expert panel on food security to advise the commission "how humankind can be insulated from hunger on an ecologically sustainable basis." The panel's review, led by M. S. Swaminathan, concluded that the key to action for food security should be the aim of increasing *sustainable livelihood security,* explained as follows:

> Livelihood is defined as adequate stocks and flows of food and cash to meet basic needs. Security refers to secure ownership of, or access to, resources and income earning activities, including reserves and assets to offset risk, ease shocks and meet contingencies. Sustainable refers to the maintenance or enhancement of resource productivity on a long-term basis.[63]

That is a good starting place, but ending world hunger involves still more. The challenges ahead are enormous. The obstacles are stubbornly entrenched. Still, change does come. To build on the increments of positive change and to improve the odds may be as much as a realist can ask.

One fact is very clear: Success in eliminating hunger comes more readily when both the hungry and the well-fed demand, and public policy recognizes and supports, what is actually needed. Neither knowledge without political will nor political will without insight will get the job done. The World Food Council has it right:

> Future progress towards the elimination of hunger will . . . depend on a better understanding of why the efforts of nations and the international community have failed to reduce the number of hungry and malnourished people. . . . the lessons of the past must form the basis for immediate and more effective action.[64]

There is work enough ahead for everyone.

Notes

1. FAO, *Food Outlook* (March 1990), 2.

2. World Food Council, President's Report to the Fifteenth Ministerial Session, *World Hunger Fifteen Years after the World Food Conference: The Challenges Ahead,* WFC/1989/2 Part One, Rome, 22 March 1989.

3. *Food Outlook* (March 1990), 2.

4. James P. Grant, *The State of the World's Children 1989* (New York: Oxford University Press for UNICEF, 1989).

5. World Food Council, *The Global State of Hunger and Malnutrition—1990 Report,* WFC/1990/2, Rome, 10 April 1990, para. 1. Hunger statistics used throughout come from this document.

6. World Bank, *World Development Report 1990* (Washington, DC: The World Bank, 1990), 28.

7. World Food Council, *Current World Food Situation,* WFC/1990/7, Rome, 12 April 1990.

8. World Food Council, *World Hunger Fifteen Years after the World Food Conference,* para. 1.

9. House Committee on Foreign Affairs, *U.N. Conference to Review and Appraise the U.N. Decade for Women, July 15–26, 1985. Report of Congressional Staff Advisors to the Nairobi Conference,* 99th Congress, 2d session, 68.

10. S. K. Kumar, *Rural Infrastructure in Bangladesh: Effects on Food Consumption and Nutrition of the Population* (Washington, DC: IFPRI, 1988), cited by John Mellor in *Environment* 30:9 (November 1988), 28.

11. *Address by Henry A. Kissinger, Secretary of State of the United States of America, before the World Food Conference, Rome, 5 November 1974* (Washington, DC: Department of State).

12. See especially two writings of development ethicist, Denis Goulet: *The Cruel Choice: A New Concept in the Theory of Development* (New York: Atheneum Press, 1971) and *The Uncertain Promise: Values and Conflict in Technology Transfer* (Washington, DC: Overseas Development Council, 1977).

13. Amartya Sen, "The Great Bengal Famine," chapter 6 in *Poverty and Famines. An Essay on Entitlement and Deprivation* (Oxford: Clarendon Press, 1981), 52ff.

14. Thomas Robert Malthus, *Essay on the Principle of Population as It Affects the Future Improvement of Society* (London, 1798), revised in 2 volumes, Patricia James, ed. (Cambridge: Cambridge University Press, 1990).

15. Congressional Research Service, *Feeding the World's Population: Developments in the Decade Following the World Food Conference of 1974,* a report prepared for the Committee on Foreign Affairs, U.S. House of Representatives, October 1984, 762.

16. W. W. Rostow, *The Stages of Economic Growth: A Non-Communist Manifesto* (Cambridge: Cambridge University Press, 1960), 7.

17. Robert S. McNamara, "Address to the Board of Governors, Nairobi, Kenya,

September 24, 1973," in *The McNamara Years: Major Policy Addresses of Robert S. McNamara 1968–1981* (Washington, DC: The World Bank, 1981).

18. Robert S. McNamara, *Address to the Board of Governors*, Belgrade, Yugoslavia, 12 October 1979 (Washington, DC: The World Bank, 1979), 26.

19. United Nations World Food Conference, *Assessment of the World Food Situation Present and Future*, E/Conf.65/3, Rome, 1974, para. 181.

20. Frances Moore Lappé and Joseph Collins, *World Hunger: Ten Myths* (San Francisco: Institute for Food and Development Policy, 1977).

21. Susan George, *How the Other Half Dies. The Real Reasons for World Hunger* (Montclair, NJ: Allenheld, Osmun & Co., 1977), 115.

22. Dan Morgan, *Merchants of Grain* (New York: Viking Press, 1979).

23. Sen, "The Great Bengal Famine," 94.

24. Susan George, "World Hunger: Asking the Right Questions," *Educational Leadership* 40:1, reprinted by the Office on Global Education, Church World Service, Baltimore, MD.

25. Shlomo Reutlinger and Jack van Holst Pellekaan, *Poverty and Hunger: Issues and Options for Food Security in Developing Countries*, a World Bank Policy Study (Washington, DC: The World Bank, 1986), 1.

26. Economic Research Service, U.S. Department of Agriculture, *Agricultural Outlook* (Jan.–Feb. 1990), 34.

27. M. S. Swaminathan, "Agricultural Prosperity—Key to Third World Progress," *Third World Quarterly* 5:3 (July 1983), 559.

28. Cited by Lester Brown, "Feeding Six Billion," *World Watch* (Sept.–Oct. 1989), 34.

29. Ibid.

30. FAO, *World Hunger*, E/685/1/4000 (1985), 13.

31. Swaminathan, "Agricultural Prosperity," 562.

32. International Labour Office, *World Labour Report*, Vol. 1 (Geneva: ILO, 1984).

33. World Food Council Secretariat, *The Global State of Hunger and Malnutrition and the Impact of Economic Adjustment on Food and Hunger Problems*, WFC/1987/2, Rome, 8 April 1987, para. 39.

34. *ILO Information* (May 1986 and August 1987).

35. FAO, *Second Progress Report on the World Conference on Agrarian Reform and Rural Development Programme of Action Including the Role of Women in Rural Development*, C 87/19, Rome, August 1987, cited in World Food Council, *World Hunger Fifteen Years after the World Food Conference*, p. 16.

36. Gross national product data throughout are from the World Bank, *World Development Report 1989* (New York: Oxford University Press, 1989).

37. Idriss Jazairy, address to the Twelfth Annual Meeting of the Governing Council of the International Fund for Agricultural Development, Rome, 24 January 1989.

38. House Committee on Foreign Affairs, 69ff.

39. Ibid., 66.

40. ILO, *World Labour Report.*

41. David Richards, testimony before the House Select Committee on Hunger, U.S. Congress, 12 March 1987, as cited in *Hunger Notes* 13:11–12 (April–May 1988), 18–19.

42. Muhammad Yunus, founder of the Grameen Bank, testimony before the House Select Committee on Hunger, U.S. Congress, 25 February 1986, as cited in *Hunger Notes* 13:11–12, 15.

43. Idriss Jazairy, in an interview with the author cited in *Hunger Notes* 13:11–12.

44. Swaminathan, "Agricultural Prosperity," 565. Research on women's expenditures from increased income show different patterns, giving priority to increased household food and children's education and health.

45. P. B. R. Hazell and A. Roell, *Rural Growth Linkages: Household Expenditure Patterns in Malaysia and Nigeria,* IFPRI Research Report 41 (Washington, DC: IFPRI, 1983).

46. R. Ahmed and M. Hossain, *Infrastructure and the Development of a Rural Economy* (Washington, DC: IFPRI, 1987).

47. Kumar, *Rural Infrastructure in Bangladesh.*

48. Swaminathan, "Agricultural Prosperity."

49. FAO, *Food Outlook* (March 1990), 30ff.

50. Swaminathan, "Agricultural Prosperity," 562.

51. World Food Council, *Additional and More Effective Measures by Governments to Alleviate Hunger and Poverty. Report by the Executive Director,* WFC/1990/3, Rome, 6 April 1990, para. 22.

52. S. K. Kumar and D. Hotchkiss, *Energy and Nutrition Links to Agriculture in a Hill Region of Nepal* (Washington, DC: IFPRI, 1988), as cited by Mellor in *Environment* 30:9 (November 1988), 10.

53. FAO, *Food Outlook* (March 1990), 21.

54. Economic Research Service, USDA, *World Food Needs and Availabilities 1989/90: Winter,* 6.

55. Charles E. Hanrahan, *Foreign Food Aid: Reauthorization Issues,* Congressional Research Service, Library of Congress, updated 23 May 1989, Table 2.

56. Reutlinger and van Holst Pellekaan, *Poverty and Hunger,* 39.

57. FAO, *Food Outlook* (February 1990).

58. Paul VI, *On the Development of Peoples,* papal encyclical (Rome: The Vatican, 1967).

59. Among the more widely read writers and works on the world hunger problem from the perspective of Christian biblical theology are Bruce C. Birch and Larry L. Rasmussen, *The Predicament of the Prosperous* (1978); Mary Evelyn Jegen and Brunno V. Mannos, eds., *The Earth Is the Lord's* (1978); Adam Daniel Finnerty, *No More Plastic Jesus: Global Justice and Christian Lifestyle* (1977); Jack

Nelson, *Hungry for Justice* (1980) and *The Politics of Compassion* (1986); and Ronald J. Sider, *Rich Christians in an Age of Hunger* (1977).

60. See Henry Shue, *Basic Rights: Subsistence, Affluence and U.S. Foreign Policy* (Princeton, NJ: Princeton University Press, 1980) and Henry Shue and Peter G. Brown, eds., *Food Policy: The Responsibility of the United States in the Life and Death Choices* (New York: Macmillan Publishing Co., 1977).

61. See especially William J. Byron, S.J., "On the Protection and Promotion of the Right to Food: An Ethical Perspective"; Amartya K. Sen, "Food Entitlements and Economic Chains"; and John W. Mellor, "Toward an Ethical Redistribution of Food and Agricultural Science," all in Brian W. J. LeMay, ed., *Science, Ethics and Food,* conference proceedings (Washington, DC: Smithsonian Institution Press, 1988).

62. World Food Council Secretariat, *Global State of Hunger and Malnutrition,* para. 13.

63. M. S. Swaminathan et al., *Food 2000: Global Policies for Sustainable Agriculture* (London: Zed Books, 1987). Emphasis added.

64. World Food Council, *World Hunger Fifteen Years after the World Food Conference,* para. 3.

2

Chronology

THE THEME OF THE CHRONOLOGY sketched here is the quest for food security in all of its many aspects, both at the macro level (national and international) and at the micro level of the actual millions of hungry individuals and households.

At the macro level the quest focuses on the "big picture": the production of adequate food supplies nationally and globally; the question of sustainable balance between the number of humans to be fed and the capacity of the earth and human societies to feed them; the guarantee that food-deficit societies can obtain through trade or aid what is lacking in their own production; concern to protect the fundamental ecology of the earth, upon which all food production ultimately depends; and questions of the rights and duties of nations and of how the international community of nations can best organize to meet its moral obligations.

Achieving these macro goals, however, still can leave millions of people with a chronic lack of adequate food. As agricultural scientists, social scientists, and other deeply concerned students of the hunger problem grapple with the elusive goal of food security, therefore, we find inquiry moving ever more intently toward the micro level. There, political, social, and economic obstacles to food security become glaringly apparent as they operate to keep certain groups of people hunger-prone, even when the productive potential of the natural environment is adequate and even though ample food supplies may be available in theory. Some of these obstacles are wholly internal, but others are found to be linked to influences and forces operating globally. So new themes arise in the chronology of the world hunger problem, themes having to do with human rights, North-South relations, U.S. foreign policy, multinational corporations, the debt crisis, inequitable access to productive resources, and, above all, the autonomy and empowerment of chronically disadvantaged groups.

The world hunger problem began when the human species spread itself across the face of the planet. The chronology recorded here, however, starts with the year 1940. Most of the initiatives to end world hunger that are still operating stem from events of the 1940s. On one side are new fruits of concerns that began to grow even before World War II about the effects of malnutrition and about the long future of population growth and world food supply. On the other side are the food crises spawned by World War II and the mechanisms to cope with those crises created by churches and other volunteer agencies and by the Allied governments (who had already begun calling themselves the United Nations).

In 1940, World War II began to disrupt food systems upon which hundreds of millions of people depended for sustenance. On the European continent, the food system was disrupted so badly and for so long that more than a million Europeans died of hunger and millions of survivors would remember to the end of their days the great blessing contained in a loaf of bread. Part of that story is told below. At the same time, several million other children, women, and men starved to death in Asia, partly because of the war's attack on their food systems, but partly also because of inept comprehension by public authorities of why people were lacking food. Three million died in the Indian state of Bengal, for example, where inappropriate responses based on inaccurate assumptions permitted a terrible tragedy that could have been avoided through different policies based on different assumptions.

This chronology traces a 50-year evolution in those two facets of the world hunger problem: assumptions about the actual nature of the problem and the responses that flow from those assumptions.

Several famines mark this history, but famine is not its subject. The terrible drama of famine has a unique ability to refocus the attention of both the public and policy makers on the world's hunger problem—attention that always wanders when the sense of urgency wanes. The lasting significance, however, lies in the insights and institutions generated during famines that remain at work after most of the world turns back to "business as usual." The most important insight, always, is that famine's victims are those with little food security in the existing food system as it normally operates from day to day. Those in any society for whom the food system works adequately do not succumb to famine; those left out of the system's food security do. To make food systems work for everyone is the challenge for policy makers the world over.

This chronology may leave the reader feeling pessimistic. The speed at which the lessons learned are translated into effective policy and action can seem glacial. For example, the best that we now know about the nature and cure of the hunger problem was first stated in 1943, at least in broad terms, by the people assembled at Hot Springs, Virginia, to lay the groundwork for a United Nations Food and Agriculture Organization.

At no other time in human history, however, have so many people armed with so much knowledge and skill and so many instruments for collaboration across ethnic and political boundaries worked together to end needless human suffering. Almost all of these instruments for collective effort, as will be seen, have been created since 1940. That is one seed of hope: The international community of effort as we know it today—official and unofficial—is actually very young as historical change is measured. Another seed of hope can be seen in the worldwide awakening of the poor and the long-disadvantaged to an awareness of better possibilities and to a determination to achieve at least some measure of those possibilities. The ignorance, the fatalism, and, in some cases, the fear of reprisal that have held chronic victims of hunger imprisoned in their situation are ending.

These are two of the most important seeds of hope found in the story of these past five decades. Others will speak for themselves in the events chronicled briefly here.

1940–1949

1940   World War II begins as Germany invades Holland, Belgium, and Luxembourg on May 10 and France on May 12.

1940
cont.
The Presiding Bishop's Fund for World Relief is established by the General Convention of the Episcopal Church to receive contributions for the relief of human needs created by the war. Most other religious institutions create similar European emergency funds that, similarly, turn into long-range assistance programs for developing nations by the 1950s.

1941
The "four freedoms" declared by President Franklin Roosevelt in the Annual Address to Congress on January 6 include freedom of speech and worship and freedom from want and fear:

> The third [freedom] is freedom from want—which, translated into world terms, means economic understandings which will secure to every nation a healthy peacetime life for its inhabitants—everywhere in the world.

**1941–
1943**
Famine in Leningrad, under siege by the German Army for 872 days, kills an estimated one million.

1942
The Oxford Committee for Famine Relief is formed by volunteers in Oxford, England, to raise relief for famine in Nazi-occupied Greece. The famine kills an estimated 450,000 civilians. Made permanent as OXFAM in 1948, the organization shifts the focus of its aid to self-help organizations toward developing regions.

The Inter-American Institute for Cooperation on Agriculture is founded in Costa Rica to help member nations develop agricultural production and promote rural advancement. World War II has greatly increased demand for sugar, beef, cotton, and other exports from Latin America. Large landowners and wealthy investors expand production of such cash crops, with fateful results for smallholder peasants and Indians who cannot enforce claims to land they are cultivating. Rapid population growth, low wages, shrinking opportunity for the poor, and growing hunger set the stage for explosive conflict in the Caribbean Basin within a generation.

The "Second Memorandum on a United Nations Programme for Freedom from Want of Food" is drafted by Australian agricultural advisor Frank McDougall with encouragement from Eleanor Roosevelt. (McDougall's first memorandum, drafted for Australian High Commissioner Stanley Bruce's League of Nations address in 1935, urged the "marriage" of health and agricultural objectives in national planning.)

1942
cont.
President Roosevelt approves a conference of the Allied nations to promote cooperation in matters of food production, food supply, and nutritional health.

1943
United Nations (i.e., the Allied nations) Conference on Food and Agriculture at Hot Springs, Virginia, 18 May–3 June, appoints an interim commission (chaired by Lester Pearson, Canadian ambassador to the United States) to prepare a specific plan for a permanent international organization—the Food and Agriculture Organization of the United Nations. Conference Resolution 24, "Achievement of an Economy of Abundance," states that the first cause of hunger and malnutrition is poverty, which consequently requires

> promotion of the full employment of human and material resources, based on sound social and economic policies [as] the first condition of a general and progressive increase in production and purchasing power.

Catholic Relief Services (CRS) is founded 28 June in the United States to distribute food, clothing, and medical supplies in Europe. CRS begins with refugee aid in the United Kingdom, Portugal, and Spain, the only areas of Europe exempt from the British blockade. (The U.S. Catholic Bishops' Emergency Fund, started in 1941, was the CRS's precursor.)

The Friends Committee on National Legislation (FCNL), the first permanent faith-based humanitarian lobby in the United States, is founded 1 November and quickly gains prominence in advocacy on measures to end hunger and poverty worldwide.

The United Nations Relief and Rehabilitation Administration (UNRRA) is formed by 44 Allied nations on 9 November to aid regions damaged by World War II.

The Rockefeller Foundation and the government of Mexico begin cooperative agricultural research to increase the productivity of Mexican grain under director J. George Harrar, who later would become president of the Rockefeller Foundation. Research targets corn and wheat, with Norman Borlaug directing wheat research. This project evolves into the International Center for Improvement of Maize and Wheat (CIMMYT) in 1963.

1943–
1944
The Bengal famine, erroneously believed to be due to a food shortage, kills an estimated three million people, four times the

1943–
1944
cont.
number of Americans and Britons killed in World War II. (Research by Amartya Sen, published in 1981, demonstrates the actual cause to have been a spreading unemployment and income crisis triggered by flood damage for which government response was inadequate. See "References in Print.")

1944–
1945
Famine in the Netherlands kills approximately 10,000 people during the winter of 1944/1945 when Germany blocks the import of food supplies.

The Minnesota Starvation Experiment studies the physiological and psychological effects of gradual starvation with the aid of 32 U.S. pacifist conscientious objectors between the ages of 21 and 33, who volunteer as subjects. The research team for the one-year experiment in the Laboratory of Physiological Hygiene at the University of Minnesota is led by Ancel Keys. Keys and co-authors release a preliminary report 15 October 1945, *Experimental Starvation in Man,* and a final two-volume report in 1950 titled *The Biology of Starvation.* Observations from the experiment by pacifists Harold Steere Guetzkow and Paul Hoover Bowman, *Men and Hunger: A Psychological Manual for Relief Workers,* are published by the Church of the Brethren in 1946 to guide volunteers in postwar Europe.

1944
Heifer Project (later Heifer Project International) is founded by U.S. volunteers to rebuild livestock herds in war-devastated regions of Europe and China by shipping donated pregnant heifers from U.S. herds.

1945
Famine in Vietnam kills two million when Japanese occupation forces confiscate rice from Vietnamese peasants and burn rice fields.

The Food and Agriculture Organization of the United Nations (FAO) is established 16 October by 34 member nations at the first annual FAO conference, held at Chateau Frontenac in Quebec. The founding conference is chaired by Lester Pearson. Sir John Boyd-Orr, a noted British humanitarian and veterinary scientist with passionate concern about human malnutrition related to poverty, is chosen first FAO director-general. Temporary FAO headquarters are located in Washington, D.C.

The United Nations Charter is signed 24 October in San Francisco, establishing the General Assembly, the Economic and Social Council, and the Security Council.

1945 Cooperative for American Remittances to Europe (CARE) is
cont. formed in November by 22 members of the American Council
of Voluntary Agencies to purchase millions of surplus U.S. Army
Ten-in-One ration kits and send them to destitute Europeans as
"CARE packages." By the end of July 1946, CARE Executive
Director William N. Haskell (a retired lieutenant-general) reports that 400,000 of the 30-pound army ration kits have been
sent to 11 countries.

UNRRA begins massive postwar relief, sending 100,000 tons of
food, clothing, and medicine to China, more than 330,000 tons
to Czechoslovakia, and similar quantities to other European
countries by the end of the year. U.S. postwar relief reaches
nearly $18 billion by the end of 1947, distributed mainly
through UNRRA. (UNRRA's Displaced Persons Office evolves
into the present Office of the U.N. High Commissioner for
Refugees.)

Lutheran World Relief (LWR) is established as the overseas aid
channel for all branches of the Lutheran Church in the United
States. Like many nongovernmental agencies founded for post–
World War II relief in Europe, LWR becomes a permanent
instrument of voluntary assistance to small-scale self-help projects in developing countries.

1946 Church World Service (CWS) is formed as the overseas relief
agency for Protestant denominational members of the Federal
Council of Churches in the United States (later named the
National Council of Churches) and begins its Community
Hunger Appeal (CROP) in 1947.

International Bank for Reconstruction and Development (the
World Bank) begins operations in June.

FAO's First World Food Survey, issued in July, shows serious,
widespread lack of adequate nourishment in the world based on
prewar data from 70 countries with 90 percent of the world's
population. FAO's World Food Appraisal for 1946/1947, released 26 December, confirms a food crisis.

A World Food Board is proposed on 7 August by FAO Director-
General Boyd-Orr, who urges that "food is more than a trade
commodity; it is an essential of life." The World Food Board

1946
cont.
forms and coordinates a plan (with an emergency grain reserve, surplus food sold to needy at reduced prices, and price-stabilizing trade agreements) to ensure "that sufficient food is produced and distributed to bring the consumption of all peoples up to a health standard." Opposition from the United States comes immediately. The second FAO conference appoints a Preparatory Commission under Stanley Bruce to draft a more detailed proposal. None of the Bruce Commission's recommendations (including a famine reserve "held nationally by exporting and importing countries for use nationally and internationally under agreed conditions") is adopted by the third FAO conference in 1947. Boyd-Orr leaves FAO in 1948 to take his message to the tribune of world public opinion, writing, travelling, and speaking widely. (He is succeeded at FAO by U.S. Under-Secretary of Agriculture Norris E. Dodd for the term 1948–1953, who is followed by another USDA official, Philip V. Cardon, from 1954 to 1956.)

United Nations International Children's Emergency Fund (UNICEF) is established by the U.N. General Assembly to raise funds for 60 million needy European children. Aake Ording of Norway is named executive director.

India's Central Rice Research Institute begins scientific rice research.

The Japanese Land Reform Act is passed by the Japanese parliament in October, the most successful democratically designed and administered agrarian reform in the twentieth century. The chief advisor on land reform is Wolf Ladejinsky, a Russian-born U.S. agricultural economist loaned to General Douglas MacArthur for this purpose by the Department of State. Five million acres of agricultural land are purchased by the Japanese government at a fixed price from wealthy landlords and transferred to peasant farmers, accomplishing a far-reaching democratization of Japan's rural society that defuses growing Communist influence.

**1946–
1947**
Famine threatens Europe and Asia. In March 1946, the Allies' Combined Food Board reports to UNRRA that world food supplies are 40 percent below normal. Half a billion people are severely undernourished and at risk of starvation. Famine is occurring in Poland, Finland, and other countries. President Harry Truman forms a Famine Emergency Committee under

1946–
1947
cont.
Chester Davis, wartime U.S. food administrator, with former President Herbert Hoover (World War I food relief hero) as honorary chairman. On a fact-finding tour, Hoover warns from Paris on 26 March that starvation is imminent in France and Italy within four months unless food arrives. By May, Hoover is estimating up to 800 million people threatened by famine in Europe. The new U.N. General Assembly creates an International Emergency Food Council (IEFC) to replace the wartime Combined Food Board in securing and distributing food supplies for war-ravaged nations. Congressional ambivalence and postwar labor strife make U.S. response unreliable and inconsistent. As late as February 1948, congressional testimony from a major volunteer agency working in Europe, the American Friends Service Committee, reports European despair and loss of confidence in U.S. leadership. Food aid is insufficient. The crisis ends in 1948 with the return of good harvests.

German and Austrian food rations are below subsistence. Health professionals in the U.S. occupation authorities recommend in January 1946 that the civilian food ration be increased from 1,550 calories per day to 1,750 (compared with an average of 3,000 calories in peacetime), but President Truman resists. By April, hampered also by dockers strikes, food supplies drop to 1,050 calories per person in the French and British zones and to 1,250 calories in the U.S. zone. Workers riot in many German cities. The death rate rises, especially among children and the elderly, as undernourishment lowers disease resistance (a characteristic problem during famine). In November 1946, UNRRA Director Fiorello LaGuardia and commander of the U.S. occupation General Mark Clark succeed in raising Austrian rations from 1,200 to 1,550. U.S. public opinion and the persistence of Herbert Hoover and General Clark finally ease U.S. policy (Britain, France, and the U.S.S.R. are themselves short of food). By the spring of 1947, a mounting food crisis in all four occupation zones is officially confirmed and the U.S. War Department sets up soup kitchens "under the Hoover plan" to feed 3.5 million children and 1 million aged in the U.S. and British occupation zones.

1948
The Joint Commission for Rural Reconstruction in China, funded by the U.S. China Aid Act of 1948, seeks to improve conditions for small farmers in Szechuan by providing funding and technical assistance to projects of local government and

1948
cont.
peoples' organizations. The aid is managed in consultation with local peasants by a commission of two Americans and three Chinese, including Dr. Y. C. James Yen, for 30 years a pioneer of nonformal education and organizing for self-advancement among rural Chinese. During its one year before the Chinese Communist advance takes over Szechuan, the commission aids 216 projects in agricultural improvement, irrigation, land reform, rural industries, farmers' organizations, rural health, and citizen education. The commission's work inspires Truman's Point Four Program and agrarian reform actions during 1951–1952 by Nationalist Chinese on Taiwan.

Marshall Plan (named for U.S. Secretary of State George Marshall) begins in March to deliver massive U.S. economic aid to rebuild war-torn economies in non-Communist Europe and Asia. In FY 1949, Marshall Plan aid amounts to 11.5 percent of the federal budget, 2.79 percent of the U.S. GNP. By its close in January 1952, the Marshall Plan distributes $12 billion in economic foreign aid.

Organization for European Economic Cooperation is formed to coordinate Marshall Plan funds. Headquartered in Paris, it becomes the Organization for Economic Cooperation and Development (OECD) when the Marshall Plan ends.

1949
President Truman's Point Four Program is announced in his inaugural address 20 January as a "bold new program for making the benefits of our scientific advances and industrial progress available for the improvement and growth of underdeveloped areas." Truman names technical assistance to developing countries as the fourth point in a new strategy of U.S. foreign policy to prevent the spread of communism and promote global prosperity:

> More than half the people of the world are living in conditions approaching misery. Their food is inadequate. They are victims of disease. Their economic life is primitive and stagnant. Their poverty is a handicap and a threat both to them and to more prosperous areas.
> For the first time in history humanity possesses the knowledge and the skill to relieve the suffering of these people. . . . Greater production is the key to prosperity and peace. And the key to greater production is a wider and more vigorous application of modern scientific and technical knowledge. Only by helping the least fortunate of its members to help themselves can the human

1949
cont.   family achieve the decent, satisfying life that is the right of all people.

United Nations Expanded Program of Technical Assistance (EPTA) begins, inspired by the U.S. Point Four Program.

1949–
1950   People's Republic of China takes over all of mainland China and revolutionizes the structure of Chinese agriculture and food system.

1950–1959

1950   Point Four Program begins 5 June, administered by the Technical Cooperation Administration in the State Department. By 1961, 6,000 U.S. technicians are working in 58 countries.

1950–
1956   India suffers recurrent food crises following independence on 16 January 1950 and is the largest recipient of U.S. food aid and Point Four technical assistance. Alarmed about rapid population increase, the government of India adopts a policy to reduce population growth.

1951   Land reform becomes an issue for the U.N. General Assembly in 1950 and a joint U.N./FAO report is issued in 1951, *Land Reform—Defects in Agrarian Structure as Obstacles to Development*. The U.N. Economic and Social Council (ECOSOC) asks FAO to assume permanent responsibility within the U.N. system for problems of agrarian structure.

The International Conference on Land Tenure and Related Problems in World Agriculture is co-sponsored by the University of Wisconsin, the U.S. Department of State, the U.S. Department of Agriculture, and several other federal agencies 7 October in Madison, Wisconsin. One hundred and fifty government officials and rural development researchers from developing countries and the United States jointly examine issues, training, and administration of agrarian reform. This is the last major U.S. agrarian reform initiative until after the anticommunist witch hunts of the McCarthy era. The conference report is first published in 1963. (Agrarian reform was considered communistic in some quarters, and Wolf Ladejinsky

1951 was considered a security risk by President Dwight Eisenhower's
cont. secretary of agriculture, Ezra Taft Benson.)

Ford Foundation's Overseas Development Program begins in
South and Southeast Asia in 1951, with grants for community
development, agricultural production, and the development of
institutions for agricultural research and training (especially in
India). The foundation's efforts spread to sub-Saharan Africa in
1958 and to Latin America and the Caribbean in 1959.

1952 Brazilian rainforest conversion to farmland and new settlements, a policy initiated in 1945, gains momentum in the 1950s,
avoiding the issue of reform of highly inequitable land ownership. A thousand families move onto newly cleared land to plant
cotton, corn, and beans in early 1953.

The Mau Mau rebellion in Kenya is in full force. Recovery of
African control over agricultural land taken by European set-
tlers is a major objective. This marks the beginning of the end
of European colonization in Africa. Ghana, in 1957, is the first
colony to become independent.

FAO's second World Food Survey, published in November,
notes a fall in the world's per capita calorie supply from pre–
World War II levels and also a wider gap between developed and
developing nations in per capita food energy.

1952– North American grain surpluses are the most pressing world
1954 food problem for most policy makers, depressing crop prices
worldwide. FAO proposes a new "Guidelines and Principles of
Surplus Disposal" to prevent a recurrence of the 1930s destructive trade practice of "dumping" surpluses on the market at any
price just to get rid of them.

1953 Militarism as an obstacle to ending hunger ("guns or butter") is
highlighted in President Eisenhower's inaugural address 20
January:

> Every gun that is made, every warship launched, every rocket
> fired signifies, in the final sense, a theft from those who hunger
> and are not fed, those who are cold and not clothed.

1954 The Agricultural Trade Development and Assistance Act of
1954 (Public Law 83-480, commonly known as P.L. 480) establishes food aid as a fixture in U.S. agricultural policy. The first

1954
cont.

two of the seven purposes stated in the legislation are viewed as primary: (1) to dispose of agricultural surplus, (2) to develop export markets for U.S. commodities, (3) to expand international trade, (4) to combat hunger and malnutrition, (5) to promote educational and cultural exchange programs, (6) to promote economic development, and (7) to promote the common defense. The initial authorization earmarks $300 million for Title II grants for humanitarian use and $700 million for Title I sales on "concessionary terms" (below normal market costs) from Commodity Credit Corporation surplus grain stocks. By 1956, 18 U.S. private volunteer organizations are distributing P.L. 480 Title II commodities in 70 countries. From 1956 to the end of 1959, P.L. 480 disposes of more than 11 million tons of surplus grain each year in Title I concessional sales; consequently, the United States is accused of dumping.

The World Population Conference, the first international governmental meeting on this issue, is convened by FAO.

"Population bomb" and "population explosion" are spread as common images in public dialogue by a pamphlet published by the Hugh Moore Fund. Two million copies are distributed. (By the 1960s these figures of speech are commonplace.)

Honduran workers win a strike against U.S. banana companies for higher wages. Organizing among peasant groups and laborers increases.

Guatemalan land reform is proposed by the newly elected president, who is quickly overthrown in an army coup with CIA support. A veritable war against peasant and Indian leaders continues to be waged by the army. The conflict reaches a crescendo in the late 1970s, when armed guerrilla resistance appears. Most volunteer development assistance organizations leave to avoid exposing to even greater risk the peasants they are trying to help. An estimated 50,000 to 75,000 Guatemalans, most of them Indians, are killed by the army or by anonymous death squads in the years following 1978.

1959

The Cuban Revolution, led by Fidel Castro, is victorious on New Year's Day. Cuban President Fulgencio Batista, virtual dictator since 1934, goes into exile. The Marxist government nationalizes land ownership and institutes broad programs of nutrition assistance, free medical care, literacy, employment, and housing. Hunger decreases dramatically.

1959 The U.N. Special Fund is established to promote more volun-
cont. tary government funding for development in the South.

The General Assembly names the 1960s as the United Nations
Development Decade.

1960–1969: First United Nations Development Decade

1960 World Food Programme (WFP) is initiated by the U.N. General
Assembly. FAO Director-General B. R. Sen is asked to design
multilateral arrangements for "the mobilization of available
surplus foodstuffs and their distribution in areas of greatest
need."

International Rice Research Institute (IRRI) is established at
the University of the Philippines at Los Banos as a cooperative
venture of the Rockefeller and Ford foundations and the
Philippine government. Robert Chandler is named the first
director. Sterling Wortman, later director of agricultural research for the Rockefeller Foundation, is associate director.

International Development Association (IDA) is established at
the World Bank to channel development loans on very lenient
terms (almost as grants) to least developed countries (LDCs), a
category defined chiefly by very low levels of per capita income
and GNP.

FAO's Freedom from Hunger Campaign (FFHC) begins as a
worldwide citizens' movement to end hunger. The campaign is
proposed by FAO Director-General B. R. Sen, a noted Indian
statesman whose inspiring passion is reminiscent of FAO's first
leader, Sir John Boyd-Orr. Freedom from Hunger Committees
organized nationally by volunteers raise public consciousness,
motivate political commitment, and collect voluntary contributions for food production in developing countries.

The "peace corps" idea draws electrifying response from a
crowd of 10,000 students gathered to hear presidential candidate John Kennedy on 14 October at the University of Michigan
in Ann Arbor. Within six months of Kennedy's inauguration,
the Peace Corps sends 12 volunteers to work with the Heifer
Project and the government of Saint Lucia in the West Indies to

1960
cont. improve animal husbandry; develop feed mills; increase vegetable production; and aid public health, vocational, and home economics programs. In 1961 volunteers also go to India, Pakistan, the Philippines, Chile, Colombia, Ghana, Nigeria, and Tanganyika (Tanzania). (Senator Hubert Humphrey and Congressman Henry Reuss had begun advocating a Peace Corps of U.S. volunteers in 1957, but Kennedy is the first to give the idea crucial publicity and a presidential mandate.)

1960–
1965 African national independence is increasing rapidly. Twenty-six newly independent African countries become members of the AO within one six-year period (1960–1965). (At FAO's founding in 1945, total membership is 34 countries. By 1985, FAO includes 158 countries, most of them in Africa, Asia, or Latin America.)

1961 U.S. Agency for International Development (USAID or A.I.D.) is created by the Foreign Aid Act of 1961, which consolidates the administration of U.S. development assistance in the new agency. The A.I.D. administrator reports directly to the president as well as to the secretary of state. Kennedy's Foreign Aid Message to Congress on 22 March urges all-out aid for democratic reforms (including agrarian reform) and economic growth in developing countries "to help make a historical demonstration that . . . economic growth and political democracy can go hand in hand."

An "Alliance for Progress" in Latin America is proposed by President Kennedy as

> a vast cooperative effort, unparalleled in magnitude and nobility of purpose, to satisfy the basic needs of the [Latin] American people for homes, work and land, health and schools.

Kennedy's expectation is that the Latin American partners in the alliance will introduce reforms, including agrarian reform, to reduce social inequities and help the poor while the United States provides capital to speed up economic development, but the anticipated reforms don't materialize. (The alliance concept first had been proposed to President Eisenhower by Juscelino Kubitschek, president of Brazil, in 1958.)

The American Freedom from Hunger Foundation (AFFHF) is formed at the urging of President Kennedy and remains active in public education, policy advocacy, and organizing on issues of world hunger until 1978. Its first major task is to help host the 1963 World Food Congress, sponsored by FAO.

1961
cont.   Food-for-work is pioneered by Church World Service, using food aid to compensate laborers for work on communal projects in an effort to promote development instead of dependency. Though it is initially contrary to USAID regulations to permit food aid to substitute for cash wages, gradually, food-for-work gains acceptance as one option for the distribution of food aid grants. (Food-for-work is the norm for the U.N./FAO WFP from the beginning of WFP's operations in 1963.)

The Development Assistance Committee (DAC) of the OECD is formed as a permanent agency to promote and improve the quality and coordination of assistance to developing nations. The DAC includes member nations of OECD that make grants or concessionary loans to developing countries.

Famine in China, starting with agricultural disruption from the Great Leap Forward in 1958, kills about 30 million people by 1961.

Sandinista National Liberation Front forms in Nicaragua to overthrow the Somoza oligarchy but makes little headway until the Nicaraguan middle class and workers in general rise up during 1978–1979.

1962   Asian Population Conference in New Delhi from 11–20 December calls on governments to take immediate steps to reduce population growth.

Land Tenure Center (LTC) is formed at the University of Wisconsin to do research on agrarian reform and the problems of small farmers worldwide. In 1963 the center publishes the proceedings of the 1951 International Conference on Land Tenure and Related Problems in World Agriculture.

1962–
1965   Vatican II, the Second Ecumenical Vatican Council, convenes in Rome under Pope John XXIII and his successor Paul VI to examine the teachings of the Church in the context of the present historical moment. Some 2,500 bishops worldwide along with lay leaders and members of religious orders are involved in the assessment, the most important event in the Catholic Church in this century. A dynamic new emphasis is given to the moral obligation and spiritual need to end the misery of poverty among all people everywhere, to protect basic human rights (social, economic, and spiritual), to act in solidarity with the poor and oppressed, and to create a more just world order among nations as well as within them. These missions of

1962–
1965
cont.
Christian faith are articulated eloquently in Vatican II documents and in papal encyclicals addressed also to "men of goodwill everywhere":

> [T]here must be made available to all . . . everything necessary for leading a life truly human [Vatican II, *Constitute on the Church in the Modern World*]. [A]nd this must be specially emphasized— the worker has a right to a wage determined according to criteria of justice, and sufficient . . . to give the worker and [the worker's] family a standard of living in keeping with the dignity of the human person [John XXIII, *Pacem in terris*, 11 April 1963].

1963 First World Food Congress is convened by FAO's Freedom from Hunger Campaign in Washington, D.C., 4–18 June, commemorating the twentieth anniversary of the Hot Springs conference that led to FAO's founding. More than 1,200 governmental and nongovernmental representatives attend. At opening ceremonies in the U.S. State Department auditorium, FAO Director-General Sen asks for a moment of silent homage to the recently deceased Pope John XXIII, "this great and good man" who had given his blessing to the Freedom from Hunger Campaign and "immeasurably strengthened its spiritual and moral message to all mankind." President Kennedy's keynote address is remembered for its stirring challenge:

> So long as freedom from hunger is only half achieved, so long as two thirds of the nations have food deficits, no citizen, no nation can afford to be satisfied. . . . We have the means, we have the capacity to eliminate hunger from the face of the earth in our lifetime. We need only the will.

In their closing declaration, congressional participants pledge

> to take up the challenge of eliminating hunger and malnutrition as a primary task of this generation, thus creating basic conditions for peace and progress for all mankind.

A planned world attack on poverty and inequities between nations is called for by Julius Nyerere, president of Tanzania (formerly Tanganyika), at the Twelfth Session of the FAO Conference meeting in November.

Centro Internacional por Mejoriamento de Maiz y Trigo (CIMMYT) is chartered by the Mexican government and supported jointly by the Rockefeller and Ford foundations on the successful pattern of IRRI. It continues the wheat and corn research at Chipingo, near Mexico City, that had been started

1963
cont.
20 years earlier by the Rockefeller Foundation and the Mexican government. Norman Borlaug directs the wheat research.

1964
The U.N. Conference on Trade and Development (UNCTAD) meets for the first time. The U.N. General Assembly creates UNCTAD in 1963 as a perpetual international forum to help negotiate better terms of trade for U.N. members from the South. UNCTAD's first secretary-general, Raul Prebisch, becomes a leading exponent of the South's views on the international economic order (IEO) as dominated by OECD (capitalist) nations. Prebisch argues that an IEO based on "comparative advantage" at the present does not maximize production and distribute the fruits equitably. Rather, the present IEO enriches the "center" (the industrialized OECD nations) at the expense of the "periphery" (the South, developing nations that produce mostly primary products). The IEO reinforces the persistent and growing inequity between rich and poor nations, because industrialized goods (in which OECD nations dominate the market) will always have higher trade value than the primary commodities that the South offers. To progress toward equity with the North, therefore, the nations of the South must obtain more favorable prices for their commodities and be helped to diversify their economies. (This assessment forms the basis of the demands raised in the U.N. General Assembly a decade later for a new international economic order.)

1965
The United Nations Development Programme (UNDP) is formed (merging the U.N. Special Fund and the Expanded Program for Technical Assistance) to be the principal coordinator and broker for technical and financial assistance from agencies of the U.N. system for development in the South.

An Indicative World Plan (IWP) for agricultural development is approved as an FAO project by the FAO conference. Work on the IWP begins under FAO Director-General B. R. Sen. Preparation of the IWP first had been proposed by the 1963 World Food Congress to be reviewed at the second World Food Congress in 1970. However, the IWP objective to ensure food adequacy in all nations through international cooperation based on an analysis of the world food system as a whole is never fulfilled. Strong resistance to the concept from the United States and other countries prevents the IWP from becoming a "plan" and converts it to a mere report published in 1969 indicating major problems to be expected in the next 10 to 15 years.

1965 A World Population Conference is held under U.N. auspices
cont. (smaller than the one to come in 1974).

1965– Anxiety about impending environmental crises due to over-
1975 population grows, fed by a proliferation of publications, public
interest organizations, and radio programs. The population
movement and the environmental movement draw large support. To the commonplace imagery of *population explosion* and
population bomb is added the "fragile spaceship," as in the words
of Adlai Stevenson in 1965:

> We travel together, passengers on a little spaceship, dependent
> on its vulnerable reserves of air and soil; all committed for our
> safety to its security and peace; preserved from annihilation only
> by the care, the work and, I will say, the love we give our fragile
> craft.

Among the more influential publications of this period are
Georg Borgstrom's *The Hungry Planet* (1965), *Famine—1975!* by
William and Paul Paddock (1967), and Paul Ehrlich's *The Popu-
lation Bomb* (1968). Following publication of "Tragedy of the
Commons" in *Scientific American* (13 December 1968), Garrett
Hardin's popularity as a speaker takes his Malthusian message
of doom (barring immediate and stringent birth control measures) to thousands of campuses and public gatherings across
the United States. Hardin's didactic novel *Exploring the New
Ethics for Survival: The Voyage of Spaceship Beagle* (1972) is widely
read. Lester Brown's *Man, Land, and Food: Looking Ahead at
World Food Needs* (1963) is a U.S. Department of Agriculture
report for specialists, but his *In the Human Interest* (1974) and *By
Bread Alone* (with Erik Eckholm, 1974) have a significant public
readership.

1966 IRRI releases IR-8 as a high-yielding variety (HYV) of rice and
launches the "Green Revolution." The HYVs produced at IRRI
and later at CIMMYT (for wheat) are a new plant type: dwarf
varieties with erect leaves to absorb extra sunshine and stiff
straw with a strong root system able to utilize large doses of
fertilizer. When properly irrigated and cultivated, the HYV
dwarfs give five to six times more yield per hectare than traditional varieties and mature more quickly so that three to four
crops per year can be produced. The world press greets IR-8
with great enthusiasm as a miraculous solution to Asia's
impending Malthusian disaster. Recalling this response ten
years later for the World Food Conference at Ames, Iowa,
Philippine rural sociologist Gelia Castillo says: "[H]opes ran

1966
cont.
wild. The press dubbed it 'miracle rice' and endowed it with unimaginable virtues. The only thing it could not do was fly."

The United Nations declares freedom from hunger a "fundamental right" in Article 11 of the International Covenant on Economic, Social and Cultural Rights, prepared by the U.N. Commission on Human Rights. The covenant is adopted by the U.N. General Assembly in 1966 and is opened for signature and ratification by U.N. members. (The U.S. government chooses not to ratify the covenant.)

The Food for Peace Act of 1966 deletes surplus disposal as an objective of U.S. food aid under P.L. 480 and requires recipient countries to undertake "self-help" measures to increase agricultural production, improve agricultural marketing, and reduce population growth rates.

A U.N./FAO Conference on Land Reform is held in association with the International Labour Organization.

**1966–
1967**
Famine in India is averted by successful relief. When a severe two-year drought causes a harvest shortfall of nearly 30 million tons of grain and food stocks are depleted widely, the Indian government and international agencies organize one of the biggest and most successful programs of disaster relief ever undertaken. Conditions are particularly bad in the state of Bihar. At the peak of the crisis nearly six million children and mothers are being fed daily in Bihar alone. Permanent programs to improve child and maternal nutrition in India receive important impetus from the experience gained in the relief effort.

1967
The "Peace and Justice Programme" of the Catholic Church is begun by Pope Paul VI with a pontifical commission in the Vatican to help carry out the intentions of Vatican II. Many local peace and justice centers and consciousness-raising programs are established by Catholic laity and members of religious orders throughout the United States and other countries. The message of the peace and justice movement is articulated especially in the papal encyclical *On the Development of Peoples,* issued by Paul VI on Easter Sunday, 26 March 1967:

> Today the principal fact that we must all recognise is that the
> social question has become worldwide. . . . Today the peoples in

1967
cont.

hunger are making a dramatic appeal to the peoples blessed with abundance. The Church shudders at this cry of anguish. . . . We must make haste: too many are suffering; . . . the present situation must be faced with courage and the injustices linked with it must be fought against and overcome. Development demands bold transformations, innovations that go deep. Urgent reforms should be undertaken without delay. It is for each one . . . to share in them with generosity, particularly those whose education, position and opportunities afford them wide scope for action. . . . To speak of development is, in effect, to show as much concern for social progress as for economic growth. . . . There can be no progress toward the complete development of man without the simultaneous development of all humanity in the spirit of solidarity. . . . Development is the new name for peace. . . . To wage war on misery and to struggle against injustice is to promote, along with improved conditions, the human and spiritual progress of all . . . and therefore the common good of humanity.

The U.S. President's Science Advisory Committee report *The World Food Problem* is presented to President Lyndon B. Johnson. The 3 volumes contain reports by 22 panels of experts on nearly every aspect of food production and commodity trade. Aggregate food supply is the central focus. Social, economic, and political obstacles that keep people hungry are scarcely mentioned.

**1967–
1969**

Famine in Biafra kills an estimated 1.5 million. Caused by war between the Nigerian government and secessionists in the province of Biafra, the famine is viewed by the government as a weapon of war and relief action is not permitted. Questions of diplomatic protocol toward an internal conflict in a sovereign nation inhibit official international action, UNICEF notably excepted. Volunteer North American and European humanitarian agencies (many of them ad hoc) airlift food and medical teams from the neighboring Ivory Coast into Biafra by night at great risk and evacuate starving children to impromptu rehabilitation centers the same way.

1968

The International Institute of Tropical Agriculture (IITA) is established in Nigeria for research on rainfed and irrigated crops of the lowland tropics, becoming the third agency in the growing network of international agricultural research centers (IARCs) on the pattern of IRRI and CIMMYT.

1968
cont.
Social transformation "with an option for the poor" becomes official Catholic Church teaching in Latin America at the Second General Conference of Latin American Bishops meeting at Medellin, Colombia, 24 August–8 September. Translating the message of Vatican II into the particular realities of Latin America, the bishops state:

> Our pastoral mission is essentially a service of encouraging and educating the conscience of believers [*conscientizacion*], to help them to perceive the responsibilities of their faith in their personal life and in their social life . . . [including responsibilities for] the human promotion of the peasants and Indians.

Acts of solidarity across class and ethnic boundaries are urged as part of the *conscientizacion*. Informal groups of laity and clergy begin to meet everywhere as *communidades eclesiales de base* (base communities) for communal worship and Bible study in relationship to their daily experience. Such base communities become the inspirational vehicle of grassroots solidarity and commitment to undertake nonviolent social change. Liberation theology evolves out of this experience. Leaders of such worship groups and the bishops and clergy who encourage them are targeted especially, therefore, as "subversives" by those forces resisting economic and social democratization. In what will become an often quoted statement, Dom Helder Camara—archbishop of Recife, Brazil, and one of the most outspoken bishops at Medellin—says, "When I give food to the poor I am called a saint; when I ask why the poor have no food I am called a communist."

Seven years of drought begin in the Sahel region of sub-Saharan Africa, a drought that will become one of the greatest natural disasters of the twentieth century.

1969
Centro Internacional por Agricultura Tropical (CIAT) is established in Colombia, the fourth agency of the IARC network, as an international agricultural research center for rainfed tropical crops growing between sea level and an altitude of 1,000 meters (approximately 3,250 feet).

The Inter-American Foundation (IAF), a low-profile U.S. public corporation, is created by Congress as an experiment in channeling development assistance to the poor in Latin America

1969
cont.
through local Latin American intermediary organizations, by-passing national elites and partisan politics.

The Pearson Commission report *Partners in Development,* a review of the First U.N. Development Decade by an independent commission of "eminent persons" led by former Canadian Prime Minister Lester Pearson, is delivered to World Bank President Robert McNamara in October. The report reveals much less progress than anticipated but fails to question the trickle-down economic development strategy followed in the 1960s, a strategy that has led to little or no gain for the poor and to ever wider gaps between rich and poor. The Pearson Commission argues that less developed countries can "lift themselves out of the depths of underdevelopment" in reasonable time if only industrialized countries will "fight off their aid weariness" and bring aid up to seven-hundredths of 1 percent (.07 percent) of each donor nation's GNP. This aid target is adopted by the U.N. General Assembly for the Second Development Decade.

The Overseas Development Council (ODC) is founded in Washington, D.C., with James Grant (later to become executive director of UNICEF) as its president. ODC quickly becomes a major nongovernmental voice in advocating increased U.S. support for Third World development. To improve on the GNP-based definition of development progress, ODC develops the physical quality of life index (PQLI), based on infant mortality, literacy, and life expectancy statistics.

Presbyterian Church in the United States (PCUS) declares ending world hunger as a priority mission of the Atlanta-based Protestant denomination. PCUS Washington Office Director George Chauncey and others persuade the 1969 PCUS General Assembly to make the world hunger crisis a mission priority. In 1971 James Cogswell becomes director of a world hunger program designed to enlist church members in five kinds of response: (1) education to understand the deeper causes and implications of hunger, (2) change-oriented action "where they are," (3) support for church relief and development projects overseas, (4) political advocacy for U.S. government policies to help the hungry, and (5) a biblically based examination of lifestyle integrity that asks "How do Christians live in a hungry world?" Lay leaders are trained to serve local churches in each presbytery (district) of the church as "hunger action enablers." The PCUS World Hunger Program becomes the prototype for

1969   initiatives after the World Hunger Conference of 1974 by other
cont.   Protestant denominations. (In 1980 the "southern" and "north-
             ern" Presbyterian Hunger Programs of PCUS and the United
             Presbyterian Church U.S.A. merge under one director, Colleen
             Shannon. In 1988 the organization moves its headquarters to
             Louisville, Kentucky.)

1969-   The FAO Committee on Agrarian Reform reviews progress dur-
1971   ing the First U.N. Development Decade and issues a very
             gloomy assessment.

1970–1979: Second United Nations Development Decade

1970   CIMMYT and IRRI receive the UNESCO Science Prize for HYV
             wheat and rice.

             Norman Borlaug receives the Nobel Peace Prize for leadership
             in developing HYV wheat and is hailed as "father of the Green
             Revolution."

             Oxfam-America is formed to aid refugees and famine victims in
             East Pakistan as it becomes Bangladesh in a war of secession
             from Pakistan. Aid is soon redirected to local self-help projects
             in Asia, Africa, and Latin America.

             The International Development Research Centre (IDRC) is
             founded in Canada to support research by scientists and devel-
             opment planners of and for the South. Food and agriculture are
             primary concerns.

             Earth Day, 22 April, involves 20 million Americans, including
             members of Congress, in teach-ins and demonstrations for
             "alternative" technology, lifestyle modification, and stronger
             laws to protect the environment.

             Second World Food Congress, sponsored by the FAO's Freedom
             from Hunger/Action for Development program, meets in The

1970
cont.
Hague, Netherlands, 16–30 June, under leadership of FAO's new director-general, Addeke H. Boerma, a prominent food policy leader from the Netherlands. (Boerma had begun his civil service career as Dutch officer in charge of food distribution and management before, during, and after Nazi occupation in World War II.) Of the 1,800 participants, 1 in 6 is under the age of 30. Social justice joins agricultural productivity on the agenda. It is not enough to think only of food, the congress's final declaration insists. Rather, the total development of every man, woman, and child is at stake, "thwarted by injustice, exploitation, discrimination and all manifestations of human selfishness." In his closing statement, Boerma notes:

> There has been an atmosphere of concern, of commitment and indeed of passion that I cannot recollect having felt at any other international gathering I have attended. [The congress has] helped to build a new bridge between public opinion and the U.N. system.

The U.N. International Development Strategy (IDS) for the Second Development Decade highlights equity issues. The General Assembly Special Session, on 24 October, criticizes trickle-down, industry-led strategies of the 1960s.

The Federation of Christian Peasants of El Salvador (FECCAS) begins to spread rapidly and to become more militant in demanding official attention for the problems of El Salvador's rural poor. Guerrilla organizations also form during this year. With continued resistance to change from the landowning Salvadoran oligarchy aided by the army, violence escalates. In 1974, troops kill, arrest, and "disappear" members of a Christian community who had occupied a piece of idle land in an effort to persuade the owner to rent it to them. In 1975, troops fire on a demonstration by university students in San Salvador. Similar events are occurring simultaneously in other countries of Central and South America: Christian base communities pressing more boldly for change, intellectuals supporting reforms, armed guerrilla groups forming, and resistance growing more violent from an army linked to the wealthy elite. Many who start by advocating nonviolent efforts for change come to support the violence of the guerrillas.

1971
A "crisis" in dietary protein in developing countries is declared by the FAO/WHO Expert Panel on Nutrition in a report to the

1971
cont.
U.N. Economic and Social Council. Research is urged to increase the protein content of grain and to develop unconventional sources of protein such as algae and petroleum-based single-cell protein.

Meat-centered diets are accused of contributing to world hunger in *Diet for a Small Planet,* Frances Moore Lappé's first book, which becomes a best-seller. This book drives the first wedge in the unquestioned popular view that the hunger problem results from an imbalance between the number of people to be fed and the quantity of food that can be produced.

The International Conference on Nutrition, National Development, and Planning at the Massachusetts Institute of Technology (M.I.T.) attracts high-level officials from 55 countries. Conference planners include Nevin Scrimshaw, head of the M.I.T. Department of Nutrition and Food Science, and Alan Berg, recent chief of food and nutrition in USAID's India mission during the threatened Bihar famine.

The Food Aid Convention to promote cooperation and set mutual standards for food aid among wheat exporting nations is established when the International Wheat Association meets to negotiate changes in the 1949 International Wheat Agreement. The United States is represented in the Wheat Trade Convention by USDA and in the Food Aid Convention by the State Department.

The Consultative Group on International Agricultural Research (CGIAR) is established to support international agricultural research centers (IARCs) on the pattern of IRRI, CIMMYT, IITA, and CIAT. CGIAR is an informal association of donor governments, private foundations, U.N. agencies, and developing countries. New IARCs established in 1972 are the International Potato Center (CIP) in Peru and the International Crops Research Institute for the Semi-Arid Tropics (ICRISAT) in India. Five more will be added by the end of the decade.

1972
Infant formula promotion in the South becomes an international hunger issue. The U.N. Protein-Calorie Advisory Group warns about the sharp increases in infant illness and death from diarrhea and starvation due to spreading use of commercial infant formula. The advisory group emphasizes the "critical importance of breast-feeding in developing countries." A campaign to stop multinational corporations from promoting

1972 formula in the South begins among British activists in 1973 and
cont. spreads to Germany and Switzerland in 1974 (Nestlé wins a libel
suit against Arbeitsgruppe Dritte Welt for the slogan "Nestlé
kills babies" but is chastised by the Swiss judge for its promo-
tional practices). Shareholder actions against formula
corporations begin in the United States.

LANDSAT 1 is launched by the United States, the first major
earth resources satellite. *LANDSAT* eventually helps the United
States and FAO monitor rainfall and crop conditions in areas
too remote for regular onsite reports.

The Self-Employed Women's Association (SEWA) in
Ahmedabad, India, pioneers a new approach to ending the
poverty of the poorest of the poor in the urban slums of
the South: a union for women working as construction laborers, street vendors, or in cottage industries as lacemakers,
seamstresses, or cigarette manufacturers. Considered "unemployed" or only "informally" employed by traditional labor
unions and government economists alike, such women are discovered by Ela Bhatt, Ph.D. economist appointed to direct the
women's wing of the Gandhian Textile Labour Association, to
be arduously employed in efforts to provide food, clothing, and
shelter for themselves, their children, and often their unemployed or physically handicapped husbands as well. They are
also found to be working at starvation wages, often harassed by
police, illiterate, and without societal protection of any kind.
SEWA, soon managed by leaders elected by its members, quietly
begins to change all of this and gradually becomes a model for
similar efforts elsewhere in India (still the home of most of the
world's chronically undernourished despite dramatic gains in
national agricultural production).

United Nations Conference on the Environment meets in
Stockholm. The South forces poverty issues onto the agenda,
asserting that the immediate, urgent needs of hungry people
and poor countries must be included in plans to save the environment. A new consensus begins to form about the goal: no
longer simply conservation but now sustainability of ecosystems
that support human life.

U.N. General Assembly calls for a World Population Year in
1974. The first World Fertility Survey begins, an integrated
population research program in more than 50 countries, to
provide a better database on human fertility choices and
behavior.

1972
cont.

The Club of Rome's pessimistic global projections receive wide attention with publication of *The Limits to Growth* (principal editor, Donella Meadows), a computer modelling projection of the future outcome of current trends in population and the consumption of natural resources.

Food production declines worldwide for the first time in two decades. In the United States, government policy to reduce surpluses takes land out of cultivation at the same time that bad weather reduces harvests in Australia (normally a grain exporter), Russia, India, China, and other parts of Asia. Simultaneous crop failures in Russia, India, and China put a particularly great stress on world food supplies, since these are the world's three largest producers and consumers of grain. The Sahelian drought in Africa enters its fourth year.

1972–
1973

World grain stocks drop drastically. In 1971 President Richard Nixon devaluates the dollar, and market demand for cheaper U.S. exports, including food, increases as expected. Surplus grain stocks decline. Meanwhile, India uses up its record grain surplus in 1971 and 1972, feeding an estimated 8 million to 10 million refugees from East Pakistan (Bangladesh), and must depend on grain imports when the monsoon fails in 1972. China and the Soviet Union also enter the market to purchase grain in unusually large quantities. In the summer of 1972, the U.S.S.R. contracts for 24.2 million tons of grain, mostly wheat, to be delivered in 1973 by the "Big Five" grain corporations: Cargill, Cook, Continental, Dreyfus, and Bunge. The United States will supply 17.5 million tons of this grain and the rest will come from Canada, France, Australia, and Sweden. (This triples Soviet grain imports during fiscal year 1972 and doubles the amount imported after the disastrous harvests of 1963 and 1965.) In mid-1972, the United States has 23.5 million metric tons of wheat in stock; by the fall of 1973, less than 7 million tons remain. Harvests in most world regions improve in 1973 but not enough to replenish stocks. Therefore, between mid-1972 and mid-1974, world stocks of grain (wheat, rice, and coarse grains) decline by 40 million metric tons. If customary market demand is translated into "consumer-days of world supply," the world has a 20- to 27-day supply of grain on hand at the peak of the crisis in 1974 (compared with a 95-day supply held by the United States alone in 1961 at the height of the glut).

1972–
1974

World grain prices skyrocket. In mid-1972 before the massive Soviet grain purchases, the world price of wheat averages $60

1972–
1974
cont.
per metric ton. By January 1973, wheat is $108 a ton and by January 1974, $210 a ton. Inflation in the cost of rice is similar: from $131 a ton for Thai rice in January 1972 to $179 a year later and $438 by January 1974. Grain market speculation is very active in anticipation of continued world food shortages. Consultations between major grain exporting and importing countries organized by FAO Director-General Boerma reveal that the exceptionally high market price of grain, not an absolute lack of grain available for sale, is the main problem for food-deficit developing countries.

1973
The Organization of Petroleum Exporting Countries (OPEC) succeeds for the first time in driving up the world price of petroleum. This greatly aids developing countries that export oil but puts oil-importing countries of the South in double jeopardy of economic crisis. A new U.N. term is coined: MSAs, or most seriously affected countries, meaning those short of both food and petroleum. Petroleum products are essential not only for industrial development but also—as fertilizers and fuel to operate irrigation pumps—for increased food production. Higher petroleum prices make it harder for MSAs to produce food, to keep their economies going, and to stretch limited foreign exchange to buy both food and fuel.

Sahelian drought assistance forges new patterns of international collaboration. The momentum of destitution and deprivation reaches a peak in 1973, the fifth year of the drought. Famine deaths are estimated at 100,000. In January, Upper Volta's Minister of Agriculture and Livestock Antoine Dakouré, in New York City as a member of the UNDP Governing Council, asks U.N. Secretary-General Kurt Waldheim for U.N. action. Advised that a regional appeal will be more effective, Dakouré invites other Sahelian countries to join Upper Volta (later renamed Burkina Faso) in forming a Permanent Inter-State Committee for Drought Control in the Sahel (CILSS). In March, CILSS asks FAO to organize emergency relief. In May, FAO Director-General Boerma issues the first appeal for international aid on behalf of CILSS and creates the FAO Office for Sahelian Relief Operations. The campaign that follows is the first major attempt to coordinate U.N. agencies, bilateral national donors, private voluntary organizations, and national governments of affected countries in a concerted crisis effort. The work is hampered by poor infrastructure and lack of transport to remote areas and, amid much administrative confusion, many mistakes are made, but much is learned of importance for

1973
cont.

African food crises to come. (The return of good rains in 1974 ends this particular Sahelian crisis, but drought and a new crisis return 10 years later.)

BBC news exposes famine in Ethiopia being ignored by the government of Emperor Haile Selassie. With the failure of rains in Wollo (Welo) and Tigray provinces in 1972 and again early in 1973, the impoverishment of farmers and herders begins spiraling downward. In March, police break up a demonstration in Addis Ababa of 1,500 farmers demanding government aid. By August 1973, more than 60,000 famine refugees are crowded into towns and squalid relief camps. Volunteer relief by nongovernmental Ethiopian organizations cannot meet the need. Despite ample food available in Ethiopian markets, 100,000 die. Army officers depose Selassie 12 September in a bloodless revolt with wide popular support. The first international relief arrives in October (two months after the famine has peaked) and continues into 1975.

International Undertaking on World Food Security is proposed by FAO Director-General Boerma, including organized food reserves, special assistance to help developing countries expand food production, international exchange of information on threats to national food security, and formal arrangements for international consultation to protect food security before crises develop. The undertaking is adopted by the FAO Conference in November 1974 and endorsed by the World Food Conference. Seventy-five governments and the European Economic Community sign on.

The Algiers Summit of the Group of 77 (the Fourth Conference of Heads of State of Non-Aligned Countries, 5–9 September) proposes a "new international economic order" (NIEO) and an "emergency meeting on the serious food crisis." An "Action Programme for Economic Development" is drafted to present to the U.N. General Assembly. FAO and UNCTAD are asked to sponsor the food crisis meeting.

"Absolute poverty" and "the basic needs of the bottom 40 percent" are declared priority concerns for the World Bank by World Bank President Robert McNamara in his "Address to the Board of Governors, Nairobi, Kenya," on 24 September. Absolute poverty is defined as inability to purchase the minimum essentials to meet basic needs for food, shelter, clothing, schooling, and medical care. It becomes the bank's operational term for the chronically hungry and undernourished. All wealthy

1973
cont.
nations and their citizens are urged to end the poverty of "the bottom 40 percent," who live in "a condition of life so limited as to prevent realization of the potential of the genes with which one is born, . . . so degrading as to insult human dignity." The bank becomes an advocate of a basic human needs (BHN) development strategy to replace the trickle-down, capital-intensive industrial strategy of the 1950s and 1960s.

"New Directions" in U.S. foreign aid are legislated by the Foreign Assistance Act of 1973. Senator Hubert Humphrey, a principal author of the New Directions language, explains the purpose as being "to change our whole approach to development by concentrating on the needs of the poor" and "to help improve the lives of the masses of people who live under conditions of extreme poverty, malnutrition and disease." Aid funding is shifted from high-tech, capital-intensive, industry-based economic projects favored in the previous two decades toward more emphasis on food production and nutrition, population reduction and health programs, and education and skills development.

The World Hunger Action Coalition (WHAC) is formed by 75 U.S. NGOs as a humanitarian citizens' lobby in anticipation of the World Food Conference. WHAC chairperson is Herbert J. Waters, president of the American Freedom from Hunger Foundation; executive director is Martin McLaughlin, senior fellow of the Overseas Development Council. Senator Charles Percy of Illinois and Governor Milton Schapp of Pennsylvania are honorary co-chairs. WHAC obtains the signatures of 30,000 Americans on petitions urging generous U.S. policies, even if they mean personal sacrifices for U.S. citizens.

Bread for the World, "a Christian citizens' lobby to end hunger," is founded in New York City by Lutheran pastor Arthur Simon and others. National organizing begins in May 1974. By 1989 membership will reach 50,000.

1973–
1974
Food aid drops because of higher grain prices. The U.N./FAO World Food Programme's food resources are cut 50 percent in 1973. U.S. food aid delivers only a third as much grain in 1974 as in 1972, although hunger distress has reached the famine stage in parts of Africa and Bangladesh and is worsening among the poor everywhere. In 1972, a $1.1 billion appropriation for P.L. 480 "Food for Peace" provides 9.9 million metric tons of grain; in 1974, the appropriation of $860 million provides only 3.3 million tons. To make matters worse, U.S. foreign policy

1973–
1974
cont.
priorities in 1974 allocate about 70 percent of P.L. 480 Title I (concessionary sales) and 42 percent of all Title II (grant) food aid to just two countries, Cambodia and South Vietnam, representing only 0.8 percent of the world's population. South Vietnam resells the Title I grain to help finance the war against North Vietnam.

A U.N. World Food Conference develops. On 24 September, U.S. Secretary of State Henry Kissinger addresses the U.N. General Assembly and proposes a U.N. conference to discuss ways "to maintain adequate [food] supplies and . . . meet hunger and malnutrition resulting from natural disasters." On 18 October, the U.N. Economic and Social Council (ECOSOC) endorses a world food conference but with a much broader agenda. In November, the FAO Conference and the International Labour Organization endorse ECOSOC's recommendation and the U.N. General Assembly establishes a preparatory committee to plan an intergovernmental conference at the ministerial level, giving ECOSOC overall responsibility. In February 1974, U.N. Secretary-General Kurt Waldheim appoints Sayed Ahmed Marei of Egypt as secretary-general of the World Food Conference and John Hannah, former administrator of USAID, as executive secretary. At its second session (4–8 June 1974) the preparatory committee adopts the provisional agenda (circulated to all U.N. member nations and U.N. agencies) and the "Preliminary Assessment of the World Food Situation, Present and Future," which becomes the major background document for the conference. "History records more acute shortages in individual countries," the preliminary assessment states, "but it is doubtful whether such a critical food situation has ever been so worldwide."

1974
The Shakertown Pledge triggers electrifying response through the grapevine of U.S. religious organizations after its appearance in April in *Fellowship Magazine*. Named for Shakertown, Kentucky, where a small group of retreat center leaders first conceive it, the pledge articulates values thoroughly at odds with conventional U.S. lifestyle and culture but values, nonetheless, that drive the explosion of politically conscious grassroots hunger activism in the 1970s and make personal lifestyle issues an integral part of that activism. Adam Finnerty and others form the Shakertown Pledge Group in Minneapolis to service the great demand that arises for speakers, workshop leaders, and social change trainers. The pledge says, in part:

1974
cont.

Recognizing that the earth and the fulness thereof is a gift from our gracious God, and that we are called to cherish, nurture, and provide loving stewardship for the earth's resources, and recognizing that life itself is a gift, and a call to responsibility, joy, and celebration, I make the following declarations:

I declare myself to be a world citizen. I commit myself to lead an ecologically sound life. I commit myself to lead a life of creative simplicity and to share my personal wealth with the poor. I commit myself to join with others in the reshaping of institutions to bring about a more just global society in which all people have full access to the needed resources for their physical, emotional, intellectual, and spiritual growth.

A new model of empowerment for women in poverty in India occurs when the Self-Employed Women's Association of Madras establishes a cooperative bank. (Conventional banks are intimidating and ill-adapted to the women's hours and conditions of work.) SEWA's bank is needed to protect the women's earnings from theft or appropriation by husbands. Most of the depositors are illiterate and have to be identified by photographs on their deposit books. With its own bank, SEWA also begins to make small loans to help members upgrade the productivity of their enterprises and provides training in micro-enterprise management.

The Cocoyoc (Mexico) Symposium on Patterns of Resource Use, Environment and Development Strategies adds more ferment to the reevaluation of purpose and strategies characteristic of the 1970s. Social scientists and U.N. officials from North and South have been gathered by the U.N. Environment Programme and UNCTAD to examine the purposes that should inform development decisions. The purpose of development in the South, the symposium participants agree, should not be "to catch up with the North" but rather "to ensure the quality of life for all with a productive base compatible with the needs of future generations." Development should satisfy basic human needs (including needs for freedom of expression and meaningful work), emphasize self-reliance, and bring about fundamental economic, social, and political changes to permit a decentralization of both world and national economies to broaden popular participation. A "temporary detachment from the present economic system" may be necessary in order to move beyond it.

1974
cont.
Sixth Special Session of the U.N. General Assembly on Raw Materials and Resources, 9 April–2 May, adopts the Group of 77's "Declaration and Programme of Action on the Establishment of a New International Economic Order." The objective is to redress the imbalance of economic power between rich and poor nations and achieve a more equitable global economy. Opposition to most of the NIEO proposals is led by the United States. (Canada, the Netherlands, and the Scandinavian countries take a middle ground.) NIEO politics influences negotiations at the World Food Conference and in all other U.N. venues for the rest of the decade.

U.N. World Population Conference meets in Bucharest, 19–30 August, as the high point of the World Population Year declared by the General Assembly.

Famine is declared by the government of Bangladesh in September, having been triggered by loss of income and employment due to summer floods. Mortality estimates range up to one million people between August 1974 and January 1975. A massive relief effort by governments and volunteer organizations prevents even greater disaster. (U.S. food aid is interrupted at the peak of the crisis because Bangladesh is selling jute, its main source of foreign exchange, to Cuba. Only after Bangladesh yields to U.S. pressure and cancels trade with Cuba is U.S. food aid resumed; by then, the autumn famine is largely over.)

The Rome Forum on World Food Problems, a group of 25 eminent persons, meets 1–2 November at the invitation of World Food Conference Secretary-General Sayed Marei. The forum is led by Lady Barbara Ward Jackson, a prominent British writer and speaker on ethical issues in North-South relations and global interdependence. "The Declaration of the Rome Forum" is distributed to all World Food Conference participants. In it Lady Jackson, Norman Borlaug, Lester Brown, René Dumont, Orville Freeman, Mahbub-Ul-Haq, Jean Meyer, Margaret Mead, and other forum members conclude:

> The issue is finally one of political will. . . . We do not believe that either the "old rich" of the industrialized world or the "new rich" within OPEC could live in peace and self-respect on a planet moving towards recurrent famine.

The World Food Conference meets 5–16 November at FAO in Rome. The three major tasks defined by ECOSOC are reiterated

1974
cont.
in opening ceremonies by U.N. Secretary-General Waldheim: (1) to increase food production especially in developing countries, (2) to improve consumption and distribution of food, and (3) to build a global system of food security. FAO's research for the conference estimates there are 460 million chronically undernourished people. In his address (5 November), Kissinger urges, "let us make global cooperation in food a model for our response to other challenges of an interdependent world—energy, inflation, population, protection of the environment." Kissinger's words also inspire the "bold objective" that becomes the conference's watchword (repeated in the first resolution of "The Universal Declaration on the Eradication of Hunger and Malnutrition," issued at the close of the conference on 16 November):

> The profound promise of our era is that for the first time we may have the technical capacity to free mankind from the scourge of hunger. Therefore, today we must proclaim a bold objective—*that within a decade no child will go to bed hungry, that no family will fear for its next day's bread, and that no human being's future and capacities will be stunted by malnutrition* [emphasis added].

The U.S. delegation is led by Secretary of Agriculture Earl Butz, assisted by Don Paarlberg, assistant secretary of agriculture for economics and economic policy. Gerald Ford has been president for only three months following Richard Nixon's resignation. Congressional representation includes senators Hubert Humphrey, George McGovern, Dick Clark, Robert Dole, Pete Domenici, Mark Hatfield, Jesse Helms, and Howard Metzenbaum; and representatives John Breaux, Kiki de la Garza, and Thomas Foley. Coordinator of U.S. preparations is Ambassador Edward Martin, assisted by Daniel Shaughnessy, recently director of USAID's Food and Nutrition Division in India and later to be executive director of President Jimmy Carter's Commission on World Hunger.

Representing U.S. NGOs as observers are Frances Moore Lappé (Friends of the Earth), Susan George (Transnational Institute), Larry Minear (Church World Service), Jane Blewett (Center of Concern), Herbert Waters (American Freedom from Hunger Foundation), and Patricia Young (World Hunger Action Coalition), among others. Activity by more than 400 representatives from at least 107 international and 53 national NGOs is intense and lively. For the first time at a U.N. conference, NGO representatives help draft proposals taken up as official business and help prepare official reports. Following precedents at the U.N. Environment and Population conferences, a daily conference newspaper, *PAN*, is published by the

1974 International Council of Voluntary Agencies (ICVA), with fi-
cont. nancial support principally from Oxfam, Christian Aid, and
Friends of the Earth, while FAO provides office space.

Conference resolutions approve two major new agencies, a
World Food Council of high-ranking government ministers (as
close to the rank of prime minister as possible), and an International Fund for Agricultural Development (IFAD). The World
Food Council is to address issues of national and global food
security through research, new proposals, and political persuasion. The International Fund for Agricultural Development is
to direct funds from both OPEC and OECD donors for self-
reliant development to help exclusively the rural poor and
small farmers, groups whose unfulfilled potential and great
need are highlighted by the conference but whose needs are
not the entire agenda of any existing official agency.

Conference documents and resolutions affirm that hunger is
more a function of poverty and faulty distribution than of
climate and production, more a consequence of an inequitable
international economic system and mistaken national policies
than of the decisions of individual farmers and families, more
related to social and cultural constraints than to technical
input, and more related to technology than to geography.

A Rural Development Taskforce is established in the U.N. ACC
(the Administrative Coordinating Committee on which each
U.N. agency is represented). The ACC issues a recommendation that all U.N. organizations "orient or reorient their
programmes in rural development to ensure that the benefits
accrue primarily to the rural poor."

1974– The Interreligious Taskforce on U.S. Food Policy and the Na-
1975 tional Council of Churches' (NCC) Coordinating Council on
Hunger Concerns are formed, two major initiatives of the U.S.
religious community with far-reaching influence. Under the
leadership of George Chauncey, director of the Washington,
D.C., Office of the Presbyterian Church in the United States,
the Interreligious Taskforce on U.S. Food Policy begins to speak
with the combined knowledge and talent of Washington-based
staff from more than 25 religious agencies—Protestant,
Catholic, Jewish, Unitarian, and Quaker. It becomes a highly
respected voice in congressional deliberations, as well as a
major source of political education for the U.S. religious community. (The task force is renamed Interfaith Action for
Economic Justice in 1983.)

1974-
1975
cont.

The NCC Coordinating Council on Hunger Concerns evolves from an NCC ecumenical Working Session on World Hunger, 16–17 December, at the Graymoor Christian Unity Center in New York State, attended by representatives of Lutheran, Episcopal, Presbyterian, United Methodist, Christian Reformed, and other denominational and ecumenical agencies. The working session establishes a World Hunger Taskforce to follow up its decisions and issues a prophetic statement, "The Graymoor Covenant." The covenant stresses the structural causes of hunger and the obligation of Christians to respond in ways of justice more than charity. Signers of the Graymoor Covenant confess:

> over the years we have tended to reduce love to charity. We also have participated in economic, political and ecclesiastical systems that too frequently have been instruments of oppression. We rejoice that by the grace of God, new possibilities exist.

Evangelical and Third World Christians contribute significantly to the new economic and political content of church education on the world hunger problem. Campaigns to educate and mobilize members of major U.S. Protestant denominations for response to the world hunger problem follow Graymoor. For example, in the spring of 1975 the Episcopal Church conducts four-day training events to which each bishop in the United States sends a team of clergy and laity to be responsible for hunger education/action programs in the local diocese. Among the speakers at the training events are Episcopal clergy flown in from developing countries to explain the various forms of injustice that oppress the poor they serve. For more than a decade following this initial training, an active hunger network within the Episcopal Church is supported by a professional national coordinator, further training opportunities, a regular newsletter, and other instructional resources.

Twice a year for eight years beginning in 1975, the NCC Coordinating Council on Hunger Concerns brings together NCC staff and denominational staff to share information and perspectives on new developments in the hunger issue and also to collaborate in planning programs of education and action. Joining these discussions are representatives from unaffiliated organizations working closely with the churches, such as Bread for the World, Clergy and Laity Concerned, the Interreligious Taskforce on U.S. Food Policy, and World Hunger Education

1974- Service. One of the most ambitious ecumenical outcomes of the
1975 coordinating council's work is the WHE/AT project (World
cont. Hunger Education/Action Together), 1976–1980, in which
interdenominational training events with specially prepared
educational materials are conducted for church volunteers in
every region of the United States.

1975 The first scholarly journal devoted exclusively to issues of world
food security, *Food Policy*, begins publication in England. With a
stellar international editorial board, it quickly becomes a premier forum for food policy specialists.

The International Food Policy Research Institute (IFPRI) is
formed by a group of major foundations to support
policy-oriented research by social scientists who can work
independently of existing bilateral and multilateral policy
institutions. Dale Hathaway is first executive director,
succeeded in 1977 by John Mellor. In 1979 IFPRI becomes
the social science research center of the CGIAR.

AGRIS, the online bibliographical database of the International
Information System for the Agricultural Sciences and Technology, becomes operational at FAO with 120 countries and 14
regional and international research centers participating.

The World Food Council's First Ministerial Session meets in
Rome under Executive Director John Hannah. Five areas are
selected for analysis and advocacy: production, aid, trade, food
security, and adequate consumption.

The Consultative Group on Food Production and Investment is
formed in February by the World Bank, U.N. Development
Programme, and FAO with Edward Martin, U.S. State Department coordinator for the World Food Conference, as director.
(Martin also had been assistant secretary of state for economic
affairs.) The purpose is to increase, coordinate, and improve
the efficiency of financial and technological assistance to agricultural production in developing countries. However, FAO
contests the necessity for the new organization, claiming dupli-
cation, and the consultative group is phased out in 1978.

1975
cont. FAO's Global Information and Early Warning System (GIEWS) begins to monitor crop conditions and food security prospects for developing countries in the present and the near future. Monthly reports are issued to governments in the North and South.

The International Emergency Food Reserve (IEFR) is established by the U.N. General Assembly at its Seventh Special Session after a resolution to create such a reserve is defeated at the World Food Conference. The IEFR is a minimum food aid reserve of 500,000 metric tons of grain annually, administered by the U.N./FAO World Food Programme.

Honduras enacts land reform to distribute nearly 1.5 billion acres to 125,000 landless families. Ten years later, however, titles have been issued to only about a quarter of those 125,000 families. Meanwhile, the expanding market for cheap beef to feed the U.S. fast-food industry provides economic incentive to convert food cropland to cattle ranches. The more prosperous farmers and investors benefit, but thousands of peasant cultivators lose the land they are farming through this process, becoming further impoverished.

New U.S. NGOs stress policy changes to end hunger. NGOs formed in 1975 are the Institute for Food and Development Policy (Food First), led by Frances Moore Lappé and Joseph Collins; World Hunger Year (WHY), led by Harry Chapin and Bill Ayres; the Food Action Center of the National Student Association, led by Edith Wilson; and, in 1976, World Hunger Education Service (WHES), led by Patricia Kutzner. NGOs, NCC Coordinating Council member churches, and similar groups at the local level conduct consciousness-raising activities, such as Food Day, sponsored from 1975 to 1978 by the Center for Science in the Public Interest, and nonformal adult education through publications, conferences, workshops, and leadership training such as the two-week Seminar/Praxis on the Politics of Hunger (conducted by WHES from 1978 to 1983). These groups also engage in federal policy advocacy. A relative late-comer, Results, begins in 1980 to target editorial pages of U.S. newspapers as a vehicle for building political will; trained volunteers become adept at writing op-ed pieces and letters on world hunger topics that are published locally and nationally.

1975
cont.
The International Women's Year (IWY) Conference in Mexico City in July persuades the U.N. General Assembly to declare 1976–1985 the U.N. Decade for Women, keeping the IWY themes "Equality, Development, and Peace." Women from developing nations surprise many by naming access to agricultural technology and training as one of their chief concerns. Ester Boserup's study *Woman's Role in Economic Development* (1970) is still a pioneer in 1975, but following Mexico City and the IWY, women agriculturalists will seldom be again as invisible to researchers and planners concerned with hunger as they were at the 1974 World Food Conference. Three far-reaching initiatives of the IWY are two small new U.N. agencies—the International Research and Training Institute for the Advancement of Women (INSTRAW) and the U.N. Voluntary Fund for Women (UNIFEM), which attempts to generate more funding for innovative projects and programs to empower women's groups in the South—and a new international NGO, Women's World Banking, which helps women entrepreneurs in the South obtain investment capital for their enterprises.

The National University Conference on Hunger meets at Austin, Texas, 21–23 November. In addition to the University of Texas, sponsors include the Institute for World Order, the Carnegie Endowment for Peace, and the Food Action Center of the National Student Association. The conference program is action-oriented. The participants—500 students, campus ministers, faculty, and deans—organize into regional task forces to follow up specific issues and courses of action when they return to their campuses. The success of the conference in getting concern for world hunger permanently and broadly institutionalized in academic curricula and campus life varies greatly from campus to campus, but many U.S. colleges and universities are marked by increased, lively, and creative hunger activism.

1976
Congress passes a Right to Food Resolution affirming that all people have a right to a nutritionally adequate diet. The resolution is initiated by Bread for the World.

The World Food Conference at Ames, Iowa, 27 June–1 July, assembles 1,600 researchers and specialists from 70 countries to examine the topic "The Role of the Professional in Feeding Mankind." Planning for the event begins in 1972 at Iowa State University, independently of the U.N. World Food Conference. Major topics are the impact of the world food situation on people, environment, and development; the effect and role of

1976
cont.
national and international policy; the development of natural and human resources; and technology and change.

The World Hunger Programme of the United Nations University (UNU) is formed. Four neglected areas are selected in which to promote international scholarly research through the UNU program: (1) post-harvest conservation of food, (2) human nutritional needs and their fulfillment in practice, (3) nutrition and food objectives in national development planning, and (4) the interfaces between food science and technology and between nutrition and agricultural production. Nevin Scrimshaw is senior advisor.

"Food-priority country" as a new policy category is proposed by the World Food Council. A food-priority country is defined by low per capita income (under $500 in 1975), a projected cereals deficit of 500,000 tons or more by 1985, average food consumption of less than 100 percent of basic nutritional requirements, a critical balance of payments problem making it difficult to import food, a slow rate of growth in food production from 1965 to 1975, and underutilized potential to produce food. The council urges particular focus by the international community on aiding these countries to develop. (The "food-priority country" concept is never adopted by the U.N. General Assembly and therefore gradually ceases to be used by the World Food Council.)

The ILO World Employment Conference broadens and refines the concept of basic human needs (BHN) as a development objective, giving the concept three dimensions: basic needs in household consumption (especially of food), basic needs for access to communal social services, and the basic need of people to participate in making the decisions that will affect them. All three BHN dimensions are linked with the need to raise levels of productive employment, as none can be fulfilled without such employment. The conference places the basic needs issue on the agenda of international development planning more firmly than ever before while agreeing that meeting basic needs is a minimum objective for any society, not the only goal of development.

The RIO (or Tinbergen) Report, *Reshaping the International Order,* issues the challenge that the primary aim of the world community should be "to achieve a life of dignity and well-being for all people" and sets specific minimum targets for each

1976
cont. country by the year 2000 in basic needs indicators: life expectancy of 65 or older, an adult literacy rate of at least 75 percent, IMR of 50 deaths or fewer, and a birth rate of 25 or less per year per 1,000 population. After studying trends in the arms race, population, food supply and distribution, environment, and energy resources and consumption, the RIO Conference concludes that the challenge can be met if countries adopt new economic and social priorities emphasizing BHN, poverty elimination, and balanced eco-development. The RIO project is coordinated by Jan Tinbergen of the Netherlands.

The Bariloche Foundation issues *Catastrophe or New Society? A Latin American World Model* as an answer to the Club of Rome's *Limits to Growth.* Using computer modelling of various global trends (as did the Club of Rome's study), the foundation's Latin American researchers conclude that it is indeed possible to satisfy the basic needs of the world's population without endangering the environment or exhausting material resources, but only providing that "the goal of egalitarian society is accepted and controls are in place to prevent attainment of power through property ownership." Using specific targets for food, housing, education, and health, the Bariloche group's mathematical models determine that BHN can be achieved in Latin America by 1990 and in Africa by 2000, but not in Asia until much later.

The government of El Salvador proposes land reform in an experiment to begin with 12,000 peasant families (out of 112,000 families with no land and another 236,000 families with very little land). Opposition from most of the wealthy families forces the government to back down.

The Grameen Bank begins for Bangladesh's rural poor, initiated by Muhammad Yunus, professor of economics at the University of Chittagong, as an experiment in poverty eradication among the "poorest of the poor." (*Grameen* means "rural" in Bengali.) Disillusioned by the lack of development progress in Bangladesh, Yunus turns away from academic theory to examine firsthand the lives of the poor in villages near the university. His observations suggest that loans to help the self-employed poor to increase the productivity of their labor could make an important difference. The experiment begins with funds loaned by the university's bank, distributed and guaranteed by Yunus himself. Loans as small as one U.S. dollar, invested appropriately, prove capable of making sustained improvement in earned income among the poorest people. By

1976
cont.
1979, the Grameen Bank Project is receiving capital also from the national Bank of Bangladesh.

The Club du Sahel is formed by the OECD, based in Paris, and CILSS, based in Oagadougou, the capital of Burkina Faso. The purpose is to facilitate dialogue and coordinated action between Sahelian governments and donors toward the goal of self-reliant food security for the Sahel region by the end of the century.

1976–
1977
The International Fund for Agricultural Development (IFAD), first proposed by a World Food Conference resolution in 1974, finally—through efforts of the World Food Council—receives donor pledges for the minimum $1 billion, three-year start-up budget. Forty-three percent of the pledges come from OPEC donors and 57 percent from OECD donors. On 20 December 1976, U.N. Secretary-General Waldheim opens the IFAD agreement for government signature and ratification. The only U.N. agency whose work is focused exclusively on aiding the progress of small farmers and the rural poor becomes operational in 1977 and holds the first session of its governing council.

1977
Violence against clergy and nuns supporting the poor in El Salvador escalates with the arrest and torture of several priests in January. They are accused of fomenting subversion. Violence by forces opposing the precepts of Vatican II will evoke outrage repeatedly, especially with the 1980 assassination of Archbishop Oscar Romero in the cathedral while he is celebrating Mass, the murders of four U.S. nuns, and the November 1989 murders by masked men in army uniforms of six Jesuit faculty members of the University of Central America, including the rector.

The U.N. Water Conference meets in Mar Del Plata in Argentina and declares the 1980s the U.N. Water Decade with the goal of bringing adequate and safe water within reach of everyone. (Diarrheal disease from poor water and poor sanitation is a major cause of undernutrition in infants of developing countries.)

The National Academy of Sciences completes a major report on hunger, *World Food and Nutrition Study: The Potential Contributions of Research.* The report is requested by President Ford in 1975. Study chairman Harrison Brown of the California Institute of Technology expresses the new consensus of the scientific community: Even if food production could be doubled within a year starting from the day after the report is released, the majority

1977
cont.
of people hungry that year would still be hungry the next, because the real problem is poverty. The technology and science to end hunger are already known, says the report; the missing ingredient is political will.

INFACT (Infant Formula Action Together), formed at a meeting of U.S. hunger activists in Minneapolis in January, organizes support in the United States for the lengthy, hard-fought Nestlé boycott to compel policy changes by the industry leader. The objective of the international Infant Formula Campaign, widely supported by the health profession, is to force major formula manufacturers to stop marketing formula in developing countries, or at least to keep the companies from marketing to poor consumers and using misleading methods. The campaign peaks in 1979 and then subsides after an apparent victory in 1981 with the World Health Organization's Infant Formula Marketing Code.

Skeptical analysis or unbounded optimism—sharply contrasting stances emerge in U.S. hunger activism. Susan George's food trade and agribusiness exposé, *How the Other Half Dies: The Real Reasons for World Hunger,* and *Food First: Beyond the Myth of Scarcity* by Frances Moore Lappé and Joseph Collins both appear this year and profoundly alter the nature of hunger policy debates with their radical criticism of conventional views. The Hunger Project also debuts with a diametrically opposite approach, avoiding analysis of structural causes or policy issues and expressly refusing to be critical of any assumption except one: that it is impossible to end hunger. Werner Erhard and associates of Erhard Seminar Training (EST) launch the new organization by delivering inspiring messages to large audiences of EST alumni and their friends who attend celebrity-style events in major cities: "The end of hunger is an idea whose time has come" and hunger can be ended by the year 1990 if enough people pledge to "take responsibility." Joan Holmes becomes executive director of The Hunger Project in 1978. Asserting its independence from EST, the organization wins millions of adherents first in the United States and then abroad. Increased volunteerism for existing projects, hundreds of new projects, and a few new independently operated organizations are initiated by people inspired by The Hunger Project's appeal. From now on, world hunger activism among NGOs in the United States will tend to fall into one of two camps: either Hunger Project noncritical enthusiasm or a George-Lappé-Collins political economy critique that advocates the democratization of national and global food systems.

1977
cont.

President Carter appoints a World Hunger Working Group chaired by Peter Bourne. The group's report *World Hunger and Malnutrition: Improving the U.S. Response* is submitted in 1978 but receives little attention.

Congress establishes a U.S. farmer-held grain reserve. Up to 35 million tons of wheat and coarse grains owned by farmers (not by the federal Commodity Credit Corporation) can be stored on farms with the aid of government loans for storage costs. When the world market price reaches a certain level, farmers must sell the grain and repay the loans.

FAO's fourth World Food Survey stresses the inadequacy of national data on actual food consumption and the distribution of consumption among different groups within societies. Nutritionists, economists, and statisticians are seeking ways to improve the database on the world food problem. In a disturbing trend, many more countries than in the 1960s are showing a decline in per capita food production.

The first U.N. Conference on Desertification takes place at the headquarters of the U.N. Environment Programme in Nairobi. Desertification is rapidly destroying crop and grazing land in the Sahel region of Africa.

UNIFEM, the U.N. Voluntary Fund for Women proposed at the International Women's Year Conference, becomes operational and begins channelling funds to women's organizations and economic projects (including agriculture) in developing countries. In 1985, "development" replaces "voluntary" in the agency's name.

The Independent Commission on International Development Issues, chaired by Willy Brandt, is formed at the suggestion of World Bank President Robert McNamara. The objective is to examine the world's gap between rich and poor and to propose solutions. The 21 prominent commissioners from 20 countries, all serving as volunteers in their own capacity as individuals, issue two reports that are widely read and discussed: *North-South: A Program for Survival* (1980) and *Common Crisis North-South: Co-operation for World Recovery* (1983).

1977–1979

Negotiations for an International Wheat Reserve are conducted under the auspices of UNCTAD and the International Wheat Council as part of a new Wheat Trade Convention. The concept is to create an internationally coordinated system of reserves.

1977–
1979
cont.
The purpose is to reduce the short-term variability of the price of wheat in international markets so that food-deficit developing countries can manage their food needs rationally and avoid crises. No agreement can be reached between wheat exporting countries and importing countries, however, and the negotiations are closed permanently in 1979.

1978
Food sector strategies in national development planning become the focus of major advocacy and consultations with developing countries by the World Food Council. Food sector strategies would differ significantly from conventional planning for agricultural development by integrating food production, food security, and adequate consumption and nutrition.

Food security: from grain reserves or grain insurance? This is the main question for specialists in food policy planning and the international grain trade at a conference sponsored by IFPRI and CIMMYT. The two CGIAR centers define food security as "the ability of food deficit countries or regions, or households within these countries, to meet target consumption levels on a year-to-year basis." D. Gale Johnson of the University of Chicago proposes a system of grain insurance instead of grain reserves, on the grounds that it is a more efficient use of limited funds for a food-deficit country to purchase grain on the open market than to store it. By the time negotiations—led by UNCTAD and the International Wheat Council—on an international system of grain reserves collapse in 1979, the grain insurance scheme has been researched thoroughly by economists at IFPRI and the World Bank. Promoted also by the World Food Council, the insurance system will form the basis of the International Monetary Fund's new Cereal Facility in 1981.

NGO Coalition on Agrarian Reform and Rural Development, led by the World Hunger Education Service, is formed by 26 U.S. NGOs in September, when U.S. government disinterest in the 1979 World Conference on Agrarian Reform and Rural Development (WCARRD) becomes apparent. The coalition arouses greater attention for the WCARRD in Congress and fresh commitment to the WCARRD agenda in USAID, the Department of State, and the Department of Agriculture. Official preparations for U.S. participation include discussions with the NGO Coalition. The coalition also focuses attention by U.S. news media and other networks on the significance of the WCARRD agenda for the elimination of hunger, poverty, and rural inequity within the United States as well as in developing countries.

1978
cont.
The Presidential Commission on World Hunger is established by President Carter after an overwhelming majority vote in favor of a Congressional Resolution introduced by senators Robert Dole and Patrick Leahy and representatives Benjamin Gilman and Richard Nolan. Lobbying for a commission had been initiated in 1977 by Harry Chapin and Bill Ayres of World Hunger Year and supported actively by an ad hoc NGO coalition. As paraphrased from President Carter's executive order of 5 September, the purposes of the commission are: (1) to determine the basic causes of, and relationships between, domestic and international hunger and malnutrition; (2) to identify and evaluate existing programs and policies that affect these causes and relationships; (3) to focus national and international attention on and to improve understanding about such findings; (4) to recommend policies, legislation, or other actions; and (5) to carry out educational and other activities to publicize such recommendations and assist in their implementation. Along with the four original congressional sponsors, the commission includes prominent scientists and leaders in business, academia, and the Church. Pop singers Harry Chapin and John Denver (a director of The Hunger Project) also are appointed to bring grassroots concerns into the commission's deliberations and to generate broad public interest. An overly ambitious agenda and strong disagreements among commissioners slow the commission's progress. The agenda cannot be completed and *Overcoming World Hunger: The Challenge Ahead,* the final report delivered in 1980, contains numerous qualifying comments added by individual commissioners.

Famine threatens in Vietnam. Official U.S. aid is embargoed. Church World Service withdraws from long-standing participation in the U.S. Food for Peace program and defies official policy by shipping 10,000 tons of wheat donated by U.S. farmers or purchased with funds from private U.S. contributors.

Debt relief for the poorest countries is agreed to "in principle" by OECD nations for the first time at the March ministerial meeting of UNCTAD but no specific commitments are made. In the South, debt relief has been part of NIEO negotiations from the beginning.

1978–
1979
The Somoza oligarchy in Nicaragua is overthrown by a general uprising in which the Sandinista National Liberation Front is the most organized group. Somoza's land and that of other exiles is confiscated and redistributed in a land reform that favors cooperatives.

1979   U.S. military advisors are sent to El Salvador by President Carter
to aid the Salvadoran Army's efforts to crush the guerrillas, now
united as the FMLN (Farabundo Martí National Liberation
Front).

The World Conference on Agrarian Reform and Rural Development (WCARRD) meets 4–11 July at FAO in Rome. "Growth
with equity and participation" is the catch phrase. Advance
preparations involve all U.N. agencies and include 115 case
studies, as well as surveys by each FAO Regional Conference of
the current status of rural development and agrarian equity.
FAO Director-General Edouard Saouma calls the final Declaration of Principles and Programme of Action "The People's
Charter" because of its emphasis on the rights of people at the
grassroots to form their own organizations and to share in both
the planning and the benefits of rural development. The
WCARRD declaration breaks new and progressive ground also
by expressly recognizing the importance of women's economic
activity and empowerment for the first time in a major intergovernmental meeting on development. Despite favorable
rhetoric, however, women's participation at WCARRD is rare
among both the official delegations and NGOs, and NGOs at
WCARRD are permitted much less voice in official dialogue
than is the case at the World Food Conference five years earlier.

The Joint UNICEF/WHO Meeting on Infant Formula Marketing, 9–12 October in Geneva, hears representatives from all
sides of the issue: formula corporation executives, citizen critics
from the Infant Formula Campaign, nutritionists and medical
experts, and government representatives from formula exporting and importing nations. In May 1981, after circulating
several drafts of a fair marketing code and making efforts to
obtain voluntary compliance by the formula companies, the
WHO Council adopts the International Code of Marketing of
Breastmilk Substitutes.

International grain reserve negotiations collapse permanently,
after four years of fruitless effort by negotiators from grain
exporting and importing countries. The main sticking point is
the method of determining the conditions under which grain
will be released from the reserve and enter the commercial
market—one proposed method favors grain exporters, another
favors food-deficit nations. No compromise is acceptable to all
parties.

1979 Famine in Cambodia evokes scant international response when
cont. the Red Cross and UNICEF first appeal for relief assistance,
after they have finally obtained agreement from the
Kampuchean government to admit outside aid. Then an out-
pouring of public concern by private citizens and popular
entertainers galvanizes Congress. Within 10 days the U.S.
government's pledge rises from $7 million to $69 million, and
within 2 weeks the figure reaches $105 million. This triggers a
worldwide reaction. Ultimately $500 million is mobilized in
relief for 5 million starving Cambodians (called Kampucheans
at that time). "This was not on the initiative of governments; it
was on the initiative of people," reports UNICEF Executive
Director James Grant a year later. The famine is the outcome of
nearly 6 years of genocidal oppression by the Khmer Rouge.

1980–1989: Third United Nations Development Decade

1980 A U.S. government-owned Food Security Wheat Reserve of 4
million tons is established by Congress after intense lobbying
from NGOs. The reserve is to ensure that food aid will be
available to low-income food-deficit countries even when worldwide stocks decline and grain prices rise as happened in the
1972–1974 crisis.

A minimum food aid target for donor nations is established
under the Food Aid Convention at the urging of the World Food
Council. The minimum pledged is 7.6 million metric tons of
wheat, of which the U.S. share is approximately 4.5 million tons.
The Food Aid Convention of 1986 retains this level. In practice,
food aid exceeds this minimum throughout the decade, with
more than half of the total going to Africa.

BHN is the emphasis of the international development strategy
(IDS) for the Third Development Decade, as established by the
General Assembly Special Session on Development Cooperation in September. The South's NIEO demands make little
progress. North-South polarization is more entrenched than
ever.

1980
cont.

The South's economic crisis worsens as the flow of capital reverses: more capital—$10.9 billion more—flows from South to North in debt payments than from North to South for new development investments. This negative pattern continues to undermine economic progress throughout the decade. Net capital outflows from South to North occur each year ranging from approximately $6.5 billion to more than $14.5 billion.

Attention to women in development (WID) issues, including hunger and agriculture, is growing in both official and NGO circles, as demonstrated by the U.N. Mid-Decade Conference for Women and the NGO Forum, 14–30 July, in Copenhagen. At the official U.N. meeting delegates from the South and many U.N. agency reports stress women's role in producing food (accounting for up to 80 percent of all food produced in some countries) and providing for other survival needs of rural households. At the NGO Forum, women leaders and researchers from Asia, Africa, and the Caribbean Basin—aided by travel grants from foundations and OECD donor nations—are prominent among the 8,000 women attending from 200 countries. One of the most significant aspects of the forum is a series of seminars conducted by women development professionals from many different countries of the South, in which they discuss their experience and research. A dynamic transnational network of development researchers and trainers, who are able to bring to their work unique sensitivity to the socioeconomic status and role of women, is clearly building under the aegis of the U.N. Women's Decade. Planning begins for a U.S.-based Association for Women in Development (AWID), established in 1982 to provide a permanent forum for WID specialists worldwide.

Refugees in Africa strain food systems severely. Africa now has more refugees than Southeast Asia. Wars, ethnic conflict, political upheavals, and drought displace more than 5 million Africans during the 1970s. Refugee camps dot the landscape of more than 25 African countries in 1980. The worst case is Somalia in the Horn of Africa, a semi-arid, very low income country, whose population suddenly swells by more than a third as a million people (mostly ethnic Somalis) flee from war in the disputed Ogaden region of Ethiopia. Voluntary, bilateral, and international aid agencies are swamped by needs for immediate relief and longer range resettlement and rehabilitation.

1980
cont.

CGIAR is honored by the King Badouin Prize for International Development and adds two more IARCs—the West Africa Rice Development Association (WARDA) in Ivory Coast and the International Service for National Agricultural Research (ISNAR) in The Hague, Netherlands. For sustainable agricultural progress that is widely shared by rural populations, there can be no adequate international substitute for national research systems with many local sites. Only within such national systems can research be applied consistently over many years to the specific soils, specific ecology, and within the specific constraints and priorities of farming households and rural communities at the local level. To further the development of such national systems of applied research is the function of ISNAR.

The U.S. Supreme Court ruling in *Diamond v. Chakrabarty* accelerates the race for genetic engineering in agriculture. The Court rules that when a microorganism engineered in the laboratory does not exist in nature, it can be patented. Major corporations, especially petrochemical firms, begin investing large sums to develop or secure control of new organisms affecting agricultural plants and animals. Advocates of self-reliant development for limited-resource, smallholder farmers, both North and South, worry about the economic and social impacts of the new technology and join environmentalists in worrying about the biological impact. These and other anxieties are spelled out for the general public by Jack Doyle, director of the Agricultural Resources Project of the Environmental Policy Institute, in *Altered Harvest: Agriculture, Genetics, and the Fate of the World's Food Supply* (Viking Press, 1985).

1981

Reforming U.S. food aid to reduce its harm to local agriculture and its dependency-forming characteristics is a major policy objective of U.S. hunger activists and their congressional allies. New language in the 1981 Foreign Aid Act specifies that 1.7 million tons of food aid be reserved for "development to promote self-reliance." Congress asks USAID and USDA to report on the impact of U.S. food aid on economic development and on ways food aid can promote food self-reliance.

The FAO Conference adopts the World Soil Charter as a general policy framework for government planning and action to prevent further soil degradation and to reclaim soil fertility wherever possible.

1981 The fuelwood crisis, linking hunger and environment issues, is
cont. on the agenda of the U.N. Conference on New and Renewable
Sources of Energy. Soil erosion, declining precipitation, drop-
ping water tables, desertification, and worsening household
nutrition are interrelated in the dilemma of poor households.
These poor households have no source of fuel for cooking other
than fuelwood, little to eat that does not have to be cooked, and
no alternative means of obtaining fuelwood but to further de-
nude fragile soils of the protecting trees and shrubs, which
consequently grow ever more sparse.

A Cereal Facility for LDC food security is enacted by the International Monetary Fund in May at the urging of the World Food
Council. The Cereal Facility provides LDC members of the IMF
with balance-of-payments support for grain imports to meet
national food deficits during times of crop failure and rising
international grain prices.

The first World Food Day is observed 16 October, on the anniversary of FAO's founding. (World Food Day was established as
an annual observance of world food needs, problems, and progress by the 1979 FAO Conference.) A U.S. National Committee
for World Food Day is formed by 17 NGOs at the initiative of the
Community Nutrition Institute and World Hunger Education
Service to stimulate World Food Day observances by federal and
local government agencies and by schools, colleges, churches,
and civic associations across the country. Organizational membership in the U.S. committee swells to 250 in the first year and
then doubles in the next year. Beginning in 1984, a World Food
Day teleconference is broadcast annually to participating universities and other institutions across the United States.

1982 The Presidential End Hunger Awards begin as an annual event,
administered by the U.S. Agency for International Development to honor service by Americans toward ending hunger at
home and abroad.

The right to food gains attention from prominent international
law specialists after the U.N. Subcommittee for the Prevention
of Discrimination and the Protection of Minorities launches a
study on this right led by Asbjorn Eide of Norway. The Netherlands Institute of Human Rights (SIM) begins a Right to Food
Project in 1983. In June 1984, SIM, the Netherlands Ministry of
Development, the Norwegian Ministry of Foreign Affairs, and

1982
cont.
Oxfam U.K. sponsor the conference, "The Right to Food: From Soft to Hard Law." Also in 1984, *Food as a Human Right* is published by the United Nations University, an international bibliography is published by Eide's research team, and the International Law Association creates a Right to Food Committee to investigate possibilities to make the right to food enforceable ("hard law") instead of only normative ("soft law"). In 1985, the College of Law of the University of Iowa conducts a symposium titled "International Law and World Hunger" (*Iowa Law Review*, July 1985), and in 1986, Howard University Law School holds a World Food Day conference titled "The Legal Faces of the Hunger Problem" (*Howard Law Journal*, volume 30, 1987).

The South's debt crisis deepens as trade earnings plummet. Between 1980 and 1982, prices received by developing countries for their commodity exports drop 30 percent on agricultural food commodities, 24 percent on agricultural nonfood commodities, and 17 percent on metals and minerals. Perennially poor terms of trade for developing countries is one reason for the South's NIEO campaign. The international prices of primary commodities, the South's major exports, are always lower than the prices of industrial products from the North. During the 1980s economic slowdown and new technologies reduce the North's demand for the South's exports.

Thirty years of development progress begins to unravel and reverse in the South. Mexico's default on debt payments in August 1982 is only a harbinger of the wider crisis ahead, as debt burdens and shrinking trade earnings bring African and Latin American countries to the brink of collapse. In 1982, 50 percent of the debt from loans received by developing countries is due to be paid back as these loans mature—this figure is 24 percent of all the money owed to official development agencies (such as the World Bank) and 70 percent of all the money owed to private banks. By 1989 the combined debt burden of the South will be $1.3 trillion. The economic development progress of the past 30 years slows to a halt and actually reverses in 40 nations (mainly in Africa) that seem likely to have lower per capita GNP at the end of the 1980s than they had at the beginning. Real incomes are dropping and unemployment is skyrocketing.

1983
Fifteen million more people are chronically underfed than at the time of the 1974 World Food Conference, bringing the total

1983 number to 450 million, according to the World Food Council's
cont. June ministerial session. The council also estimates that 40
million die from malnutrition every year, about 7 million of
them children.

The Grameen Bank "takes off" with IFAD support. When the
World Bank and the Asian Development Bank turn down the
Grameen Bank's request for new capital as too risky, IFAD offers
$3.4 million at only 3 percent interest to the Central Bank of
Bangladesh as a 50–50 matching fund for the Grameen Bank.
In 1985, Grameen Bank enters into a second loan agreement
with IFAD for about $23.6 million. IFAD persuades the Ford
Foundation, the Norwegian Agency for Development, and the
Swedish International Development Agency to add $15 million
more. The net result is 530 new village branches carrying the
Grameen Bank's service of loans and training for micro-
entrepreneurs to hundreds of thousands of the rural poor.

The African food crisis returns after eight fairly normal years.
Drought begins in 1980 and spreads from east to west across the
continent. Early in 1983, FAO reports abnormal food shortages
in more than half the countries of sub-Saharan Africa, placing
as many as 30 million people at risk, or 16 percent of the total
population. By December, official estimates soar, warning that
150 million to 225 million face starvation if massive shipments
of food aid do not arrive in the next few months. Famine
continues well into 1985, although half of the world's total food
aid is going to Africa by then.

Danger to the world's crop genetic resources becomes a major
concern of the FAO Conference through an international
network of NGOs led by Canadian development activist and
seed specialist Pat Mooney and Cary Fowler of the Rural
Advancement Fund in North Carolina. The alarming loss of
agriculture's diversity under the influence of international seed
marketing gains widespread attention through Mooney's
exposé *Seeds of the Earth: A Private or Public Resource?*, published
in 1980 by the International Coalition for Development Action.
In 1984, Rural Advancement Fund International (RAFI) is
created with FAO assistance to conduct the RAFI International
Genetic Resources Programme of consultation to governments
and NGOs in the South to help them preserve the genetic
diversity of traditional food crops in their regions. (Cary Fowler
and Pat Mooney receive the Right Livelihood Award in 1985, a

1983
cont.
kind of "alternative Nobel Prize" offered since 1980 by a committee of representatives from the parliaments of Sweden and Great Britain, the European Community, and several foundations.)

1984
The plight of the landless rural poor is highlighted in ILO's *World Labour Report*. Improving the productivity of smallholder farmers is seen as necessary but not sufficient to end hunger. Landlessness is increasing everywhere. The International Labour Office's research shows a widespread rural employment crisis. In Bangladesh, for example, 26 percent of the rural labor force own no land and another 11 percent own so little land that they depend entirely on earnings from wage-labor. The ILO finds that very small industries located in rural areas account for from 50 percent to almost 90 percent of manufacturing employment in many countries of the South. The ripple effect of an increase in smallholder prosperity, wherever it occurs, reduces hunger indirectly by increasing incentive for rural manufacturing employment.

A Select Committee on Hunger is established in the U.S. House of Representatives on 22 February by a vote of 309 to 78. The resolution to establish the select committee is introduced early in 1982 by representatives Mickey Leland and Benjamin Gilman. The two-year lobbying effort for the committee is led by World Hunger Year and Bread for the World. Leland serves as the select committee's first chairperson until his death in an airplane crash in August 1989, which occurs while he is visiting relief camps in Ethiopia.

The DAWN Project, "Development Alternatives with Women for a New Era," begins, initiated by the Institute of Social Studies Trust in New Delhi, India. A wide network of activists and researchers (mainly women from Asia, Africa, the Caribbean, and Latin America) begins intellectual collaboration to articulate new methods and conceptual paradigms for economic and social justice, peace, and development free from all forms of oppression by gender, class, race, and nationality—goals not well served by the conventional thinking and methods of the mainstream institutions dominating global development. With help from the Norwegian Agency for International Development, DAWN produces its first collective book in time for the 1985 U.N. Women's Decade Conference in Nairobi: *Development, Crises, and Alternative Visions: Third World Women's Perspectives* (principal editor, Gita Sen).

1984   The African Development Foundation (ADF) is established by
cont.   Congress, following the pattern of the Inter-American Founda-
             tion of 1969. A public enterprise accountable directly to
             Congress, ADF channels development assistance to indigenous
             African associations at the local level for economic and social
             development projects.

             U.N. Office of Emergency Operations in Africa (OEOA) is
             created in December by U.N. Secretary-General Javier Perez de
             Cuellar to coordinate stepped up U.N. assistance to Africa. The
             OEOA director is Bradford Morse, who is also director of the
             U.N. Development Programme. Morse is assisted by Adebayo
             Adedji, executive secretary of the U.N.'s Economic Commission
             for Africa, and Maurice Strong, former director of the U.N.
             Environment Programme, as executive coordinator. The office
             wins universal acclaim for its effectiveness during the height of
             the emergency but when needs turn to rehabilitation and
             longer range development again the OEOA is closed in the fall
             of 1987.

1984–   After BBC broadcasts gruesome scenes of a new Ethiopian
1985   famine, pop artists in Britain and the United States trigger
             massive aid for Africa, exceeding any previous humanitarian
             campaign in history. Band Aid's recording under the leadership
             of Bob Geldof in late 1984, "Do They Know It's Christmas?," and
             Live Aid concerts the following summer generate more than
             $90 million. The funds are distributed by the Band Aid Trust
             partly for Ethiopian famine relief but mainly to strengthen
             African self-help development organizations. In the United
             States, "We Are the World," composed by Lionel Ritchie and
             Michael Jackson, is recorded on 28 January 1985 by 45 U.S. pop
             stars in a televised session organized by Harry Belafonte and
             Ken Kragen. The effort raises more than $58 million, which is
             distributed similarly to Band Aid Trust by the nonprofit organi-
             zation United States for Africa, created expressly for this
             purpose.

1985   The Geneva Conference on the Africa Emergency, called by
             U.N. Secretary-General Perez de Cuellar, is organized by the
             Office on Emergency Operations in Africa on 11–12 March to
             describe comprehensively the continent-wide emergency needs
             to the international donor community. The conference is at-
             tended by representatives of 125 countries (the United States is
             represented by Vice-President George Bush), 30 NGOs deeply
             involved in the African emergency, and hundreds of journalists.

1985   A special facility for Africa at the World Bank is established.
cont.   Development specialists, donor agencies, and African governments agree that Africa's persistent food crisis is a development
crisis, not a temporary crisis of weather conditions. Of all developing regions, only in Africa has food production failed to keep
pace with population growth. Poorly conceived agricultural
technologies and development strategies on the advice of
development agency "experts" as well as misguided priorities by
African governments share the blame for Africa's steady decline
in food self-reliance.

Rising rates of infant mortality and child malnutrition are attributed to the South's debt crisis and related structural adjustment
programs. The World Health Organization, UNICEF, and the
World Food Council express alarm over accumulating evidence
that the world's rate of progress in reducing infant mortality
and child malnutrition is slowing down and even reversing. The
annual rate of decrease in infant mortality for the years 1950–
1980 averages 2.5 percent. For the period 1980–1985, the IMR
decrease averages only 1.7 percent. In São Paulo, Brazil, IMR
rises in 1985 for the first time in many years, and in Zambia
nutrition-related deaths of infants and children double between
1980 and 1984. Nutrition surveys in several countries also show
rising percentages of children who are seriously malnourished,
reversing trends of steady progress over many years in reducing
child malnutrition. A combination of lower family incomes,
higher real costs for all consumer goods (especially food), and
reduced public health services is held responsible—characteristic socioeconomic results of changes in national fiscal and
budgetary policies ("structural adjustment") required by the
IMF and World Bank as conditions of new assistance for debt-
ridden countries.

The Child Survival Action Program of USAID is created, pat-
terned on UNICEF's Child Survival Campaign: immunization
against childhood diseases, promotion of birth spacing, breast
feeding and nutritious weaning practices using local foods, oral
rehydration therapy (ORT) for infant diarrhea, and maternal
health education.

FAO's fifth World Food Survey estimates the number of the
chronically undernourished at 512 million. The survey finds
that growth of per capita food supplies in developing countries
(especially in the more populous countries of China, India, and
Indonesia) has reduced the proportion of the world's people
suffering from malnutrition since 1974, although the absolute

1985   number of chronically hungry people is higher because of
cont.   population growth.

The World Conference to Review and Appraise the Achievements of the United Nations Decade for Women meets 15–26
July in Nairobi and adopts the document "Forward-Looking
Strategies," which contains national and multilateral actions to
continue progress. Bilateral and multilateral support for the
decade has generated an enormous body of research on the
economic, social, and political status of women in all countries.
It is known widely by now that women agriculturalists produce
about 50 percent of the world's food and between 60 percent
and 80 percent of all the food produced in Africa. More than
40,000 people, including thousands of African women and men,
attend Forum '85, the NGO conference on the campus of the
University of Nairobi, from 10–19 July. Preparations for Nairobi,
especially by women's NGOs, are extensive and intense. More
policy-oriented data on women is generated than ever before,
especially on rural women. Bilateral and private donor funding
and national government support greatly strengthen the capacity for continued research and influence by African women's
organizations. A highlight of Forum '85 are discussions led by
the DAWN group: "The Global Economic, Political, and Cultural Crisis" and "Alternative Vision, Strategies, and Methods."

The World Hunger Program at Brown University is founded
under Director Robert W. Kates, the first permanent interdisciplinary university program to promote research expressly
toward ending hunger. A Hunger Research and Briefing Exchange begins annually in 1988, sponsored jointly with the
American Council for Voluntary International Action (Inter-
Action). In 1987, the first annual Alan Shawn Feinstein Award
for the Prevention and Reduction of World Hunger (named for
the principal benefactor of the Brown University program) goes
to A. T. Ariyaratne, founder of the Sarvodaya Shramadana rural
self-help movement in Sri Lanka.

1986   IFAD establishes a Special Fund for Africa. U.S. NGOs obtaining
congressional support for this fund—$10 million in the 1986
Foreign Aid Act—claim that IFAD can enable African farmers
to produce two tons of food each year for the rest of their lives
at half the cost of sending one ton of food from the United
States to Africa as famine relief.

1986
cont.
The U.N. General Assembly's Special Session on the African Emergency meets at the end of May and adopts the U.N. Programme of Action for Africa's Economic Recovery and Development. Based on economic and social priorities established by African heads of state, the recovery program gives top priority to agriculture at the national level and "[p]rimary focus will be on women farmers who contribute significantly to agriculture productivity."

The first annual World Food Prize, sponsored by the General Foods Fund, is awarded to M. S. Swaminathan, leader of India's Green Revolution and director of the International Rice Research Institute (IRRI). At Norman Borlaug's urging, General Foods Corporation created the prize in 1985 to recognize and reward outstanding achievement in improving the world's food supply.

Scientific interest in "low-input agriculture" is growing as it becomes apparent that the high-input technology required for the HYVs is too costly or is otherwise unsuitable for many smallholder farmers. The HYVs have been least adaptable to African growing conditions. By the 1980s the production gains from "miracle varieties" of high-yielding wheat and rice have slowed. Nearly 1.4 billion people in Asia, Africa, and Latin America are not using the HYVs. Low-input agriculture seeks to increase production through means less dependent on chemical fertilizers, irrigation, or other capital expenses. *Biological* or *regenerative* are other terms applied to such alternative technologies for this form of agriculture that is nonconventional in a modern Western sense but is still commercial in the sense of attempting to produce a surplus beyond subsistence. Rodale International and the Winrock Foundation are among the promoters of such research.

1987
The World Food Council finds an accelerating increase of hunger in the 1980s. Between 1980 and 1985, the number of undernourished people increased by some 40 million, in contrast to a 15 million increase during the entire decade of the 1970s. The burden of economic adjustment placed on the poor in countries in a debt crisis is held to be the cause. The necessary measures to eliminate hunger are known and the resources can be made available, says the council at its Thirteenth Ministerial Session in Beijing, but the governments of the world's

1987
cont.

nations have not yet chosen to make the elimination of hunger a high priority. Political will is still the missing key.

IFAD celebrates its tenth anniversary, widely acclaimed by NGOs in South and North as the multilateral agency that has accomplished the most progress toward ending hunger since the World Food Conference by working closely with NGOs and emphasizing credit schemes for micro- or small-scale enterprise, including but not limited to farming. In appealing for renewed and larger funding from donor nations, IFAD's president, Idriss Jazairy of Algeria, explains:

> The poor are not a problem; they are a largely untapped asset for development. [IFAD targets] the most backward regions of the countries which are already extremely poor, where roads are often non-existent and communications inadequate and we design projects there to help people who have been left out of the mainstream of economic development.

The Africa Prize for Leadership in Ending Hunger is launched by The Hunger Project. The first awards go to President Abdou Diouf of Senegal and Thomas R. Odhiambo, founder-director of the International Centre for Insect Physiology in Kenya.

African women agriculturalists are actively recruited by IITA (the International Institute of Tropical Agriculture) for practical training and advanced academic degrees in agricultural research at the IITA in Nigeria. Scholarship support for 39 women is provided by the Ford Foundation. Since IITA's training program began in 1971, women from 24 countries have comprised only 18 percent of the master of science candidates, 12 percent of the Ph.D. candidates, and merely 9 percent of the farmers in the applied agriculture, nondegree training program.

The World Commission on Environment and Development issues its report, *Our Common Future,* in April. The commission had been created by the U.N. General Assembly in 1983 under the leadership of Mrs. Gro Harlem Brundtland (leader of the Norwegian Labour Party and later Norwegian prime minister) for three tasks: (1) to reexamine the critical issues of environment and development and formulate new and concrete action proposals to deal with these issues, (2) to assess and propose new forms of international cooperation that could break out of existing patterns and foster needed change, and (3) to raise the

1987
cont.
level of understanding and commitment everywhere. When asked "how humankind can be insulated from hunger on an ecologically sustainable basis," a special panel led by M. S. Swaminathan answers that the key to action should be the aim of increasing "sustainable livelihood security":

> Livelihood is defined as adequate stocks and flows of food and cash to meet basic needs. Security refers to secure ownership of, or access to, resources and income earning activities, including reserves and assets to offset risk, ease shocks and meet contingencies. Sustainable refers to the maintenance or enhancement of resource productivity on a long-term basis.

1988
The World Food Council's Cyprus Initiative against Hunger in the World reaffirms that hunger is the council's primary concern, rather than economic development or agriculture. The absolute number of the world's undernourished population is growing. The initiative notes the need to understand better why the efforts of nations and the international community have failed to reduce the number of hungry and malnourished people. The lessons of the past must form the basis for immediate and more effective action. The agency's president is asked to present a full action-oriented report at the council's Fifteenth Ministerial Session in Cairo in 1989.

Three million more Latin Americans have become unemployed since 1980 and urban minimum wages have dropped 16 percent in the region, reports ILO's Regional Employment Program for Latin America and the Caribbean. Another 8 million workers have been forced into precarious, low-paying jobs or self-employment in micro-enterprises because of the debt crisis and structural adjustment programs undertaken to secure International Monetary Fund assistance.

1989
IFAD assesses 12 years of experience in attempting to reduce rural poverty. At the Twelfth Annual Meeting of the Governing Council in Rome, 24 January, IFAD President Jazairy reports:

> From the beginning of its operations, the International Fund for Agricultural Development has sought to bring an internal dynamism to the task of rural poverty alleviation. Relying on the skills, traditions and creativity of the poor themselves, the Fund has explored new ways of mobilizing the poor, enlisting their participation and activating their productive potential. So immense is the worldwide extent of rural poverty that it is only by releasing an internal dynamism of self-reliance that the poor

1989
cont.

can hope to attain durable food security for themselves. IFAD has played the role of catalyst in this effort to tackle poverty alleviation from the grassroots upwards. . . . While the rural development effort in general still has a long way to go, it is fair to say that IFAD has clearly reached the point where its approach offers an important agenda for action in the 1990s by the international development community at large.

World Hunger Fifteen Years after the World Food Conference: The Challenge Ahead is the fitting title of the World Food Council president's report to the Fifteenth Ministerial Session, 22–25 May in Cairo. The review concludes with these words:

The above review is a sad testimony to the deterioration of the human condition in terms of hunger, malnutrition and poverty since the World Food Conference. Its message for the decade ahead is clearly that these problems will not diminish in the prevailing policy environment. On the contrary, with population growth, ecological deterioration and a mixed outlook for the world economy and the economies of developing countries, the challenges of dealing with hunger and poverty will be increasing.

When there were ample global food stocks, the world did not feed its millions of hungry and malnourished people. The above-normal stocks have now disappeared and, in the light of sharply increased international food prices and the prospect of a reduction in food-aid levels, at least in the short run, many low-income food-deficit countries will face even greater difficulties in feeding their people in the next few years.

At the same time, this review is encouraging testimony to the progress that can be realized if governments are truly determined to eliminate hunger, malnutrition and poverty. It illustrates remarkable achievements, even at low levels of economic activity, by countries which have made the improvement of the human condition the central objective of development and which have set specific goals for the reduction of hunger and malnutrition in their plans.

The *Bellagio Declaration: Overcoming Hunger in the 1990s* is produced and adopted by a group of 23 prominent development and food policy planners, development practitioners, opinion leaders, and scientists who meet 13–16 November at the Rockefeller Foundation Study and Conference Center in Bellagio, Italy. Participants come from 14 countries, North and South, and are affiliated with nine national or international agencies, eight advocacy and grassroots organizations, and five

1989
cont.

universities and research institutes. The participants see new opportunity for progress against hunger as the Cold War ends, the arms race declines, and democratization spreads rapidly. They note four major obstacles remaining: unequal trade relations between the North and the South, heavy debt burdens still growing, environmental degradation, and continued rapid population growth. With the Bellagio Declaration, distributed widely to policy leaders and hunger activists on many levels, they challenge world leaders to meet the following goals:

> We believe that it is possible and imperative in the 1990s (1) to eliminate deaths from famine, (2) to end hunger in half of the poorest households, (3) to cut malnutrition in half for mothers and small children, and (4) to eradicate iodine and vitamin A deficiencies. Together, they comprise a comprehensive yet still practical program that can end half of world hunger in the 1990s.

3

Biographies

THE WOMEN AND MEN IN THIS CHAPTER illustrate the diverse fields of expertise that contribute to a food systems understanding of world hunger. They are nutritionists, anthropologists, historians, political scientists, agriculturalists, economists, pastors, politicians, international civil servants, and private-citizen activists. They work within universities, voluntary nongovernmental organizations, international agencies, independent research institutes, and national governments. They come from North America, Europe, Asia, the Caribbean, and Africa. All of them share a passionate concern about people who are hungry.

Space limits these biographical sketches to a small representative selection of people influencing efforts to end hunger since the World Food Conference of 1974. Many important leaders, whose primary work took place before 1974, are omitted. Among those missing are Sir John Boyd-Orr, Dr. B. R. Sen, and Dr. Addeke H. Boerma, three outstanding directors-general of FAO; Dr. Jimmie Yen, a pioneer in the empowerment of rural people for self-reliant progress; Wolf Ladejinsky, the leading post–World War II agrarian reform authority and advocate; Lady Barbara Ward Jackson, British economist famed as a voice of conscience for the North in its dealings with the postcolonial South; and René Dumont, French agronomist and ecologist.

Many others whose current or recent contributions deserve recognition are also missing. A few have won renown and some appear in other chapters. Most remain quietly behind the scenes, their persistent and valuable influence known only to a relatively small network of colleagues, policy makers, and specialists.

Alan Berg (1932–)

Alan Berg is a leader in the effort to help development economists understand the importance of nutrition for national development progress, a role established by his first major publication, *The Nutrition Factor: Its Role in National Development* (1973), written while he was a senior fellow at the Brookings Institution (1970–1972). Berg's interest in these relationships began when he was deputy director of the U.S. Food for Peace Program in the Kennedy administration, co-leading a White House Inter-Agency Nutrition Task Force. He then directed the Food and Nutrition program in the USAID mission in India and coordinated 1966–1967 famine relief, receiving an award for outstanding service in public administration.

He has worked in nutrition planning at the World Bank since 1972, becoming senior nutrition advisor in 1975. He has taught nutrition policy and planning at the Massachusetts Institute of Technology, where he co-led the International Conference on Nutrition, National Development and Planning (1972). He chaired the Nutrition Committee for the World Food and Nutrition Study of the National Academy of Sciences (1975–1977) and served on the International Nutrition Committee of the National Academy of Sciences Food and Nutrition Board. He has authored numerous articles for major newspapers, magazines, and scholarly journals. Other books include *Nutrition, National Development and Planning* (1973, senior editor Alan Berg, with Nevin Scrimshaw and David Call); *Malnourished People: A Policy View* (1981); *International Agricultural Research and Human Nutrition* (1984, co-edited with Per Pinstrup-Andersen and Martin Forman); and *Malnutrition: What Can Be Done?* (1987).

Norman Borlaug (1914–)

"Father of the Green Revolution" is a term popularly applied to this agricultural scientist born in Cresco, Iowa, and educated at the University of Minnesota. Norman Borlaug received the Nobel Peace Prize in 1970 for his work as director of wheat research at CIMMYT. The high-yielding varieties developed there began to sweep across the wheat regions of the world in 1968, dramatically increasing harvests in Pakistan, India, Mexico, Turkey, and other developing countries. Borlaug began his research on wheat in Mexico in 1944 as a plant pathologist with the Rockefeller Foundation. In addition to his own research, he has trained scores of young scientists from Latin America and the Middle East. He retired from CIMMYT in 1979 but keeps that agency as his base while advising on agricultural projects in many developing countries. He was a member of the Rome Forum at the World Food Conference in 1974 and served on the Presidential Commission on World Hunger in the Carter administration. He presently chairs the selection committee for the annual World Food Prize, a project he instigated in 1985.

Lester Brown (1934–)

Early in his career as an agricultural economist, Lester Brown became known for raising public alarm about threats posed to the earth's food-producing resources from environmentally unsound agricultural technologies and unchecked population growth. Later he added the environmental impact of growing affluence on the world's food, forest, and energy resources to his list. His first major analysis, *Man, Land, and Food,* was published for the U.S. Department of Agriculture in 1963.

Brown left his position as administrator of USDA's International Agriculture Development Service in 1969 to become a senior fellow at the new Overseas Development Council (ODC), an independent research and advocacy center on global development and interdependence. In 1974, with major foundation support and former agriculture secretary Orville Freeman as chairman of the board of directors, Brown became president and senior researcher of his own center, Worldwatch Institute, whose efforts are devoted entirely to research on problems and trends in the world's population-resource balance. *Worldwatch Papers,* short, nontechnical, interdisciplinary reports, began in 1975. *State of the World,* an annual overview that Brown directs, began in 1984.

He was born in Bridgeton, New Jersey, and educated at Rutgers University (B.S., 1955; M.A., 1959) and Harvard University (M.P.A., 1962). Among his many writings are *In the Human Interest* (1974), *By Bread Alone* (1974, with Erik Eckholm), *The Twenty-Ninth Day* (1978), and *Building a Sustainable Society* (1981).

Carol Capps (1936–)

Carol Capps is associate for development policy in the Washington, D.C., public policy advocacy office jointly sponsored by Church World Service and Lutheran World Relief, a position she has held since January 1979. She is an outspoken and internationally recognized leader in advocacy for policy and actions by United Nations agencies and the U.S. government to support equitable and participatory development. She serves as a spokesperson for the NGO community at congressional hearings, at World Bank consultations, and in many other forums such as the International Conference on Popular Participation in Arusha, Tanzania, in 1989, sponsored by the U.N. Economic Commission of Africa. She participates actively in the advocacy work of Interfaith Action for Economic Justice, the Coalition for Women in International Development, the U.S. Committee for UNIFEM, and the U.S. Committee for INSTRAW. Prior to 1979, she worked as an analyst in International Organization Affairs and a consultant for the Congressional Research Service of the Library of Congress. A native of Putnam, Connecticut, she studied American history at Brown University (B.A., 1958) and international relations at the Fletcher School of Law and Diplomacy (M.A., 1960).

Harry Chapin (1942–1981)

Among the many entertainment celebrities making contributions to end hunger, singer-songwriter Harry Chapin's impact remains unique. His dedication began during the Bangladesh famine of 1973. It was spurred by discussions with a friend who became his partner in hunger work, New York television and radio talkshow host Bill Ayres. Chapin's engagement as a hunger activist continued with unmatched intensity until his untimely death in a car accident 16 July 1981. During those eight years, he donated almost $8 million of personal income to this effort, including a grant to Frances Moore Lappé and Joseph Collins as they researched and wrote *Food First*. Chapin early became convinced that donations were not the most effective means to help hungry people. He began to spend many hours buttonholing members of Congress and appearing as a witness before committees, arguing for U.S. policies that addressed the powerlessness of the poor and the political and economic causes of hunger. In 1975 Chapin and Ayres became co-founders of a new organization, World Hunger Year (WHY), to carry similar messages to the American people and to develop the kinds of programs and public policies needed to end hunger. The purpose of the organization's name was to emphasize that as long as people anywhere remain hungry, every year was world hunger year and the most important question was "why." Chapin and Ayres co-hosted hunger radiothons in a dozen cities across the United States, 24-hour music and talk shows that reached some 15 million people and gave a media voice to more than 500 anti-hunger activists, for many their first major publicity. At the same time, Chapin set out to persuade Congress and President Jimmy Carter to establish a Presidential Commission on World Hunger. Many other organizations joined WHY in this campaign, but Chapin remained its prime mover and, appointed by President Carter, served as the commission's most active member when it was established in 1978.

A native of New York City, Chapin was educated in New York's public schools and briefly attended the Air Force Academy and Cornell University but did not complete a degree. Chapin is survived by his wife, Sandy, and five children. His oldest brother, James B. Chapin, chairs the WHY board of directors. Sandy Chapin and two other brothers, Stephen Chapin and Tom Chapin, are also active on the board in supporting the organization Harry founded. In 1989, Sandy Chapin and the Harry Chapin Foundation established the annual Harry Chapin Food Self-Reliance Award, a cash grant of $5,000 to the community-based organization that has done the most during the year to promote food self-reliance in the United States.

James A. Cogswell (1922–)

James Cogswell, presently a consultant to the Global 2000 Project of the Jimmy Carter Presidential Center, provided outstanding leadership and inspiration from 1971 to 1988 to ecumenical ministry on behalf of just, peaceful, and sustainable solutions to global hunger and poverty. In 1971 he became the first director of the Task Force on World Hunger of the Presbyterian Church, U.S. (PCUS), and then served as director of the PCUS Office of

World Service and World Hunger (1973–1984). He chaired the National Council of Churches (NCC) Task Force on World Hunger (1974–1976) and was vice-chair of the NCC Division of Overseas Ministries. He was president of Agricultural Missions (an NCC affiliate agency supporting self-help organized by small-holder farmers) for 6 of his 11 years on that agency's board. During the same period (1973–1983) he served on the board of Church World Service (CWS), NCC's overseas relief and development agency, and represented CWS at the World Food Conference.

As associate general secretary of the NCC for the Division of Overseas Ministries from 1984 to 1988, Cogswell was a frequent consultant to the World Council of Churches and a leader in ecumenical consultations among NCC member churches, the Orthodox Church, and the U.S. Catholic Mission Association. In 1988 he became the first non-Catholic to receive the Sixth Annual Mission Award of the U.S. Catholic Mission Association.

Cogswell was ordained a minister of the Presbyterian Church, U.S., in Mississippi in June 1945. Thirteen years as a missionary in Japan during the recovery from World War II and seven more years as area secretary for Asia of the PCUS Board of World Missions brought abiding affection and understanding for peoples of non-Western cultures and deep insight into the struggles of people everywhere for dignity and autonomous development.

Joseph Collins (1945–)

Joseph Collins is co-founder of the Institute for Food and Development Policy and an independent researcher who specializes in agricultural policies and the causes of world hunger. His background in hunger and poverty issues began as a Catholic missionary-in-training in the late 1950s and early 1960s, assisting Maryknoll parish priests in the slums of Santiago, Chile, and Lima, Peru, in remote Mayan villages of the Yucatan peninsula, the highlands of Guatemala, and on the island of Mindanao in the Philippines. It was during these experiences that he chose his life work: communicating the reality of underdevelopment. "I began to see how all of our lives are interconnected," Collins says; "I decided I wanted to help more of my fellow Americans understand how our choices, our society, and our government affect people's lives in the rest of the world." From 1971 to 1973, Collins was a researcher at the Institute of Policy Studies (IPS) in Washington, D.C., helping to complete *Global Reach,* the first major study of the globe-spanning power of multinational corporations. In 1974 he represented IPS as an observer at the World Food Conference in Rome, where he met Frances Moore Lappé with whom he subsequently co-authored *Food First* (1975, revised 1977) and founded the Institute for Food and Development Policy. Asked in 1979 by the new Sandinista government of Nicaragua to advise the Nicaraguan Ministry of Agriculture on agrarian reform and food policies, Collins wrote *Nicaragua: What Difference Could a Revolution Make?* (1979), a sympathetic but also sharply critical look at Sandinista food policy successes and failures. Other major publications include *No Free Lunch: Food and Revolution in Cuba Today* (1984, with Lappé), *World Hunger: Twelve Myths* (1986, with Lappé), and *The Philippines: Fire on the Rim* (1989). Current research focuses on food and development policy in Chile. Collins is a graduate of Maryknoll College. He holds an M.A. and a Ph.D. in public policy from Columbia University. A native of Cincinnati, he now resides in Santa Cruz, California.

Walter P. Falcon (1936–)

Walter Falcon is a development economist specializing in the agricultural development problems of less developed countries. He has been prominent in this field since the mid-1960s, joining the Development Advisory Service of Harvard University as director of research and research associates in 1966. In 1972 he became director of the Food Research Institute at Stanford University, one of the oldest and most prestigious centers of interdisciplinary research in the United States. He was a member of the Presidential Commission on World Hunger during the Carter administration and was a consultant to the President's Science Advisory Committee as it prepared its massive report on the world food problem for President Lyndon Johnson. He has been a frequent consultant to the World Bank, the Ford Foundation, the U.S. government, and national governments in Asia, especially in Indonesia, Malaysia, and Pakistan, where he was a Fulbright scholar from 1961 to 1962. He was born in Cedar

Rapids, Iowa, and holds degrees from Iowa State University (B.Sc., 1954) and Harvard University (M.A. and Ph.D. in economics, 1960 and 1962), where he became a member of the economics faculty immediately upon receiving his doctorate. He is married, has three children, and lives in Stanford, California.

Susan George (1934–)

Susan George has been a fellow of the Transnational Institute (TNI) since it was founded in 1973 in Amsterdam, Holland, as an affiliate of the Institute for Policy Studies in Washington, D.C. Her special field of expertise is the impact on the world food system by agribusiness and multinational corporations. She participated in preparing the TNI analysis for the 1974 World Food Conference that radically countered the official view of the food crisis. The TNI report traced the roots of hunger to the actions of multinational corporations and powerful national elites. Subsequent research led to her first book, *How the Other Half Dies: The Real Reasons for World Hunger* (1977), which quickly established her as a major spokesperson for strategies to end hunger by empowering the poor rather than by food aid or by "more of the same" agricultural and rural development. Other publications include *Feeding the Few: Corporate Control of Food* (1978), *Food for Beginners* (with Nigel Paige, 1982), *Ill Fares the Land: Essays on Food, Hunger, and Power* (1984), and *A Fate Worse than Debt—The World Financial Crisis and the Poor* (1988). George serves on the international editorial board of *Food Policy* and is a frequent consultant to agencies of the European Economic Community and the United Nations.

Born in Akron, Ohio, Susan George was graduated from Smith College, where she was elected to Phi Beta Kappa, and received a "Licence" in philosophy from the Sorbonne. She completed a doctorate at the École des Hautes Études en Sciences Sociales of the University of Paris. She lives in Paris, is married, and has three children. Explaining her own development, George says:

> My political education came about through the Vietnam War against which I was an active militant. Moving from [that] toward a general concern with poverty and oppression in the underdeveloped countries was natural—and hunger is the most basic of oppressions.

James P. Grant (1922–)

James Grant became executive director of UNICEF in 1980. An eloquent advocate of development justice and aid for the suffering poor, he is principal author of *The State of the World's Children,* a series of annual policy-oriented reports in nontechnical language that he initiated in 1981. In 1982 he was instrumental in launching the Child Survival Campaign to muster governments, NGOs, women's groups, primary school classes, radio and television personalities, and health professionals the world over for the prevention of millions of needless deaths through "GOBI." GOBI stands for a combination of low-cost interventions that even illiterate parents can understand and apply: G = growth monitoring, with a simple chart to discover early signs of undernutrition; O = oral rehydration of diarrheal children with a simple preparation of boiled water, table salt, and sugar; B = breast feeding and birth spacing for healthier infants; and I = immunization of children against major infectious diseases by public health workers. For his leadership at UNICEF Grant received the 1988–1989 Alan Shawn Feinstein Award for the Prevention and Reduction of World Hunger.

Grant came to UNICEF after 11 years as president and chief executive of the Overseas Development Council (ODC), a private research and policy advocacy center in Washington, D.C., that he helped to found. At ODC he made many important contributions to human needs–oriented development strategy. He was on the steering committee for the National Academy of Sciences World Food and Nutrition Study (1975–1977). He also served for several years as the international president of the Society for International Development.

James Grant is a U.S. citizen who was born in China of missionary parents. After graduating from the University of California at Berkeley in 1943, he returned to China, first in the U.S. armed forces and then for three years in relief and development programs of UNRRA and the U.S. Economic Aid Mission. In 1951 he earned a doctorate in jurisprudence from Harvard University and then worked on U.S. aid programs in South Asia, becoming director of the U.S. economic aid mission in Sri Lanka. Returning to Washington, he served as deputy to the director of the International Cooperation Administration in the State Department (a predecessor of the U.S. Agency for International Development), deputy assistant secretary of state for Near East and South Asian affairs, director of the USAID program in Turkey, and assistant administrator of USAID from 1967 to 1969. In 1969 Grant left government service to become president and chief executive of the newly founded Overseas Development Council.

Richard R. Harwood (1937–)

Richard Harwood is regional director for Asia at the Winrock International Institute for Agricultural Development. He specializes in smallholder farming systems, multiple cropping, appropriate technologies, and low-input (organic/biological) cropping systems with little or no use of chemicals. He was previously deputy director of Winrock International's Technical Cooperation Division, coordinating research and technical support for programs in Nepal, Pakistan, and the Philippines. He is a former director of the Department of Multiple Cropping at IRRI in the Philippines and served on the field staff of Rockefeller University at Kasetsart University in Thailand, directing the sorghum-improvement program.

Formerly Harwood directed the Rodale Horticultural Research Center in Pennsylvania and taught vegetable gardening, plant breeding, and tropical agriculture at Loma Linda University in California. He has served on a variety of research and scholarly panels at the U.S. National Academy of Sciences, the International Agricultural Development Service, USAID, and the Congressional Office of Technology Assessment and as a consultant on projects in Indonesia, India, Tanzania, Bangladesh, and Costa Rica.

Born in Manchester, New Hampshire, he holds agriculture degrees with specialty in vegetable crops from Cornell University (B.Sc., 1964) and Michigan State University (M.Sc. and Ph.D, 1966 and 1967). Publications include *Small Farm Development: Understanding and Improving Farming Systems in the Humid Tropics* (1979) and *Lessons from Organic Gardening* (with W. C. Liebhardt, 1989).

Joan Holmes (1935–)

Joan Holmes is global executive director of The Hunger Project, coordinating activities among groups organized in 22 countries in North and Central America, Europe, Africa, Asia, and Australia, volunteers who are "creating the context for responsibility and sufficiency" to end hunger by the year 2000. Under her leadership major media campaigns have drawn attention to food crises in Cambodia and East Africa, resulting in donations of more than a million dollars to relief and development agencies. In 1983, she launched The Hunger Project in India, inspiring receptive audiences in six major cities to "take responsibility for ending hunger." The African food crisis became a major focus of her efforts to mobilize global commitment as early as 1980. In 1987, she helped inaugurate the annual Africa Prize for Leadership for the Sustainable End of Hunger, by which outstanding Africans and their initiatives are given both international prominence and a generous cash grant to further their success. She was managing editor of *Ending Hunger: An Idea Whose Time Has Come* (1985), written and produced by many contributing authors and editors as an illustrated introduction for the general public to major facts, viewpoints, and controversies involved in the hunger issue. She serves on the boards of the Overseas Development Council and the International Development Conference and is a member of the executive committee of the American Council for Voluntary International Action.

Prior to becoming executive director of The Hunger Project at its founding in 1977, Holmes's career was in humanistic psychology, counseling, and education. A native of Colorado, she holds a B.A. in psychology from the University of Colorado and an M.A. in psychology from San Francisco State University.

Barbara Huddleston (1939–)

Barbara Huddleston, an economist, is chief of the Food Security and Information Service, Commodities and Trade Division of the Economic and Social Policy Department of the FAO in Rome. She supervises FAO's Food Security Assistance Scheme and the Committee on World Food Security. Prior to joining FAO, she did research and policy analysis on issues of food aid, food insurance, and food security programs in developing nations as a fellow of the International Food Policy Research Institute; served as an economist with the Africa Division in the U.S. Department of Commerce; and directed the Trade Negotiations Division of the U.S. Department of Agriculture. She has been a consultant to the U.S. Presidential Commission on World Hunger, the Rockefeller

Foundation, the Agriculture Development Council, the American Universities Field Service, and the U.N. World Food Council. She is a member of the international editorial board of *Food Policy*.

A native of Malone, New York, Huddleston holds degrees from the College of Wooster (B.A., 1961), Johns Hopkins School of Advanced International Studies (M.A., 1963), and George Washington University (M.Phil., 1975). Publications include *International Finance for Food Security* (co-authored with D. Gale Johnson, Shlomo Reutlinger, and Alberto Valdes, 1984), *Closing the Cereals Gap with Trade and Food Aid* (1984), and *Food Policy—Frameworks for Analysis and Action* (co-edited with Charles P. Mann, 1985).

Idriss Jazairy (1936–)

Idriss Jazairy became the second president of the International Fund for Agricultural Development (IFAD) in 1984. Under his leadership, diplomatic skill, and dedicated and enthusiastic articulation of IFAD's mission, the agency has gained steadily in recognition and support for its innovative, uniquely effective approach to development assistance for smallholder farmers and the rural poor. Before being elected by the IFAD Ministerial Council to this post, Jazairy had chaired the U.N. General Assembly's Committee of the Whole on the North-South Dialogue in 1978 and 1979 and had been a member of various expert groups appointed by the United Nations on world inflation and development (1975), science and technology (1977), social aspects of development (1980), desertification (1984), and regional and inter-regional cooperation (1983–1984). He has held prominent positions also in the Non-Aligned Movement of the Group of 77.

A native of Algeria, Jazairy was Algerian Ambassador to Belgium, Luxembourg, and the European Communities (1979–1982); ambassador-at-large in the Ministry of Foreign Affairs of Algeria (1982–1984), specializing in international economic affairs; and led Algeria's delegations to many international meetings, including several sessions of the U.N. General Assembly, the U.N. Economic and Social Council, and the U.N. Conference on Trade and Development. He is an alumnus of the National School for Administration in Paris and holds master of arts degrees in political science (Oxford University) and public administration (Harvard University).

Norge W. Jerome (1930–)

Norge Jerome is director of the Office of Nutrition in the Bureau of Science and Technology of USAID. Before coming to this post, she was an associate professor of nutritional anthropology in the Department of Community Health and then director of the Department of Preventive Medicine in the Community Nutrition Division, School of Medicine, at the University of Kansas Medical Center in Kansas City. Her research specializes in the dietary patterns of population groups and the effect of modernization on diet and health. She participated in the 1975–1977 World Food and Nutrition Study of the National Academy of Sciences. Since 1980 she has been a member of the Man–Food Systems Interaction Committee of the National Research Council.

She was born in Grenada, West Indies, and holds degrees from Howard University (B.S., 1960) and the University of Wisconsin at Madison (M.Sc., 1962; Ph.D. in nutrition and anthropology, 1967). She is a fellow of the American Anthropology Association and holds membership in the American Public Health Association and the Society of Medical Anthropology, among other professional associations. She is co-editor of *Nutritional Anthropology* (Marcel Dekker, 1978), introducing an area of nutritional research she helped to pioneer.

Richard Jolly (1934–)

Richard Jolly has been deputy executive director of UNICEF in charge of programs since 1982. In this capacity he is concerned with all aspects of UNICEF's programs in more than 100 countries, including the Child Survival and Development campaign and programs in support of women. Since 1985, he has been a key spokesperson in UNICEF's challenge to conventional World Bank and IMF structural adjustment policies and a major architect of alternative policies described in the study titled *Adjustment with a Human Face*. Alternative kinds of structural adjustment, Jolly argues, promote economic growth in debt-ridden countries but not at the cost of harming their most precious resource: their children.

Before joining UNICEF, Jolly was director of the Institute of Development Studies at the University of Sussex for nine years. During this period, he was closely involved with the ILO's World Employment Programme, participating in the employment missions to Colombia (1970), Sri Lanka (1971), and Zambia (1975). He co-led the ILO mission to Kenya (1972) (published as *Employment, Incomes and Equality*) and headed the mission to Zambia, whose report *Basic Needs in an Economy under Pressure* was published in 1981. Work on the early ILO employment missions led in 1974 to the joint IDS/World Bank publication *Redistribution with Growth,* of which Jolly is a co-author. He is also editor of *Disarmament and World Development* (1978) and a contributor to *Rich Country Interests and Third World Development* (1982), among many other publications.

After graduating from Cambridge University in economics in 1956, he began his career as a development economist by serving for two years as a community development officer in Baringo District, Kenya, where he was concerned with literacy, women's activities, village water supplies, and other community action. Jolly's African experience during the 1960s includes a year in Makerere College, Uganda, and several years in the Office of National Development and Planning of the government of Zambia. He has held office in the Society for International Development since 1975. In 1987 he became chair of SID's North/South Roundtable. He holds a doctorate in economics from Yale University.

Frances Moore Lappé (1944–)

Frances Moore Lappé, probably North America's most widely read writer on the world hunger problem, is co-founder (with Joseph Collins) of the Institute for Food and Development Policy (IFDP), a research and educational institute also known as Food First. Coming to the hunger issue as an environmental activist, she wrote the best-selling *Diet for a Small Planet* (1971) under the assumption of a food scarcity. She became convinced that scarcity was not the problem while attending the World Food Conference of 1974 as an observer for Friends of the Earth. She teamed up with Joseph Collins, who represented the Institute for Policy Studies at the conference, to write *Food First: Beyond the Myth of Scarcity* (revised 1977).

The assumption expressed in that book and in most of her

subsequent work is that the real cause of hunger is control of agricultural land by elite interests, abetted by the greed of the national and international agribusiness establishment that determines what happens with food from production to the final consumer. Other publications include *Aid as Obstacle* (with Joseph Collins and David Kinley, 1980); *What Can We Do?* (with William Valentine, 1980); *Mozambique and Tanzania: Asking the Big Questions* (with Adele Beccary-Varela, 1980); *World Hunger Myths* (1982); *Food and Farming in the New Nicaragua* (with Joseph Collins, 1982); *World Hunger: Twelve Myths* (with Joseph Collins, 1986); and *The Missing Piece in the Population Puzzle* (with Rachel Schurman, 1988).

Lappé was born in Pendleton, Oregon, and grew up in Fort Worth, Texas, in a socially conscious family with strong ethical convictions. Politicized by her private study of the Vietnam War while attending Earlham College, a Quaker institution in Indiana, she developed the habits of independent inquiry and skepticism toward "establishment" views and motives that have remained hallmarks of her work. These characteristics were reinforced by experiences as community organizer and social worker first in Philadelphia, then in California, where she began graduate study in the School of Social Work at the University of California at Berkeley. Pursuit of a personal inquiry into the political economy of food, using the agriculture library on the Berkeley campus, led to her present career as a writer and lecturer on the world hunger problem.

Besides a B.A. in history from Earlham College (1966), Lappé has been awarded honorary doctorates from the University of California at Berkeley, Notre Dame University, Bucknell University, Lewis and Clark College, and St. Mary's College. In 1981 she was named to the Nutrition Hall of Fame by the Center for Science in the Public Interest. She lives in the San Francisco Bay Area with a teenage son and daughter from her first marriage to Marc Lappé and commutes for part of each month to Stevens Point, Wisconsin, where her present husband, Baird Callicott, is a philosophy professor at the University of Wisconsin.

Mickey Leland (1944–1989)

Congressman Mickey Leland was the first chairman of the House Select Committee on Hunger during its crucial formative years from 1984 to 1989. Jointly with Benjamin Gilman (Republican congressman from New York and member of the 1979–1980 Presidential Commission on World Hunger), Leland introduced the resolution establishing the select committee in 1983. As committee chairman, he set high standards of policy-oriented investigation and reporting that won praise and overwhelming majorities for reauthorization of the committee from both Democrats and Republicans in three succeeding congresses.

Leland's devotion to the cause of ending hunger became legendary. "He wore his feelings and compassion right out in the open"; "Leland represented the best in compassion that we as a nation possess"; "Mickey Leland died as he lived, on a mission of mercy and hope for victims of poverty, injustice, racism, and hunger. Wherever suffering people existed on our planet, Mickey Leland wanted to be there to help"—these are the words reported after Leland's death from Representative Ronald Dellums, Speaker of the House Thomas Foley, and Senator Edward Kennedy, who typify the regard in which he was held by his colleagues.

In addition to the normal duties of studying staff reports and presiding over hearings to investigate hunger in the United States and developing countries, Leland also repeatedly visited Ethiopia to examine firsthand the condition and treatment of famine victims. His personal witness from such direct exposure to the ravages of hunger was all the more powerful because of his sincerity and lack of political grandstanding.

Born in Lubbock, Texas, Leland was a black civil rights activist who grew up in a fatherless family in one of the poorest neighborhoods of Houston. He championed the needs of poor people throughout his career, a career that included being arrested and jailed for protesting police brutality against minorities in Houston in 1970. Leland graduated in 1970 from Texas Southern University with a degree in pharmacy but soon entered politics. He was elected to the state legislature in 1972. He was sent to the House of Representatives by voters from the 18th district of Texas for the first time in 1978 and was reelected five times, serving in his sixth term at the time of his death.

The manner of Leland's death fits his inspiring legend. Only hours after Congress adjourned for summer recess on 5 August 1989, instead of going home to rest, Leland was on his way for the sixth time to investigate hunger in the Horn of Africa. Two days later, during thunderstorms over rugged mountains in a remote region southwest of Addis Ababa, the Ethiopian Relief and

Rehabilitation Service plane carrying Leland to refugee camps along the Ethiopian-Sudanese border disappeared. Two of the seven Americans travelling with Leland were members of the Select Committee staff; one was an aide to Congressman Dellums; and two were USAID officers stationed in Addis Ababa. When the wreckage of their plane was found after a week-long air search, none of the nine Americans and seven Ethiopians on the mission had survived.

An assessment of Leland's accomplishments that might have pleased him most came from Texas State Representative Al Edwards, during a memorial service held in Leland's former high school in Houston, attended by hundreds of classmates, colleagues, and friends who vowed to carry on his dream of ending hunger: "Millions of would-be starving children won't be starving because of Mickey Leland." He is survived by his wife, Alison, and their two young children.

C. Payne Lucas (1933–)

C. Payne Lucas is executive director of Africare, a Washington-based private development organization that he helped to found in 1971 to improve the quality of life in rural Africa. From its inception as a pioneer in U.S. NGO cooperation with Africans working on their own behalf, Africare has emphasized the leadership of Africans at national and local levels, marshalling only the funds and technical assistance needed to help them conduct their own development projects. He is a frequent lecturer on Africa and holds many awards for his work through Africare, including an honorary doctorate of laws degree from the University of Maryland (1975); the Capitol Press Club's Humanitarian of the Year Award (1980); the Presidential Hunger Award for Outstanding Achievement (1984); and the Phelps-Stokes Fund Aggrey Medal (1986) for his accomplishments in establishing enduring links of friendship and cooperation between the United States and Africa.

Lucas is a native of North Carolina and was educated at the University of Maryland (B.A.) and American University (M.A.). His experience with Africa began in 1962 when he became a Peace Corps volunteer. He received the Distinguished Federal Service Award from President Lyndon B. Johnson in 1967 for his work with the Peace Corps. From 1967 to 1969 he directed the Peace Corps's Africa Region.

Publications include *Keeping Kennedy's Promise—The Peace Corps: Unmet Promise of the New Frontier* (Westview Press, 1978, co-authored with Kevin Lowther) and many articles in newspapers and journals. Lucas serves on the board of directors of the Council on Foreign Relations, the Overseas Development Council, International Voluntary Services, and the American Council for Voluntary International Action, among other organizations.

John Mellor (1928–)

John Mellor directed the International Food Policy Research Institute (IFPRI) from 1977 to 1990 and is one of the most authoritative agricultural economists at work in the field of food policy analysis and advocacy. His research specializes in relating growth in agricultural development to growth in other sectors of society and in the role of technology in these processes. For a short time before assuming his position at IFPRI in 1977, he was chief economist for the U.S. Agency for International Development.

From 1952 through 1976 Mellor was on the faculty of Cornell University, in the later years as professor of economics, agricultural economics, and Asian studies. He also directed Cornell's Program in Comparative Economic Development. He has been a Fulbright Fellow at Oxford University, a visiting professor at Balwant Rajput College in Agra, India, and a Rockefeller Foundation researcher at the Indian Agricultural Research Institute in New Delhi. Among his numerous publications are *The Economics of Agricultural Development* and *The New Economics of Growth: A Strategy for India and the Developing World*. He has also edited and contributed chapters to *Agricultural Change and Rural Poverty: Variations on a Theme by Dharm Narain* (with G. M. Deasi), *Accelerating Food Production Growth in Sub-Saharan Africa* (with C. Delgado and M. Blackie), and *Agricultural Price Policy for Developing Countries* (with R. Ahmed).

Mellor has served as contributing editor to *Environment* and as a member of the board of directors of the Overseas Development Council. He is a fellow of the American Academy of Arts and Sciences and of the American Agricultural Economics Association. In 1985, he became the first social scientist to receive the Wihuri Foundation International Prize. For his publications and research he has received the American Agricultural Association Award three times.

Larry Minear (1936–)

Larry Minear is one of the most highly respected voices from the NGO community on issues of food and development aid and humanitarian assistance. He serves frequently as a consultant to various U.S. government and United Nations groups and agencies in his position as representative for development policy for Church World Service and Lutheran World Relief. Since 1975, he has been based in Washington, D.C., where he helped to establish the Interreligious Taskforce on U.S. Food Policy (renamed Interfaith Action for Economic Justice in 1982). He has been active in that organization's International Development Work Group since the group's founding in 1974. Prior to becoming a development policy analyst and advisor, he administered a CWS-supported refugee resettlement program in southern Sudan in 1972 at an earlier phase of that country's lingering civil war. His work as a policy analyst and advisor began as the CWS representative to the World Food Conference in 1974.

Minear was born in Evanston, Illinois, and educated at Yale University (B.A. in history and M.A. in theology) and Harvard University (M.A. in education). He began his career as a high school teacher but soon joined the "War on Poverty" during the Johnson administration, working for the Office of Economic Opportunity in Chicago and Boston before leaving to work on poverty and development at the international level. He lives with his wife and two sons in Washington, D.C. Publications include *New Hope for the Hungry?: The Challenge of the World Food Crisis* (1975), *Helping People in an Age of Conflict: Toward a New Professionalism in U.S. Voluntary Humanitarian Assistance* (1988), "The Forgotten Human Agenda," a review of the Reagan administration's stewardship of U.S. humanitarian traditions and programs that appeared in *Foreign Policy* (Winter 1988), and *Humanitarianism under Siege: A Critical Review of Operation Lifeline Sudan* (1990).

Thomas R. Odhiambo (1931–)

Thomas R. Odhiambo is director of the International Centre of Insect Physiology in Nairobi, Kenya, and president of the African Academy of Sciences. His research focuses on natural history and insect endocrinology, particularly in relation to insect reproductive biology, on which he has published more than 100 papers. Applications of his research are beginning to show great promise for ecologically benign biological control of harmful insects, which are among the greatest obstacles to the advance of African agriculture. In 1979 he received the Albert Einstein Medal for Science.

He labors tirelessly also to develop Africa's scientific research capacity, which at present is less developed than in any other region of the world, while some of agricultural science's most difficult challenges lie in the African environment. In both of these endeavors, Odhiambo's farsighted vision and initiatives address fundamental issues for sustainable food security and agricultural progress in Africa. He founded the East African Academy of Sciences and is a fellow of the Kenya National Academy of Sciences. In 1987 he received one of the first two awards of the Africa Prize for Leadership in Ending Hunger, established by The Hunger Project.

Odhiambo was born in Mombasa, Kenya, and studied at Makerere College in Kampala, Uganda, and at Cambridge University (B.A., M.A., Ph.D.). He has taught at the University of Nairobi since 1965, where he was the first professor of entomology and the first dean of the Faculty of Agriculture. He is a fellow of the Third World Academy of Sciences, the Indian National Academy of Sciences, the Italian Academia dei Quaranta, and the Royal Norwegian Academy of Science and Letters. He is a member of the international jury for the UNESCO Science Prize and a member of the Club of Rome.

Per Pinstrup-Andersen (1939–)

Per Pinstrup-Andersen is an agricultural economist with broad interests in food and nutrition policy; in the impact of macroeconomic adjustment policies on poverty, consumption, and nutritional status; and in the use of nutrition surveillance. He is professor of food economics in the Division of Nutritional Sciences and director of the Cornell Food and Nutrition Policy Program at Cornell University in Ithaca, New York. From 1980 to 1987, he was a research fellow and director of the Food Consumption and Nutrition Policy Research Program at IFPRI.

He has also been a senior research fellow and associate professor in the Economic Institute of the Royal Veterinary and Agricultural University in Copenhagen and an agricultural economist at CIAT (International Center for Tropical Agriculture) in Cali, Colombia. He is a frequent consultant on the economic aspects of food and nutrition policy for national and international agencies. He currently chairs the Food Policy Committee of the International Union of Nutrition Sciences.

Pinstrup-Andersen was born in Bislev, Denmark, and studied at the Royal Veterinary and Agricultural University (B.Sc. in agricultural economics, 1965) and at Oklahoma University (M.Sc. and Ph.D. in agricultural economics, 1967 and 1969). Publications include "The Pilot Food Price Subsidy Scheme in the Philippines: Its Impact on Income, Food Consumption, and Nutritional Status," with Marito Garcia, *IFPRI Report* (1987); *Nutrition and Development* (1985, co-edited with Margaret Biswas); and *International Agricultural Research and Human Nutrition* (1984, co-edited with Alan Berg and Martin Forman).

Shlomo Reutlinger (1925–)

Shlomo Reutlinger is a World Bank economist who specializes in questions of food security, characteristically combining highly technical economic analysis with compassionate concern and humane understanding. He has been a pioneer in the effort to define and measure hunger in terms that can have impact on the economic decisions that developing-country governments must make. In 1987, he became advisor on food security in the World Bank Office of the Vice-President for the Africa Region.

His work in international development began in 1965, when he served as economist and co-manager on a project sponsored by the United Nations Development Programme and the FAO for a pre-investment study of watershed development in Israel.

The following year he joined the Economics Department of the World Bank in the Projects and Sector Studies program. In 1971 he became chief of the new Agriculture and Rural Development Division and then, in 1974, he became senior economist in the Development Economics Department and the Agriculture and Rural Development Department. In addition to numerous journal articles on diverse aspects of hunger, he is principal author of the World Bank policy study titled *Poverty and Hunger: Issues and Options for Food Security in Developing Countries* (1986). He also co-authored *Malnutrition and Poverty* (1976, with Marcelo Selowsky) and *International Finance for Food Security* (1984, with Barbara Huddleston and D. Gale Johnson).

Born in Germany, Reutlinger emigrated to Israel and was a member of a kibbutz from 1942 to 1950 before coming to the

United States. He received a B.Sc. in economics from Cornell University in 1958 and a doctorate in agricultural economics and statistics from North Carolina State University in 1963. He worked in the Economics Research Service of the U.S. Department of Agriculture briefly before beginning his career in international economics. He is married and has two grown children.

Beatrice Lorge Rogers (1947–)

Beatrice Lorge Rogers's research in nutrition policy spotlights the dynamics of food consumption and nutritional status at the micro and intrahousehold level, an area of reality about which national policy makers commonly have very little knowledge. When income earnings rise or fall in relationship to food prices, are all members of a household affected equally? Does it matter for the nutrition of children which parent is the chief income earner or whether the mother also earns income? Rogers's research in Mali, the Dominican Republic, and other developing countries indicates that "no" is the answer to the first question and "yes" is the answer to the second. The implications of such research are very significant for food policy planning.

Rogers is associate professor of nutrition policy in the School of Nutrition of Tufts University. She has done research in the International Nutrition Planning Program of the Massachusetts Institute of Technology and for USAID, the U.S. Department of Agriculture, IFPRI, the World Bank, and the U.S. Presidential Commission on World Hunger. She serves on the Committee on International Nutrition of the National Academy of Sciences and the board of directors of the International Nutrition Foundation for Developing Countries. She is the author of numerous articles and papers, including "The Role of Women's Earnings in Determining Child Health," *Food and Nutrition Bulletin* (1987), and *Consumer Food Price Subsidies,* volume 4 of *Nutrition Intervention in Developing Countries* (1980).

Edouard Saouma (1926–)

Edouard Saouma became director-general of FAO in 1979, shortly before the United Nations World Conference on Agrarian Reform and Rural Development, hosted by FAO. He was re-elected to a third six-year term in 1987. His main concern at FAO has been to strengthen its operational role in the field as a complement to FAO's predominant functions in coordinating multilateral technical assistance, research, and consultation. He established the Technical Cooperation Programme in 1976, which enabled FAO for the first time to provide practical and timely technical assistance to developing countries out of its own resources. Saouma has also decentralized FAO's operations, establishing 74 field offices serving 100 countries. Before becoming director-general, he had been FAO Regional Representative for Southwest Asia in New Delhi and director of FAO's Land and Water Development Division.

Saouma was born in Beirut, Lebanon, where he became an agronomist serving in a number of posts with the government of Lebanon, notably as the first director-general of the National Agricultural Research Institute and later as minister of agriculture, fisheries, and forests. He holds degrees in agricultural chemistry from St. Joseph's University in Beirut and from the National School of Agronomy in Montpelier, France. He has been awarded honorary doctorates from several universities throughout the world. He is married and has two daughters and a son.

Nevin S. Scrimshaw (1918–)

There is no more prominent scientist working on food and health in developing countries than Nevin S. Scrimshaw. He currently directs the Food and Nutrition Programme of the United Nations University (UNU) and edits *Food and Nutrition Bulletin*. He has also directed the Development Studies Division and the Food, Nutrition, Biotechnology and Poverty Program of UNU and has chaired the Protein Advisory Group (PAG) of the United Nations System, the WHO Advisory Committee on Medical Research, and the Malnutrition Panel of the U.S.-Japan Cooperative Medical Sciences Program. He was on the steering committee for the 1975–1977 World Food and Nutrition Study of the National Academy of Sciences.

Scrimshaw was founding director of the Instituto de Nutricion de Centro America y Panama (INCAP), where he helped develop a protein-rich weaning food, Incaparina. Through INCAP and WHO, he led the campaign to educate health professionals on the relationship between infectious diseases and childhood nutrition. He is past president of the International Union of Nutrition Sciences and former trustee of the

Rockefeller Foundation. He has been an institute professor at Columbia University and visiting lecturer at Harvard University and is now institute professor emeritus at the Massachusetts Institute of Technology.

Scrimshaw was educated at Ohio Wesleyan University (B.A., 1938), Harvard University (M.A. and Ph.D. in biology, 1939 and 1941), and the University of Rochester (M.D., 1945). He interned at Gorgas Hospital in Panama and completed residencies at Strong Memorial and Genesee hospitals in Rochester, New York. Among his many publications are *Interactions on Nutrition and Infection* (1968, with Carl E. Taylor and John E. Gordon); *Nutrition, National Development and Planning* (1973, co-edited with Alan Berg and David L. Call); *Nutrition and Agricultural Development: Significance and Potential for the Tropics* (1976, co-edited with Moses Behar); *Diarrhea and Malnutrition: Interactions, Mechanisms, and Interventions* (1983, co-edited with Lincoln Chen); and "The Phenomenon of Famine," *Annual Review of Nutrition* (1987).

Amartya K. Sen (1933–)

Amartya K. Sen is presently Lamont Professor of economics and philosophy at Harvard University, a title that aptly describes his unique contribution to the current study of hunger. Sen the economist performs hard-headed, state-of-the-art economic analysis, applying sophisticated mathematical processes to data culled from statistical records. Sen the humanitarian philosopher wonders about the values and assumptions that underlie political and economic decisions.

His research interests include famines, food economics, endemic hunger, gender bias, welfare economics, economic development, social choice theory, ethics, and social and political philosophy. With a philosopher's independence of mind, he accepts nothing in conventional wisdom as true prior to thorough examination. He asks seemingly naive questions that, when probed with his combined skills as economist and logician, have a way of unmasking error in long-accepted views. His book *Poverty and Famines: An Essay on Entitlement and Deprivation* (1981) is a classic example. A major premise of *Hunger and Public Action* (1989, with Jean Dreze) is that because chronic hunger and famine are preventable, such conditions at this point in history signify massive failure by governments and societies. Other books include *Choice of Techniques* (1960); *Collective Choice and Social Welfare* (1970); *Choice, Welfare and Measurement* (1982); *Values and Development* (1984); and *Commodities and Capabilities* (1985).

Amartya Sen was born in India and studied at Presidency College in Calcutta (B.A., 1953) and at Trinity College, Cambridge University (B.A., 1955; M.A. and Ph.D., 1959). He has been Drummond Professor of political economy at Oxford University and has taught also at Trinity College, Cambridge; Jadavpur University in Calcutta; the London School of Economics; and Cornell University. He is a fellow of the British Academy, a fellow and past president of the Econometric Society, foreign honorary member of the American Economic Association, and president of the International Economic Association. He was awarded the Mahalanobis Prize in 1976 and the Seidman Distinguished Award in Political Economy in 1986.

Arthur Simon (1930–)

Arthur Simon is founder and president of Bread for the World, a faith-based volunteer citizens' movement credited with influencing a number of significant improvements in U.S. legislation affecting hungry people since its founding in 1974. Bread for the World now has 50,000 members organized into more than 400 local chapters corresponding to congressional districts in the United States. In 1990, Simon was awarded a Presidential End Hunger Award in the category "Lifetime Achievement."

Simon's involvement in hunger and poverty issues began in 1961 when he became Lutheran pastor of an inner-city parish on Manhattan's Lower East Side. He soon saw that relief action could never change the structural causes of the problems of hunger and poverty, not locally and not globally. Gradually he envisioned a network of Christians dedicated to influencing structural causes through political action. In 1973 he began to build that network with a core of 14 people from different Protestant denominations and from the Catholic Church and took leave from pastoral duties to write *The Politics of World Hunger* (1973) with his brother, Senator (then Representative) Paul Simon. By May 1974, Bread for the World began to organize nationally. The book Simon wrote as an introductory education on the issue for church people, *Bread for the World* (1975), won the national Religious Book Award in 1976. It was revised and reissued in 1984, with more than 300,000 copies now in print. Additional publications include *Christian Faith and Public Policy— No Grounds for Divorce* (1987), *Harvesting Peace: The Arms Race & Human Need* (1990), many articles in national magazines and journals, and two books on U.S. poverty.

Simon grew up in Eugene, Oregon, and Highland, Illinois, the son of a Lutheran pastor who had served for several years as a missionary in China. Speaking out on public policy was part of the family's life. In Oregon his father openly protested the internment of Japanese-Americans during World War II and in Illinois his brother unmasked local political corruption as a smalltown newspaper editor and entered state politics, with Arthur helping in the campaign. Simon studied theology at Concordia Seminary in St. Louis and became ordained in the Lutheran Church Missouri Synod in 1961. He holds honorary doctorates from numerous institutions, including the Loyola Universities in Chicago and New Orleans, Valparaiso University, and St. Olaf's College. He is married and the father of four children. He has made his home in Washington, D.C., since 1982, when Bread for the World moved its headquarters there from New York City.

Margaret Snyder (1929–)

Margaret Snyder was the director of the United Nations Development Fund for Women (UNIFEM) from its founding in 1978 until her retirement from the United Nations in 1989. She helped to envisage and design the proposal for UNIFEM adopted by the International Women's Year Conference in Mexico City in 1975 and then lobbied actively for UNIFEM's establishment by the U.N. General Assembly. UNIFEM promotes and enhances the recognition and involvement of women as partners in economic and social development. Under her leadership UNIFEM introduced innovative and catalytic approaches to human resource development; supported nonprofit professional and technical organizations by and for women; established community revolving credit funds; introduced more appropriate technologies for producing and processing food; strengthened environmental conservation movements; and identified improved methods of channeling resources to the poorest families.

From 1971 to 1978, she was regional advisor to the U.N. Economic Commission for Africa (ECA) in Addis Ababa, Ethiopia, heading the first ECA Voluntary Agencies Bureau. In 1975, she co-founded the ECA African Training and Research Centre for Women. She is also a co-founder of Women's World Banking, an international nongovernmental organization that seeks to overcome discrimination by private credit resources against women entrepreneurs throughout the world.

Prior to becoming an international civil servant in the United Nations, she followed a career in higher education as sociology lecturer at Trinity College in Washington, D.C.; as Dean of Women at LeMoyne College in Syracuse, New York; as consultant to the State University of New York and the Institute for International Development; and as assistant director of the Overseas Liaison Committee of the American Council on Education. During the 1960s, she worked in East Africa, advising voluntary groups in Kenya and Tanzania and directing field research on village settlements in Tanzania for the Maxwell School of Syracuse University, and was assistant director of the Maxwell School's Programme of Eastern African Studies.

She holds an M.A. degree in sociology from Catholic University in Washington, D.C., and a Ph.D. in sociology from the University of Dar es Salaam, Tanzania. A native of Syracuse, she lives in New York City.

Kathleen Staudt (1946–)

Kathleen Staudt is a prominent leader in the burgeoning field of policy-oriented research and training to inform and sensitize development planners about women in development. Africa and the role of women in food systems and rural development are prominent among her specialties. In addition to teaching and performing research as tenured professor of political science at the University of Texas at El Paso, she is frequently called upon to review and critique development research by others and to advise on the design of projects and programs of governments and volunteer agencies. For example, she has been social science analyst in the Office of Women in Development in the Bureau for Program and Policy Coordination of the U.S. Agency for International Development (1979); technical consultant for the Population Council's study in Jamaica, Dominica, and Saint

Lucia, titled "The Impact of Rural Development Schemes on Low-Income Households and the Role of Women" (1982–1983); and curriculum consultant on training courses about development policy and women for mid- to top-level management officials, taught by the Eastern and Southern African Management Institute (ESAMI) in Arusha, Tanzania (1981).

Staudt is a prolific writer, always integrating a gender perspective on data into the general discussion. Among her many publications are "Women Farmers and Inequities in Agricultural Services," *Rural Africana* (Winter 1975–1976); "Agricultural Productivity Gaps: A Case Study of Male Preference in Government Policy Implementation," *Development & Change* (July 1978); *Women and Participation in Rural Development: A Framework for Project Design and Policy-Oriented Research* (1979); *Agricultural Policy Implementation: A Case Study from Western Kenya* (1985); *Women, Foreign Assistance and Advocacy* (1985); "Uncaptured or Unmotivated? Women and the Food Crisis in Africa," *Rural Sociology* (Spring 1987); *Women and the State in Africa* (1989, co-edited with Jane Parpart); and *Development Management: State, Society and International Contexts* (forthcoming).

Her development experience began in the Philippines during 1967–1968 as an elementary math teacher with the Peace Corps, even before she attended college. She holds degrees from the University of Wisconsin at Milwaukee (B.A. in political science, 1971) and at Madison (M.A. and Ph.D. in political science, with an African studies minor, 1972 and 1976). Her Ph.D. dissertation was "Agricultural Policy, Political Power, and Women Farmers in Western Kenya."

Monkombu Sambasivan Swaminathan (1925–)

M. S. Swaminathan is acclaimed as an educator, visionary, humanitarian, and one of the world's leading agricultural scientists and science administrators. His numerous awards include the Albert Einstein Medal for Science in 1986, the Association of Women in Development Award for serving the cause of women's equality, and the Padma Shri and Padma Bhushan awards from the president of India. In 1987 he was the first laureate for the World Food Prize sponsored by the General Foods Fund. He holds honorary doctorates from 25 institutions. He chaired the panel on food and agriculture for the Brundtland Commission's report to the United Nations on environment and development and serves on the international editorial board of *Food Policy*. He is a founder and current president of the International Union for the Conservation of Nature and Natural Resources and serves on the board of directors of the Better World Society and the World Resources Institute.

While he was a cytogeneticist first at the University of Wisconsin at Madison and then from 1954 until 1972 at the Indian Agricultural Research Institute, Swaminathan's research led to improvements in the yield, quality, and stability of potatoes, wheat, and rice; identification of barriers to high yields in wheat; and initiation of the dwarf wheat breeding program. He is considered the chief architect of India's Green Revolution because of his leading role in the National Demonstration Programme, begun in 1964, under which high-yield varieties of wheat and rice seedlings were planted in demonstration plots in fields of many of India's poorest farmers, bypassing the problem of illiteracy. Largely through his efforts, a generation of Indians was converted to an understanding of the value of scientific agriculture. Within only a few years grain production quadrupled, transforming India from a chronic dependent on food aid to a nation of food self-sufficiency.

Swaminathan served as director-general of the Indian Council of Agricultural Research from 1972 to 1979, where his foresight and inspiration led to the establishment of two of the earliest efforts to promote scientific collaboration in developing countries: the International Crops Research Institute for the Semi-Arid Tropics (ICRISAT) and the International Federation of Agricultural Research Systems for Development. As secretary of the Ministry of Agriculture and Irrigation (1979–1980) and the commissioner in charge of agriculture and rural development on India's Planning Commission from 1980 to 1982, he fought for smallholder access to credit, irrigation, and extension services. From 1982 until his retirement in 1988, he was director of IRRI in the Philippines. He also served as chairman of the FAO Council from 1981 to 1985.

Born in the Indian state of Tamil Nadu, Swaminathan studied at Travancore University (B.Sc., 1944), Coimbatore Agricultural College of Madras University (B.Sc. in agriculture, 1947), and the School of Agriculture of Cambridge University (Ph.D. in genetics, 1952). He is a member of the Royal Society of London, the U.S. National Academy of Sciences, the U.S.S.R. All-Union Academy of Agricultural Sciences, and the Royal

Swedish Academy of Agriculture and Forestry. Among his many publications are *Building a National Food Security System* (1981) and *Science and Integrated Rural Development* (1982).

Charles Sykes (1934–)

Charles Sykes is a veteran of 30 years of international relief and development work with CARE. As vice-president of public policy, he currently directs CARE's Washington office and is responsible for liaison between CARE and the federal administration, Congress, the World Bank, and private international relief and development organizations in the Washington, D.C., area. He is co-chairman of the Coalition on Food Aid Policy, formed by U.S. nongovernmental organizations (NGOs), and co-founder of another cooperative NGO project called the Development Bank Assessment Network.

His work with CARE began in 1961 as a field representative in Greece. Other CARE positions include work in Algeria in 1962, helping to direct a medical aid program soon after Algeria's independence from France; country director in Poland 1963–1966, where he met his wife, an attorney (and was decorated by the Polish government); country director in Pakistan 1966–1970, during which time CARE began its first major self-help housing project in an area that is now Bangladesh; country director in Egypt 1974–1978, where he worked closely with the Egyptian Family Planning Association to develop a supplemental nutrition and health education program and with the Fishing Cooperative Association of Aswan on Lake Nasser to develop a combined shelter-health-reforestation program. His last overseas assignment with CARE was in the Dominican Republic 1978–1980, supervising CARE's relief operations following Hurricane David.

In 1974, Sykes was on CARE's delegation to the World Population Tribune (an NGO event paralleling the U.N. Population Conference) in Bucharest and served as NGO representative on a team of U.S. government aid officials reviewing the logistical management of emergency food aid in the Sahel. Similarly in 1984, he was NGO representative on the U.S. government aid team sent to India to review food aid programs, and in 1988 he served on the Agricultural Aid and Trade mission to Indonesia. His writings include articles or chapters in numerous publications such as *World Health Forum, Economic Times of India,* and many technical handbooks and reports issued by CARE. He frequently is called upon to testify to Congress on issues of food aid, foreign assistance, and world hunger.

Born in Decatur, Alabama, he spent most of his childhood in Baltimore, Maryland. He earned a B.A. at Middlebury College in Vermont in 1957 and has done graduate work at Oslo University and Columbia University.

Irene Tinker (1927–)

As a political scientist, development policy researcher, and activist, Irene Tinker is known for commitment to equity and empowerment for disadvantaged groups, especially women. She is also widely recognized for her farsighted leadership and initiative in establishing institutions to further the research and training of others toward those goals. She is a founder of the International Center for Research on Women in Washington, D.C.; the Wellesley College Center for Reserch on Women; the United States Council for INSTRAW (the United Nations Institute for Training and Research for the Advancement of Women); the Association for Women in Development, an international professional association for WID specialists; and the Equity Policy Center in Washington, D.C., which she directed from 1978 to 1989.

Most of her field research has been in India and Indonesia. Equity Policy Center's study of the role of streetfoods and streetfood vendors in urban economies and urban diets is a model and trailblazer for research on micro-enterprise in developing countries. In 1989, Tinker became tenured professor at the University of California at Berkeley, with a joint appointment in Women's Studies and the Department of Urban and Regional Planning.

She and her husband, Milledge P. Walker, also an Asian specialist, have two daughters and a son. Dr. Tinker is a native of Milwaukee, Wisconsin. She attended Radcliffe College (B.A. magna cum laude, 1949) and the London School of Economics (Ph.D., 1954). Publications include *Leadership and Political Institutions in India* (1959, revised 1968; co-edited with Richard L. Park); *Culture and Population Change* (1974); *Population: Dynamics, Ethics and Policy* (1975, co-edited with Priscilla Reining); *Women and World Development* (1975, with Michelle Bo Bramson); and *Persistent Inequalities: Women and World Development* (1989, editor).

Maurice J. Williams (1920–)

Part development economist, part diplomat, part visionary, part executive administrator, Maurice Williams uses his exceptional talents for persuasive dialogue and consensus building to promote equitable development within nations and between nations. In 1986, he became secretary general of the nongovernmental Society for International Development (SID)—the largest global forum for dialogue and cooperation on development issues—and helped prepare SID for its ambitious and successful Nineteenth World Conference in New Delhi. He is editor-in-chief of SID's international journal, *Development,* and is on the international editorial board of *Food Policy.*

As the second executive director of the U.N. World Food Council (succeeding John Hannah) from 1979 to 1986, Williams was instrumental in bringing about the new Cereal Facility at the IMF. He also urged gently but insistently that food security has little meaning at all unless it means that all people, at all times, can obtain enough to eat. Therefore, strategies for food security, while including the common official concerns for grain production, stocks, and trade, must consider also all of the other factors that affect household food supplies—jobs and household incomes, social programs of nutrition assistance, and markets and marketing infrastructure such as processing, storage, and transportation.

Born in Canada with U.S. citizenship and educated at the University of Chicago (M.A., 1950), Williams began his career in international development as a State Department economist in the early years of Truman's Point Four Program. He held many positions in the State Department and the U.S. Agency for International Development at home and overseas until 1974. In 1974 he became chairperson of the Development Assistance Committee of the OECD in Paris, a position he held until his appointment as executive director of the World Food Council. He and his wife, Betty, have three grown children and now make their home in the Washington, D.C., area.

Patricia Young (1923–)

Patricia Young, mother of 4 and grandmother of 6, has been a tireless behind-the-scenes leader in volunteer actions and policy advocacy to end hunger, poverty, and related human rights violations for almost 30 years. She is a walking encyclopedia of U.S. activism on hunger and related issues.

As national coordinator of the U.S. National Committee for World Food Day since 1981, Young manages an information clearinghouse and advisory center for hundreds of civic organizations, schools, churches, and universities planning World Food Day activities. She also coordinates the World Food Day teleconference, with more than 500 interactive sites via a special satellite hookup in the United States and Canada, an annual event that she initiated in 1984.

Her career as nearly full-time activist began with a refugee sponsorship program of the United Presbyterian Church U.S.A. and advocacy on domestic hunger and poverty programs through a coalition led by the National Council of Negro Women. In 1969 she chaired the Task Force on Women at the White House Conference on Food, Nutrition and Health. A year later she became chairperson of the board of directors of the Community Nutrition Institute, a position she still holds.

During the 1970s, she chaired the Infant Formula Project of the Interfaith Center on Corporate Responsibility of the National Council of Churches (NCC), debated Nestlé Corporation representatives publicly, and was a delegate to the 1979 joint WHO/UNICEF Meeting on Infant and Young Child Feeding (from which evolved the international Infant Formula Marketing Code). She attended the Second World Food Congress of the FAO Freedom from Hunger Campaign in The Hague (1970), the 1974 World Food Conference (as vice chairperson of the World Hunger Action Coalition in the United States), and the 1979 World Conference on Agrarian Reform and Rural Development (as chairperson of the 10-state Northeast Task Force for Food and Farm Policy).

Born in Monmouth, Illinois, Young attended Indiana State University and received its Distinguished Alumni Award in 1975. She and her husband, Joseph H. Young, make their home in Scranton, Pennsylvania.

4

Facts and Data

THE INFORMATION IN THIS CHAPTER is organized in seven
sections:

The Meaning of Food Security

The Demographics of World Hunger: (1) how many
people are hungry, (2) how many people die of hunger,
(3) the regional and national distribution of hunger, and
(4) global food supply trends

Population Trends Affecting Food Security: (1) the
population explosion, (2) population density,
people/arable land, (3) competition for economic
opportunity, (4) agrarian inequity, and (5) women's roles

Food-Deficit Nations

The Nutrition of World Hunger: (1) staple foods and
adequate diets, (2) defining "enough" food energy,
(3) the special cases of women, infants, and children, and
(4) measuring a nation's supply of food energy

Food Supplies of Developing Nations: (1) the significance
of food imports, (2) increasing food production through
applied research, and (3) environmental problems for
food production

The Role of Food Aid and Development Assistance

Tables are located in a separate section of this chapter beginning on page 193, figures in a section beginning on page 212.

The Meaning of Food Security

The opposite of being threatened by hunger is to have food security. The two basic elements of food security are, first, a regular food supply large enough (and diverse enough) to meet human nutritional needs and, second, access to a supply of food in sufficient quantity at all times to maintain a healthy, active life. The world hunger problem is the absence of food security for 10 percent to 20 percent of the world's population.

Policy makers examine food security on three levels: global food security, national food security, and household food security. The global level of analysis is the most abstract, the most simplistic, and the most hypothetical. It compares the caloric content of total world production of major staples with the estimated food energy needs of the total population. Rice and wheat, the most widely eaten staples and the grains most prominent in world trade, are usually the only staples considered in such a calculation.

Estimating the risk of hunger in this manner is to act as if food will be distributed throughout the world according to everyone's need. This, of course, is not the case in real life. The global food/people ratio, therefore, cannot describe the hunger situation accurately. It can indicate only whether it is even hypothetically possible to feed everyone (at least with rice and wheat) under the current or projected status of food production and population size. The answer for the remainder of the twentieth century and at least the first decade or two of the twenty-first century is, yes, there is enough food for all human need.

"Hungry nations" is a common figure of speech, but nations neither eat nor go hungry; only people do, individual children, women, and men (in that order of numerical significance and nutritional need). Ultimately, the world hunger problem is the problem of food insecurity in millions of households and, since not all members of a household are affected the same way, a problem of too little food for specific individuals in those households.

The national level of food analysis begins to pinpoint the location of hungry populations in the world. It helps to define the national and international policy questions involved in preventing and eliminating hunger. It also identifies those nations where the present situation handicaps food security at the household level because two essential preconditions are not being met—either an adequate national food supply is lacking, or the infrastructure is inadequate, or both are true.

Having a national food supply large enough to permit household food security means that a country is able to either produce or import sufficient food for both the nutritional needs and the market demand of its entire population. The second precondition for household food security is a national infrastructure that can process and store ample stocks of food safely and can distribute food efficiently to all communities and all groups of people in the country. Such an infrastructure implies adequate port facilities for food imports, adequate food processing and storage facilities, adequate internal transportation and communications, adequate marketing processes, and adequate procedures for distributing food to people who are too poor, too young, or too infirm to supply their own needs without help.

The Food and Agriculture Organization of the United Nations (FAO) uses the term *food-deficit nation* for countries that do not meet the supply precondition for food security. By FAO's analysis, there were 65 food-deficit nations at the time of the Fifth World Food Survey in 1985. A failure to meet the infrastructure precondition for food security is typical of countries in the early stages of modern economic development, but it is neither limited to such countries nor inevitable. A highly developed country like the United States may not meet the food security criterion of adequately distributing food to people who cannot supply their own needs without help, while some developing countries such as Cuba, Sri Lanka, and China seem to do that rather effectively.

In order to ensure food security for all people at all times, policy makers in both developed and developing nations must know which groups of people are prone to hunger and why and which policy actions within each nation's means—from its own resources, with aid, or with a combination of both—are likely to be most effective in preventing hunger.

The facts and data in this chapter illuminate some of these questions.

The Demographics of World Hunger

How Many Are Hungry

In 1989, 550 million people were too undernourished to "sustain an active, healthy life," according to the World Food Council.

The FAO estimates that the number of the world's hungry grew by 15 million during the decade of the 1970s, from 460 million to 475 million, an average annual increase of 1.5 million people. Then, during the first half of the 1980s alone, hunger increased almost eight times faster, adding 40 million people within five years for a total of 512 million by 1985. Globally, the number of undernourished children grew by almost 10 million between 1975 and 1984, mainly because of increases in Asia and Africa. In reaching its estimate of 550 million hungry people in 1989, the World Food Council assumed that, since the economic crisis of the early 1980s had continued for most developing countries, the higher rate of increase of hunger had continued also. (See Table 1.)

The World Bank prefers to use data on purchasing power for basic essentials as an instrument for estimating the extent of undernutrition. By this means, a 1986 World Bank study of the prevalence of energy-deficient diets in 87 developing countries (*Poverty and Hunger: Issues and Options for Food Security in Developing Countries*) estimated between 340 million and 730 million undernourished people in 1980 instead of FAO's 475 million. The lower figure, 340 million, included people consuming below 80 percent of the FAO/WHO recommended calorie level. The higher figure, 730 million, included people consuming below 90 percent of the FAO/WHO recommendation. The 90 percent level would not sustain "an active working life." The 80 percent level would be too low to prevent stunted growth in children or serious health risks generally. The bank's study mapped the global incidence of energy-deficient diets in 1970 and 1980, finding a decrease in the extent of intense undernutrition during that decade. (See Figure 1.)

The World Bank's *World Development Report 1990* focuses on poverty in developing countries (with 1985 data) but it does not attempt to estimate how many of the poor were also undernourished. After calculating a poverty line for each country in terms of the cost of basic essentials there, the bank finds that 1.116

billion people were living below the poverty lines of their respective countries in 1985 on annual incomes equivalent to $370 or less (adjusted for national comparison). Of those 1 billion or more "poor," a group of 633 million were "extremely poor," with annual incomes below $275.

How Many Die from Hunger

UNICEF and the World Health Organization estimate that about 14 million children under the age of five die each year from hunger-related, preventable causes. According to USAID's Child Survival Program, child health specialists believe that undernutrition affects more than 30 percent of all children in developing countries and contributes directly or indirectly to nearly three-fifths of all deaths among the under-fives.

No one really knows how many deaths of adults or children above the age of five can be attributed to hunger-related causes. Long before starvation sets in, the body loses its resistance to infections and diseases of all kinds. Public health records, if a record occurs at all, list only the immediate causes of death, causes such as respiratory failure, diarrhea, tuberculosis, measles, hemorrhage, and so on. The role of undernutrition, anemia, or vitamin A deficiency is rarely mentioned. In any case, measurements of the nutritional status of adult populations are too inadequate in most countries to draw sound conclusions about how many early deaths could have been prevented with more food. Experts in public health, nutrition, and pediatrics can say with certainty only, "many, perhaps most."

The Regional and National Distribution of Hunger

Although the largest increases in the number of hungry people during the 1980s have occurred in Africa, the majority of the world's hungry are still to be found in Asia. Eighty-three percent of the world's underfed children live in Asia. By FAO's estimate in 1985, 291 million Asians were undernourished compared with 140 million Africans. (See Tables 2, 3, and 4.)

Hunger is unevenly distributed within regions, too. For example, 66 percent of all undernourished Africans live in just 7 countries—Ethiopia, Nigeria, Zaire, Tanzania, Kenya, Uganda, and Mozambique—and in some countries a much higher percent of the population is affected by food insecurity than in other countries. More than 40 percent of the population are under-nourished in Ethiopia, Zaire, Uganda, Mozambique, Zambia, Chad, and Somalia, according to World Bank estimates.

Of Asia's undernourished, 75 percent live in the 7 countries of South Asia: Bangladesh, Bhutan, India, Maldives, Nepal, Pakistan, and Sri Lanka. India alone, one-third the size of the United States, is home to more than half of all of the world's hungry. Because of its great size, China has 15 percent of Asia's hungry although they comprise less than 6 percent of the Chinese population.

Finally, hunger is unevenly distributed within countries, with the majority being found in rural areas. (See Table 5.)

Global Food Supply Trends

Despite the growing numbers of hungry people, famine is becoming a less frequent and more limited occurrence on the globe. (See Figure 2.)

Until quite recently, the trend in world per capita grain production has also been encouraging since the end of World War II. Between 1950 and the early 1980s, yearly fluctuations fall along an upward trendline of overall growth. In other words, global food production has kept ahead of population growth. (See Figure 3.)

In the early 1980s, however, per capita food production reached a plateau and began to drop. Experts say it is too soon to know whether a per capita decline in food production will remain the new norm. Much of the per capita gain during the past 20 years has come from the success of new high-yielding varieties (HYVs) of rice and wheat, especially in Asia. But the adoption rate of these HYVs is slowing. The same rate of productivity expansion cannot be expected to continue now without similar scientific breakthroughs for other crops or for soils and climates where the present HYVs do not thrive. (See Figure 4.)

Population Trends Affecting Food Security

The Population Explosion

When Thomas Robert Malthus began to worry about the effect of population growth on the welfare of societies at the end of the eighteenth century, England was beginning to experience rapid growth. Total world population was less than 1 billion. By 1930, it was 2 billion. By 1989, there were 5.2 billion people on the earth. The world had taken almost 150 years to double in population from Malthus's day to 1930, but then in less than 60 years it doubled again. By the end of the twentieth century, world population is expected to be 6 billion. That accelerating increase in total number of people on the planet is referred to as the population explosion. (See Figure 5.)

The world's rate of growth peaked around 1960 and is declining steadily. By 1990, the rate of population was falling in every region except sub-Saharan Africa, where the downturn is expected to come before the end of the 1990s. Nevertheless, there are now 90 million more people to feed every year, a number not expected to decrease for many years to come. Current projections for peak population range between 10 billion and 14 billion by the middle of the twenty-first century before total population size—not the growth rate alone—begins to shrink. (See Figures 6 and 7.)

The population explosion began in Europe in the nineteenth century almost simultaneously with the industrial revolution. The shift from a primarily agrarian economy to a primarily industrial one generated enough new jobs to relieve much but not all of the stress of rapid population growth. European emigration to less populated parts of the world in North America, South America, Australia, and Africa relieved the remaining stress.

Population Density—People/Arable Land Ratios

Despite massive emigration in the eighteenth and nineteenth centuries, Europe's population density in certain countries became the highest in the world. As recently as 1980, there were still more people per hectare of land in the Netherlands, Belgium, West Germany, and the United Kingdom than in India, Sri Lanka, El Salvador, Haiti, or, indeed, than in any developing country except Bangladesh, South Korea, the island of Mauritius, and the city-states of Hong Kong and Singapore. (See Table 6.)

High population density in countries like Japan and Belgium causes no anxiety about food security as long as ample food is available for import from other countries—which it is still, despite the population explosion. Industrial countries can pay easily for imported food and they have all the food processing and distributing infrastructure required. (Most of them also subsidize their farmers heavily in order to have a flourishing agricultural sector.)

The picture is quite different for a low-income, low-GNP, primarily agrarian society, which is what most developing countries are. About five-sixths of the new people being added to the world now are born in developing countries. As of 1986, 78.5 percent of the world's people lived in the combined regions of Asia, Latin America, North Africa, the Near East, and sub-Saharan Africa. Fifty-four percent of the world's inhabitants are Asians. (See Table 7.)

The U.S. Department of Agriculture estimates that world cropland available per person dropped from nearly half of a hectare in 1961 to about one-third of a hectare by 1986, a substantial drop of nearly 32 percent in a quarter of a century. About 1,474 million hectares were being cropped in 1986. Estimates of the maximum potential of arable land on the planet range from 2,500 million to 3,200 million hectares. If the lower estimate is selected, there are about 1 billion arable hectares available still for expanding crop production.

The primary cause of the population explosion of the nineteenth and twentieth centuries is declining death rates, not higher birth rates. High birth rates are a lingering pattern from an era of much higher death rates and from traditions that severely restrict the roles of women. Continued high birth rates exacerbate the population explosion but they are not its primary cause. Improved public health is the chief culprit—improved sanitation, prevention of communicable diseases, reduced infant mortality, and better treatment of disease.

These improvements affected Europe and North America first, moving almost in tandem with expanding economic opportunity from industrialization. Voluntarily, couples began gradually to desire smaller families. Rapid population growth always creates social and economic strains within a society. However, low-income societies heavily dependent on agriculture (or other primary production such as mining or forestry) are least able to accommodate rapid population increase without deepening poverty and a heightened risk of food insecurity. When improved public health measures began to spread in Asia, Africa, and Latin America in the twentieth century, the impact of those measures on death rates grew much more rapidly than the economic development that would have cushioned developing societies' explosive increase in the need for jobs, education, housing, food, and all manner of social and economic infrastructure to accommodate rapid population growth. Population change has come much more rapidly, too, than changes in long-standing traditional assumptions regarding desirable family size (or the desirable number of male children). Consequently, developing countries are having to evolve social and economic patterns within one or two generations that took almost 200 years to develop in Europe and North America.

For two reasons, the people/arable land ratio is a much more significant factor for food security in developing countries than it is in the industrialized countries. First, the capacity to pay for imports is more severely limited in developing countries, and, second, the land itself is the primary source of sustenance—both because of the food produced on it and also because most livelihoods in an agrarian society depend directly or indirectly on producing food. Without alternative sources of income for sustenance, poverty and hunger must increase when population density outstrips the land's capacity to support the people dependent on that land. Only in Latin America today are there large reserves of uncultivated or undercultivated arable land, and these reserves are controlled by an elite minority of landowners. (See Tables 8 and 9.)

Increased Competition for Economic Opportunity

In all developing regions, more and more job seekers with each new generation experience futility in competing for jobs in circumstances of very limited agricultural and nonagricultural economic opportunity. This situation is the driving force behind the reverse wave of emigration occurring in the second half of the twentieth century: no longer emigration from Europe to "underdeveloped" regions (from a European perspective) as in earlier centuries but now emigration from those regions to Europe—or to North America and Australia, which were "underdeveloped" regions themselves not so very long ago.

The International Labour Office (ILO) reports that, just to accommodate population growth, an average of 47 million new jobs must be created each year from now on. In India, records show an increase of 10 million unemployed workers between 1980 and 1985. In Indonesia and Thailand, unemployment increased 6 to 7 times in the 1970s, a trend continuing into the 1980s.

In Latin America the number of the rural poor has been increasing since 1970 and now accounts for two-thirds of the rural population. Between 1970 and 1985, population growth, a high concentration of land ownership and economic power, and the economic recession of the 1980s combined to add 31 million more to the population of the rural poor in that region, according to the U.N. Economic Commission for Latin America and the Caribbean.

The World Bank finds that in Asia, despite relatively high rates of economic growth in the 1970s and 1980s, about half of the rural population still lives in poverty and from 80 percent to 90 percent of all the poor live in rural areas.

Agrarian Inequity

Most of the world's poor live in rural areas, and within those areas social and economic inequity tends to be the rule rather than the exception. Patterns of access to productive land and water resources are the key to understanding gaps between the prosperous and the poor in rural areas. The details are complex and varied from region to region and from country to country, and they can be accurately understood only within the particular historical context of each country.

A certain pattern repeats itself so universally, however, that one lesson is clear: if scientific or economic innovations make new crops or new ways of using the land more profitable than traditional farming in the region, rural inequity will increase rapidly—those who own more land will come to own more land still, those who own little land will lose it, and those who were farming as tenants on someone else's land will become wage-laborers no longer able to farm at all—unless government programs to prevent these social outcomes of agricultural innovation are in place, well designed, and implemented vigorously.

The following information from India, Bangladesh, and the Philippines indicates the extreme rural inequity that characterizes Asian societies (where the majority of the world's hungry live) and suggests some of the difficulty faced by agrarian reform programs.

In India's federal system, the laws affecting land ownership and tenant rights are under the jurisdiction of each state's authority. The state of Kerala is the only one where land reform has been carried through effectively. Karnataka and West Bengal have also made some progress in "land to the tiller" policies. An Asian NGO Coalition preparing a report on 7 countries for distribution at the U.N. World Conference on Agrarian Reform and Rural Development found the following: In 1971–1972, approximately 26 million rural households owned less than 1 hectare and about 22 million rural households owned no land. Together, these households comprised 55 percent of the rural households of India. When the 20 percent of rural households that owned between 1 and 2 hectares were added, these three groups of rural poor comprised 75 percent of all rural households. The Asian NGO Coalition found also that whenever agriculture with hired workers became profitable because of new technology and marketing opportunities, or whenever a serious possibility of land reform arose in state politics, landlords tended to evict tenants and become "self-cultivators" in order to avoid loss of land as "noncultivating owners" in land-to-the-tiller reforms (Asian NGO Coalition, *The Case for Alternative Development: Of the People, for the People, by the People*, Bangkok, 1979).

In Bangladesh, the Asian NGO Coalition found that the percent of rural households without any land at all increased from 16 percent in 1961 to 44 percent by 1977. When a land reform program was enacted by the government, it applied only to farmers who already owned land. The legal ceiling on landholdings set by the reform (but not always implemented) was approximately 34 acres—a very large farm in Bangladesh. In 1974, just 2 percent of all farmers had landholdings of more than 25 acres, covering 11 percent of all farmland. A ceiling below 7.5 acres, not 34, would have been necessary to extend the benefits of land reform to landless rural households and sharecropping tenant farmers.

In the Philippines, 10 percent of the population owned 90 percent of the land in 1971, according to a government estimate. Land reform was promised at a constitutional convention that year. In 1972, with World Bank encouragement and credit, President Ferdinand Marcos announced a program to requisition (with reimbursement) 1.8 million hectares of land in rice- and corn-producing areas owned by large absentee landlords for redistribution to 1 million smallholders and sharecropping tenant farmers (by purchase over a 15-year period). (These ambitious targets in hectares and beneficiaries were soon reduced.) In 1986, the Ministry (now Department) of Agrarian Reform issued the following statistics: Of the intended 630,680 Emancipation Patents (new land titles), 3.5 percent had been issued, encompassing 1.5 percent of the intended land. More than 5 million hectares of "alienable and disposable" land had not yet been titled to any new owners. Land reform financing had been extended to 12,391 smallholders and 136,268 tenants—out of a farming population of 1.5 million owner-cultivators with titles, another 1.5 million nonowning cultivators on public land, and 2 million sharecroppers and lease-holding tenants. The one target that had been reached as planned was the number of lease-hold contracts issued to tenants to improve their conditions of tenure short of actual ownership.

An IFPRI study released in January 1990 (*Effects of Agricultural Commercializaion on Land Tenure, Household Resource Allocation, and Nutrition in the Philippines*) found that the introduction of sugar as an export crop in a previously subsistence corn-farming area had a profound effect on land tenure patterns. Eight years after a sugar mill began operating in the area, most of those who were sugar landowners or tenants had the same land tenure status as in earlier years when they were growing mainly corn. Of the landless laborers on sugar farms by this time, however, 42 percent had lost the access to land they had (either as landowners or tenants) before the shift to sugar production in the region. When landlords switched from corn to sugar, they found it more profitable to hire labor than to rent their land to sharecroppers, as had been the custom for corn. Sugar production gradually replaced corn production in the region as larger landowners, who were in a better financial position to take advantage of the new commercial opportunity, purchased and rented additional lands, consolidating small farms into larger ones. The nutritional effects of these changes were mixed. Higher income sugar-farming households tended to spend increased income on higher cost foods and nonfood items that did not improve the nutrition of their children, while lower income corn households who were still farming tended to feed their small children as well as or better than the higher income sugar households. The diets of children in landless households, on the other hand, suffered greatly because of the greater poverty of those households and because working adults were given preference in access to the household's limited food.

By inference if not directly, IFPRI's study supports the Asian NGO Coalition's findings that laws offering even minimal protection for the rights of farm laborers in the Philippines remain unenforced. In the politics of agriculture there (as often also elsewhere), farm workers are "voiceless, powerless, and defenceless."

Women's Economic Roles

Population statistics are beginning to document women in their economic roles, no longer solely as producers of children. Women's economic roles have an immediate bearing on food security. First, women play a much larger role in food production than was previously recognized. Where women are registered as workers in the formal labor force of a country, the overwhelming majority of them in Asia and Africa are employed in agriculture (to a lesser degree in Latin America and the Caribbean). (See Figure 8.)

Outside of the formal labor force, sociological research at the household level in countries as diverse as Pakistan and Zambia reveals that many hours of women's daily labor are devoted to food production. (See Figures 9 and 10.)

For many of the reasons sketched above, more and more households in developing countries depend upon income earned in off-farm employment. The great majority of off-farm workers in developing countries work in the "informal" sector—the economic sector of small-scale manufacture and trade in goods and services ignored or denigrated by most national economic plans and policies. The ILO estimates that in some countries, the informal sector produces as much as a third of all local wealth. In this sector, as in food production itself, women form a large proportion of the workers and managing entrepreneurs. (See Figure 11.)

Food-Deficit Nations

In 1985, FAO's fifth World Food Survey identified 65 food-deficit countries. The two criteria for that classification are, first, that total available cereal supplies (from domestic production and import capability) fall below FAO's minimum daily per capita calorie standard, and, second, that average incomes are very low as indicated by per capita GNP, below the cut-off level for IDA lending. (IDA-eligible countries currently must have less than $1,070 per capita GNP in 1988 prices.) Hunger and malnutrition are presumed by FAO's method of analysis to be widespread in countries with fewer than 2,400 calories available per day per person in the national food supply and to be extremely serious in countries below 2,000 calories per capita. Some countries in the range of 2,401 to 2,800 calories per capita also fall within FAO's food-deficit country category because of IDA eligibility. (See Figure 12.)

Classified by per capita GNP, 56 of these food-deficit countries fall under the World Bank's category of low-income country (per capita GNP $480 or less in 1987 U.S. dollars). Only 5 low-income countries (with populations of 1 million or more) are not also FAO food-deficit countries. These 5 low-income, *non*-food-deficit countries are: in sub-Saharan Africa—Burundi, GNP $250; Liberia, GNP $450; and Malawi, GNP $160; and in Asia—Burma, GNP unstated; and Pakistan, GNP $350.

Nine on FAO's food-deficit country list are lower-middle-income countries with per capita GNP between $481 and $2,000 in 1987 dollars and 1 million population or more: in north Africa—Egypt, GNP $680; and Morocco, GNP $610; in sub-Saharan Africa—Ivory Coast, GNP $740; and Senegal, GNP $520; in Asia—the Philippines, GNP $590; in Oceania—Papua New Guinea, GNP $700; and in Latin America—Bolivia, GNP $580; El Salvador, GNP $860; and Honduras, GNP $810.

FAO's food-deficit country list includes 12 nations that do not appear on the World Bank's 1989 table of basic development indicators because their populations are under 1 million people: in Africa—Cape Verde, GNP $500; Comoros, GNP $370; Djibouti, estimated GNP between $481 and $2,000; Equatorial Guinea, estimated GNP below $481; the Gambia, GNP $220; and Guinea Bissau, GNP $160; in Asia—Maldives, GNP $300; and in Oceania—Kiribati, GNP $480; Solomon Islands, GNP $420; Tonga, GNP $720; Vanuatu, estimated GNP below $481; and Western Samoa, GNP $550. Angola is also declared a food-deficit country but no development indicators are given in the 1989 data of the World Bank.

Average per capita calories available and average per capita GNP, of course, do not determine whether or not hunger is a

serious problem within a country. UNICEF points out that, measured by per capita GNP, Kenya is twice as rich as Bangladesh,
Brazil is twice as rich as Thailand, and Peru is twice as rich as Sri
Lanka. But when these same countries are compared using the
per capita GNP of *just the poorest 40 percent,* one sees that the poor
are as badly off in Kenya as in Bangladesh, in Brazil as in Thailand, and in Peru as in Sri Lanka. Furthermore, some low-GNP
countries have achieved higher levels of well-being as measured
by health, education, and nutrition than other countries with
much higher per capita incomes. China and Sri Lanka, low-
income countries, and Costa Rica, a lower-middle-income
country, all have higher levels of child health (a significant indicator also of nutritional standards) than many countries even five
times richer by GNP measurement.

A classic study in 1960 compared calorie consumption
among population groups at different income levels in Brazil, an
upper-middle-income country with one of the world's most inequitable income distribution patterns. The analysis revealed that
the 12 percent of the Brazilian population in the 2 lowest income
groups were consuming less than 73 percent of the FAO/WHO
recommended calorie minimum. These 8.5 million Brazilians
were presumably too severely undernourished for normal growth
among children or for children and adults alike to escape serious
health risks. Meanwhile, 88 percent of the Brazilian population
were either adequately fed or overfed. By neither GNP nor total
food supply could Brazil be called a food-deficit nation, yet 8.5
million chronically and severely undernourished Brazilians
would account for more than 2 percent of the world's hungry in
FAO's assessment at that time. (See Table 10.)

Granting these exceptions and warnings, however, GNP does
provide a useful measure of a nation's economic capacity to
address the needs of its people effectively. (Economic capacity, of
course, says nothing about political will.) When grouped by GNP,
developing countries, as groups, also tend to show similar patterns within various social indicators such as fertility rates among
women, infant mortality rate (IMR), and life expectancy. The last
two social indicators correlate positively with levels of nutritional
adequacy within countries. Generally speaking, both indicators
improve with gains in GNP—the IMR drops and life expectancy
rises. (See Figure 13.)

The correlation of rising IMR with economic decline in
debt-burdened countries is illustrated in Figures 14 and 15. The

structural adjustment program Brazil adopted in the early 1980s to qualify for aid from the International Monetary Fund (IMF) reversed Brazil's previous progress in reducing its infant mortality rate.

The IMF's "Selected Economic Indicators for Developing Countries, 1970–1989" shows the severity of economic decline for most developing countries during the 1980s. The decade of the 1970s is used as the basis for comparison. Per capita GNP declined in all regions except Asia in almost every year of the decade. The improvement from one year to the next in export earnings compared with the cost of imports (the terms of trade) was either very modest or actually negative: national earnings from trade dropped. Only the Middle East showed significant trade improvements, and in only three years out of ten. Meanwhile, the size of national debts grew steadily in all regions as countries rescheduled debts for longer repayment (and greater total interest) or borrowed new money to sustain any economic growth potential at all. For most of the 1980s, Africa was paying approximately one-quarter of all of its export earnings merely to service its debt, and in Latin America the situation was even worse. The interest on Latin American debt took minimally one-third, and in one year more than half, of everything Latin American nations earned from exports. The extreme difficulty experienced by low-income food-deficit nations in meeting their own needs must be seen against the background of the Third World debt crisis. (See Table 11.)

In Table 12, a slightly adapted World Bank table of basic indicators of development progress, food-deficit countries listed in FAO's fifth World Food Survey are indicated with an asterisk.

The Nutrition of World Hunger

Hunger is the discomfort that comes from a lack of food—discomfort that is both physiological and psychological. It is a subjective phenomenon. Analyzing the problem in terms of nutrition, malnutrition, and undernutrition helps to target preventive and curative actions toward the objective harm caused by hunger. The current working definition of hunger for many food policy specialists—"lack of enough food to sustain an active working life"—is a rough translation of the more precise terms used by the nutrition scientist.

The major forms of malnutrition in developing countries are protein-energy malnutrition (PEM); vitamin A deficiency, which increases vulnerability to infectious diseases and xerophthalmia, a leading cause of blindness in children; anemia, a major factor in the high death rate of pregnant women; and iodine deficiency, which causes goiter and sometimes brain impairment. Of these four major nutritional problems, vitamin A deficiency is the easiest to prevent by simple and inexpensive means, while PEM is the most widespread and serious in almost all developing countries.

The term PEM reflects the importance of both protein and calories (the measure for food energy) in human health and survival. The young children whose swollen bellies carried on matchstick legs typify the disease called kwashiorkor and the infants whose shrivelled bodies and wizened faces characterize marasmus are both victims of severe PEM, as are the living skeletons of all ages witnessed wherever there is famine. Even at far less severe levels, PEM stunts growth, limits brain development, reduces energy and alertness, and weakens resistance to disease.

The term PEM also reflects the intimate relationship between calories and proteins. When calories from carbohydrates or fats are insufficient to cover the energy a body expends in its daily activities, the body will convert its protein into calories. A diet with enough energy from staple foods usually supplies also enough protein. On the other hand, a person whose diet is seriously lacking in calories typically does not consume enough protein nor enough vitamins and minerals. Consequently, malnutrition from a calorie deficiency (often specified as undernutrition or undernourishment) is found most commonly together with symptoms of other nutritional deficiencies. The major food policy objective in hunger prevention, therefore, is to ensure adequate intake of food energy from staples while diversifying the diet with small amounts of other foods.

Staple Foods and Adequate Diets

A few decades ago, protein was considered the nutrient most critically lacking in the diets of poor people in developing countries. Much research and thought was applied to finding ways to reduce this deficiency. More recent research shows, however, that protein is not as lacking as was once supposed. Generally speaking, when commonly consumed cereal-based diets meet human energy needs, they meet protein needs also.

Grains are the cheapest, most nutritious, and—in the ratio of amount of food produced per unit of land, labor, and other agricultural inputs—the most efficient source of food energy for the world's people. International trade divides grains into "cereal" grains (wheat and rice) and "coarse" grains (sorghum, maize, millet, oats, rye), but in fact, all grains are eaten as cereals on the world's menu, if not in one culture then in another.

The bran and germ of grain are rich sources of B vitamins, minerals, and vitamin E, while the endosperm surrounding the germ provides the complex carbohydrates that are the healthiest source of calories. Unfortunately for human health, wheat and rice, the most widely consumed grains, are eaten primarily in highly milled forms in which the bran and germ are lost, leaving carbohydrates and protein and removing most of the vitamin and mineral content.

All grains contain protein, although the proportion of protein to carbohydrates and the quality of protein vary from one grain to another. Protein "quality" refers to the composition of essential amino acids in the grain. All amino acids must be present in the right proportions in order to build the "complete" protein needed for optimum tissue growth and repair. The "essential" amino acids are those that must be consumed in food because the body cannot produce them itself.

Food scientists are reviving interest in two staples native to the Western Hemisphere that were nearly eradicated by the Spanish conquistadors: amaranth, the most important grain in the Aztec culture, and quinoa (botanically an herb), considered sacred by the Incas. Both have more complete protein than cow's milk. Quinoa is extremely rich in minerals and vitamins. Amaranth has the highest protein content of all natural grains, 16 percent. Only triticale, a manmade grain formed by crossing wheat and rye, equals amaranth in protein. The protein in triticale has a quality considered biologically superior to soy protein (itself more complete than meat protein).

Millet and sorghum, which is known also as milo or Guinea corn, are food staples in semi-arid regions of Africa and Asia where other grains cannot thrive. Sorghum is the third largest grain crop in the world, but most of it is fed to meat animals in

North America, Europe, Japan, and elsewhere. Nevertheless, sorghum is high in protein, lacking only the amino acid lysine (found in many legumes, especially beans). Millet has exceptionally complete protein and is high in B vitamins, potassium, magnesium, phosphorus, and iron.

Wheat is the most widely cultivated food crop globally and is the grain produced in greatest quantity. Rice, however, is the major source of both calories and proteins for more than 1.5 billion low-income people in Asia and hundreds of millions in Africa and Latin America.

Modest amounts of beans, soy products, nuts, or seeds are needed in a grain-based diet to complement the protein of those grains (maize, rice, and sorghum in particular) lacking one or more of the essential amino acids required to form complete protein. Tubers that are eaten as staples such as cassava (manioc), yams, or taro are severely deficient in protein although they are good sources of food energy. Common legumes (or pulses) in traditional African, Asian, and Latin American diets include chickpeas (garbanzos), lentils, turtlebeans (black beans), cowpeas (blackeyed peas), redbeans, and groundnuts (peanuts). Soybeans, a staple in the Far East eaten in curd form (tofu) and in many different sauces, are now being promoted by food planners in all developing countries because of their excellent protein.

Agricultural planning that is not integrated with nutrition planning tends to value grains and other crops solely in market terms. This kind of planning can easily overlook the importance in the diets of the poor of both coarse grains and pulses and therefore can interfere with the production of these grains. In low-income countries, the poorest 20 percent of the population spend 60 percent to 80 percent of their income on food. Compared with the richest 10 percent of the population, the poorest 10 percent get a larger share of their food energy (also their protein, minerals, and vitamins) from staple foods and devote a larger share of their food expenditures to staples. (See Figure 16.)

Figure 17 compares the roles of cereals, animal products, roots, and tubers as staple foods in major regions. Figure 18 shows the most commercially significant producers of staples in terms of world trade. The same staples are produced for local consumption, of course, in a great number of additional countries not shown in the figure.

Defining "Enough" Food Energy

All scientific definitions of undernutrition involve the basal metabolism rate (BMR) and calories. The basal metabolism rate is the amount of energy used up by any organism merely to sustain its life. A kilocalorie (kcal, the scientific term for calorie), of energy is the amount of heat required to raise the temperature of 1 kilogram of water from 15 degrees centigrade to 16 degrees centigrade. BMR in humans is found by measuring (as kcals per hour) the heat emanating from a person who is awake and resting in a warm place 12 to 18 hours after eating.

Prior to 1981, FAO used 1.2 times the BMR (1.2BMR) as the minimum essential requirement for dietary energy in order not to starve. In 1981, the FAO/WHO/UNU standing committee of nutritional experts decided that a more useful minimum to guide policy decisions would be a "maintenance requirement" that covered the energy expended by a person eating, bathing, dressing, speaking, and listening—for example, the energy expended by someone idled in a refugee camp. Such a maintenance requirement was found to be 1.4BMR. (FAO's fifth World Food Survey in 1985 calculates national food deficits in terms of both 1.2BMR and 1.4BMR.)

The obvious defect in using 1.4BMR to estimate minimum essential calories needed by the hungry, of course, is that most hungry people cannot sit around idly waiting for international relief agencies to feed them. On the contrary, they have to expend significant amounts of energy to produce food themselves, to build or repair their homes, to collect fuelwood and water, to grind or pound grain until it can become edible by cooking, to earn income, and to accomplish other necessities of daily life. In 1985, the FAO/WHO/UNU expert committee agreed that a more realistic standard should cover the amount of energy that is expended in "essential human activities." "Essential," the committee stated, means activities that are "economically necessary and socially desirable." This common-sense standard appeals to nutrition specialists and nonspecialists alike. However, to give measurable statistical meaning to such common sense for food policy planning is another story.

The scientific task now is to identify in terms of BMR how many calories men, women, and children need in different cultures, climates, and environments of sub-Saharan Africa, in northern India versus southern India, in Haiti versus Bolivia, and so on. Economically necessary and socially desirable activities vary from culture to culture (and among different population groups within a culture). The energy required of the body varies also according to climate, degree of stress, and the technology used by people to accomplish their myriad tasks. To make the new common-sense standard practical for food policy planners and health workers, nutrition scientists are going back to the drawing board to establish new guidelines for adequate food energy. The standard nutrition reference books must be rewritten. The old dietary guidelines are too specifically European and North American to apply equally well to the needs of populations in developing countries. Nutrition science at some future date will reflect more accurately the realities of the pluralistic world community.

However much the specific kcal guidelines for adequate energy intake will change to reflect specific cultural conditions, energy requirements will continue to differ among individuals within any given culture and will continue to depend upon age, sex, and whether a woman's body is nourishing one person or two. In terms of kcals per kilogram of body weight, an infant in the first year of life, a child, an adolescent, and a nursing mother all need higher proportions of calories in their daily diets than does an adult man. (See Figure 19.)

The Special Cases of Women, Infants, and Children

While many factors other than the nourishment of mother or child can reduce or increase the infant mortality rate (IMR) in a country, the intimate relationship between nutrition and maternal and infant health makes the IMR a sensitive indicator of nutritional well-being within a culture.

Undernourished women do not produce well-developed babies and their breastmilk is less likely to provide adequate nutrition for the infant's optimal development after birth. Low birthweight infants have less chance of surviving infancy, and infants who are not breast fed adequately have lower resistance to the attacks of infection that are bound to occur in the first years of life.

Mothers in low-income countries are 50 to 100 times more likely to die in pregnancy and childbirth than mothers in affluent countries, according to the World Health Organization. Part of the explanation has to do with septic conditions surrounding many home-based births and the limited access to medical assistance when birth complications arise. Another reason stems from cultural pressure (combined with low status accorded women) that causes women to have too many children, too closely spaced. Much of the explanation, however, is chronic lack of adequate food in the mother's diet, starting often in her own early childhood. Women who are undernourished or anemic or both are less likely to survive the physiological stresses of pregnancy and childbirth.

Tables 13 and 14 illustrate the relationship between maternal nutrition and pregnancy outcome in Bangladesh and other developing countries. Table 15 shows the incidence of undernutrition in children and anemia in women in Africa, Asia, and Latin America. Chronic, long-standing undernourishment is suspected in children whose height is low for their age group ("stunting"); recent, but not long-standing, undernourishment is indicated by low weight for height ("wasting").

Measuring a Nation's Supply of Food Energy

Precise assessments of national nutritional levels are difficult. Food consumption and household expenditure surveys are potentially the most revealing sources of information, but the cost of such surveys makes them impractical in most developing countries, hence very little such data is available.

The FAO estimate of national average per capita dietary energy supply (DES) uses the nation's "food balance sheet." The food balance sheet calculates the total quantity of calories available for human consumption in one year from national records of agricultural production, agricultural exports, agricultural imports, and the intended use of these various agricultural items—livestock feed, green manure, raw materials for manufactured products, fuel, or human consumption. Food balance sheet calculations are enormously complex and can be no more accurate than the data that goes into them. Such data is sometimes subject, for reasons of perceived self-interest, to over- or understatement by farmers or governments. FAO's food balance sheets continue to be used because no more reliable source of information on national food supply seems to be available.

On the basis of DES calculations, FAO's Fifth World Food Survey concludes that for the period of 1981–1983 the world's average daily DES was 2,660 kcals per person—a rise of 14 percent over the previous 2 decades. The average person in industrialized countries had access to 3,390 kcals a day, some 9 percent more than in the early 1960s, while the average person in the developing countries had access to 2,400 kcals a day, a gain of 21 percent over the 1,980 kcals available 20 years earlier. By the early 1980s, Africa replaced Asia as the region with the largest proportion of population undernourished, although Asia still accounted for nearly three-fifths of the world's hungry. The Near East (or Middle East) replaced Latin America as the region with the smallest proportion of population undernourished. The Near East was also the only region with a decline in the absolute number of undernourished people, an indirect result of higher oil revenues through OPEC. (See Figure 20.)

Food Supplies of Developing Nations

Significance of Food Imports

Among low-income food-deficit countries as defined by FAO, per capita staple food production declined in all regions except the Far East between 1970 and 1986. In all other regions, per capita consumption gains were made possible only by expanding food imports—in Africa, only very marginally possible, at that. FAO's data indicates only food availability, not degree of actual access by the poor to supplies. Dietary improvement among the poor is unlikely when national supply averages improve so slightly. (See Table 16.)

The largest exporters and importers of rice, wheat, and other (coarse) grains at the end of the 1980s are shown in Tables 17 and 18. Thai rice and Argentinian wheat provide 85 percent of all exports by developing countries of staple food commodities. Thailand, in fact, so dominates world trade in rice that the price of Thai rice sets the world market price.

Developing countries, collectively, are both the largest producers and largest importers of the world's grain. In the crop year 1989/90, for example, farm households in Asia, Africa, and Latin America produced about 95 percent of the world's rice crop, 42 percent of the world's wheat, and 34 percent of all coarse grains (mainly millet, sorghum, and maize). At the same time, developing countries imported almost 59 percent of all the grain that moved in international trade, paying normal commercial prices for about 85 percent of this and receiving the balance as food aid.

China and India, giants in size, are also giants in agricultural production. Together they produce more than half of the world's rice. China alone produces more wheat than Canada and the United States combined (as does the U.S.S.R. in normal years). India, with about one-third of the world's undernourished people, produces nearly twice as much wheat as Canada and almost as much as the United States. Only in coarse grains does the United States outproduce the two Asian countries.

The great significance of the United States and Canada as world sources of grain is not in high grain production relative to other countries but rather in low consumption relative to production. China, the U.S.S.R., India, and other grain importers need more grain than they produce. Canada and the United States produce much more grain than their own populations need. Therefore, they have the largest stocks of surplus available for exporting commercially or as food aid.

The size of world grain stocks carried over from one crop year to another strongly affects the next year's price of grain and, consequently, the ability of low-income food-deficit countries to import food either commercially or as aid. The quantity of staple foods available in the markets of a country affects the price for consumers. Therefore, even though disparate incomes mean that food supplies distributed through the market will be distributed unevenly, the food purchasing power of low-income people is greatly diminished by higher food prices and greatly improved by lower prices. The sheer quantity of national food supplies, while not guaranteeing nutritionally adequate distribution in the absence of nonmarket policy mechanisms, affects hunger through the interaction among quantity, price, and low-income purchasing power. A study done in India by the International Food Policy Research Institute showed that the higher prices that resulted when food stocks dropped 10 percent below average reduced food consumption among the poorest fifth of the population by 40 percent; among the wealthiest fifth, food consumption dropped only 8 percent. (See also Figure 16, "Staple Foods and the Poor.")

FAO recommends a stock carryover of 18 percent of normal world consumption to prevent price shocks for low-income importers. Table 19 shows that when carryover stocks were between

24 percent and 26 percent of normal consumption in the period 1985–1988, low-income food-deficit countries were able to cover 21 percent to 24 percent of their import requirements with food aid. In the 1988/89 and 1989/90 crop years, however, when carryover stocks dropped to an estimated 17 percent or 18 percent of normal world consumption, food aid also dropped as a percentage of low-income country imports. More foreign exchange had to be used to pay full (higher) prices for food imports, with less help from affluent countries.

Increasing Food Production through Applied Research

The primary reason that the Far East, alone of all the developing regions, has been able to make steady per capita gains in staple food production over the past 30 years has been the expanded use of high-yielding varieties (HYVs) of rice and wheat. (See Figure 21.)

The HYVs were developed by genetic crossbreeding of traditional varieties at the International Rice Research Institute (IRRI) in the Philippines and the Centro Internacional de Mejoramiento de Maize y Trigo (CIMMYT) in Mexico, the first international agricultural research centers in a network that now numbers 13. In 1965, HYV rice was in use only in China and Latin America and only on 27.6 percent and 1.4 percent of all land under cultivation in rice in those regions, respectively. HYV wheat was not yet in use anywhere. Table 20 shows how greatly this changed in less than 20 years.

In 1960, the population explosion in Asia seemed to be on an unavoidable collision course with famine. Keeping that in mind, it is easy to understand the worldwide euphoria that greeted news of genetically engineered rice strains that could multiply Asia's harvests 5 or 6 times on the same amount of land. The increase in productivity per hectare turned out to be rarely that high under actual field conditions for most farmers. However, the 40 percent average increase in rice harvested per unit of land and the 60 percent overall increase in Asia's rice production in just 20 years seem sufficiently dramatic to merit the name "Green Revolution." Figure 22 shows how close the actual race has been between rice production and Asia's 55 percent population growth.

The rapid increase in additional food grain made possible by HYV rice and wheat is illustrated in Figure 23.

HYV rice was developed by crossbreeding many different traditional varieties to obtain the blend of genes that created the most productive plant under the intended growing conditions. Japanese and Chinese scientists had been doing genetic and agronomic research for many years to improve the productivity of their rice. IRRI built upon this and other Asian research, using Chinese scientists joined by many others. One objective was to maximize a rice plant's ability to absorb energy from the sun even on cloudy days. Genes from varieties with erect, rather than drooping, leaves aided that process. Another objective was to enable rice plants to benefit from greater use of fertilizer. In theory, fertilizer could increase yields per hectare, but in reality, the taller stalks caused by fertilizing traditional varieties tended to bend or break ("lodge") under the weight of the grain, thereby reducing the harvest. Genes from Chinese dwarf varieties with short, stiff stalks solved that problem.

By now there are many different HYV rice and wheat varieties, each with its own particular advantages and disadvantages for various growing conditions depending on soil types, local insects and plant diseases, rainfall patterns, amounts and kinds of fertilizer applications, and so on. While the first HYV rice strains required large amounts of fertilizer and irrigation to thrive and were highly susceptible to pests and diseases, more recent varieties have been bred to reduce fertilizer requirements and increase pest resistance genetically, without pesticides. The newer varieties can utilize fertilizer better than the traditional varieties, but they outproduce traditional varieties even without fertilizer.

HYV rice matures so quickly even when days are short and skies are cloudy that farmers can plant two or three crops a year where only one could be harvested before. If adequate water is assured, even three and four crops can be grown within the same year. In some parts of Asia, HYV wheat can be grown between rice crops when climate conditions are unfavorable for rice, greatly expanding again how much food one farmer can produce on a given piece of land in one year. Fast-maturing wheat suitable for tropical conditions has enabled farmers in Bangladesh, for example, to utilize their land year-round. The total area in Bangladesh that is planted in wheat has expanded nearly fivefold since 1970. Multiple crops and shorter crop cycles increase the need for farm labor and create more jobs than did the traditional varieties.

When the HYVs were first introduced, only relatively prosperous farmers could afford to adopt them—farmers with
assured access to irrigation and the ability to buy fertilizer and
pesticides. Over time, however, with new HYVs that need less
irrigation and fewer purchased inputs and with more enlight-
ened government programs of credit and extension services for
small farmers, the adoption of HYVs has spread among farmers
in all income groups and on farms of all sizes. In some areas, the
proportion of HYV adopters is higher among the smallest farms
than among the largest landowners. (See Figure 24.)

The rate of gain in food production from HYV rice and
wheat varieties has slowed in recent years. As the areas for which
their characteristics are most appropriate become gradually sat-
urated with HYV use, the rate of new increase in production
approaches zero.

Research on rice and wheat continues to attempt to make it
possible to raise these crops in places where they cannot grow at
this point. Research at the international centers and elsewhere is
trying to increase also the productivity of sorghum, millet,
triticale, and pulses in the diverse growing conditions of sub-
Saharan Africa, Asia, the Near East, North Africa, and Latin
America. The discovery or development of improved forage
grasses could increase livestock production and permit milk and
meat animals to graze on land where animals now cannot survive.
Other research is probing effective, low-cost alternatives to chemical fertilizer through biological nitrogen fixation; biological
pest control to avoid the use of pesticides; the protection of
fragile tropical soils; dryland farming and agronomic practices
that reduce the use of irrigation; and intercropping, farming
systems, and other means to increase both the productivity of
agriculture and the income of farm households in developing
countries.

The need is very pressing for increased food production in
developing countries, both to keep pace with population growth
and to meet rising demand from those in the population whose
income is rising. The slightest gain in income among the poor in
developing countries is translated overwhelmingly into the purchase of more food.

National economies will benefit most, overall, when the
greatest possible number of small, poor farmers share in the
increased productivity. However, experience shows that unless

those small farmers are protected by enforceable land tenure rights, fair rents demanded from tenants and sharecroppers, and fair sources of credit, the profits from increased productivity on the part of small farmers will flow to the landlords and village money lenders. Without these protections, productivity may rise without reducing hunger among those who till the land.

Research that leads to increased agricultural productivity is a slow process, because it must work in partnership with the natural growing cycles and seasons of the crop under scrutiny. More than 20 years of persistent effort preceded the first HYV wheat strains, for example. The various steps in developing a new crop variety at one of the international agricultural research centers today require 6 to 14 years to complete: (1) collection and characterization of existing germplasm, 1–4 years; (2) selection of germplasm for breeding material, 1–3 years; (3) generation of segregating lines through crossing, 1 growing season; (4) screening segregating lines against stresses, 3–6 seasons; (5) selection of elite lines, 2–4 seasons; (6) preliminary and advanced yield testing, 2–4 seasons; and, finally, (7) distribution in international field trials before being released to national governments for dissemination to their own farmers.

Environmental Problems for Food Production

Salinization of soil, loss of soil fertility, pollution of soil and water from agricultural chemicals, and erosion from deforestation and poor cultivation practices are among the most serious causes of the land degradation that threatens sustained food production in developing countries (as elsewhere).

FAO finds that the loss of soil fertility in many developing countries already poses a serious threat to food production. An average grain crop removes from 100 to 150 kilograms of important plant nutrients from the soil per hectare, according to FAO. Those nutrients must be restored by some form of fertilization, whether organic (biological) or inorganic (chemical), if the land is to remain productive. Some developed countries are using up to 700 kilograms of inorganic fertilizer per hectare of arable land, endangering the soil and creating serious water pollution through run-off. In contrast, African countries use an average of 11 kilograms per hectare, Latin American countries use 48 kilograms, and Asian countries use 62 kilograms—not enough to restore the nutrient loss from cropping.

Irrigation was long hailed as a major answer to the world's need to expand agriculture. Deserts, it was thought, could be made to bloom. Many large-scale irrigation schemes have been funded by development assistance in Asia and Africa. The area of arable cropland by regions and the percent of land that is irrigated are shown in Table 21 as estimated by the Economic Research Service of the U.S. Department of Agriculture. Table 22 shows the darker side: the percent of irrigated soils that have become salty and unproductive as a result of irrigation. Over-use of irrigation and poorly designed and operated irrigation systems have reduced crop production in some areas to less than it was before irrigation was introduced.

The Global 2000 study of the sustainability of world ecological systems conducted for President Jimmy Carter found that continuation of current agricultural practices and erosion rates could reduce agricultural production by 25 percent in Central America and Africa, 21 percent in South America, 12 percent in Southeast Asia, and 5 percent in Southwest Asia (the Near East) by the year 2000.

Soils in Africa are inherently poor, highly leached, and low in nutrients, clay content, fertility, and water-holding capacity. Some 130 million acres of cultivable land are at risk of possibly irreversible degradation there from practices that include overgrazing, especially around waterholes, shortened fallow periods, removal of trees for fuelwood, and cultivation of hillsides. Desertification is advancing in arid southwestern Asia from overgrazing, abandonment of irrigated land because of salinization, and wind erosion. Wind erosion is severe also in western China, Pakistan, and India. Water erosion is also severe in hilly areas and from deforestation both of the foothills of the Himalayas and of steep mountain slopes in Central America. Because mountain and tropical forest soils are generally thin with limited levels of natural fertility, cultivation of these soils can exhaust soil productivity in less than 5 years. This is happening rapidly in large areas of Brazil and Central America where tropical forests have been cleared.

There seem to be no real shortcuts in agricultural progress for developing countries. The Green Revolution may have been an anomaly, a one-time leap in the long-term, slow-but-steady trendline of gains in food production.

The Role of Food Aid and Development Assistance

Food Aid

The World Food Conference of 1974 set a target of 10 million tons of cereals as the minimum safe level of food aid pledges annually. The Food Aid Convention, an agreement negotiated among major donor nations, sets a lower target of 7.6 million tons in annual food aid commitments (an amount provided unilaterally by the United States in 1962). FAO estimates that actual food aid shipments in the 1988/89 crop year were less than 9.8 million tons and, with continued strong world prices for wheat and rice, were likely to fall below the U.N.'s 10-million-ton target again in 1989/90. Meanwhile, the Economic Research Service of the U.S. Department of Agriculture (USDA/ERS) found that food aid needs were 17 million tons in low-income countries in 1989/90—just to maintain typical, not nutritionally adequate, consumption. Obviously, food aid dependency is a poor answer to the needs of hungry people.

Fortunately, food aid dependence is declining. In the 1970/71 crop year, the LDCs relied on food aid for 35 percent of their cereal imports, while in 1987/88, food aid provided 15 percent of the cereals imported by LDCs.

The United States is the largest source of food aid overall. As a group, the nations of the European Economic Community are the second largest donor, Canada is the third largest, and Japan is the fourth. Japan is the only donor that conducts all of its bilateral food aid through triangular transactions—buying food aid commodities from one country (rice from Thailand, wheat from the United States, maize from Zimbabwe) to donate to another country. Table 23 shows the volume of food aid commodity contributions from all countries during the 1980s, multilateral and bilateral combined. All donor countries except the United States conduct food aid entirely as grants.

The two most important food aid programs in the world are the U.S. P.L. 480 program and the UN/FAO World Food Programme (WFP). The WFP administers "food-for-development" grants to developing countries and emergency food aid, including the International Emergency Food Reserve (IEFR) established by the U.N. General Assembly in 1975. The annual target for the IEFR is 500,000 metric tons of cereals.

The World Food Programme

Aid through the WFP is always provided as a grant. The biannual target for donor commitments (in cash or commodities) is $1.4 billion in addition to support for the IEFR. Canada is typically the largest donor to the WFP in most years, with the United States a close second. (See Table 24.)

The WFP provides most of its aid as food-for-work on various public works projects, for which the recipient country pays laborers in food rather than cash. Some food-for-development WFP grants feed schoolchildren and university students. Recipient countries are encouraged to involve local women's groups and other local organizations in the administration of food aid. Food-for-work jobs assist only the poorest people, those who have no alternative employment at the time. These public works projects are supposed to support rural development and agriculture by constructing or improving infrastructure such as roads, irrigation canals, dams, and terracing or reforestation schemes to halt erosion. Many food-for-work laborers are women of the poorest households, who are often supporting children as a single parent.

Critics of food-for-work argue that food-for-work laborers are undercompensated for their labor and that cash payments would meet their needs better than a small bag of rice or wheat. These critics also doubt the development value of many infrastructure projects, claiming that the projects benefit rural elites rather than the poor and widen the poverty gap. Advocates of food-for-work schemes reply that payment in rice or wheat for otherwise impoverished workers is better than nothing at all coming into their households and that resources to pay cash for labor on public works projects simply are not as available as food aid. Food-for-work defenders maintain also that infrastructure improvements help everyone, including the poor.

Emergency food aid projects approved by the WFP in 1988 involved more than 15 million people in 29 countries. In 1989, there were 46 emergency projects—29 in Africa, 5 in Asia, 8 in the Near East, and 4 in Latin America. Many of these were for refugees. Table 25 shows estimated 1990 food aid requirements for refugees under the supervision of the U.N. High Commissioner for Refugees (UNHCR), more than half of them in Africa. Donors contributing to the IEFR as shown in Table 26 include 4 low-income, developing countries—India, Sri Lanka, Mauritius, and Lesotho. The 500,000-ton cereal goal was not met in the 1988–1989 period, when lowered world grain stocks and higher grain prices inhibited contributions.

Food for Peace: P.L. 480

The P.L. 480 program is administered jointly by USAID and the Department of Agriculture. The annual budget is usually around $1.5 billion. The actual volume of food shipped depends on world commodity prices. A 4-million-ton Food Security Wheat Reserve mandated by Congress guarantees the availability of at least that volume, regardless of prices. During the rise in world wheat prices in 1988 and 1989, the Food Security Wheat Reserve was drawn upon twice to meet special needs in Africa.

Aid through P.L. 480 may be either a grant (Title II) or a concessional sale (Title I). There are two or three "aid" elements in a concessional sale: first, very low interest (2 percent to 4 percent) is charged on the credit extended to the developing country purchasing the food; second, a much longer time (up to 40 years) is allowed for repaying the loan than normal market transactions permit; and occasionally, a 10-year grace period with 2 percent annual service charge is allowed before repayment begins. Congress amended the P.L. 480 legislation in 1985 to allow also for payments to be made in a developing country's own currency rather than in harder to obtain U.S. dollars. Since 1988, all Title I sales must permit at least partial repayment in the recipient country's currency. The local currencies paid to the U.S. government are to be loaned to private businesses or cooperatives in the recipient country to promote private sector development.

Title II food commodities are used for emergency relief and humanitarian purposes such as maternal and child nutrition programs. Title II food is distributed chiefly through U.S. private volunteer organizations (PVOs) that meet specific administrative qualifications. The most active PVO distributors of Title II food are Catholic Relief Services, Cooperative for American Relief Everywhere (CARE), World Vision Relief Organization, and the

Adventist Development and Relief Agency. (The proportion of U.S. government funding in the 1986 revenues of these PVOs ranged from approximately 55 percent to nearly 88 percent, most of this coming from P.L. 480.)

Most P.L. 480 food is distributed under Title I purchase contracts. During fiscal year (FY) 1989, Title I accounted for slightly more than 53 percent of the value of all commodities shipped compared with approximately 39 percent under Title II. An addition to P.L. 480 legislation in the late 1970s, Title III, turns a concessionary sale agreement into a development assistance grant. In a Title III contract, the recipient country commits itself at the time of the contract to "repay" the food purchase loan by applying the value of the loan to a specific development project or program. Only 8 percent of the value of P.L. 480 commodities shipped in FY 1989 were for Title III contracts. (See Table 27.)

When a developing country purchases P.L. 480 Title I food aid, one purpose may be to increase the total food available in domestic markets, but another purpose usually is to generate government revenue through resale of U.S. food grains. Once the arbiters of U.S. foreign policy have cleared a developing country to receive food aid, there are few strings attached to the purposes for which the recipient government can use Title I resale revenues. There is no legislative requirement that U.S. food aid go to the neediest countries.

In practice, P.L. 480 allocations often serve strategic foreign policy purposes more than they do actual food need. The degree of political skewing of U.S. food aid varies according to the politics of the current administration. For fiscal year 1990, P.L. 480 planned for El Salvador amounted to $7.31 for each Salvadoran, while in sub-Saharan Africa, where food shortfalls and hunger are most dire, each person was allocated only 34 cents worth of food aid. Fortunately, the needs of sub-Saharan Africa currently receive primary consideration by the World Food Programme and most other donor nations. (See Table 28.)

The reason that the United States is the largest donor of food aid is obvious from Figure 25. Although not the world's largest producer of wheat, the United States utilizes relatively little of its wheat domestically and is by far the largest exporter, accounting for about 36 percent of the world's food grain exports. The United States usually has also the largest carryover stocks of any country that are not needed for domestic consumption from one crop year to the next.

Very large surplus grain stocks in the United States during the 1950s and 1960s provided a *de facto* world food reserve for emergencies or harvest shortfalls in any country. The uncharacteristically large Soviet grain purchases in the early 1970s, the general world food crisis of 1972–1974, and deliberate U.S. policy to reduce carryover stocks ended the era of a unilateral world food reserve stored in U.S. grain elevators. In 1962, food aid accounted for 84.5 percent of all U.S. food grain exports; by 1987, that figure had shrunk to 24.5 percent. The volume of food aid also declined from more than 7.6 million metric tons in 1962 to 4.3 million tons in 1987. (See Figure 26.)

Thus, U.S. food aid has been declining during the same period that food deficits in many developing countries are increasing along with the total number of undernourished people in the world. Food-deficit countries are having to go deeper into debt or to pay increasing amounts of scarce foreign exchange for food imports. On the other hand, the urgency of improving the capacity of their own farmers to produce food is very clear to developing-country leaders, who may have been inclined to slight agricultural development in the days of vast U.S. surpluses and food aid largesse.

Development Assistance

Development assistance is critically needed by low-income countries to improve their farmers' capacity to produce food, to build the economy and create more income-earning opportunity for everyone, to build infrastructure to facilitate the transportation and marketing of food and other goods, to implement programs of special nutrition assistance for the poorest people and the most vulnerable groups (infants, small children, and pregnant or lactating women), and to increase the health and education of their people generally.

While it may well be true that every country has the potential to meet its own needs, it is also true that this potential is sadly underdeveloped in low-income food-deficit countries. With declining foreign exchange earnings for many countries during the 1980s, external financing was doubly needed to obtain materials to build the economy, to import food to supplement domestic production, and to maintain or improve social programs. Rather than increasing, however, external financing for developing countries shrank during the decade. (See Figure 27.)

Official development assistance (ODA) is aid to developing countries for economic and social development provided by other governments as grants or loans on very concessional terms. It does not include military aid, export credits (helping firms in the donor country that export to developing countries), direct investment, bank lending, or aid from private organizations. ODA to sub-Saharan Africa has increased markedly in the past two decades and aid to Asia and Latin America has changed very slightly, but aid to North Africa has dropped by more than 50 percent. (See Table 29.)

The 18 industrialized donor countries apparently are giving priority not to the poorest developing countries, however, but rather to middle-income and richer developing countries. Using data from the World Bank and the OECD for 1985–1986, UNICEF found that the 30 poorest countries, with 64 percent of the population of all developing countries, received only 32 percent of ODA. (See Figure 28.)

The most generous aid donors in 1987 in terms of aid capacity as measured by GNP were Norway (1.09 percent of GNP), the Netherlands (0.98 percent of GNP), and Denmark and Sweden (0.88 percent of GNP each). All four exceeded the donor target of 0.07 percent of GNP established by the U.N. General Assembly at the beginning of the Second United Nations Development Decade (the 1970s). The least generous of the 18 donors in 1987 by GNP capacity were the United States (0.20 percent of GNP) and Austria (0.17 percent). In total spending, the United States was the largest aid donor at $8.95 billion in 1987. Japan was second largest at $7.45 billion. When ODA performance is measured in relation to economic potential for aiding developing countries, however, the United States ranks nearly at the bottom. Norway's ODA in dollar amount was only a tenth of the $8.95 billion from the United States; but by size Norway is only 4 percent of the United States and has only 2 percent of the U.S. population. U.S. ODA performance has not always been so poor. In 1967, it came close to 6 percent of GNP, but it has declined steadily over the past 20 years. (The U.S. "foreign aid" budget, not to be confused with official development assistance, includes a great amount of military aid and general budgetary support to strategically valued countries; the development significance of the latter is subject to debate. See Figure 29.)

Concessional lending for economic and social development is a major source of development assistance. Most of this lending comes through multilateral institutions, some of which are supported by monetary "subscriptions" from member governments and some by contributions. The most important of these concessional lending institutions for low-income food-deficit countries are the International Development Association (IDA), administered by the World Bank, and the International Fund for Agricultural Development (IFAD), created by the World Food Conference of 1974. IDA's very long term, very low interest loans are restricted to developing countries with per capita GNP less than $1,070 in 1988 dollars. IFAD makes loans only for projects serving small farmers or the rural poor. IFAD's budget is among the smallest of all multilateral institutions, but its significance is enhanced by creative and insightful targeting to groups and projects with high "pay-off" in terms of self-reliant, sustainable poverty reduction and enhanced food production by the poor themselves. During the later half of the 1980s, both the International Monetary Fund (IMF) and the World Bank created special new lending programs to assist countries badly hurt by debt-related structural adjustment efforts.

The U.N. Development Fund for Women (UNIFEM), although not a lending institution, operates with a budget even smaller than IFAD's. UNIFEM resembles IFAD in its creative use of a very small budget to empower a particular group that has been overlooked and even, at times, harmed by mainstream development assistance. Women food producers and micro-entrepreneurs are among the primary beneficiaries of UNIFEM assistance.

Major Sources for This Chapter

Asian NGO Coalition for Agrarian Reform and Rural Development. *The Case for Alternative Development of the People, for the People, by the People.* Thailand: C. J. L. Miramit, for the Asian NGO Coalition, 1979.

Berg, Alan. *Malnourished People. A Policy View.* Poverty and Basic Needs Series. Washington, DC: The World Bank, 1981.

———. *Malnutrition. What Can Be Done? Lessons from World Bank Experience.* Baltimore, MD: Johns Hopkins University Press for the World Bank, 1987.

Brown, Lester R., et al. *State of the World 1989*. New York: Company for Worldwatch Institute, 1989.

Consultative Group on International Agricultural Research. *Ir cultural Research Centers: A Study of Achievements and Poter* Washington, DC: The World Bank, 1985.

Food and Agriculture Organization of the United Nations. *F٦ ٠d Survey*. 1985.

——. *Food Outlook*. No. 1/2 (February 1990) and No. 3 (March 1990).

——. *Guide to Staple Foods of the World*. I/Q4937/E/1.84/1/20,000. 1984.

——. *State of Food and Agriculture 1987–1988*. Special topic: Changing priorities for agricultural science and technology in developing countries.

——. *State of Food and Agriculture 1989*. Special topic: Sustainable development and natural resource management.

——. *Women in Agriculture*. A report prepared by Mary Roodkowsky. I/Q5245/E/12.83/1/20,000. 1983.

Grant, James P. *The State of the World's Children 1989*. A report by the executive director of UNICEF. Oxford: Oxford University Press for UNICEF, 1989.

Hirschoff, Paula M., and Neil G. Kotler, eds. *Completing the Food Chain. Strategies for Combatting Hunger and Malnutrition*. Papers by John Mellor, Nevin Scrimshaw, Uma Lele, Aree Valyasevi, and others in the proceedings of a colloquium organized by the Smithsonian Institution. Washington, DC: Smithsonian Institution Press, 1989.

International Labour Office (ILO). *World Labour Report*. Volume 1. Geneva: ILO, 1984.

Library of Congress, Congressional Research Service (CRS). *The Effectiveness of Food Aid: Implications of Changes in Farm, Food Aid, and Trade Legislation. Proceedings of a CRS Workshop Held on April 25, 1988*. 88-4923 ENR. CRS Report for Congress, 1 June 1988, prepared by Charles E. Hanrahan.

Organization for Economic Development and Cooperation, Development Assistance Committee. *Development Cooperation 1989*. Paris: OECD, 1989.

Poleman, Thomas T. "Quantifying the Nutrition Situation in Developing Countries." *Food Research Institute Studies* 18:1 (1981), 1–58.

Reutlinger, Shlomo, Jack van Holst Pellekaan, et al. *Poverty and Hunger. Issues and Options for Food Security in Developing Countries*. A World Bank Policy Study. Washington, DC: The World Bank, 1986.

Sadik, Nafis. *The State of World Population 1989*. A report prepared by the executive director of UNFPA. New York: United Nations Population Fund, 1989.

United Nations. *World Survey on the Role of Women in Development. Report of the Secretary-General*. Item 7 of the provisional agenda of the World Conference to Review and Appraise the Achievements of the United Nations Decade for Women. A/Conf.116/4. 11 December 1984.

U.S. Department of Agriculture, Economic Research Service. *1989 Agricultural Chartbook*. Agricultural Handbook No. 684.

World Agriculture. Situation and Outlook Report. Special Issue: "Are We Approaching a World Food Crisis Again?" WAS-55. June 1989.

——. *World Food Needs and Availabilities, 1989/90: Summer Update.* August 1989.

——. *World Food Needs and Availabilities, 1989/90: Winter.* December 1989.

Woods, Alan. *Development and the National Interest: U.S. Economic Assistance into the 21st Century.* A report by the administrator, Agency for International Development. Washington, DC: USAID, 1989.

World Bank. *World Development Report 1989.* Oxford: Oxford University Press for the World Bank, 1989.

World Food Council. *The Cyprus Initiative against Hunger in the World. President's Report to the Fifteenth Ministerial Session.* Introduction and Part One: "World Hunger Fifteen Years after the World Food Conference—The Challenges Ahead." WFC/1989/2 (Part One), 22 March 1989.

TABLES

TABLE 1   The Undernourished[*]

REGION	1969–1971 (a)	1969–1971 (b)	1979–1981 (a)	1979–1981 (b)	1983–1985 (a)	1983–1985 (b)
			(millions)			
Africa	92	32	110	29	140	32
Far East	281	29	288	24	291	22
Latin America	51	18	52	15	55	14
Near East	35	22	24	12	26	11
TOTAL	460		475		512	

(a) = Numbers
(b) = Percentage of population

[*]"Cut-off" point with 1.4 BMR for adults and adolescents.

SOURCE: FAO. Cited in *President's Report to the Fifteenth Ministerial Session of the World Food Council,* WFC/1989/2 (Part One Annex), 22 March 1989.

TABLE 2   Regional Distribution of Hunger

REGION	PERCENT OF ALL HUNGRY
Far East	57
Africa	27
Latin America	11
Near East/North Africa	5

SOURCE: FAO. Revised and updated estimates based on methodology of the Fifth World Food Survey. World Food Council, WFC/1989/2, 22 March 1989.

TABLE 3   Protein-Energy Malnutrition among Children
under the Age of Five in Developing Countries*

Region	Numbers (in millions)			Percent of Age Group		
	1975	1980	1984	1975	1980	1984
Sub-Saharan Africa	14.8	16.1	19.5	24.7	23.6	25.3
Near East/ North Africa	4.3	3.4	3.2	17.1	12.3	10.2
Middle America/ Caribbean	1.9	1.8	1.7	12.7	10.2	8.9
South America	2.3	2.0	2.3	7.8	6.4	6.4
South Asia	89.3	93.8	97.7	73.9	70.0	66.7
South-East Asia	16.1	16.4	17.5	37.1	34.0	32.7
China	20.6	19.0	16.0	25.8	22.1	17.7
All Developing Regions	149.3	152.5	157.9	–	–	–

*Children significantly underweight for their age.

SOURCE: United Nations ACC/SCN. World Food Council, WFC/1989/2, 22 March 1989.

TABLE 4   Percentage of Infants with Low Birth Weights
by Regions (1982–1987)

Sub-Saharan Africa	14
Near East and North Africa	8
Middle America/Caribbean	15
South America	9
South Asia	27
Southeast Asia	17
China	6

SOURCE: UNICEF. State of the World's Children 1989.

TABLE 5   Rural/Urban Distribution of Hunger

REGION	HUNGRY WHO ARE RURAL	HUNGRY WHO ARE URBAN
Far East	80–90%	10–20%
Africa	80–90%	10–20%
Latin America	60%	40%
Near East/North Africa	70%	30%

SOURCE: John Mellor, "Ending Hunger: An Implementable Program for Self-Reliant Growth." 1988 draft cited in World Food Council, WFC/1989/2, 22 March 1989.

TABLE 6   World's Most Densely Populated Countries (persons/sq. km)

1960		1980		2000	
Hong Kong	2,943	Hong Kong	4,635	Hong Kong	6,132
Singapore	2,812	Singapore	4,178	Singapore	5,327
Malta	1,041	Malta	1,075	Malta	1,224
Barbados	535	Bangladesh	621	Bangladesh	1,074
Bangladesh	360	Barbados	588	Barbados	689
Mauritius	324	Mauritius	487	Mauritius	645
Belgium	300	Korea, Rep. of	386	Korea, Rep. of	516
Netherlands	281	Puerto Rico	386	Puerto Rico	495
Puerto Rico	265	Netherlands	345	Lebanon	470
Martinique	260	Belgium	325	El Salvador	407
Korea, Rep. of	251	Japan	308	Netherlands	379
Japan	249	Lebanon	304	Haiti	356
Germany, Fed. Rep. of	223	Martinique	297	Belgium	353
United Kingdom	215	Germany Fed. Rep. of	245	Japan	342
Lebanon	179	United Kingdom	229	Rwanda	342
Italy	167	Sri Lanka	227	Martinique	326
Trinidad & Tobago	164	El Salvador	224	India	316
German Dem. Rep.	159	Trinidad & Tobago	222	Sri Lanka	306
Guadeloupe	153	India	212	Burundi	281
Windward Islands	152	Haiti	210	Philippines	278
Sri Lanka	151	Reunion	209	Reunion	273
Jamaica	149	Jamaica	200	Israel	272
Haiti	134	Israel	191	Trinidad & Tobago	268
India	133	Italy	189	Jamaica	262
Reunion	132	Guadeloupe	188	Germany, Fed. Rep. of	240

SOURCE: U.N., *Selected World Demographic Indicators by Countries, 1950–2000*, ST/ESA/SER.R, 1979.

TABLE 7   Population and Current and Potential Arable Land

Region/country	Population		Arable land	
	1986	2050	1986	Potential
	--- Million ---		Million ha	
World	4,967	10,805	1,474	2,500
		Percent of total		
North America	5.4	3.0	16.1	15.0
Latin America	8.5	8.9	12.1	23.4
Europe 1/	9.9	4.3	9.5	5.7
USSR	5.7	3.6	15.7	11.1
North Africa and Middle East	5.6	9.7	7.3	10.4
Sub-Saharan Africa	9.7	21.6	10.8	12.4
Asia	54.7	48.5	25.0	22.0
Oceania	.5	.4	3.5	4.6

1/ Excludes USSR.

SOURCE: USDA/ERS, *World Agriculture Situation and Outlook,* June 1989.

TABLE 8   Cropland per Inhabitant by Region

Region/country	Ha per capita		Percent change
	1961	1986	1961-86
	------ Ha -----		Percent
World	0.44	0.30	- 32
North America	1.11	.88	- 21
Latin America 1/	.59	.43	- 27
Europe 2/	.35	.28	- 28
USSR	1.05	.83	- 21
Sub-Saharan Africa	.54	.33	- 39
North Africa and Middle East	.58	.31	- 47
South Asia	.33	.20	- 39
Southeast Asia	.25	.18	- 28
China 3/	.16	.09	- 44
Other East Asia	.08	.05	- 38
Oceania	1.93	1.96	2

1/ Includes Mexico. 2/ Excludes USSR. 3/ Excludes Taiwan.

SOURCE: USDA/ERS *World Agriculture Situation and Outlook,* June 1989.

TABLE 9   Arable Land Farmed per Farm Worker (in hectares)

	1961-65	1978	2000
Africa	2.37	2.15	2.04
Asia and the Pacific	0.97	0.88	0.76
Latin America	4.18	4.59	6.05
Near East	2.89	2.67	2.21
Industrialized countries	5.73	9.30	. . .

Note: Data cover 90 developing countries, excluding China.

SOURCE: FAO, World Hunger, 1/R4200/E/685/1/40000, 1985.

TABLE 10   Calorie Consumption and Deficit by Income Groups, Brazil, 1960

Annual family income (new cruzeiros)	Population		Daily calorie consumption		Daily calorie deficit [a]	
	Number (thousands)	Percent of total	Amount (millions)	Percent of total	Per capita	Total (millions)
Under 100	3,583	5.05	5,172	2.87	1,006	3,604
100–149	4,873	6.87	8,847	4.91	634	3,089
150–249	12,235	17.25	25,940	14.41	330	4,037
250–349	10,197	14.37	23,378	12.98	157	1,601
350–499	11,145	15.71	28,293	15.71		
500–799	12,884	18.16	34,958	19.41		
800–1,199	7,198	10.14	22,689	12.60		
1,200–2,499	6,840	9.65	23,022	12.78		
2,500 and over	1,986	2.80	7,800	4.33		
Total	70,941	100.00	180,099	100.00		12,331

a. Deficits are defined as the difference between daily calorie requirements (2,450 calories) and actual consumption.

SOURCE: World Bank. Shlomo Reutlinger and Marcelo Selowsky, Malnutrition and Poverty, 1976, data from the Fundacio Getúlio Vargas.

TABLE 11   Selected Economic Indicators for Developing Countries, 1970–1989

	Average 1970–79	1980	1981	1982	1983	1984	1985	1986	1987	1988	1989 (est. f'cast)
PER CAPITA REAL GNP % change											
Africa	1.6	0.9	-0.7	-1.5	-4.4	-1.3	-0.8	-1.9	-1.6	0.2	0.3
L. America	3.1	2.8	-1.9	-3.5	-4.5	1.2	0.8	1.7	0.1	-0.2	1.2
Asia	3.4	3.3	3.6	3.2	6.0	6.4	4.8	4.8	4.9	5.3	4.4
Middle East	2.9	-6.6	-6.9	-4.5	-3.4	-2.9	-4.3	-1.6	-3.8	-1.5	-1.4
TERMS OF TRADE % change											
Africa	2.6	16.6	1.6	-5.4	-2.3	1.6	-3.8	-24.9	1.4	-3.1	-0.4
L. America	3.8	77.2	-4.4	-4.8	-3.0	3.8	-2.8	-13.9	1.2	-2.9	0.33
Asia	-0.2	-1.6	-2.7	-	-0.1	3.0	-3.2	-8.0	3.7	1.5	-0.5
Middle East	13.2	41.1	13.5	2.2	-8.5	0.2	-0.1	-48.3	10.7	-11.1	-0.1
TOTAL DEBT $US billions											
Africa		99.3	110.1	123.6	132.0	134.8	147.2	165.7	186.3	195.5	203.9
L. America		231.1	287.8	329.9	341.7	357.0	367.6	380.6	400.0	410.7	421.7
Asia		137.9	157.9	183.7	203.2	217.1	246.9	272.3	306.7	312.4	318.4
Middle East		73.9	89.9	102.5	112.6	122.4	128.4	137.4	143.8	149.4	154.0
DEBT SERVICE (as % of exports)											
Africa		14.4	17.1	21.1	23.3	26.7	28.8	27.8	25.5	26.6	24.9
L. America		33.2	41.6	50.7	40.5	40.6	40.3	45.1	37.8	42.1	37.9
Asia		8.6	9.7	11.5	11.3	11.4	12.5	13.5	12.6	11.3	9.9
Middle East		3.5	4.7	6.3	7.6	9.1	9.5	12.9	11.5	12.5	13.1

SOURCE: IMF, *World Economic Outlook,* Statistical Appendix, April 1988.

TABLE 12   Basic Indicators

		Population (millions) mid-1987	Area (thousands of square kilometers)	GNP per capita			Average annual rate of inflation (percent)		Life expectancy at birth (years) 1987
				Dollars 1987	Average annual growth rate (percent) 1965-87		1965-80	1980-87	
	Low-income economies	2,822.9 t	37,015 t	290 w	3.1 w		8.9 w	8.6 w	61 w
	China and India	1,866.1 t	12,849 t	300 w	3.9 w		2.9 w	5.5 w	65 w
	Other low-income	956.9 t	24,166 t	280 w	1.5 w		18.2 w	13.3 w	54 w
★ 1	Ethiopia	44.8	1,222	130	0.1		3.4	2.6	47
★ 2	Bhutan	1.3	47	150	..		..	..	48
★ 3	Chad	5.3	1,284	150	-2.0		6.3	5.3	46
★ 4	Zaire	32.6	2,345	150	-2.4		24.7	53.5	52
★ 5	Bangladesh	106.1	144	160	0.3		14.9	11.1	51
6	Malawi	7.9	118	160	1.4		7.0	12.4	46
★ 7	Nepal	17.6	141	160	0.5		7.8	8.8	51
★ 8	Lao PDR	3.8	237	170	..		..	46.5	48
★ 9	Mozambique	14.6	802	170	..		..	26.9	48
★10	Tanzania	23.9	945	180	-0.4		9.9	24.9	53
★11	Burkina Faso	8.3	274	190	1.6		6.2	4.4	47
★12	Madagascar	10.9	587	210	-1.8		7.9	17.4	54
★13	Mali	7.8	1,240	210	..		..	4.2	47
14	Burundi	5.0	28	250	1.6		8.5	7.5	49
★15	Zambia	7.2	753	250	-2.1		6.4	28.7	53
★16	Niger	6.8	1,267	260	-2.2		7.5	4.1	45
★17	Uganda	15.7	236	260	-2.7		21.2	95.2	48
★18	China	1,068.5	9,561	290	5.2		0.0	4.2	69
★19	Somalia	5.7	638	290	0.3		10.5	37.8	47
★20	Togo	3.2	57	290	0.0		6.9	6.6	53
★21	India	797.5	3,288	300	1.8		7.6	7.7	58
★22	Rwanda	6.4	26	300	1.6		12.4	4.5	49
★23	Sierra Leone	3.8	72	300	0.2		8.0	50.0	41
★24	Benin	4.3	113	310	0.2		7.4	8.2	50
★25	Central African Rep.	2.7	623	330	-0.3		8.5	7.9	50
★26	Kenya	22.1	583	330	1.9		7.3	10.3	58
★27	Sudan	23.1	2,506	330	-0.5		11.5	31.7	50
28	Pakistan	102.5	796	350	2.5		10.3	7.3	55
★29	Haiti	6.1	28	360	0.5		7.3	7.9	55
★30	Lesotho	1.6	30	370	4.7		8.0	12.3	56
★31	Nigeria	106.6	924	370	1.1		13.7	10.1	51
★32	Ghana	13.6	239	390	-1.6		22.8	48.3	54
★33	Sri Lanka	16.4	66	400	3.0		9.4	11.8	70
★34	Yemen, PDR	2.3	333	420	..		..	5.0	51
★35	Mauritania	1.9	1,031	440	-0.4		7.7	9.8	46
★36	Indonesia	171.4	1,905	450	4.5		34.2	8.5	60
★37	Liberia	2.3	111	450	-1.6		6.3	1.5	54
★38	Afghanistan	..	648	..	..		4.9	..	..
39	Burma	39.3	677	..	..		..	..	60
★40	Guinea	6.5	246	..	..		2.9	..	42
★41	Kampuchea, Dem.	..	181	..	..		..	..	..
★42	Viet Nam	65.0	330	..	..		..	..	66
	Middle-income economies	1,038.5 t	36,118 t	1,810 w	2.5 w		20.4 w	62.3 w	65 w
	Lower-middle-income	609.6 t	16,781 t	1,200 w	2.2 w		16.9 w	36.7 w	64 w
43	Senegal	7.0	196	520	-0.6		6.5	9.1	48
★44	Bolivia	6.7	1,099	580	-0.5		15.7	601.8	53
45	Zimbabwe	9.0	391	580	0.9		6.4	12.4	58
★46	Philippines	58.4	300	590	1.7		11.7	16.7	63
★47	Yemen Arab Rep.	8.5	195	590	..		..	11.4	51
★48	Morocco	23.3	447	610	1.8		6.1	7.3	61
★49	Egypt, Arab Rep.	50.1	1,002	680	3.5		7.3	9.2	61
★50	Papua New Guinea	3.7	462	700	0.8		7.5	4.4	54
51	Dominican Rep.	6.7	49	730	2.3		6.8	16.3	66
★52	Côte d'Ivoire	11.1	322	740	1.0		9.5	4.4	52
★53	Honduras	4.7	112	810	0.7		5.6	4.9	64
54	Nicaragua	3.5	130	830	-2.5		8.9	86.6	63
55	Thailand	53.6	514	850	3.9		6.3	2.8	64
★56	El Salvador	4.9	21	860	-0.4		7.0	16.5	62
57	Congo, People's Rep.	2.0	342	870	4.2		6.6	1.8	59
58	Jamaica	2.4	11	940	-1.5		12.8	19.4	74
59	Guatemala	8.4	109	950	1.2		7.1	12.7	62
60	Cameroon	10.9	475	970	3.8		8.9	8.1	56
61	Paraguay	3.9	407	990	3.4		9.4	21.0	67
62	Ecuador	9.9	284	1,040	3.2		10.9	29.5	65
63	Botswana	1.1	582	1,050	8.9		8.1	8.4	59
64	Tunisia	7.6	164	1,180	3.6		6.7	8.2	65
65	Turkey	52.6	781	1,210	2.6		20.7	37.4	64
66	Colombia	29.5	1,139	1,240	2.7		17.4	23.7	66
67	Chile	12.5	757	1,310	0.2		129.9	20.6	72

CONTINUED ON NEXT PAGE

TABLE 12   *continued*

	Population (millions) mid-1987	Area (thousands of square kilometers)	GNP per capita Dollars 1987	GNP per capita Average annual growth rate (percent) 1965-87	Average annual rate of inflation (percent) 1965-80	Average annual rate of inflation (percent) 1980-87	Life expectancy at birth (years) 1987
68 Peru	20.2	1,285	1,470	0.2	20.5	101.5	61
69 Mauritius	1.0	2	1,490	3.2	11.4	8.1	67
70 Jordan	3.8	98	1,560	..	..	2.8	66
71 Costa Rica	2.6	51	1,610	1.5	11.3	28.6	74
72 Syrian Arab Rep.	11.2	185	1,640	3.3	8.3	11.0	65
73 Malaysia	16.5	330	1,810	4.1	4.9	1.1	70
74 Mexico	81.9	1,973	1,830	2.5	13.0	68.9	69
75 South Africa	33.1	1,221	1,890	0.6	10.0	13.8	60
76 Poland	37.7	313	1,930	..	..	29.2	71
77 Lebanon	..	10	..	..	9.3	..	..
Upper-middle-income	432.5 *t*	20,272 *t*	2,710 *w*	2.9 *w*	23.2 *w*	86.8 *w*	67 *w*
78 Brazil	141.4	8,512	2,020	4.1	31.3	166.3	65
79 Uruguay	3.0	176	2,190	1.4	57.8	54.5	71
80 Hungary	10.6	93	2,240	3.8	2.6	5.7	70
81 Panama	2.3	77	2,240	2.4	5.4	3.3	72
82 Argentina	31.1	2,767	2,390	0.1	78.2	298.7	71
83 Yugoslavia	23.4	256	2,480	3.7	15.3	57.2	71
84 Algeria	23.1	2,382	2,680	3.2	9.8	5.6	63
85 Korea, Rep.	42.1	98	2,690	6.4	18.8	5.0	69
86 Gabon	1.1	268	2,700	1.1	12.7	2.6	52
87 Portugal	10.2	92	2,830	3.2	11.5	20.8	73
88 Venezuela	18.3	912	3,230	−0.9	10.4	11.4	70
89 Greece	10.0	132	4,020	3.1	10.5	19.7	76
90 Trinidad and Tobago	1.2	5	4,210	1.3	14.0	6.2	70
91 Libya	4.1	1,760	5,460	−2.3	15.4	0.1	61
92 Oman	1.3	212	5,810	8.0	17.6	−6.5	55
93 Iran, Islamic Rep.	47.0	1,648	..	..	15.6	..	63
94 Iraq	17.1	435	..	..	..	..	64
95 Romania	22.9	238	..	..	..	..	70
High-income economies	777.2 *t*	33,757 *t*	14,430 *w*	2.3 *w*	7.9 *w*	5.2 *w*	76 *w*
OECD members	746.6 *t*	31,085 *t*	14,670 *w*	2.3 *w*	7.6 *w*	5.0 *w*	76 *w*
†Other	30.6 *t*	2,673 *t*	7,880 *w*	3.5 *w*	15.9 *w*	13.3 *w*	70 *w*
96 Spain	38.8	505	6,010	2.3	12.3	10.7	77
97 Ireland	3.6	70	6,120	2.0	12.0	10.2	74
98 †Saudi Arabia	12.6	2,150	6,200	4.0	17.2	−2.8	63
99 †Israel	4.4	21	6,800	2.5	25.2	159.0	75
100 New Zealand	3.3	269	7,750	0.9	10.2	11.5	75
101 †Singapore	2.6	1	7,940	7.2	4.9	1.3	73
102 †Hong Kong	5.6	1	8,070	6.2	8.1	6.7	76
103 Italy	57.4	301	10,350	2.7	11.2	11.5	77
104 United Kingdom	56.9	245	10,420	1.7	11.2	5.7	75
105 Australia	16.2	7,687	11,100	1.8	9.2	7.8	76
106 Belgium	9.9	31	11,480	2.6	6.7	5.1	75
107 Netherlands	14.7	37	11,860	2.1	7.3	2.3	77
108 Austria	7.6	84	11,980	3.1	5.8	4.3	74
109 France	55.6	547	12,790	2.7	8.0	7.7	77
110 Germany, Fed. Rep.	61.2	249	14,400	2.5	5.2	2.9	75
111 Finland	4.9	337	14,470	3.2	10.5	7.2	76
112 †Kuwait	1.9	18	14,610	−4.0	16.3	−4.6	73
113 Denmark	5.1	43	14,930	1.9	9.3	6.8	75
114 Canada	25.9	9,976	15,160	2.7	7.1	5.0	77
115 Sweden	8.4	450	15,550	1.8	8.0	7.9	77
116 Japan	122.1	378	15,760	4.2	7.8	1.4	78
117 †United Arab Emirates	1.5	84	15,830	..	..	−0.3	71
118 Norway	4.2	324	17,190	3.5	7.7	6.1	77
119 United States	243.8	9,373	18,530	1.5	6.5	4.3	75
120 Switzerland	6.5	41	21,330	1.4	5.3	3.9	77

*   FAO "Food Deficit Country"
†   Economies classified by the United Nations or otherwise regarded by their authorities as developing
w weighted averages
t totals

SOURCE: World Bank, *World Development Report 1989*.

TABLE 13   Bangladesh: Mother's Nutrition and
Pregnancy Outcome

	Mother's Weight Under 42 Kgs	Over 42 Kgs
% of pregnancies ending in: miscarriage/stillbirth/ infant death	43	7
Live child after 1 year	57	93

SOURCE: UNFPA, *State of World Population 1989,* citing M. Asaduzzaman, 1987.

TABLE 14   Food, Pregnancy, and Infant Mortality

		PER CENT		
	Food % of calorie requirements	Anaemic	Low Birth Weight	Infant Mortality
Tanzania	83	59	13	10
Bangladesh	84	66	50	13
Zambia	93	60	14	11
Mali	72	50	13	13
India	86	68	30	9
Zimbabwe	90	27	15	8
Pakistan	106	65	27	12
Indonesia	110	65	18	10
Peru	98	35	9	8
Kenya	88	48	18	8
Papua New Guinea	92	55	25	10
Egypt	116	75	14	10
Colombia	108	22	10	5
Philippines	116	47	11	5
Thailand	105	48	13	5

SOURCE: UNFPA, *State of World Population 1989.*

TABLE 15   Undernourishment in Children and Anemia in Women

Region	Children under 5 years				Low birth weight	Anemia in women
	Low height-for-age		Low weight-for-age			
	(millions)	(%)	(millions)	(%)	(%)	(%)
Africa	22	26	4	7	14	40
Asia	115	54	33	16	19	58
Latin America	9	18	2	4	10	17

SOURCE: FAO, *Food and Nutrition* 11:2 (1985).

TABLE 16   Changes per Person Staple Food Production, Imports, and Consumption in Developing Countries 1970–1986/1987

	Production (1970 – 1987)	Imports	Consumption (1970–1986)
	Average annual percent change		
Low–income food–deficit countries *	0.81	2.89	1.39
Africa	−1.25	4.82	0.37
Near East	−1.23	7.87	0.78
Far East	1.22	0.75	1.59
Latin America	−0.66	3.53	0.88
Oceania	−0.86	2.71	2.99
Developing countries	0.71	4.32	1.24

*   69 countries with GNP/per caput of up to $940 in 1987, net cereal importers on average during 1983/84 – 1987/88

SOURCE: FAO, *Agrostat,* in World Food Council, WFC/1989/2, Part One, 22 March 1989.

TABLE 17   World Trade in Rice

	Exports				Imports		
	1988 estim.	1989 f'cast	1990		1988 estim.	1989 f'cast	1990
	(..... million tons .....)				(..... million tons .....)		
ASIA	7.2	9.4	8.7	**ASIA**	5.4	7.5	5.9
China 1/	0.8	0.3		Bangladesh	0.1	0.3	
India	0.3	0.3		China	0.3	1.3	
Indonesia	-	0.1		Hong Kong	0.4	0.4	
Japan	-	-		India	0.7	0.7	
Korea, D.P.R.	0.1	0.1		Indonesia	-	0.4	
Myanmar (Burma)	0.1	0.2		Iraq	0.6	0.7	
Pakistan	0.9	0.8		Korea, Rep. of	-	-	
Thailand	4.8	6.0		Malaysia	0.3	0.3	
Viet Nam	0.1	1.4		Philippines	0.2	0.2	
				Saudi Arabia	0.4	0.6	
				Singapore	0.2	0.2	
AFRICA	0.1	-	-	Sri Lanka	0.2	0.2	
Egypt	0.1	-					
CENTRAL AMERICA	-	-	-	**AFRICA**	2.5	3.1	3.1
SOUTH AMERICA	0.5	0.5	0.4	Cote d'Ivoire	0.2	0.4	
Suriname	0.1	0.1		Madagascar	-	0.1	
Uruguay	0.2	0.2		Senegal	0.3	0.4	
NORTH AMERICA	2.2	2.9	2.6	**CENTRAL AMERICA**	0.4	0.7	0.7
United States	2.2	2.9		**SOUTH AMERICA**	0.5	0.4	0.8
				Brazil	0.1	0.2	
WESTERN EUROPE	0.3	0.3	0.3	Peru	0.2	0.1	
EEC 2/	0.3	0.3		**NORTH AMERICA**	0.3	0.3	0.3
EASTERN EUROPE	-	-	-	**WESTERN EUROPE** 2/	0.7	0.9	0.9
U.S.S.R.	-	-	-	**EASTERN EUROPE**	0.2	0.2	0.3
OCEANIA	0.3	0.5	0.4	**U.S.S.R.**	0.5	0.5	0.5
Australia	0.3	0.5		**OCEANIA**	0.2	0.2	0.2
WORLD	10.7	13.7	12.6	**WORLD**	10.7	13.7	12.7
Developing countries	7.8	10.0	9.2	Developing countries	8.7	11.7	10.4
Developed countries	2.9	3.7	3.4	Developed countries	2.0	2.0	2.3

Note: Totals computed from unrounded data.

1/ Including Taiwan Province.
2/ Excluding trade between the twelve EEC member countries.

SOURCE: FAO, *Food Outlook,* March 1990.

TABLE 18   World Trade in Wheat and Coarse Grains

	Wheat 1/			Coarse Grains		
	1987/88	1988/89 estim.	1989/90 f'cast	1987/88	1988/89 estim.	1989/90 f'cast
EXPORTS	(........................... million tons ....)					
ASIA	4.0	4.6	2.1	5.2	7.2	4.7
China 2/	-	-	-	4.1	4.1	3.5
Thailand	-	-	-	0.8	1.6	0.9
AFRICA	0.7	1.3	0.1	3.3	2.7	5.2
South Africa	0.3	1.2	-	1.9	1.1	4.3
CENTRAL AMERICA	0.1	0.2	-	-	-	-
SOUTH AMERICA	3.9	3.6	6.2	4.5	4.6	3.4
Argentina	3.8	3.5	6.0	4.4	4.5	3.3
NORTH AMERICA	67.1	51.1	51.9	57.0	64.9	70.0
Canada	23.7	13.5	17.0	5.3	3.3	4.9
United States	43.4	37.6	34.9	51.7	61.6	65.1
WESTERN EUROPE	15.9	22.1	21.7	8.1	13.3	11.1
EEC 3/	14.7	20.0	20.5	7.0	12.4	9.3
EASTERN EUROPE	1.2	2.7	2.0	1.0	0.8	0.9
U.S.S.R.	0.6	0.5	1.0	-	-	-
OCEANIA	12.2	10.8	11.0	2.3	2.2	2.7
Australia	12.2	10.8	11.0	2.2	2.1	2.6
WORLD	105.8	96.8	96.0	81.4	95.7	98.0
Developing countries	8.0	8.1	8.0	11.1	13.4	9.0
Developed countries	97.7	88.7	88.0	70.3	82.3	89.0
IMPORTS						
ASIA	47.0	47.8	48.6	46.6	44.3	47.0
Bangladesh	2.3	2.1	1.8	-	-	-
China 2/	15.2	17.0	16.0	5.8	4.8	5.1
Iran, Islamic Rep. of	4.0	3.0	3.0	0.9	0.9	0.9
Japan	5.8	5.6	5.4	22.1	21.9	21.7
Korea, Rep. of	4.6	2.6	2.5	5.0	6.1	7.1
Pakistan	0.4	2.2	1.6	-	-	-
Saudi Arabia	0.1	0.1	0.1	6.0	4.7	5.0
AFRICA	19.2	18.0	17.9	6.5	6.1	5.9
Egypt	7.1	7.2	7.0	1.8	1.1	1.0
CENTRAL AMERICA	3.9	3.9	3.7	5.3	6.6	7.0
Mexico	0.7	1.0	0.6	3.7	5.0	5.3
SOUTH AMERICA	5.9	4.5	5.5	2.8	2.7	2.2
Brazil	2.0	0.8	2.2	0.1	0.3	0.1
NORTH AMERICA	0.4	0.6	0.6	1.0	2.2	1.9
WESTERN EUROPE	3.1	3.1	2.8	6.9	5.6	4.9
EEC 3/	2.0	2.3	2.1	5.1	4.4	4.0
EASTERN EUROPE	3.5	2.6	2.6	3.6	4.8	5.2
U.S.S.R.	21.3	15.0	12.0	8.5	24.0	23.0
OCEANIA	0.4	0.3	0.3	0.1	0.1	-
Unspecified	-	-	1.9	-	-	1.0
WORLD	104.7	95.9	96.0	81.4	96.6	98.0
Developing countries	69.6	68.4	71.3	37.9	37.1	39.5
Developed countries	35.1	27.5	24.7	43.5	59.5	58.5

Note: Totals computed from unrounded data.

1/ Including wheat flour in wheat equivalent. 2/ Including Taiwan Province. 3/ Excluding trade between the twelve EEC member countries.

SOURCE: FAO, *Food Outlook,* March 1990.

TABLE 19 Basic Facts of the World Cereal Situation

	1985/86	1986/87	1987/88	1988/89 estimate	1989/90 forecast	Change 1989/90 over 1988/89
WORLD PRODUCTION 1/	(.		*million tons*		)	(*. . percentage . .*)
Rice (paddy)	474	471	466	491	509	+ 3.7
Wheat	506	536	511	506	537	+ 6.0
Coarse grains	862	848	814	748	822	+ 9.8
All cereals	1 842	1 855	1 791	1 746	1 868	+ 7.0
Developing countries	928	941	934	983	991	+ 0.9
Developed countries	914	914	857	763	876	+14.8
WORLD IMPORTS 2/						
Rice (milled)	12	12	11	14	13	− 7.3
Wheat	84	88	105	96	96	+ 0.1
Coarse grains	85	86	81	97	98	+ 1.4
All cereals	181	185	197	206	207	+ 0.3
Developing countries	99	107	116	117	121	+ 3.5
Developed countries	82	78	81	89	86	− 4.0
FOOD AID IN CEREALS 3/	10.9	12.6	13.5	10.0	11.6	+16.0
WORLD STOCKS 4/						
Rice (milled)	58	54	44	46	51	+11.8
Wheat	161	167	142	116	116	− 0.3
Coarse grains	208	234	212	144	126	−12.5
All cereals	426	455	399	306	293	− 4.2
Developing countries	137	136	123	123	129	+ 5.3
Developed countries	289	319	276	183	164	−10.6
Stocks as % of world cereal consumption	(.	*percentage*			)	
	26	27	24	18	17	
EXPORT PRICES 3/	(.	*U.S.$/ton*			)	
Rice (Thai, 100%) 1/	188	186	220	284	305 5/	+ 7.4 7/
Wheat (U.S. No.1 Hard Winter)	128	109	122	166	166 6/	+ 3.4 7/
Maize (U.S. No.2 Yellow)	105	73	86	118	106 6/	−11.4 7/
OCEAN FREIGHT RATES 3/						
From U.S. Gulf to Egypt	21.3	21.2	20.7	26.6	30.6 6/	+22.4 7/
LOW-INCOME FOOD-DEFICIT COUNTRIES 8/	(.	*million tons*			)	
Roots & tubers production 1/	286	280	291	293	296	+ 1.0
Pulses production 1/	26	28	24	26	27	+ 3.8
Cereal Production 1/	705	726	715	758	786	+ 3.6
Per caput production (kg.)	242	245	236	245	249	+ 1.6
Cereal imports 2/	44	47	54	57	52	− 8.9
of which: Food aid 3/	10.0	11.1	11.5	8.3	8.5	+ 2.4
Proportion of cereal imports covered by food aid	(.	*percentage*			)	
	23	24	21	15	16	
Value of commercial cereal imports 3/	(.	*million U.S.$.*			)	
	5 500	4 800	6 900	10 100	9 000	−10.9
Prices of selected major exports 1/	(.	*U.S.$/ton*			)	
Coffee (I.C.O., 1979, daily price)	2 942	3 768	2 379	2 735	2 022 5/	−26.1 7/
Cocoa (I.C.C.O., daily price)	2 241	2 068	1 997	1 504	1 240 5/	−17.6 7/
Sugar (I.S.A., daily price)	90	133	148	247	282 5/	+14.2 7/
Jute (B.W.C., f.o.b. C.-Chalna)	613	326	389	440	440 5/	− 7/
Tea (London, all tea)	2 014	1 930	1 688	1 790	2 054 5/	+14.7 7/

Note: Totals and percentages computed from unrounded data.

1/ Data refer to the calendar year of the first year shown. 2/ July/June except for rice for which the data refer to the calendar year of the second year shown. 3/ July/June. 4/ Stock data are based on aggregate of national carryover levels at the end of national crop years. 5/ Average of quotations for January-December 1989. 6/ Average of quotations for July 1989-January 1990. 7/ Change from corresponding period of previous year for which figures are not shown. 8/ Includes all food deficit countries with per caput income below the level used by the World Bank to determine eligibility for IDA assistance (i.e. U.S.$ 1070 in 1988), which in accordance with the guidelines and criteria agreed to by the CFA should be given priority in the allocation of food aid.

SOURCE: FAO, *Food Outlook,* March 1990.

TABLE 20   Percent of Rice/Wheat Acreage in HYVs by 1983

REGION	RICE	WHEAT
China	95	18
India	54	80
Other Asia	40	70
Near East/North Africa	11	34
Sub-Saharan Africa	15	57
Latin America	29	82

SOURCE: CGIAR Secretariat, World Bank. *International Agricultural Research Centers: A Study of Achievements and Potential. Summary,* 1985.

TABLE 21   Total and Irrigated Cropland by Region

Region/country	Cropland 1961-65	1986	Irrigated area 1961-65	1986	Irrigated area as percent of cropland 1961-65	1986
	--------- Million ha ---------				Percent	
World	1,334	1,474	149	228	11	15
North America	222	236	15	19	7	8
Latin America	116	176	10	15	9	8
Europe 1/	152	140	9	16	6	11
USSR	229	232	10	20	4	9
Sub-Saharan Africa	123	159	3	7	2	4
N. Africa and M. East	81	108	14	23	17	21
South Asia	201	209	40	66	20	32
Southeast Asia	62	74	9	13	15	18
China 2/	104	98	39	45	38	46
Other East Asia	80	70	22	20	28	29
Oceania	34	49	1	2	3	4

1/ Excludes USSR.   2/ Excludes Taiwan.

SOURCE: USDA/ERS, *World Agriculture Situation and Outlook,* June 1989.

TABLE 22 Percentage of Irrigated Land Affected by Salinization, 1984

Region/country	Percent	Region/country	Percent
Africa:		**Europe:**	
Egypt	30-40	Portugal	10-15
Senegal	10-15	Spain	10-15
Sudan	15-20		
		United States	20-25
Asia:			
China	15	**South America:**	
India	27	Colombia	20
Iraq	50	Peru	12
Iran	25-30		
Pakistan	35-40	Australia	15-20

SOURCE: USDA/ERS, *World Agriculture Situation and Outlook,* June 1989.

TABLE 23 Volume of Food Aid Contributions, Principal Commodities

Commodity/country	1981/82	1982/83	1983/84	1984/85	1985/86	1986/87	1987/88	Estimated shipments [1]/ 1988/89	1989/90
				1,000 metric tons (grain equivalent [2])					
Grains [3]	9140	9238	9849	12510	10949	12579	13382	9757	9400
Argentina	20	33	30	51	44	24	25	35	30
Australia	485	349	460	466	345	368	328	330	300
Canada	600	843	817	943	1216	1240	1062	1000	900
European Community [4]	1602	1596	1917	2505	1614	1863	2450	2000	2000
Finland	9	28	40	20	5	41	3	25	25
Japan	507	517	445	295	450	529	547	380	350
Norway	36	36	17	45	31	46	54	30	30
Sweden	119	87	83	88	69	74	115	80	40
Switzerland	22	29	30	39	22	58	74	27	27
United States	5341	5375	5655	7536	6675	7861	7946	5500	5400
Others	399	345	355	522	478	455	778	350	298
Other commodities [5]	1982	1983	1984	1985	1986	1987	1988	1989	1990
Vegetable oils	346	342	345	384	513	600	NA	NA	NA
United States	300	290	271	310	418	501	NA	NA	NA
Others	46	52	74	74	95	99	NA	NA	NA
Dairy products	334	320	463	432	436	371	NA	NA	NA
United States	129	168	196	273	293	226	NA	NA	NA
Others	205	152	267	159	143	145	NA	NA	NA

NA = Not available.

1 / Estimates based on minimum contributions under the 1986 Food Aid Convention, budgetary allocations, historical patterns, current food aid policies, and other sources.

2 / To express cereal food aid in grain equivalent, wheat, rice and coarse grains are counted on a one-to-one basis; for grain products, appropriate conversion factors are used to determine the grain equivalent.

3 July-June trade years

4 Aid from individual members as well as Community actions. Ten member countries, prior to accession of Portugal and Spain.

5 Calendar years.

SOURCE: USDA/ERS, *World Food Needs & Availabilities 1989/90,* Summer Update.

TABLE 24   Major Donors to WFP by Type of Pledge or Contribution

BIENNIUM 1987-88 AS OF 31/12/1988[1]
US$ million

RANK	TOTAL		REGULAR PLEDGES		IEFR		NON-FOOD ITEMS	
	DONOR	VALUE	DONOR	VALUE	DONOR	VALUE	DONOR	VALUE
1	UNITED STATES	346.0	CANADA	257.9	UNITED STATES	95.6	NETHERLANDS	10.3
2	CANADA	293.5	UNITED STATES	250.0	CEC[2]	40.4	SWEDEN	7.9
3	CEC[2]	186.7	CEC[2]	146.0	CANADA	34.7	ITALY	2.4
4	NETHERLANDS	112.0	NETHERLANDS	85.4	GERMANY, F. REP.	30.4	JAPAN	2.1
5	GERMANY, F. REP.	88.9	AUSTRALIA	70.7	SWEDEN	28.0	NORWAY	2.0
6	SWEDEN	86.7	GERMANY, F. REP.	58.0	SWITZERLAND	19.6	FRANCE	1.9
7	AUSTRALIA	81.8	DENMARK	57.3	NETHERLANDS	16.3	FINLAND	1.5
8	NORWAY	69.9	FINLAND	52.0	UNITED KINDOM	13.6	AUSTRALIA	1.2
9	FINLAND	66.9	SWEDEN	50.8	FINLAND	133	CANADA	0.9
							SWITZERLAND	0.9
10	DENMARK	61.2	NORWAY	49.1	ITALY	9.9	GERMANY, F.REP	0.5
					AUSTRALIA	9.9		
11	ITALY	47.9	ITALY	35.6	JAPAN	8.0	UNITED STATES	0.4
12	JAPAN	36.1	SAUDI ARABIA	30.0	FRANCE	7.7	CEC[2]	0.3
							UNITED KINGDOM	0.3
							INDIVIDUALS	0.3
13	SWITZERLAND	31.3	JAPAN	26.0	NORWAY	6.8	UNESCO	0.2
							AJWS[3]	0.2
14	UNITED KINGDOM	30.9	UNITED KINGDOM	17.0	DENMARK	3.9	BAND AID	0.1
							USAFA[4]	0.1
15	SAUDI ARABIA	30.0	FRANCE	12.3	SPAIN	3.4	SOROPTIMIST INT	0.0[5]
16	FRANCE	22.0	SWITZERLAND	10.8	BELGIUM	1.9		
17	BELGIUM	9.4	BELGIUM	7.5	AUSTRIA	1.1		
18	AUSTRIA	8.1	AUSTRIA	7.0	GREECE	0.2		
19	ARGENTINA	4.0	ARGENTINA	4.0	LESOTHO	0.0[5]		
20	SPAIN	3.9	IRELAND	2.1				

1 Details and percentages do not necessarily add
   to totals because of rounding.
2 Commission of the European Communities
3 American Jewish World Service
4 U.S. Artists for Africa
5 A zero indicates that the magnitude is less than
   half the unit used

SOURCE: WFP, *Annual Report 1988.*

TABLE 25 1990 Food Aid Requirements for Persons of Concern to UNHCR

Sub-Region/ Country	1990 Food Aid Requirements	
	Cereals	Non-cereals
	(thousand tons)	
Sub-Saharan Africa	459.0	128.6
of which:		
Ethiopia (west)	76.7	28.3
Ethiopia (east)	63.9	20.6
Malawi	119.0	34.2
Somalia	92.0	15.4
Sudan	31.0	10.1
North Africa, Near East[1]	551.5	62.0
of which:		
Iran, Isl. Rep. of[2]	45.4	5.4
Pakistan	493.0	49.0
Asia, Oceania	35.6	14.3
of which:		
Thailand	17.5	0.2
Latin America, Caribbean	11.0	6.4
of which:		
Mexico	4.2	1.7
TOTAL	1,057.1	211.3

[1]Excluding Afghanistan
[2]Afghan and Iraqi Kurds

SOURCE: FAO, *Food Outlook,* March 1990.

TABLE 26   International Emergency Food Reserve, 1988 and 1989

Commodity/ Donor		Channelled through UN/FAO WFP	of which: Donated specifically for Afghan refugees	Bilateral	Total Contributions
		(.......................... tons ....)			
Year 1988					
Cereals 1/		439 998	94 000	27 000	466 998
Non cereals		92 718	6 725	2 195	94 913
Year 1989					
Cereals 1/		365 616	—	25 000	390 616
Australia		5 000	—	25 000	30 000
Austria		2 080	—	—	2 080
Canada		13 080	—	—	13 080
Denmark		2 976	—	—	2 976
EEC		55 564	—	—	55 564
Finland		1 135	—	—	1 135
Germany, F.R.		32 000	—	—	32 000
Greece		549	—	—	549
Iceland		17	—	—	17
India		200	—	—	200
Italy		7 500	—	—	7 500
Japan		22 000	—	—	22 000
Lesotho		27	—	—	27
Mauritius		4	—	—	4
Netherlands		7 372	—	—	7 372
Norway		8 388	—	—	8 388
Spain		4 000	—	—	4 000
Sri Lanka		178	—	—	178
Sweden		40 000	—	—	40 000
Switzerland		8 169	—	—	8 169
United Kingdom		15 464	—	—	15 464
United States		139 913	—	—	139 913
Pulses		**12 052**	—	—	**12 052**
Canada		1 811	—	—	1 811
Denmark		2 030	—	—	2 030
EEC		3 390	—	—	3 390
Finland		1 150	—	—	1 150
Germany, Fed. Rep.		1 716	—	—	1 716
United States		1 955	—	—	1 955
Vegetable oils/edible fat		**14 774**	—	—	**14 774**
Denmark		124	—	—	124
EEC		4 000	—	—	4 000
Finland		2 500	—	—	2 500
Sweden		2 500	—	—	2 500
United States		5 650	—	—	5 650
Dried skim milk/whole milk		**437**	—	—	**437**
Canada		137	—	—	137
Finland		100	—	—	100
Switzerland		200	—	—	200
Others		**6 850**	—	—	**6 850**
Canada	(fish)	275	—	—	275
Denmark	(sugar)	2 000	—	—	2 000
EEC	(sugar)	108	—	—	108
Finland	(canned meat)	250	—	—	250
"	(butteroil)	1 600	—	—	1 600
Norway	(biscuits)	18	—	—	18
Switzerland	(fish)	200	—	—	200
United States	(corn soya milk)	2 399	—	—	2 399
Total non cereals		**34 113**	—	—	**34 113**

1/ Includes wheat, coarse grains and rice.

SOURCE: FAO, *Food Outlook,* March 1990.

TABLE 27   Allocation of P.L. 480 Aid by Program, 1989

FY 1989, PL-480 Value of Commodities Shipped

($ in Millions)

Program	Total	% of Total
Title I	642.9	53.4%
Title II		38.6%
Food for Development		
MCH-CF	98.8	8.2%
SF	78.6	6.5%
FFW	70.8	5.9%
Emergency	186.0	15.4%
Refugee and Other	30.0	2.5%
Title III	97.0	8.1%
	1,204.1	100.1%

Notes: MCH-CF (Maternal Child Health-Child Feeding), SF (School Feeding), FFW (Food for Work). Source: Table 16b of USAID FY89 approvals of P.L.-480 TitleI/II Section 416 aid, December 29, 1989.

SOURCE: National Council for International Health, *Healthlink,* May 1990, based on data from USAID, *Report to Congress FY89.*

TABLE 28   Allocation of P.L. 480 Aid by Recipients

	($US millions) total	($US) per capita
Africa	173,627	0.34
Asia	331,357	0.12
Latin America	242,024	0.56
El Salvador	39,413	7.31
Egypt	171,295	3.21

SOURCE: National Council for International Health, *Healthlink,* May 1990, based on data from USAID, *Congressional Presentation for FY 1990.*

Table 29   Regional Distribution of ODA by Percent

REGION	1975–1976	1980–1981	1987–1988
Sub-Saharan Africa	19.7	25.8	34.5
North Africa	29.2	24.6	14.3
Asia	34.2	31.8	33.4
Latin America	12.2	11.3	13.0

SOURCE: IMF, *IMF Survey,* 5 February 1990, from data in OECD/DAC, *Development Cooperation,* 1989.

FIGURES

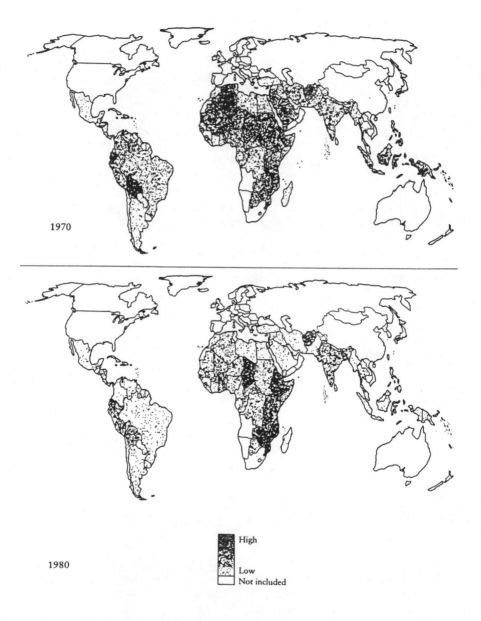

1970

1980

High

Low
Not included

FIGURE 1   The Prevalence of Energy-Deficient Diets, 1970 and 1980.
Source: World Bank, *Poverty and Hunger,* 1986.

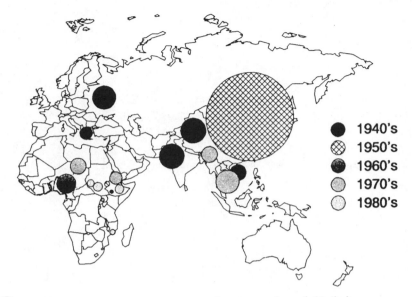

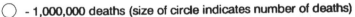

○ - 1,000,000 deaths (size of circle indicates number of deaths)

FIGURE 2   Major Famines. *Source:* USDA/ERS, *World Agriculture Situation and Outlook,* June 1989.

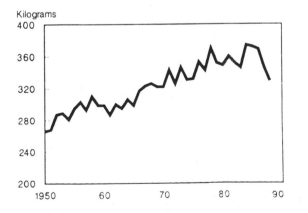

FIGURE 3   World per Capita Grain Production, 1950–1990. *Source:* USDA/ERS, *World Agriculture Situation and Outlook,* June 1989.

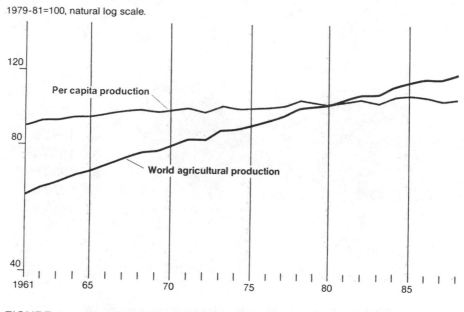

1979-81=100, natural log scale.

FIGURE 4   World Agricultural Output Plateaus. *Source:* USDA/ERS, *Agricultural Outlook,* Jan.–Feb. 1990.

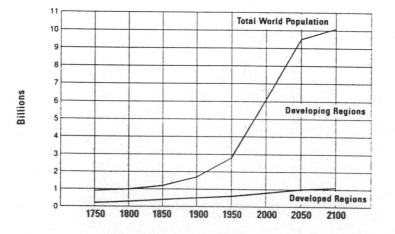

FIGURE 5   Population Growth, 1750–2100. *Source:* Thomas W. Merrick, "World Population in Transition," *Population Bulletin* 4:2, Population Reference Bureau.

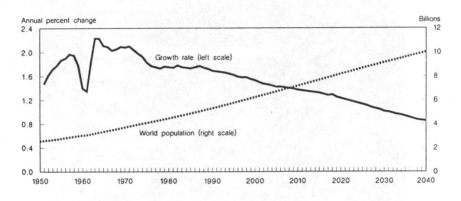

FIGURE 6   World Population and Population Growth Rate. *Source:*
              USDA/ERS, *World Agriculture Situation and Outlook,*
              June 1989.

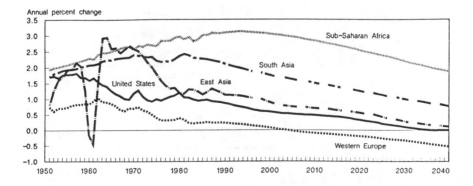

FIGURE 7   Population Growth Rates: Selected Regions. *Source:*
              USDA/ERS, *World Agriculture Situation and Outlook,*
              June 1989.

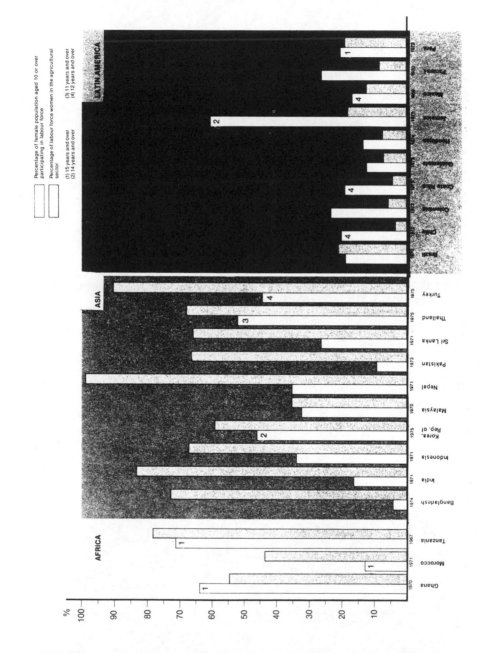

FIGURE 8   Women in Agricultural Production. *Source:* FAO, *Women in Agriculture,* 1983, from U.S. Census Bureau data in *Revised Illustrative Statistics on Women in Selected Developing Countries,* 1980.

Total waking hours: 15 hrs 30 mins

FIGURE 9   Time Spent on Daily Domestic Activities in a Pakistani Village. *Source:* FAO, *Women in Agriculture,* 1983, based on Ruth Dixon, *Rural Women at Work.*

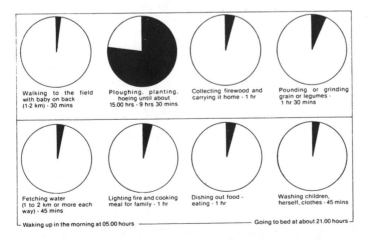

FIGURE 10   Typical Workday for Zambian Women during the Planting Season. *Source:* FAO, *Women in Agriculture,* with data from the Women's Programme Unit, U.N. Economic Commission for Africa, 1974.

In many countries it is women who dominate the
informal sector – the small-scale trade in goods and
services not usually counted in national economic
statistics.
In many Third World cities the informal sector
generates up to a third of local wealth.

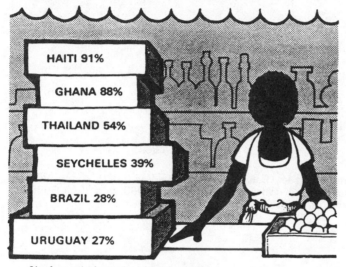

HAITI 91%

GHANA 88%

THAILAND 54%

SEYCHELLES 39%

BRAZIL 28%

URUGUAY 27%

% of people in trade who are women

FIGURE 11   The Entrepreneur. *Source:* U.N. Population Fund,
State of the World's Women Report 1985.

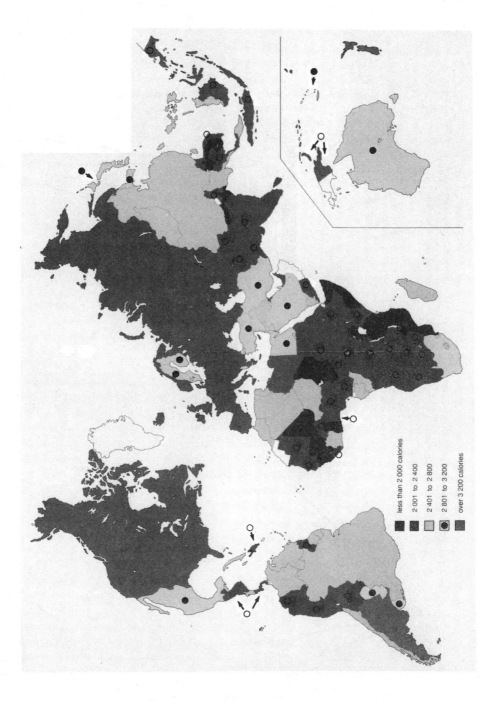

FIGURE 12   Average Daily Calorie Supply per Person 1979–1981.
Source: FAO, *World Hunger,* 1985.

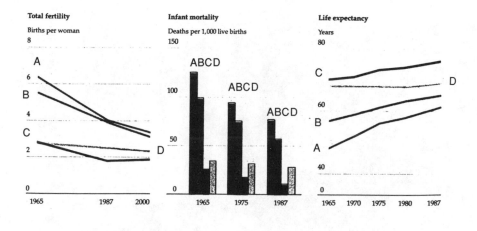

Total fertility

Births per woman

Infant mortality

Deaths per 1,000 live births

Life expectancy

Years

A Low-income economies
B Middle-income economies

C High-income economies
D Nonreporting nonmember economies

FIGURE 13   Fertility and Mortality. *Source:* World Bank,
World Development Report 1989.

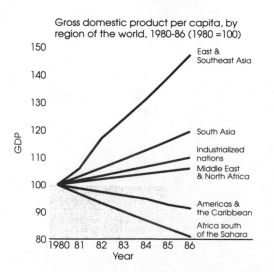

Gross domestic product per capita, by
region of the world, 1980-86 (1980 =100)

East &
Southeast Asia

South Asia

Industrialized
nations

Middle East
& North Africa

Americas &
the Caribbean

Africa south
of the Sahara

GDP

Year

FIGURE 14   Economic Trends. *Source:* UNICEF, *State of the
World's Children 1989.*

The infant mortality rate (the number of deaths before the age of one per 1,000 live births) is an indicator not just of the quantity of deaths but also of the quality of life for surviving mothers and children. The chart below, showing changes in the infant mortality rate for the different regions of Brazil, shows that it is the poorest groups who are carrying the heaviest burden of the present economic crisis. The great majority of Brazil's poorest live in the northern, and especially the north-eastern, regions.

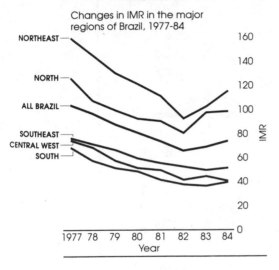

Changes in IMR in the major regions of Brazil, 1977-84

FIGURE 15   Rising Infant Deaths in Brazil. *Source:* UNICEF, *State of the World's Children 1989.*

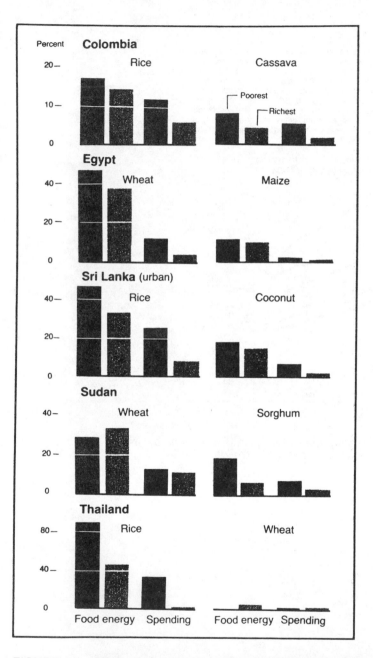

FIGURE 16   Staple Foods and the Poor. Compared with the richest 10 percent of the population, the poorest 10 percent get a larger share of their food energy from staple foods and devote a larger share of their food expenditures to staples. *Source:* CGIAR Secretariat, World Bank, *International Agricultural Research Centers: A Study of Achievements and Potential. Summary,* 1985.

AFRICA

Cereals..	46%
Animal products......................	7%
Roots and tubers....................	20%

LATIN AMERICA

Cereals..	41%
Animal products......................	18%
Roots and tubers....................	6%

NEAR EAST

Cereals..	61%
Animal products......................	10%
Roots and tubers....................	2%

FAR EAST

Cereals..	69%
Animal products......................	5%
Roots and tubers....................	3%

ASIAN CENTRALLY PLANNED ECONOMIES

Cereals..	67%
Animal products......................	10%
Roots and tubers....................	8%

OTHER DEVELOPING COUNTRIES

Cereals..	22%
Animal products......................	13%
Roots and tubers....................	28%

NORTH AMERICA

Cereals..	19%
Animal products......................	38%
Roots and tubers....................	3%

WESTERN EUROPE

Cereals..	26%
Animal products......................	33%
Roots and tubers....................	4%

OCEANIA

Cereals..	25%
Animal products......................	37%
Roots and tubers....................	4%

EASTERN EUROPE AND THE USSR

Cereals..	38%
Animal products......................	28%
Roots and tubers....................	6%

OTHER DEVELOPED COUNTRIES

Cereals..	46%
Animal products......................	19%
Roots and tubers....................	2%

FIGURE 17   Percentage of Major Staple Foods in the Diet.
Source: FAO, *A Guide to Staple Foods of the World,* 1984.

Where rice is grown...

China	34%
India	20%
Indonesia	7%
Bangladesh	5%

Other producers include: Japan. Thailand. Viet Nam. Brazil. Burma. the Republic of Korea. Philippines. USA. the Democratic People's Republic of Korea. Pakistan.

Where wheat is grown...

USSR	19%
USA	17%
China	12%
India	8%
Canada	5%

Other producers include: Turkey. France. Australia. Argentina. Italy. Pakistan. Germany F-R.. Romania. Iran. Portugal. Yugoslavia. Hungary. Czechoslovakia. U.K.. Spain.

Where millet is grown...

India	35%
China	19%
Nigeria	11%
USSR	6%

Other producers include: the Niger. Egypt. Mali. Uganda. Chad. Senegal.

Where sorghum is grown...

USA	36%
India	17%
Argentina	10%
Nigeria	7%
Mexico	7%

Other producers include: the Sudan. the Yemen Arab Republic. Ethiopia the Upper Volta. Uganda.

Where cassava is grown...

Brazil	20%
Thailand	14%
Indonesia	11%
Zaire	10%
Nigeria	9%

Other producers include: Tanzania. Viet Nam. China. Mozambique. Philippines. Colombia. Paragay.

Where maize is grown...

USA	47%
China	10%
Brazil	5%

Other producers include: Romania. the USSR. Mexico. Yugoslavia. S. Africa. India. Argentina. France. Hungary. Italy. Canada.

Where cow-milk is produced...

USSR	21%
USA	14%
France	8%
Germany F-R.	6%
U.K.	4%
Poland	4%

Other producers include: India, the Netherlands. Brazil. Italy. Canada. Mexico. New Zealand. Spain. Japan. Czechoslovakia. China.

Where potatoes are grown...

USSR	30%
Poland	17%
China	6%
USA	6%

Other producers include: Germany F-R.. India. Spain. Germany D-R.. the Netherlands. UK. Czechoslovakia. France. Japan. Romania. Italy.

Where meat is produced...

USA	18%
China	16%
USSR	11%
France	4%
Brazil	3%
Germany F-R.	3%

Other producers include: Argentina. Italy. Japan. U.K.. Australia. Spain. Canada. Poland.

FIGURE 18   Major Producers of Staple Foods. *Source:* FAO, *A Guide to Staple Foods of the World,* 1984.

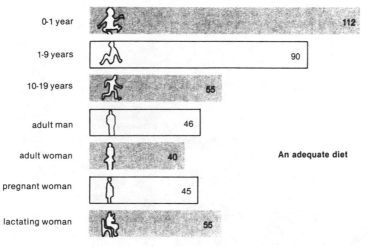

0-1 year	112
1-9 years	90
10-19 years	55
adult man	46
adult woman	40
pregnant woman	45
lactating woman	55

An adequate diet

energy requirement (kcal/kg bodyweight/day)

FIGURE 19   An Adequate Diet. *Source:* FAO, *A Guide to Staple Foods of the World,* 1984.

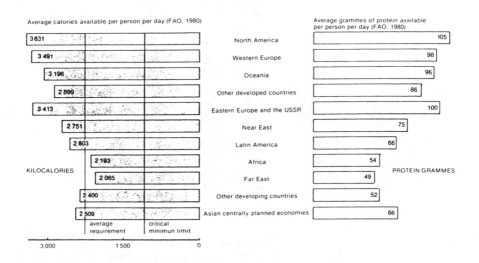

Average calories available per person per day (FAO. 1980)

Average grammes of protein available per person per day (FAO. 1980)

Region	Kilocalories	Protein grammes
North America	3 631	105
Western Europe	3 491	98
Oceania	3 196	96
Other developed countries	2 899	86
Eastern Europe and the USSR	3 413	100
Near East	2 751	75
Latin America	2 603	66
Africa	2 193	54
Far East	2 085	49
Other developing countries	2 400	52
Asian centrally planned economies	2 509	66

average requirement   critical minimun limit

3 000   1 500   0

FIGURE 20   How Diets Differ. *Source:* FAO, *A Guide to Staple Foods of the World,* 1984.

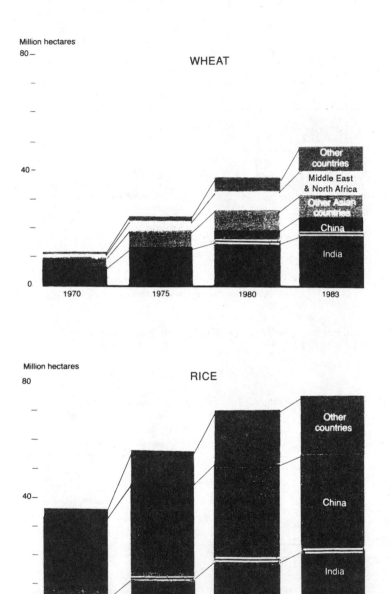

FIGURE 21 Land in New Wheats and New Rices. Estimated area planted to modern wheat or rice, respectively, in developing countries. *Source:* CGIAR Secretariat, World Bank, *International Agricultural Research Centers: A Study of Achievements and Potential. Summary,* 1985.

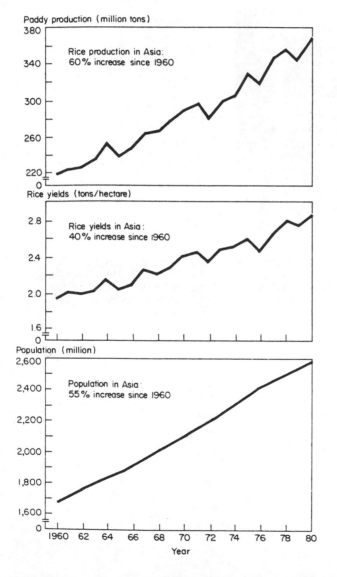

FIGURE 22   The Race between Population and Rice in Asia. *Source:*
M. S. Swaminathan, Third World Foundation Lecture, 1983.

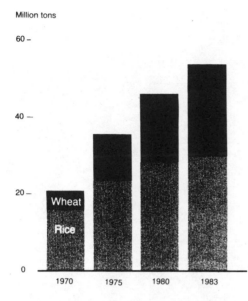

Million tons

60 –

40 —

20 –

0

Wheat

Rice

1970   1975   1980   1983

FIGURE 23   More Food. Estimated additional foodgrain produced by
modern wheat and rice varieties.*Source:* CGIAR Secretariat,
World Bank, *International Agricultural Research Centers:
A Study of Achievements and Potential. Summary,* 1985.

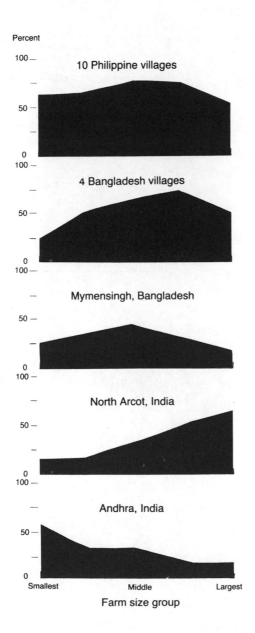

FIGURE 24   Farm Size and Adopters of Modern Varieties. Proportion of farmers in different farm-size groups who grow modern rice varieties. *Source:* CGIAR Secretariat, World Bank, *International Agricultural Research Centers: A Study of Achievements and Potential. Summary,* 1985.

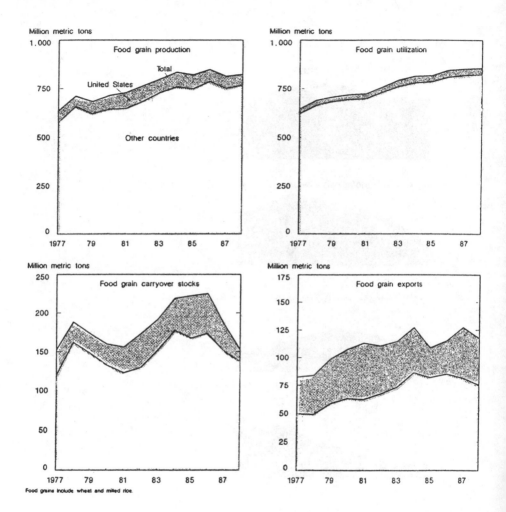

FIGURE 25   World and U.S. Food Grain Production, Utilization, Carryover, and Exports. *Source:* USDA/ERS, *1989 Agriculture Chartbook.*

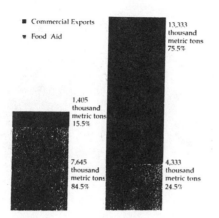

- ■ Commercial Exports
- ▼ Food Aid

1,405
thousand
metric tons
15.5%

13,333
thousand
metric tons
75.5%

7,645
thousand
metric tons
84.5%

4,333
thousand
metric tons
24.5%

FIGURE 26 · U.S. Food Exports: Increasingly Commercial. 1962 and 1987,
U.S. Wheat Exports to LDCs. *Source:* USAID, *Development
and the National Interest. A Report by the Administrator,* 1989.

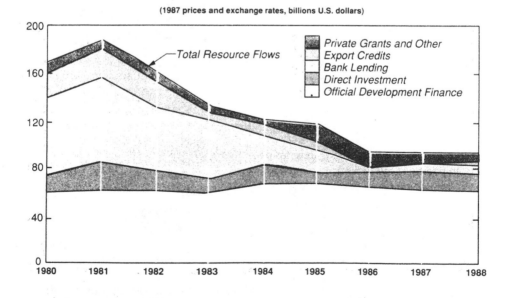

(1987 prices and exchange rates, billions U.S. dollars)

Total Resource Flows

- Private Grants and Other
- Export Credits
- Bank Lending
- Direct Investment
- Official Development Finance

FIGURE 27 Total Net Resource Flows from All Sources. *Source:* IMF,
IMF Survey, 5 February 1990, data from OECD/DAC,
Development Cooperation, 1989.

OECD aid distribution by groups of
developing countries at different
income levels,1985/86

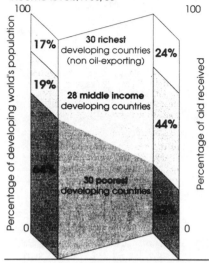

FIGURE 28   Where Aid Goes.
              Source: UNICEF,
              State of the World's
              Children 1989.

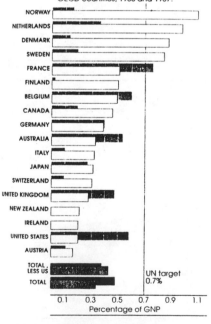

The chart below lists the aid-giving nations in order
of the percentage of their GNP's given in official
development aid. The shadow bar shows the
percentage given in 1965. Only four out of eighteen
countries have reached the UN target of 0.7% of GNP

Official development assistance
as percentage of donor GNP,
OECD countries, 1965 and 1987.

FIGURE 29   The Aid League. *Source:*
              UNICEF, *State of the*
              World's Children 1989,
              from OECD/DAC data,
              1988.

5

Organizations

THE PROGRAMMATIC APPROACHES AND OPERATING STYLES of organizations working to end hunger truly run the gamut: from top-down, centrally administered, multimillion-dollar food aid administration to low-key, small-scale support for disadvantaged groups who manage their own food security; from technical research in biological and social sciences to voluntary efforts to educate the populations of industrialized countries about the systemic causes of hunger; from high-level policy analysis for United Nations agencies and government ministries to advocacy from humanitarian organizations pressuring governments and other agencies for more effective responses to the problem of hunger.

Research, problem analysis, and policy advocacy are emphasized in this chapter, rather than material aid and technical assistance or public information and education. A few of the organizations described—such as UNICEF, the World Bank, and USAID—do all of these things. However, the only organizations included here are those that play a major role in influencing the policies of governments and development agencies that affect hungry people.

This criterion omits more than 100 organizations in the United States alone that are doing other important things about hunger, among them such well-known agencies as CARE, The Hunger Project, Save the Children, World Vision, Heifer Project, Oxfam America, World Neighbors, World Hunger Year, and

many, many more. Readers seeking information about these miss-
ing organizations are referred to *Who's Involved with Hunger—An
Organization Guide for Education and Advocacy* (World Hunger
Education Service, P.O. Box 29056, Washington, DC 20017) and
InterAction Member Profiles, 1989 (American Council for Voluntary
International Action, 200 Park Avenue South, New York, NY
10003).

Agencies of the United Nations

Multifaceted Involvement with Hunger

Food and Agriculture Organization of the United Nations (FAO)
Via delle Terme di Caracalla
00100 Rome, Italy
(011-396) 5797 3434
Edouard Saouma, Director-General

FAO North American Liaison Office
1001 Twenty-second Street, NW, Suite 300
Washington, DC 20437
(202) 653-2400
Roger Sorenson, Director

FAO is the oldest, largest, and most diversified of U.N. agencies doing
research and providing technical assistance to increase agricultural
production, promote human nutrition, and better the conditions of
rural populations. Proposed at the International Conference on Food
and Agriculture (attended by World War II Allied Powers) in 1943 at Hot
Springs, Virginia, and founded at the first FAO Conference in Quebec,
Canada, on 16 October 1945, FAO is a cooperative association governed
and funded by its 144 member nations. Funding for particular projects
and special services comes also from the U.N. Development Programme,
other U.N. agencies, and governments requesting technical assistance.
World Food Day, a consciousness-raising event observed worldwide each
year since 1981, falls on 16 October to commemorate FAO's founding.

Among the institutions of world agriculture, FAO is exceeded in
size only by the U.S. Department of Agriculture. The FAO secretariat
includes more than 3,000 professional planners, researchers, database
managers, nutrition and agriculture scientists, and technicians: 1,000
working in Rome and 2,000 in regional offices and field projects.

Early in its history, FAO created the concept of a national "food
balance sheet" to analyze food adequacy in terms of the adequacy of
annual dietary energy supplies available per capita. A global assess-

ment, similarly conceived, is done periodically. The fifth World Food Survey was published in 1985.

In the 1950s, as U.N. attention shifted from postwar recovery in Europe to the needs of the poor in countries of the less economically developed regions, the U.N. General Assembly asked FAO to be the U.N.'s representative in promoting agrarian reform and rural development. In this role, FAO hosted the U.N.'s 1979 World Conference on Agrarian Reform and Rural Development (WCARRD). FAO continues to monitor national implementation of WCARRD resolutions advocating greater equity for the poor majority in rural development policy and programs. Prior to WCARRD, concern for women in FAO's work was limited to conventional concepts of home economics. Since 1979, the economic roles and potential of women in rural development have gained more prominence at FAO, as they have elsewhere.

FAO's Global Information and Early Warning System (GIEWS) was initiated immediately following the World Food Conference of 1974 (which FAO also hosted) to help prevent food crises in developing countries. The GIEWS provides all participating governments with periodic data on current and projected food requirements and supplies in critical countries. Weather and crop data from remote sensing by satellite programs of the United States, European Space Agency, France, Japan, and the U.S.S.R. contribute to GIEWS assessments and projections.

Together with the U.N. General Assembly, FAO sponsors the World Food Programme, the food aid agency designed by FAO in 1961 at the request of the General Assembly.

"Agriculture" at FAO includes forestry and fisheries along with animal husbandry, food, forage, and fiber crops. Research and technical assistance focus on products and projects considered significant by FAO's member governments. The national delegations who determine FAO's policies are dominated by ministries of agriculture. Agricultural significance has been viewed by agricultural ministries traditionally in terms of conventional commerce and expansion of profitable exports. A serious deficiency in agricultural planning from that perspective alone is that it tends to bypass the needs and potential of smallholder farmers (including women) and landless rural households. It also tends to ignore crops of little interest for international trade, regardless of the importance of such crops in local consumption.

The dominance of conventional agricultural commerce in the priorities and perspectives of FAO's activities helps explain the creation following the 1974 World Food Conference of the International Fund for Agricultural Development and of the World Food Council. FAO assists both of these newer organizations in the U.N. system.

FAO's Investment Centre helps countries prepare agricultural development projects and works closely with the World Bank, regional development banks, Arab investment funds, and national banks to secure financing. Increasingly, such projects emphasize investments that will directly assist poor farmers.

FAO is governed by the FAO Conference, the all-member legislative body that meets every two years, and a 49-member Council that meets at least once a year as an interim governing body. Various committees of the Council work continuously. The Council and the FAO director-general are elected by the FAO Conference, which also establishes FAO's budget and policies.

PUBLICATIONS: Periodicals include *Ceres: The FAO Review, Food and Nutrition, The State of Food and Agriculture, Production Yearbook, Trade Yearbook, Food Outlook* (the GIEWS monthly report), the *Quarterly Bulletin of Statistics,* and *Agrindex,* prepared by the Agricultural Information System for Agricultural Sciences and Technology—AGRIS—which is hosted at FAO. (*Ideas and Action,* a popular forum for grassroots experience in developing countries sponsored by FAO's Freedom from Hunger/Action for Development Campaign, was discontinued in 1988.) Book-length reports of general interest include *FAO: Its Origins, Formation and Evolution 1945–1981,* by Ralph W. Phillips, and *FAO: The First 40 Years 1945–1985,* by the FAO staff.

The World Bank (International Bank for Reconstruction and Development—IBRD)
1818 H Street, NW
Washington, DC 20433
(202) 477-1234
Barber Conable, President

The World Bank (or IBRD) is involved with world hunger in four ways: (1) development policy advocacy, (2) loans to developing countries, (3) policy-oriented research and publications, and (4) participation in multi-agency activities such as the U.N. Administrative Committee on Coordination, Subcommittee on Nutrition (ACC/SCN) and the Consultative Group on International Agricultural Research (CGIAR) (see below for information about both agencies).

Founded in 1945, initially to promote post–World War II recovery, the IBRD is now owned by the governments of 151 member countries. The United States is the largest subscriber with Japan second. The IBRD finances its lending operations by borrowing (issuing bonds) in the world capital markets, backed by guarantees from its member governments. All World Bank loans are to support development progress in the less industrialized countries. China and India are currently the largest borrowers. More than 50 percent of the latest replenishment for funding by the International Development Association (IDA)—a subsidiary of the World Bank—is earmarked for Africa.

Regular IBRD loans charge normal interest, have a grace period of 5 years, and are repayable over 15 years or less. In 1961, the International Development Association (IDA) was established to make it possible for credit to be provided to lower income countries who could not afford regular loans from the bank and who could not qualify for credit from any other source. Membership in IDA is open to all members of the IBRD; 137 countries had joined the IDA by 1989. IDA loans, called credits, are extended only to governments; the terms include 10-year grace periods before repayment begins, 40 to 50 years to repay, and no interest charges. The funds for IDA credits come from contributions by IDA's more industrialized members and from transfers from the net earnings of the IBRD. The IBRD has made a profit every year since 1948. In allocating earnings, the bank's member countries give first priority to strengthening the bank's reserves; the balance is generally transferred to IDA.

The World Bank is not the largest source of financing for programs and projects in developing countries—private commercial banks lend far more—but it is the largest source of credit for agricultural development and the largest source of development financing for low-income countries (through IDA). By fiscal year 1988, cumulative lending to countries qualifying for IDA credits was $47.8 billion.

In the early 1970s, the bank began to concentrate more of its effort on activities that would benefit poor people directly. There was a major expansion of IDA and an expansion of lending for agriculture and rural development with the aim of increasing productivity and income among millions of small-scale farmers. When the momentum of Third World development halted under the impact of severe recession in the industrial countries and the international debt crisis in the early 1980s, the bank turned its attention to reforms of national policy in developing countries ("structural adjustment") as a means of combatting economic decline. To critics who claim that the bank has abandoned its 1970s zeal to aid the poor, the bank replies that economic decline is the greatest threat to the poor and that reforms can still protect those public expenditures of greatest importance to the poorest groups within national populations. (Note: The main author of the structural reform packages for debt-ridden developing countries that have added greatly to the burdens on the poor is the International Monetary Fund (IMF), a separate institution from the World Bank, but the two consult regularly and tend to share the same assumptions about economic growth. The IMF is a country's last resort for financial assistance in economic crisis.)

Since the early 1970s, the relationships between economic policy, poverty, and basic human needs have been frequent topics in the bank's research program. Environmental issues and participatory development were added to the research agenda in the 1980s. The link between the bank's research program and its lending operations, however, is tenuous. The board of directors, who determine lending policy and approve individual loans, are not bound by the findings of the bank's researchers.

PUBLICATIONS: (The bank is a prolific publisher; a free newsletter about its publications, *Publications Update,* is issued quarterly.) Periodicals include *The World Bank Economic Review* and *The World Bank Research Observer.* The annual *World Development Report* features a different topic each year (in 1990, the focus was "Poverty and Development"). Pertinent monographs include (among many others) *Fighting Malnutrition: An Evaluation of Brazilian Food and Nutrition Programs,* by Philip Musgrove (World Bank Discussion Paper No. 60, 1989); *Poverty and Hunger. Issues and Options for Food Security in Developing Countries,* by Shlomo Reutlinger and Jack van Holst Pellekaan (1986); and *Malnutrition. What Can Be Done?—Lessons from World Bank Experience,* by Alan Berg (1987).

World Food Council (WFC)
Via delle Terme di Caracalla
00100 Rome, Italy
(011-396) 5797 4510
Youssef Amin Wally, President
Gerald Ion Trant, Executive Director

World Food Council U.N. Liaison
United Nations
New York, NY 10017
(212) 963-4245

The World Food Council is the highest ministerial body within the U.N. system that deals with food. It was established by the U.N. General Assembly on 17 December 1974 to monitor and promote national and international implementation of the resolutions passed by the World Food Conference of November 1974 to eliminate hunger and prevent food crises. The overall objective is to establish reliable food security in every sense of that term. The power of persuasion is the council's only tool, a power derived from international consensus at the World Food Conference and from the prestige of the WFC delegates, president, and executive director. During its first two years, the council was critically instrumental in securing the financial commitments needed from donor nations to launch the International Fund for Agricultural Development (IFAD), the second new agency mandated by resolution of the 1974 World Food Conference.

The membership of the WFC consists of 36 nations, 12 of them newly nominated each year to the General Assembly by the U.N. Economic and Social Council. Each national delegation is led by a high-ranking minister with the ability to influence political will and raise financial resources in his or her home country to back the council's recommendations. The WFC meets in full Ministerial Session in May or June each year, hosted by a different country each time. For example, the Sixteenth Ministerial Session took place 21–24 May 1990 in Bangkok, Thailand. (WFC documents or actions commonly are referred to by location and number of the session.) WFC delegates may meet also in regional consultations between Ministerial Sessions, and the WFC executive director is in nearly constant consultation on concerns of the WFC with other U.N. agency leaders and with national governments.

The WFC secretariat is based at the headquarters of the Food and Agriculture Organization of the U.N., but the WFC is funded and administered separately from FAO. The background reports prepared for the annual Ministerial Session of the WFC by the WFC secretariat provide the most current and authoritative assessment available of the state of world progress toward the elimination of hunger. The WFC secretariat is assisted greatly in this annual research by FAO but also by other agencies within the U.N. system as needed.

PUBLICATIONS: The only WFC publications are reports prepared for the Ministerial Sessions. A few additional copies are available to researchers at no charge.

Specialty Agencies

Administrative Committee on Coordination–Subcommittee on Nutrition (ACC/SCN)
ACC/SCN Secretariat, Room X 48
c/o WHO Headquarters
Avenue Appia, 20
CH-1211 Geneva 27
Switzerland
(011-41-22) 7910456
Dr. John B. Mason, Technical Secretary

Dr. Abraham Horwitz, Chairman, ACC/SCN
Director Emeritus, Pan American Health Organization
525 Twenty-third Street, NW
Washington, DC 20037
(202) 861-3181

The ACC/SCN is the focal point for harmonizing the policies and activities in nutrition of the United Nations system. The Administrative Committee on Coordination (ACC), which is comprised of the heads of the U.N. agencies, recommended the establishment of the Subcommittee on Nutrition in 1977, with particular reference to Resolution V on food and nutrition at the 1974 World Food Conference. Establishment of the subcommittee was approved by the Economic and Social Council of the U.N. (ECOSOC). The role of the SCN is to serve as a coordinating mechanism for exchange of information and technical guidance and to act dynamically to help the U.N. respond to nutritional problems.

U.N.-system members of the SCN include FAO, World Food Programme, World Bank, UNICEF, WHO, World Food Council, IFAD, United Nations University, U.N. High Commissioner for Refugees, ILO, U.N. Development Programme, U.N. Environment Programme, UNESCO, U.N. Research Institute for Social Development, International Atomic Energy Commission, and the U.N. itself. The SCN is assisted by the Advisory Group on Nutrition (AGN), which is composed of 6 to 8 experienced individuals drawn from relevant disciplines and with wide geographical representation. Annual meetings of the SCN begin with symposia on topics of current policy importance and are attended by representatives of concerned U.N. agencies, representatives from 10 to 20 non-U.N. donor agencies, the AGN, and invitees on specific topics. The SCN sponsors working groups on specific problems.

PUBLICATIONS: *SCN News* (semi-annual); *World Nutrition Situation* (annual); and *Supplement on Methods and Statistics* (December 1989, re: the *First Report on the World Nutrition Situation*). ACC/SCN also publishes monographs in its State-of-the-Art series, for example, Nutrition Policy Discussion Papers 4 and 5: *Women's Roles in Food Chain Activities and Their Implications for Nutrition,* by Gerd Holmboe-Ottesen, Ophelia Mascarenhas, and Margareta Wandel (May 1989); and *Malnutrition and Infection—A Review,* by A. Tomkins and F. Watson (October 1989). The SCN also collaborates with the United Nations University in UNU's publication of *Food and Nutrition Bulletin,* edited by Nevin Scrimshaw (see Chapter 6, "References").

Consultative Group on International Agricultural Research (CGIAR)
CGIAR Secretariat
The World Bank
1818 H Street, NW
Washington, DC 20433
(202) 473-8949
Wilfried P. Thalwitz, Chairperson
Alexander von der Osten, Executive Secretary

CGIAR, established in 1971, is an association of countries, international and regional organizations, and private foundations dedicated to supporting a system of international agricultural research centers (IARCs) and programs around the world. The objective of the IARCs is to increase the quantity and improve the quality of food produced by farmers in developing countries. Each IARC sets its own agenda and is self-managed and independent of governments. The members of IARC governing boards usually serve as individuals rather than as representatives of their countries. The research teams are highly international. Research is problem-focused and interdisciplinary, and research findings are shared freely with governments and other agricultural research centers around the world.

Although not a U.N. agency, the CGIAR is closely affiliated with the U.N. system through its three sponsors: the World Bank, FAO, and the U.N. Development Programme (UNDP). The World Bank provides the CGIAR's chairperson and secretariat. A technical advisory committee is based at FAO. CGIAR has 50 members, most of whom also contribute funds. Private foundation members include the Ford Foundation, Kellogg Foundation, Leverhulme Trust, and Rockefeller Foundation.

Four CGIAR research centers were founded before CGIAR itself: IRRI, 1960; CIMMYT, 1963; IITA, 1968; and CIAT, 1969 (acronyms are explained below). IRRI and CIMMYT are best known to the public for the "Green Revolution" based on semi-dwarf rice and wheat varieties developed at these agencies. IRRI was sponsored by the Ford Foundation and the government of the Philippines; CIMMYT was started when the Ford Foundation joined the Rockefeller Foundation and the government of Mexico in revising a 20-year program of wheat and maize research in Mexico along the international pattern of IRRI.

The names of the 13 IARCs of the CGIAR system, the locations of their headquarters, and their research specialties are as follows: CIAT (Centro Internacional de Agricultura Tropical), in Cali, Colombia—phaseolus beans, cassava, rice, and tropical pastures; CIMMYT (Centro Internacional de Mejoramiento de Maiz y Trigo), in Mexico City—wheat, maize, triticale, and barley; CIP (Centro Internacional de la Papa), in Lima, Peru—potatoes; IBPGR (International Board for Plant Genetic Resources), at FAO in Rome—germplasm collection and conservation; ICARDA (International Center for Agricultural Research in the Dry Areas), in Aleppo, Syria—dryland farming systems of North Africa and the Middle East, barley, lentils, broadbeans, wheat, and chickpeas; ICRISAT (International Crops Research Institute for the Semi-Arid Tropics), in Hyderabad, India—sorghum, pigeonpeas, groundnuts, millet, chickpeas, and farming systems in the semi-arid tropics; IFPRI (International Food Policy Research Institute), 1776 Massachusetts Avenue, NW, Washington, D.C. 20036—food policy studies and responsibilities as the social science research center of CGIAR; IITA (International Institute of Tropical Agriculture), in Ibadan, Nigeria—rice, maize, cassava, cocoyam, cowpeas, yams, sweet potatoes, soybeans, and farming systems in the humid and sub-humid African tropics; ILRAD (International Laboratory for Research on Animal Diseases), in Nairobi, Kenya—trypanosomiasis (sleeping sickness) and theileriosis (a livestock disease); ILCA (International Livestock Center for Africa), in Addis Ababa, Ethiopia—livestock production systems in Africa; IRRI (International Rice Research Institute), in Manila, Philippines—rice and farming systems; ISNAR (International Service for National Agricultural Research), in The Hague, Netherlands—research development assistance for developing countries; and WARDA (West Africa Rice Development Association), in Monrovia, Liberia—rice.

IFPRI, under Director John Mellor, merits a special description. IFPRI was formed with private foundation support in 1975 as an independent, hunger-focused center of social science research in response to the need for such research that was revealed by the world food crisis of 1972–1974 and the 1974 World Food Conference. It became part of the CGIAR system in 1979. IFPRI's five key areas of research are national and international food data evaluation, national food production policy, agricultural growth linkages and development policy, food consumption and nutrition policy, and international food trade and food security. Since 1982 IFPRI has expanded its microeconomic research capabilities through involvement in data collection in the field at the level of households and farms.

PUBLICATIONS: Summary (34 pp.) of *International Agricultural Research Centers: A Study of Achievements and Potential* (1985); *Partners against Hunger,* by Warren C. Baum (1986); and *Annual Report.* Several IARCs also publish their own newsletters and other reports. IFPRI publications: *IFPRI Abstract* (a monthly 4-page summary of the policy implications of a recent research report); monographs in four series—Research Reports, Food Policy Statements, Working Papers, and IFPRI Policy Briefs; and *IFPRI Reports* (a quarterly newsletter).

International Fund for Agricultural Development (IFAD)
107, Via del Serafico
00142 Rome, Italy
(011-39-6) 54591
Idriss Jazairy, President

IFAD Information
c/o U.N. Information Center
1889 F Street, NW
Washington, DC 20006
(202) 289-8670
Vera Gathright, Information Officer

IFAD is the only agency in the U.N. system with a mandate to work exclusively to increase food production in the least developed countries, especially concentrating on production by smallholders and landless households. IFAD has gradually redefined its mission in terms of overall rural poverty alleviation rather than merely food production.

One of the smallest U.N. agencies (approximately 84 development professionals and 106 support staff), IFAD specializes in identifying effective ways to unleash and mobilize the potential for self-reliant, sustainable development by disadvantaged rural populations, including women. It draws frequently on the knowledge and experience of nongovernmental voluntary organizations or associations. Local village councils or other representative groups are involved in project design and management to ensure sustainability when IFAD's support ends. IFAD's funding authority is used to require equal representation of women in such project-managing groups if a village association does not do so on its own initiative.

IFAD acts as a catalyst among official development agencies and national planners, testing and demonstrating effective ways to increase food production and decrease poverty through enterprises managed by the poor themselves, thereby improving nutritional levels and living conditions, often in the remotest, most neglected areas of a country. By such demonstration, IFAD obtains additional funds for the projects it supports from foundations, national governments, and other U.N. agencies. IFAD also funds and promotes research to increase the productivity and quality of local food crops that are significant in the diets of low-income households.

IFAD, an OPEC initiative that gradually gained wider support, is one of the major outcomes of the 1974 World Food Conference and is internationally unique in its structure. The governing council, elected by the U.N. General Assembly, consists one-third of OPEC nations, one-third of non–oil exporting developing countries, and one-third of OECD countries. Each country has 1 vote. Two years of negotiation were required to obtain the full $1 billion of start-up funding, 43 percent coming from OPEC nations and 57 percent from members of the Development Assistance Committee of the OECD (industrialized, market-economy, donor nations). The U.N. secretary general opened the IFAD agreement for signing by national governments on 20 December 1976. The first session of IFAD's governing council met 1 year later, in December 1977, and the first loans were approved in April 1978. During the 3 years of IFAD's formation, the World Food Council served as the agency's secretariat.

PUBLICATIONS: *Annual Report.*

International Labour Office (ILO)
4 Route des Morillons
CH-1211 Geneva 22
Switzerland
(011-41-22) 7998537
Michel Hansenne, Director-General

ILO—Washington Branch
1828 L Street, NW, Suite 801
Washington, DC 20036
(202) 653-7652
Stephen Schlossberg, Director

The acronym ILO represents both the International Labour Organization (formed in 1919) and the International Labour Office that serves the organization. The International Labour Office sponsors many studies about hunger, poverty, and development from the perspective of the opportunities, wages, and working conditions of labour, including self-employed entrepreneurs in farming and nonfarm micro-enterprise. The basic human needs strategy for development, although not initiated by ILO, was most thoroughly articulated by the ILO World Employment Conference of 1976. Amartya Sen's seminal study *Poverty and Famines. An Essay on Entitlement and Deprivation* (1981) was commissioned under ILO's World Employment Programme.

PUBLICATIONS: *World Labour Report* (annual), *ILO Information* (5 times a year), *ILO Spotlight on Publications* (semi-annual publications announcement), and many topical reports.

United Nations Childrens Fund (UNICEF)
UNICEF House, 3 U.N. Plaza
New York, NY 10017
(212) 326-7000
James P. Grant, Executive Director

UNICEF is a network of national and regional offices serving 121 countries in the developing world. UNICEF cooperates with governments in their efforts to meet the needs of children, particularly children under five. The agency's advocacy work focuses on the world's high levels of infant and young child death and disease, with special attention to contributing factors characteristic of the least developed countries: maternal and child malnutrition; low status of women (little education, little economic opportunity, frequent pregnancies); lack of primary health care; lack of safe water; and lack of sanitation. UNICEF is unique among U.N. agencies in that a significant part of its funding (roughly 20 percent) comes from the public directly through partner National Committees (currently there are 34 such committees, such as the U.S. Committee for UNICEF) and through other volunteer organizations in the industrialized world. The balance comes from voluntary contributions by governments. UNICEF is an integral but semi-autonomous part of the U.N. system, with its own 41-member Executive Board that sets policy, reviews programs, and approves budgets.

PUBLICATIONS: *State of the World's Children,* by the UNICEF executive director (annual), and *UNICEF News* (quarterly, distributed by partner National Committees such as the U.S. Committee for UNICEF in New York City).

United Nations Population Fund (UNFPA)
220 East 42nd Street
New York, NY 10017
(212) 850-5842
Dr. Nafis Sadik, Executive Director

UNFPA is the largest multilateral population agency. It conducts demographic research, assists governments in designing family planning programs, and publishes current analyses of world population trends.

PUBLICATIONS: *The State of World Population,* by the UNFPA executive director (annual).

The World Food Programme (WFP)
Via delle Terme di Caracalla
00100 Rome, Italy
(011-396) 5797 3030
James Ingram, Executive Director

WFP was created by the U.N. General Assembly in 1963 to provide food aid both to support economic and social development projects and to meet emergency needs. Since 1975, it has also administered the U.N.'s International Emergency Food Reserve. It is sponsored jointly by the FAO and the U.N. General Assembly.

PUBLICATIONS: *World Food Programme Journal* (bimonthly), *Annual Report.*

The World Health Organization (WHO)
20 Avenue Appia
CH-1211 Geneva 27
Switzerland
(011-41-22) 7912111
Dr. Hiroshi Nakajima, Director-General

Regional Office for the Americas
Pan American Health Organization (PAHO)
525 Twenty-third Street, NW
Washington, DC 20037
(202) 861-3200
Dr. Carlyle Guerra de Macedo, Director

WHO is linked to efforts to end hunger through its role in advancing nutrition and pediatrics research, training, and the application of the health sciences to major public health problems. In 1955 WHO established a Protein Advisory Group (PAG) to study the nutritional and safety aspects of protein in foods. In 1960 FAO and UNICEF added their sponsorship and the focus broadened to include technological, marketing, and economic aspects of nutrition, particularly as these affect infants and other high-risk groups. In 1971 the World Bank's sponsorship was added to PAG. Since 1977, PAG has merged with the ACC/SCN (see above). WHO operates through six regional offices located in Washington, D.C.; Brazzaville, the Congo; Alexandria, Egypt; New Delhi, India; Copenhagen, Denmark; and Manila, Philippines. WHO assists national governments to develop programs in areas of nutrition, safe water and basic sanitation, maternal and child health, and the control of major diseases. WHO's founding on 7 April 1948 is commemorated annually by World Health Day.

PUBLICATIONS: *World Health* (bimonthly, for nonspecialists).

U.S. Federal Agencies

African Development Foundation (ADF)
1625 Massachusetts Avenue, NW, Suite 600
Washington, DC 20036
(202) 673-3916
Leonard H. Robinson, Jr., President

The ADF was established by Congress in 1980 for the purpose of funding self-reliant development initiatives in Africa, with explicit encouragement of African participation in the conception, implementation, management, and evaluation of development projects. ADF assists local communities in the execution of projects of their own design and initiation. Development proposals are sent directly to ADF from local communities and organizations. All projects funded by ADF must serve to improve the quality of life for both the rural and the urban poor. ADF also promotes development research by Africans and the transfer of development resources, expertise, and knowledge within Africa among Africans. ADF is responsible directly to Congress.

PUBLICATIONS: *Beyond Relief* (quarterly newsletter).

Inter-American Foundation (IAF)
1515 Wilson Boulevard
Rosslyn, VA 22209

(703) 841-3800
Deborah Szekely, President

IAF was created by Congress in 1969 to support the self-help efforts of poor people in Latin America and the Caribbean. Rather than working through governments, IAF responds directly to the initiatives of the poor by supporting local private organizations. IAF's funding comes from Congress and from the Social Progress Trust Fund of the Inter-American Development Bank (IDB). IAF is responsible solely to the U.S. Congress.

PUBLICATIONS: *Grassroots Development* (three times a year) and *Annual Report.*

Select Committee on Hunger
House of Representatives
H2-505, Annex 2
Washington, DC 20515
(202) 226-5470
Representative Tony P. Hall, Chairman

The Select Committee on Hunger was created 22 February 1984 by a vote of 309 to 78 in the House of Representatives. More than 250 representatives joined original sponsors Mickey Leland and Benjamin Gilman in co-sponsoring the authorizing resolution, which was supported by a diverse coalition of 60 national organizations. The Select Committee has been reauthorized by each succeeding Congress. The committee's mandate is to conduct a continuing, comprehensive study and review of the problems of domestic and international hunger and malnutrition as a background for congressional deliberation and action. The Select Committee holds hearings, seminars, and briefings and publishes reports. The committee itself does not introduce bills but individual members of the committee are active sponsors of hunger-related legislation.

PUBLICATIONS: *Hunger Report* (monthly newsletter), hearings reports, and other reports. An overview of the first four years is given in *Progress Report of the Select Committee on Hunger,* Report 100-1107, 13 December 1988 (U.S. Government Printing Office).

U.S. Agency for International Development (USAID)
320 Twenty-first Street, NW
Washington, DC 20523
(202) 647-9620
Ronald W. Roskens, Administrator

USAID Center for Development and Information Exchange
(703) 875-4836

USAID (called A.I.D. in the United States) is the U.S. government's primary administrator of economic and social (wholly nonmilitary) assistance for developing countries. It was established by the Foreign Assistance Act of 1961 during the administration of President John F. Kennedy. Under some U.S. presidents (e.g., the Bush administration), USAID has been in the Department of State; in other administrations (e.g., the Carter administration), USAID has been autonomous and responsible directly to the president. All of USAID's work affects hunger directly or indirectly. There are bureaus for Africa, Asia, and Latin America. The Bureau of Food for Peace and Voluntary Assistance includes the Office of Private Voluntary Cooperation, the government's liaison to U.S. private voluntary organizations; the Office of Development Education, which makes grants to U.S. NGOs for projects to educate the U.S. public about development; and the Office of Foreign Disaster Assistance (OFDA). The Office of Women in Development falls within the Bureau of Program and Policy Coordination. A Bureau of Science and Technology includes the Offices on Agriculture, Education, Forestry, Environment and Natural Resources, Nutrition, Population, Microenterprise, and Rural and Institutional Development. An autonomous but affiliated organization is the Board for International Food and Agricultural Development (BIFAD), which is responsible for utilizing the resources of the U.S. land-grant universities for research, extension, and education in USAID's programs in international food, nutrition, and agricultural development. Since 1985, USAID has conducted a special Child Survival Program involving several bureaus. The A.I.D. library in Rosslyn, Virginia, is open to the public.

PUBLICATIONS: *Child Survival. Report to Congress* (annual), *Front Lines* (monthly newsletter), and many research monographs.

U.S. Department of Agriculture (USDA)
14th Street and Independence Avenue, SW
Washington, DC 20250
(202) 447-2791
Clayton Yeutter, Secretary of Agriculture

Economic Research Service (ERS)
(202) 786-3300, Publications information (202) 786-1515 or
(800) 999-6779
Foreign Agriculture Service
(202) 447-7115
National Agriculture Library (NAL)
(301) 344-3755
Office of International Cooperation and Development (OICD)
(202) 638-4661

USDA, augmented by the affiliated U.S. land-grant university system, is the world's largest center of agricultural research. Through its Office of International Cooperation and Development (OICD), USDA provides technical assistance and training for agricultural researchers in developing countries and other services to national governments and international development agencies. Within the U.S. government, USDA is the agency responsible for assessing U.S. and global agricultural conditions that affect world food security. In practice, USDA focuses primarily on countries and regions that are major commercial producers and exporters of agricultural commodities. However, because USDA shares with USAID responsibility for administering P.L. 480 food aid, USDA also carries out monitoring and forecasting for areas of the world most prone to droughts, food shortages, and famine conditions.

The four main units within USDA that are involved in monitoring and forecasting world food supply and demand are the Foreign Agricultural Service (FAS), the Economic Research Service (ERS), the World Agricultural Outlook Board, and the National Agricultural Statistical Service (NASS). NASS focuses only on U.S. agriculture, but it is also important to global forecasting because of its research to develop methods for using satellite data in making crop supply estimates.

FAS maintains a worldwide intelligence and reporting program to develop and disseminate information on world agricultural production and trade. The core of FAS information comes from agricultural counselors and attachés in 75 posts throughout the world covering 110 countries. FAS information plays a significant role in P.L. 480 food aid allocations. Satellite data are used increasingly in FAS analyses.

ERS is the agency primarily responsible for economic research and analysis of factors underlying supply and demand for agricultural commodities and food products both domestically and internationally. (FAS examines only supply.) ERS uses data on income and population in assessing foreign food demand. In addition, ERS uses information on export earnings and foreign exchange reserves in assessing the capacity of countries to finance imports. Within ERS, the Commodity Economics Division and the Agriculture and Trade Analysis Division analyze foreign food supply and demand conditions. The Agriculture and Trade Analysis Division prepares the annual report on world food needs and availabilities mandated by Congress in P.L. 480. (The more official designation is P.L. 83-480, referring to the 83rd Congress, which originated P.L. 480 in 1954.) ERS assessments of world, U.S., and foreign national agricultural conditions are available regularly in published form as well as via public access computer networks.

The World Agricultural Outlook Board, a USDA agency that reports to the assistant secretary of agriculture for economics, has responsibility for review and clearance of all aggregate estimates released by the USDA on commodities, food, and agriculture. The World Board chairs the commodity estimates committee of representatives from FAS, ERS, NASS, and the Agricultural Stabilization and Conservation Service (the agency responsible for administering U.S. domestic price support programs). At these meetings, differences in estimates must be ironed out for an all-USDA consensus before any reports can be released. The World Board coordinates research on weather, climate, and remote sensing. It also coordinates cooperation in these activities with agencies outside USDA.

USDA assists researchers worldwide through the National Agricultural Library. The NAL is the largest agricultural library in the world. About 60 percent of its total collection comes from outside the United States. Its computerized bibliographic database, AGRICOLA, contains subfiles on agricultural economics, food and nutrition, and other topics (see Chapter 7, "Nonprint Resources"). The NAL sends monthly tapes from AGRICOLA to Vienna, Austria, for incorporation in AGRIS, the FAO database for an international information system for the agricultural sciences and technology. The NAL provides individualized reference service to users on a fee basis.

PUBLICATIONS: The several Situation and Outlook series by ERS (each with an individual title) focus on major world regions, major food commodities, and the world as a whole. ERS also publishes other monographs. A 12-page guide, "Information Contacts and Periodicals," is available from ERS at no charge.

Nongovernmental Research Centers

Board on Science and Technology for International Development (BOSTID)
Office of International Affairs
National Research Council
2101 Constitution Avenue, NW
Washington, DC 20418
(202) 334-2633
John Hurley, Director
Noel Vietmayer, Chair, Advisory Committee on Technology Innovation

The National Research Council (NRC), a private, nonacademic scientific institution, serves as the operating arm of the U.S. National Academy of Sciences, the National Academy of Engineering, and the Institute of Medicine. BOSTID was established within the NRC Office of International Affairs in 1969 to further the application of science and technology to problems of economic and social development. It makes grants to scientists and scientific institutions in developing countries, conducts studies, issues publications, organizes conferences, and holds seminars and briefings for government officials and policy makers in Washington, D.C. BOSTID's food research focuses on biological nitrogen fixation, grain amaranth, fast-growing tropical trees (such as leucaena), and other neglected food plants indigenous to developing countries. (Of the 3,000 plant species that have been eaten by humans throughout history, only 20 major crops currently feed most of the people on earth—due to neglect of the other options!) BOSTID's support comes primarily from USAID and private foundations. BOSTID also mobilizes volunteers from within the U.S. scientific community.

PUBLICATIONS: *BOSTID Development Review* (biannual report), *Quality-Protein Maize* (1988), *Triticale—A Promising Addition to the World's Cereal Grains* (1989), *Saline Agriculture* (1990), *Lost Crops of the Incas* (1990), *Improvement of Tropical and Subtropical Rangelands* (1990), and other monographs. *(BOSTID Developments,* a semi-annual journal, was discontinued in 1989.)

Food Research Institute (FRI)
Stanford University
Stanford, CA 94305
(415) 723-2300
Walter P. Falcon, Director

FRI is a research and teaching department within the School of Humanities and Sciences at Stanford University. It was established in 1921 to investigate the production, distribution, and consumption of food, with particular attention to economic analysis of agricultural commodities and marketing systems. Included on its diverse research agenda are the economic behavior of peasant farmers and questions of income growth and distribution within developing countries.

PUBLICATIONS: *Food Research Institute Studies* (3–4 studies per volume; a volume covers 1–2 years) and books by institute authors.

Institute for Development Anthropology (IDA)
99 Collier Street, Suite 302
Binghamton, NY 13902
(607) 772-6244
David W. Brokensha, Michael M. Horowitz, and Thayer Scudder, Co-Directors

IDA (not to be confused with IDA/World Bank, a lending institution) was founded in 1976 to promote fuller inclusion of the knowledge, perspective, and skills of anthropologists in development planning and implementation. IDA staff conduct research, technical assistance, and policy advocacy with official development agencies to secure full consideration of the values, self-defined needs, and self-determination of local peoples. IDA also encourages social scientists and institutions in developing countries to undertake development-related research and to become involved in the conceptualization, design, implementation, and evaluation of policies.

PUBLICATIONS: *Development Anthropology Network* (newsletter).

Institute for Food and Development Policy (IFDP)
145 Ninth Street
San Francisco, CA 94103
(415) 864-8555
Frances Moore Lappé, Executive Director

IFDP is also popularly known as Food First, the title of its first publication. IFDP is an independent research and education center that addresses the human-made roots of hunger, poverty, and environmental degradation. IFDP specializes in studies of antidemocratic social and economic structures that concentrate power and deny people access to the resources they need to achieve dignity and self-reliance.

PUBLICATIONS: *Food First News* (quarterly newsletter), *Progress Report* (annual report), *Action Alerts, Hunger Myths and Facts* (flier), and many books.

International Development Research Centre (IDRC)
250 Albert Street
Ottawa, Canada K1G 3H9
(613) 236-6163
Ivan L. Head, President and Chief Executive Officer

IDRC is a public corporation created by the Parliament of Canada in 1970 to support researchers in developing countries working in agriculture, health, earth sciences, engineering, information, communications, and social sciences. The emphasis in all areas is on technology that is not only scientifically effective but also user-friendly and appropriate within the communities where it is to be applied. A Women in Development Unit was established in 1987 to support integration of WID awareness into all IDRC programs and to act as a resource for gender-specific and gender-related research. The emphasis in agriculture is on local food crops, including revival and improvement of indigenous crops whose potential nutritional value previously was overlooked or underrated. Regional offices are located in Colombia, Egypt, India, Kenya, Senegal, and Singapore.

PUBLICATIONS: The quarterly magazine *IDRC Reports* was discontinued with the July 1989 issue. Many scientific monographs, technical reports, and general-interest materials on the role of research in international development are listed in the IDRC catalog.

International Institute of Rural Reconstruction (IIRR)
Silang, Cavite
Philippines
Juan Flavier, President

U.S. Headquarters
475 Riverside Drive, Room 1270
New York, NY 10115
(212) 870-2992
Robert F. O'Brien, Vice-President

IIRR is a world training center for executives and staff of governmental
and nongovernmental rural development organizations and programs
in Asia, Africa, and Latin America seeking to improve the quality of life
of the rural poor. IIRR focuses on sustainable development strategies
that enable rural people to tap their own potential (including fully
participatory self-government by local groups). Its program is based on
the grassroots development movement founded by Dr. Y. C. James Yen
in 1911 in China. IIRR conducts field operations and research and
incorporates the experiences of similar agencies into its leadership
training programs to maintain the practical relevance of IIRR training
to current situations.

PUBLICATIONS: *IIRR Report* (semi-annual newsletter).

Land Tenure Center (LTC)
University of Wisconsin–Madison
1300 University Avenue
Madison, WI 53706
(608) 262-3657
John W. Bruce, Director

The LTC administers an integrated program of research, teaching,
information dissemination, and consultation with governments and
official development agencies on a wide range of development problems
in all regions of the world. Established in May 1962, LTC focuses its
research on the interdisciplinary issues of land tenure, agrarian reform,
and related institutional aspects of rural development, with an emphasis
on access by the rural poor to land, water, and other resources.

PUBLICATIONS: Monographs in three series—LTC Research Papers,
LTC Papers, and LTC Training and Methods; also special bibliographies (e.g., *Trees and Tenure* and *Land, Trees and Tenure*).

Overseas Development Council (ODC)
1717 Massachusetts Avenue, NW
Washington, DC 20036
(202) 234-8701
John W. Sewell, President

ODC is the leading private, nonprofit institution in the United States for comprehensive analysis of the economic and political issues of interdependence between the United States and developing countries. It was founded in 1969. It conducts analytical studies on current issues, publishes reports, and provides briefings for policy makers.

PUBLICATIONS: *Policy Focus* (briefing papers for U.S. policy makers and journalists, 8–10 times a year); also *Environment and the Poor: Development Strategies for a Common Agenda* (1989), *Strengthening the Poor: What Have We Learned?* (1988), *Development Strategies Reconsidered* (1986), and other books.

Winrock International Institute for Agricultural Development
Petit Jean Mountain
Route 3, Box 376
Morrilton, AR 72110
(501) 727-5435
Robert D. Havener, President

Washington, D.C., Regional Office
1611 North Kent Street
Arlington, VA 22209
(703) 525-9430
Ned Raun, Director

The mission of Winrock International (initiated by Winthrop Rockefeller) is to reduce hunger and poverty through sustainable agriculture and rural development. Smallholder farming systems, agroforestry, on-farm seed production, and low-input sustainable agriculture are typical subjects of research and training in the field by Winrock staff (funded often by IFAD or USAID). Winrock International manages a fellowship program for advanced study by developing-country scientists and science administrators to help them obtain training in the most appropriate institutions for their specialties; conducts colloquia on food, hunger, and agriculture for public policy decision-makers and development specialists; and produces agricultural books intended for authorities in developing countries and assistance agencies. From 1986 until 1990, Winrock International administered the World Food Prize, founded by General Foods Foundation to recognize outstanding individual achievement in increasing world food supplies. The Winrock Agribookstore, a worldwide mail-order service for publications from 20 international research and development organizations, is managed from the Washington Regional Office.

PUBLICATIONS: *Strategy for the 1990s, Agribookstore Catalog,* annual reports, technical papers, and project profiles.

World Hunger Program
Brown University
Box 1831
Providence, RI 02912
(401) 863-2700
Robert W. Kates, Director

The Alan Shawn Feinstein World Hunger Program at Brown University, named in honor of its founding benefactor, is the only major university research center with the elimination of hunger as its primary objective. It was established in 1985. The World Hunger Program hosts an annual Hunger Research and Briefing Exchange at a conference for researchers and managers of official and nongovernmental relief and development programs; administers the Hunger Research Exchange, linking approximately 60 groups studying hunger in more than 15 countries; and presents the annual Alan Shawn Feinstein World Hunger Award to provide public recognition for extraordinary efforts and achievements in the reduction and prevention of hunger. The World Hunger Program also conducts and publishes studies and helps to sponsor collaborative studies such as the Beyond Hunger project to catalyze, in conjunction with leading groups of African scholars, a distinctive and positive African vision of the long-term future. The World Hunger Program's own research is focused in three areas: the history of hunger, analyses of how trends within key world regions will affect hunger, and assessments of the values, policies, and institutions needed to prevent hunger.

PUBLICATIONS: *The Hunger Report: 1988, Hunger Report: Update 1989, Hunger in History—A Selected Bibliography* (1989), *Current Perspectives on Africa's Future 1957–2057* (1989), and *Hunger in History—Food Shortage, Poverty, and Deprivation* (Oxford: Basil Blackwell, 1990). Also occasional papers and reprint series.

U.S. Political Advocacy

Bread for the World
802 Rhode Island Avenue, NE
Washington, DC 20018
(202) 269-0200
Arthur Simon, President

Bread for the World is a national grassroots political movement among Christians in the United States to influence congressional action on behalf of hungry people at home and in developing countries. Members are recruited primarily through churches and expressions of Christian faith and worship practices are used in the organization's membership literature and activities. Current membership numbers about 42,000 people organized by congressional district. Regional offices are located in Los Angeles, Denver, Minneapolis, and Chicago. Bread for the World members and national staff apply influence through letter-writing campaigns and meetings with members of Congress and as citizens voting in the electoral process.

PUBLICATIONS: *Bread for the World Newsletter* (10 per year), Offering of Letters organizing kit (annual), also miscellaneous action alerts, congressional voting records, issue papers, worship aids, and other items. (The Bread for the World Institute on Hunger and Development, an educational affiliate at the same address, produces additional publications.)

Interfaith Action for Economic Justice
110 Maryland Avenue, NE
Washington, DC 20002
(202) 543-2800
Arthur B. Keys, Jr., Executive Director

Interfaith Action began in 1974 as the Interreligious Taskforce on U.S. Food Policy. The name was changed in 1983 to reflect the broader agenda that developed as disempowerment of the poor became more clearly perceived as a root cause of hunger. Interfaith Action is a coalition of 34 Protestant, Roman Catholic, and Jewish religious agencies that work together to develop and implement U.S. domestic and international policies and programs that extend greater justice and support to the poor. Coalition member agencies contribute funds and the time of staff, who serve on Interfaith Action's four issue workgroups: Food and Agriculture Policy, International Development Policy, Domestic Human Needs and Economic Policy, and the Churches' Committee for Voter Registration/Education. Interfaith Action maintains a Legislative Update toll-free telephone line. Spokespersons for Interfaith Action and its member agencies testify before congressional committees and meet frequently with individual members of Congress to discuss particular legislation. Campaigns of letters or telephone calls from voters are conducted through individual member agencies rather than by Interfaith Action itself. In the spring of 1991, Interfaith Action will merge with Impact, a multi-issue ecumenical public policy organization, to form a new entity called Interfaith Impact for Justice and Peace.

PUBLICATIONS: *Interfaith Action* (bimonthly newsletter), *Networker* (monthly legislative updates), issue analysis monographs in the Policy Notes series, and other reports.

Results
236 Massachusetts Avenue, NE, Suite 110
Washington, DC 20002
(202) 543-9340
Sam Harris, Executive Director

Results is a grassroots organization whose members train to generate political will to end hunger by public speaking on legislative issues and by writing op-ed pieces for newspapers. Founded in the United States in 1980, Results now has approximately 110 groups across the country as well as chapters in Canada, the United Kingdom, and Australia. The network in each country operates similarly but independently. Members meet in local groups three times each month to study and practice explaining an issue upon which their legislators will soon be acting (examples: funding for IFAD and UNICEF, foreign aid for micro-enterprise, and child nutrition); to generate letters to elected officials and editorial writers; to participate in national conference calls with lawmakers or experts in the field of hunger; and to make presentations to other groups in their community. An international members' conference is held annually in Washington, D.C., during which Results members from outside the United States meet with their country's representative at the World Bank while U.S. members talk with their representatives in Congress. Articles about a featured hunger policy issue that have been prepared by Results members now appear in local and national news media at the rate of about one a day.

PUBLICATIONS: *Entry Point* (quarterly newsletter for members).

6

References in Print

THE REFERENCES LISTED HERE include something for everyone—from the seasoned specialist to the student or general reader who is approaching the study of world hunger for the first time. The descriptions provided in the annotations guide researchers to the most appropriate materials for their individual purposes.

References in this chapter are arranged as follows: (1) Bibliographies, Indexes, and Abstracts, (2) Yearbooks and Statistical References, (3) Periodicals, (4) Monograph and Occasional Paper Series, and (5) Landmark Monographs.

Bibliographies, Indexes, and Abstracts

Agricultural Information System for Agricultural Sciences and Technology (Agris). **Agrindex.** Rome: Agris, Food and Agriculture Organization of the United Nations. Monthly. $400. ISSN 0254-8801.

Publications from more than 100 national and international agricultural research centers are included in this bibliography intended for scientists and policy makers. It is updated monthly and available also as a computer-readable database. Bibliographical categories most relevant to hunger are "Economics, Development and Rural Sociology" and "Human Nutrition."

Alternative Press Center. **Alternative Press Index.** Baltimore, MD: Alternative Press Center, Inc., P.O. Box 33109, Baltimore, MD 21218. Quarterly. Individuals $30, institutions $110. ISSN 0002-662X.

Self-described as an index of "alternative and radical publications," this reference began in 1969. It provides a subject index for issue-oriented periodicals that address a popular audience. Monitored periodicals with frequent material on world hunger include *New Internationalist, Multinational Monitor, The Ecologist, Science for the People,* and *WHY.*

American Economics Association. **Journal of Economic Literature.** Nashville, TN: American Economics Association, 1313 Twenty-first Avenue, Suite 809, Nashville, TN 37212-2786. Quarterly. Individuals $72, institutions $125. ISSN 0022-0515.

Articles from approximately 300 journals are indexed by subject in each issue of this indispensable bibliographic resource for scholars. Recent doctoral dissertations in economics are listed in the final issue of each volume. A large number of selected journal articles are abstracted. Each issue contains approximately 40 book reviews and descriptions of another 50 or more new books in the field. Publication began in 1963.

Ball, Nicole. **World Hunger: A Guide to the Economic and Political Dimensions.** Santa Barbara, CA: ABC-CLIO, 1981. 386p., index. $46.50. ISBN 0-87436-308-X.

This is the most comprehensive guide to the hunger-related literature of the 1970s, with more than 3,000 entries. Major topical divisions are (1) economic development, (2) rural development, (3) constraints on rural development (for example, land tenure patterns, neocolonialism, ecology, credit), (4) food, (5) country-specific studies, and (6) resources.

Baywood. **Abstracts in Anthropology.** Farmingdale, NY: Baywood Publishing Company. Eight times a year. $190. ISSN 0001-3455.

Summaries of journal articles are indexed by author and subject. Indexes are cumulative within each volume year. Abstracts relating to hunger appear under a variety of subject headings such as food, farming, malnutrition, Africa, and even women.

British Library of Political and Economic Science. **A London Bibliography of the Social Sciences.** London: British Library of Political and Economic Science. Annual. $180. ISSN 0076-051X.

This extensive guide to current social science literature published in English is a rich hunting ground for books, articles, reports, and documents relating to world hunger. A wide range of European, North American, and international sources is included. Relevant items are easily identified under subject categories such as agriculture-developing countries, famines, food relief, food supply, malnutrition, and nutrition policy.

Commonwealth Agricultural Bureaux International (CAB). **Rural Development Abstracts.** CAB, Wallingford, Oxon OX10 8DE, United Kingdom. Distributed in the United States by CAB International, 845 North Park Avenue, Tucson, AZ 85719. Quarterly. $145. ISSN 0140-4768.

This excellent reference for development professionals monitors approximately 180 journals and the working papers of many institutes around the world. Summaries of articles are indexed by author and subject. Hunger material is plentiful in the subject index under topics such as famine, food aid, food consumption, income distribution, and women and agriculture or by specific country. Publication began in 1978.

————. **World Agricultural Economics and Rural Sociology Abstracts.** Monthly. $440. ISSN 0043-8219.

Of all bibliographical aids available for hunger research, this may well be the most fruitful. CAB began in 1959 as an association of information exchange among 28 governments in the British Commonwealth and has since expanded. For this reference, CAB summarizes articles from more than 1,000 journals in fields expressly pertinent to the world hunger problem. Abstracts are indexed by author and subject. The subject index is unusually well organized for hunger research by main topics and subtopics such as agricultural development—Africa (Asia, Caribbean, etc.); food policy—general (food aid, food industry, nutrition, etc.); and rural sociology, similarly subdivided.

Fenton, Thomas P., and Mary J. Heffron, eds. **Food, Hunger, Agribusiness: A Directory of Resources.** Maryknoll, NY: Orbis Books, 1987. 132p. $9.95. ISBN 0-88344-531-X.

The resources included here emphasize socioeconomic justice questions, the political and economic roots of hunger, and criticism of dominant power structures in the world economy. The intended audience is more activist and change-oriented than scholarly. Informative annotations by the editors evaluate a wide range of organizations, books, periodicals, pamphlets, articles, audiovisuals, and materials designed for worship groups or classrooms, as well as other resource guides.

Geo Abstracts. **Geographical Abstracts: Human Geography.** Elsevier Science Publishers, Ltd., Crown House, Linton Road, Barking, Essex

IG11 8JU, United Kingdom. Monthly. British £253. ISSN 0953-9611.

In 1989, *Economic Geography, Social and Historical Geography,* and several other of the seven geographical abstract series published by Geo Abstracts were merged under one title, *Human Geography.* Prior to the merger, hunger-related materials appeared most frequently in the two above-named abstract series. Both began in 1966. Pertinent articles are found under various subject headings such as agriculture, consumers, farming, and food. Using the regional index—e.g., Africa, Asia, Latin America—will narrow the search.

Gran, Guy. **An Annotated Guide to Global Development: Capacity Building for Effective Social Change.** Olney, MD: Resources for Development and Democracy, 17119 Old Baltimore Road, Olney, MD 20832. 1987. 154p. $7.95. ISBN 0-9618388-0-9.

More than 700 books, bibliographies, and computer-readable databases are described and indexed by author and country. The author's selection is based on an understanding of development as a process of democratic social change. Works relating to world hunger are most plentiful in the chapters titled "Food Systems" and "Social Dimensions." Beginners in the study of development will find the author's introduction helpful. The guide is co-published with the Economic and Social Development Program, Graduate School of Public and International Affairs, University of Pittsburgh.

H. W. Wilson Co. **Social Sciences Index.** Bronx, NY: H. W. Wilson Co. Quarterly. $140. ISSN 0094-4920.

Author and subject indexes are provided for articles from 353 international English-language periodicals. Academic fields include anthropology, economics, geography, international relations, political science, and sociology. To find hunger material in the subject index, try topics such as agriculture, famine, farmers, food crops, malnutrition, peasants, villages, and women (in developing countries).

International Committee for Social Science Documentation. **International Bibliography of the Social Sciences.** Published annually as four distinct series, primarily for established scholars:

International Bibliography of Economics. Annually since 1955. $110. ISSN 0085-204X. Distributed by Tavistock, London, and Aldine, Chicago.

International Bibliography of Political Science. Annually since 1953. $110. ISSN 0085-2058. Distributed by Tavistock, London, and Aldine, Chicago.

International Bibliography of Social and Cultural Anthropology.

Annually since 1955. $110. ISSN 0085-2074. Distributed since 1988 by Routledge, Chapman & Hall, New York. Prepared under the auspices of the International Union of Anthropological and Ethnological Sciences. Of the four bibliographies, this one contains by far the most material on hunger.

International Bibliography of Sociology. Annually since 1952. $110. ISSN 0085-2066. Distributed by Routledge, Chapman & Hall, New York. Prepared under the auspices of the International Sociological Association.

Each bibliography consists of an extensive list of books, pamphlets, periodical articles, and official government publications in various languages, including Slavic and Asian languages. Entries are indexed by author and subject. The most useful subject headings for hunger are agriculture, food, food aid, development assistance, drought, famine, or geographical names.

International Labour Office. **Bibliography of Published Research of the World Employment Program.** 7th ed. Geneva: International Labour Office, 1988. 125p. $12.15. ISBN 92-2-106390-9.

ILO is the acronym for both the International Labour Office and the International Labour Organization, which the International Labour Office serves. The World Employment Program (WEP) of the International Labour Organization (ILO) emphasizes fulfillment of basic human needs, including food, as the primary objective of development. The WEP was launched in 1969 as a project to evaluate development progress. It was ILO's main contribution to the International Development Strategy for the Second United Nations Development Decade (the 1970s). This bibliography includes all WEP studies, monographs, articles, and working papers published through the end of 1987.

Kutzner, Patricia L., and Nickola Lagoudakis, eds. **Who's Involved with Hunger: An Organization Guide for Education and Advocacy.** 4th ed. Washington, DC: World Hunger Education Service, P.O. Box 29056, Washington, DC 20017. 1985. 50p., index. $5.

Information on publications is included in brief descriptions of approximately 300 organizations in the United States concerned with world or domestic food and hunger issues—United Nations agencies, U.S. government agencies, and private agencies engaged in public education, policy research, political advocacy, and appropriate technology.

Public Affairs Information Service (PAIS). **PAIS Bulletin.** New York: PAIS. Monthly. $395. ISSN 0898-2201.

PAIS indexes English-language books and articles on issues of public policy from many countries. Items related to hunger in developing countries are surprisingly scarce. The more fruitful index subjects to search are agricultural assistance, basic needs, food consumption, food relief, food supply, and malnutrition.

Sociological Abstracts. **Sociological Abstracts.** San Diego, CA: Sociological Abstracts. Five times a year. $385. ISSN 0038-0202.

Articles from 1,250 journals are summarized and indexed according to author, subject, and source of publication. Although hunger material appears infrequently, it can be found in the subject index under agriculture, famine, food, and hunger (a rare topic heading in indexes of any kind). Publication began in 1963.

Third World Resources. **Third World Resources.** Oakland, CA: Third World Resources, DataCenter, 464 19th Street, Oakland, CA 94612. Quarterly. $25. ISSN 8755-8831.

Beginning in 1985, editors Thomas Fenton and Mary Heffron have provided current information in this quarterly publication on books, periodicals, pamphlets, articles, audiovisuals, and organizations having to do with a wide range of developing-country issues. The pattern will be familiar to users of Fenton and Heffron's numerous reference books. The editors select items on the basis of suitability for a popular audience and sensitivity to human rights.

Transnational Network for Appropriate/Alternative Technologies (TRANET). **TRANET.** Rangeley, ME: TRANET, Box 567, Rangeley, ME 04970. Bimonthly. Individuals $30, libraries and nonprofit organizations $50. ISSN 0739-0971.

This unusual resource can be viewed as a bulletin board of current, brief announcements (most frequently of new publications) by and for an international network of more than 50,000 people "participating in social transformation . . . [by] adopting alternative technologies." Many announcements are from readers in Africa, Asia, the Pacific, and Latin America and provide access not easily found elsewhere to publications from those regions. Food, agriculture, health, development, and environment are regular topics.

United Nations. **Directory of UN Databases and Information Systems.** New York: United Nations, 1990. Distributed by Bernan-Unipub, 4611-F Assembly Drive, Lanham, MD 20706-4391. $40. ISBN 92-1-100349-0.

This guide to the world's largest and most detailed system of data collection on hunger and development is available to the public only in print. To researchers within U.N. agencies it is also available online as "DUNIS."

U.S. Agency for International Development. **AID Research and Development Abstracts.** Washington, DC: Center for Development Information and Evaluation, Bureau for Program and Policy Coordination, USAID. Distributed by ARDA Subs, A.I.D./DIHF, 7222 47th Street, Suite 102, Chevy Chase, MD 20815-6019. Quarterly. $10. ISSN 0096-1507.

The materials summarized here include research studies funded by USAID, reports, special project evaluations, and other documents of interest to A.I.D. staff worldwide and to selected institutions in developing countries. Items are indexed by subject, geographical location, and author or institutional source. Publication began in 1975.

U.S. Congress, House, Select Committee on Hunger. **A Review of Selected Studies on World Hunger.** Washington, DC: U.S. Government Printing Office, 1985. 102p. (No longer in stock at the Government Printing Office but may be ordered at no charge from the House of Representatives Select Committee on Hunger, U.S. Congress, Washington, DC 20515.)

This report for the Select Committee on Hunger covers both domestic and international hunger. In the first part committee staff review expert opinions on the extent of hunger and various U.S. and international programs and policies to alleviate it. This review is followed by 60 pages of bibliography, giving brief descriptions of 383 books, articles, reports, and documents from a great variety of sources. Most of the titles deal with hunger in developing countries. The report was compiled by Vivian Gabor and edited by Catherine Jensen.

University of London, School of Oriental and African Studies. **International African Bibliography: Current Books, Articles and Papers in African Studies.** London: University of London, School of Oriental and African Studies. Quarterly. $49.50, individuals; $99, institutions. ISSN 0020-5877.

This bibliography for scholars is compiled at the library of the School of Oriental and African Studies and edited by David Hall. It began in 1970. Items are arranged topically within geographical regions of Africa. In the subject index, items related to African hunger appear primarily under agriculture but can be found also under other headings.

Winrock International Institute for Agricultural Development. **Agribookstore Catalog.** Arlington, VA: Winrock International, 1611 North Kent Street, Arlington, VA 22209-2134. Annual. 28p. (11 × 17). Free.

As a selective guide to recent books for development professionals on food and agriculture policies, issues, innovations, and proposals, there is no handier reference than this catalog. Each item is described clearly and succinctly. Titles are indexed topically, e.g., environment, farming systems, Green Revolution, and hunger and nutrition. Winrock International's mail-order Agribookstore is intended as a one-stop shopping service for publications from more than 30 research institutes, development agencies, and academic publishers worldwide.

Yearbooks and Statistical References

The United Nations together with its system of specialized agencies is the major collector, publisher, and manager of databases on socioeconomic aspects of world development. The sheer mass of these statistics is staggering. Direct statistics on malnutrition and hunger, however, are not plentiful, since few countries, as yet, collect that kind of information systematically. The statistics that are available reveal more about various factors that often relate to or interact with the condition of hunger than they do about hunger itself.

Both primary and secondary statistical references are included here. Secondary references are those that interpret selected facts from primary data. These are often (but not always) easier to obtain and easier to read than are the primary references. Most students and many scholars find secondary references adequate for their purposes. In the list that follows, secondary references are indicated by an asterisk.

Brown, Lester R., et al. **State of the World 1990.*** New York and London: W. W. Norton & Company, 1990. 254p., xvi, index. $9.95, paper.

Each year since 1984, Worldwatch Institute has produced a new "Report on Progress toward a Sustainable Society." Discussion of trends in the status of food-producing resources, population growth, and energy consumption figure prominently in the contents.

Food and Agriculture Organization of the United Nations (FAO). **FAO Production Yearbook.** Rome: FAO. Annual. ISSN 0071-7118.

Each yearbook is published in the year following the year of date in the title. Figures are based on information available to the Statistics Division of the Economics and Social Policy Department of FAO as of 15 April of the year of actual publication. Tables compare figures from various years within a given period to make it possible to note trends in land use, population, and food production. The period examined in the 1986 yearbook extended from 1970 to 1986.

———. **FAO Quarterly Bulletin of Statistics.** Rome: FAO. Quarterly. $14. ISSN 1011-8780.

A different special topic is featured in each issue (e.g., cereals, population, fats and oils), followed by standard statistical tables on food and agricultural production and trade.

———. **FAO Trade Yearbook.** Rome: FAO. Annual. ISSN 0071-7126.

This is similar in format and nature to the *FAO Production Yearbook.* Statistical tables permit comparisons over a six-year period of agricultural imports and exports generally and also by specific commodities, both globally and for specific countries. The 1987 yearbook, published in 1988, covered the years 1981 through 1986.

———. **The Fifth World Food Survey.** Rome: FAO, 1985 (reprinted 1986). 129p. FAO document number M/R5150/E/11.86/3/250.

The difficulty of establishing a reliable database on the nutritional status of the world's people is enormous, but that is the objective of FAO's periodic World Food Survey. Each survey represents advances in the reliability of research data and refinements in statistical analysis. Statistics cited to describe the extent of the world hunger problem are usually derived from the most recent of the FAO World Food Surveys. Five surveys have been completed so far: 1946, 1952, 1963, 1977, and 1985.

———. **Food Outlook.** Rome: FAO. Monthly. Limited distribution. Direct inquiries to Chief, Global Information and Early Warning Service, Commodities and Trade Division/ESC, FAO.

This is produced primarily for planners in governments and major aid donor agencies under the Global Information and Early Warning System on Food and Agriculture created after the World Food Conference of 1974. It gives a concise analysis of information affecting the situation and outlook for basic foodstuffs.

———. **The State of Food and Agriculture.** Rome: FAO. Annual. Single year $39. Approximately 172p. ISSN 0081-4539.

This is a comprehensive, up-to-date picture of world agriculture based on data provided to FAO by national governments. Part 1 of each yearbook reviews the world economic environment, agricultural and food production, and agricultural trade. Part 2 reviews situations prevailing in Africa, Asia and the Pacific, Latin America and the Caribbean, the Near East, Eastern Europe and the U.S.S.R., and the developed market economies. Beginning with the 1957 edition, a different special topic is included each year as Part 3. An annex of statistical tables (70 pages or more) concludes the report.

International Labour Office (ILO). **Bulletin of Labour Statistics.** Geneva: ILO. Quarterly. 80 Swiss francs. ISSN 0007-4950.

Statistical tables provide the most recent data worldwide on employment, unemployment, hours of work, wages, and consumer price indexes. When possible, figures are given separately for men and women, an important procedure for more accurate analysis of socioeconomic situations in which ILO leads most other agencies. Notes preceding the tables offer useful information about how the statistics are produced and analyzed.

———. **Yearbook of Labour Statistics.** Geneva: ILO. Annual. ISSN 0084-3857.

Beginning with the 1989 edition, each yearbook is published in the middle of the following year in order to include as much data for the year of date as possible. Tables and explanations are provided on the following: total and economically active populations; employment (various categories including agriculture); unemployment; hours of work; wages; labor cost; consumer prices (including a separate index of food prices); occupational injuries; and strikes and lock-outs. An index by countries locates country-specific data within these broad topics.

Organization for Economic Cooperation and Development, Development Assistance Committee. **Development Co-operation: Efforts and Policies of the Members of the Development Assistance Committee.** Paris: OECD, 2, rue André-Pascal, 75775 Paris 16, France. Distributed in the United States by OECD Publications, 2001 L Street, NW, Suite 700, Washington, DC 20036. Annual. Price varies. The 1988 edition (issued in 1989) costs $32. ISBN 92-64-13300-3.

Development practitioners commonly refer to this as "the DAC Report." It is the definitive source of global statistics on development assistance, particularly official development assistance (ODA), which DAC defines as being at least 25 percent in the nature of a grant rather than a loan. Numerous charts, graphs, and tables depict national and multilateral sources of development assistance, the national recipients, and the kind of development projects or programs emphasized by each donor. Special topics of current concern to aid donors are also discussed in each year's report.

Sivard, Ruth Leger. **World Military and Social Expenditures.*** Washington, DC: World Priorities, Inc., Box 25140, Washington, DC 20007. Annual. Approximately 60p. $6. ISSN 0363-4795.

This lucidly readable annual survey grew out of the author's previous work as chief of the economics division of the U.S. Arms Control and Disarmament Agency. The statistics, selected from official reports, draw contrasts and connections between military and social priorities, low-income and high-income countries, and violence and neglect of human needs.

United Nations. **Demographic Yearbook.** 40th ed. New York: U.N. Department of International Economic and Social Affairs, Statistical Office, 1988 (published in 1990). Distributed in the United States by Taylor & Francis International Publishers, New York, Philadelphia, and Washington, DC. 1,099p. $110. ISBN 92-105-107-39.

Extensive tables permit multi-year comparisons of births, birth and fertility rates, deaths and population growth rates, infant mortality and infant mortality rates, proportions of populations by gender and age groups, etc.

———. **Statistical Yearbook.** 36th ed. New York: U.N. Department of International Economic and Social Affairs, Statistical Office, 1987 (published in 1990). Distributed in the United States by Taylor & Francis International Publishers, New York, Philadelphia, and Washington, DC. 1,137p. $90. ISBN 92-106-113-14, paper.

Despite the title, this yearbook is published irregularly. The 1983/84 edition is the most recent one available. The emphasis is on economic data such as government disbursements by various categories, workforce population and employment characteristics, wages, prices, and consumption. A consumer price index is calculated for each country for the most recent decade, both (1) for all items and (2) for food, a very important hunger-related statistic.

United Nations Children's Fund (UNICEF). **State of the World's Children.*** New York: Oxford University Press for UNICEF. Annual. Approximately 120p. $6.50. ISSN 0265-718X.

Each year's edition of this popular report contains highly readable, timely discussions by UNICEF Executive Director James Grant and other staff on issues affecting the well-being of children, especially in developing countries. Its value as a statistical reference lies partly in the many clearly designed charts and graphs that illustrate these discussions and partly in the concluding statistical tables (drawn from various U.N. data sources). These tables depict the status of basic national economic and social indicators, child nutrition, maternal and child health, education, and demographic trends in most of the world's countries. Like ILO, UNICEF is a leader in advocating definitions and measurements of development that highlight development's quality-of-life impact on the poorer segments of the population.

U.S. Department of Agriculture, Economic Research Service. **Foreign Agricultural Trade of the United States.** Washington, DC: USDA, Economic Research Service. Eight times a year. $20. To obtain publications, call (800) 999-6779.

FATUS, as this report is commonly called, updates the quantity and value of U.S. farm exports and imports and indicates trends in the prices of major food grains along with other agricultural products.

——. **World Agriculture: Situation and Outlook Report.** Washington, DC: USDA, Economic Research Service. Three times a year. $10. To obtain publications, call (800) 999-6779.

Each report emphasizes information pertinent to international trade in commodities of greatest commercial value such as wheat, rice, corn, soybeans, livestock, oilseeds, and tropical products.

——. **World Food Needs and Availabilities.** Washington, DC: USDA, Economic Research Service. Three issues for 1987/88 (fall, winter, spring); two issues for 1988/89 (summer, winter). Discontinued in December 1989. To obtain publications, call (800) 999-6779.

This report was prepared to assist an Interagency Food Aid Analysis Working Group within the executive branch that was created in 1984.

World Bank. **The World Bank Atlas 1989.*** Washington, DC: World Bank, 1989. 28p. $5.95. To obtain publications, call Order Fulfillment Operations at (201) 225-2165.

Colorful and easy-to-read world maps, tables, and graphs highlight key economic and social indicators and trends in the development of 185 countries and territories. The atlas, now in its twenty-second edition, has become an international standard in statistical compilations.

——. **World Development Report.** New York: Oxford University Press for the World Bank. Annual. Approximately 260p. $12.95, paper. ISSN 0163-5085.

Each edition includes a summary of recent developments in the world economy, along with the latest world development indicators as selected and analyzed by the World Bank from databases of both the U.N. and the bank. These indicators are presented in approximately 30 statistical tables each year. Each edition also features one particular topic. Agriculture was featured in 1982; population change, in 1985. Financial systems and development is the featured topic of the 1989 report and poverty in the 1990 report.

World Food Council. **Report by the Secretariat*** or **Report by the Executive Director.*** Rome: World Food Council. Annual. Limited distribution, but may be requested from the World Food Council, United Nations, New York, NY 10017.

The World Food Council (WFC) meets in Ministerial Session every June, at a different location each time. World Food Council documents are referred to by the year and location of a particular Ministerial Session. A major purpose of the annual meeting is to review the current state of hunger and food security. For this review, WFC staff, assisted by FAO and other U.N. agencies, produce the most authoritative possible summary of recent data on the world hunger problem. The principal summary document is titled as indicated above, with slight variations from year to year. These analytical summaries by WFC staff should not be confused with the U.N. General Assembly's annual *Report of the World Food Council on the Work of Its . . . Session,* which is found in many bibliographies. The General Assembly's document is an administrative summary of WFC proceedings and is of little use for the study of world hunger.

World Health Organization (WHO). **World Health Statistics Annual. Vol. 1, Vital Statistics and Cause of Death.** Geneva: World Health Organization. Annual. ISSN 0250-3794.

Each edition contains a global overview plus some special features. Topics covered by statistical tables in the overview in recent editions include births and maternal deaths; trends in infant mortality, malaria, immunization coverage, smallpox, and yellow fever; and the service coverage of safe water supply and sanitation. The vital statistics kept in public health records do not record death from starvation or severe malnutrition as such; the immediate cause of death will be stated, rather, as a disease or pathological condition to which the hungry person was fatally vulnerable.

Periodicals

In recent years almost every major periodical has carried a discussion of world hunger. The periodicals included here, however, are only those that specialize in food policy and hunger or that average at least one article or book review related to these topics in each issue. Among academic journals, preference is given to those that use only standard English, avoiding highly technical terms or advanced mathematics and statistics. Exceptions are noted in the annotations. The annotations also indicate which periodicals are intended for scholars and which address a general audience. The organization of references in this section is alphabetical by title.

AgExporter
U.S. Department of Agriculture, Foreign Agriculture Service
Order from:
Superintendent of Documents
U.S. Government Printing Office
Washington, DC 20402
Monthly. $13.

The purpose of this relatively new periodical is to increase exports by the U.S. food industry. Not surprisingly, it contains less information relating to world hunger than did its predecessor, *Foreign Agriculture.* However, short items titled "Country Briefs" often provide news about current food consumption trends in developing countries that is not easily found elsewhere.

Agricultural Systems
Elsevier Science Publishers
Crown House, Linton Road
Barking, Essex IG11 8JU
United Kingdom

In North America:
Elsevier Science Publishers
Journal Information Center
655 Avenue of the Americas
New York, NY 10010
Quarterly. $608.
ISSN 0308-521X

The stated objective is to further the efficient use of resources to feed the world by examining research on all aspects of the human food chain from production to consumption. Although only a fourth of the articles deal with farming and food systems in developing countries rather than those in North America and Europe, they are high quality articles for a multidisciplinary audience. *Agricultural Administration and Extension,* which began in 1960, was incorporated into this journal in 1976.

Agriculture and Human Values
Agriculture and Human Values, Inc.

c/o Richard P. Haynes, Editor
Department of Philosophy
240A Dauer Hall
University of Florida
Gainesville, FL 32608
Quarterly. Students $15, individuals $20, institutions $30.
ISSN 0889-048X

The liberal arts and agricultural disciplines are combined here for educators, policy makers, and researchers interested in understanding the implications of a wide variety of actual and potential food and agricultural policies and practices, both in developed and developing economies. The journal was founded in 1983 with support from the W. K. Kellogg Foundation, the Humanities and Agriculture Program of the University of Florida, and the College of Agriculture of the Institute of Food and Agricultural Sciences (IFAS) at the University of Florida. IFAS and the Department of Rural Sociology at the University of Missouri at Columbia are the institutional sponsors.

American Journal of Agricultural Economics
American Agricultural Economics Association
Department of Economics
Iowa State University
Ames, IA 50011
Five times a year. $65.
ISSN 0002-9092

Although U.S. agriculture dominates the contents, economic aspects of food security in developing nations are discussed frequently. This is a good source for recent analyses by prominent U.S. economists on both microeconomic topics (e.g., how peasant farm households in a particular area market their surpluses) and macroeconomic issues (e.g., the effect of international trade on national food supplies or the impact of food aid on food producers in recipient nations).

Bioscience
American Institute of Biological Sciences
730 11th Street, NW
Washington, DC 20001-4584
Monthly. Individuals $43.50, institutions $96.50.
ISSN 0006-3568

A wide range of questions having to do with how farmers in developing countries can continue to produce food over the long run are frequent topics here.

Cultural Survival
Cultural Survival, Inc.

11 Divinity Avenue
Cambridge, MA 02138
Quarterly. $25 minimum contribution.
ISSN 0740-3291

Protecting the land rights and the traditional food and economic systems of indigenous peoples are difficult and pressing issues in the development of strategies to end world hunger. The journal was founded in 1976 to inform the general public and policy makers on these and related issues and to stimulate action on behalf of tribal peoples and ethnic minorities.

Culture and Agriculture: Bulletin of the Culture and Agriculture Group
Culture and Agriculture
c/o Timothy F. Frankenberger, Editor
Office of Arid Lands Studies
University of Arizona
845 North Park Avenue
Tucson, AZ 85719
Several times a year. $10.

Social, biological, and environmental aspects of agriculture, rural development, and agrarian change are the topics of discussion in this bulletin. It was started in 1984 by an interdisciplinary group of academics and development practitioners. The Culture and Agriculture Group is now affiliated with the American Anthropological Association.

Development
Society for International Development (SID)
Palazzo Civilta del Lavoro
Rome 00144, Italy

In the United States:
SID
1401 New York Avenue
Washington, DC 20005
Quarterly. Subscription is by membership in SID, individuals $25, students $5.
ISSN 1011-6370.

Issues of inequity and poverty within and between nations are discussed here in essays rather than research papers. The authors are SID members who are official and private development specialists from more than 100 countries, from both North and South. SID was formed in 1957 as an independent, nongovernmental organization to encourage a "mutually educating" development dialogue. Executive Director and Editor-in-Chief Maurice Williams was formerly executive director of the United Nations World Food Council.

Development and Change
Sage Publications
28 Banner Street
London EC1Y 8QE
United Kingdom
Quarterly. Individuals $39, institutions $99.
ISSN 0012-155X

Issues of developing-country agriculture, food, the role of women, and socioeconomic inequity are discussed frequently among the wide range of research topics appearing in this journal. It has been produced since 1969 by the Institute of Social Studies in The Hague, Netherlands.

Development Anthropology Network: Bulletin of the Institute for Development Anthropology
Institute for Development Anthropology
99 Collier Street
P.O. Box 2207
Binghamton, NY 13902
Semi-annual. $10.
ISSN 8756-0488

Articles on food and rural development share space with news about the Institute for Development Anthropology. The institute was founded in 1976 to promote attention to the significance of the knowledge, skills, and objectives of people "at the grassroots" when changes are planned in the name of development progress. The bulletin began in 1982.

Development Forum
United Nations Division for Economic and Social Information
Department of Public Information
U.N., Room 1061
New York, NY 10017
Bimonthly. $25 minimum contribution.
ISSN 0281-6632

The brief articles in this 24-page, tabloid-size news journal—on development issues, events, and ideas—typically relate to needs and activities of low-income people. They are written in nonacademic style by development specialists and journalists from both North and South. This is the only publication on economic and social development that is produced by the United Nations system collectively and on a regular basis. The views expressed are those of the authors, independent of U.N. policy.

Development Policy Review
Sage Publications
28 Banner Street
London EC1Y 8QE
United Kingdom
Quarterly. Individuals $39, institutions $91.
ISSN 0950-6764

This journal of the Overseas Development Institute in London offers unusually clear and cogent research reports, essays, and book reviews on such topics as population, trade, environment, farmers, women, debt, and aid. Publication began in 1983.

The Ecologist
Worthyvale Manor Farm
Camelford, Cornwall PL32 9TT
United Kingdom
Published by Ecosystems, Ltd.
Six times a year. $30.
ISSN 0261-3131

The relationships between deforestation and food systems, agricultural technology, famine, and the Green Revolution are among the hunger-related topics discussed frequently in this journal of the Wadebridge Ecological Centre in Cornwall. The journal incorporates *Mazingira,* formerly published by the U.N. Environment Programme in Nairobi. Back issues are available on microfilm from University Microfilms in Ann Arbor, Michigan. An index is included in issue No. 6 each year.

Ecology of Food and Nutrition
Gordon and Breach, Science Publishers, Inc.
Distributed by:
STBS, Ltd.
1 Bedford Street
London WC2E 9PP
United Kingdom
Quarterly. Individuals $152, libraries $304, corporations $444.
ISSN 0367-0244

This interdisciplinary international journal publishes both research and policy critiques, emphasizing (but not restricted to) developing countries. A recent issue included criticism of food aid, a description of food distribution customs in Nigerian families, an analysis of the nutritional impact of home gardens in Senegal, and a public health strategy for infant feeding in the Philippines.

Economic and Political Weekly
Hitkari House
284 Shahid Bhagatsingh Road
Bombay 400 038
India
Weekly. Individuals $40, institutions $60.

Reports on current events and in-depth analytical articles appear in this publication that combines aspects of a popular news magazine with those of an academic journal. The scope is international but emphasis is on India and other countries of South Asia where the majority of the world's hungry population reside. Food, nutrition, and the agrarian situation are frequent topics.

Economic Development and Cultural Change
University of Chicago Press
Journals Division
P.O. Box 37005
Chicago, IL 60637
Quarterly. Students $25, individuals $30, institutions $55.

Food production, consumption, and distribution patterns in developing countries are frequent topics of these comprehensive reports intended for scholars. This interdisciplinary journal has been published since 1951 by the Research Center in Economic Development and Cultural Change of the University of Chicago.

Environment
Heldref Publications
4000 Albemarle Street, NW
Washington, DC 20016
Ten times a year. $24.

Illustrated articles on topics affecting food supplies, hunger, and poverty in developing countries appear in nearly every issue of this magazine for a popular audience. Back issues through 1983 are available from University Microfilms in Ann Arbor, Michigan; those since 1983, from the publisher. The magazine was started in 1959 by Heldref Publications and the Scientists' Institute for Public Information in New York. Heldref is a division of the Helen Dwight Reid Educational Foundation.

Food and Nutrition
Food and Nutrition Organization of the United Nations (FAO)
Food Policy and Nutrition Division

Via delle Terme di Caracalla
00100 Rome
Italy
Semi-annual. $8.
ISSN 0304-8942

This nontechnical journal was begun in 1975 to exchange information and ideas among nutritionists, FAO staff, and non-nutritionists concerned with improving food consumption and nutrition in developing countries. The views expressed in signed articles are those of the authors and not necessarily of the FAO.

Food and Nutrition Bulletin
United Nations University
Academic Publications Services
Toho Seimei Building
15-1 Shibuya 2-chome, Shibuya-ku
Tokyo 150, Japan
Quarterly. $30.
ISSN 0379-5721

This multidisciplinary journal for scholars uses technical terms and advanced statistics. It is devoted explicitly to the problems of hunger and malnutrition in the developing countries. The contents include policy analyses, state-of-the-art summaries, and original scientific articles. The bulletin is published in collaboration with the U.N. ACC (Administrative Committee on Coordination) Subcommittee on Nutrition. It incorporates the *PAG Bulletin* of the former Protein-Calorie Advisory Group of the United Nations system. Editor Nevin S. Scrimshaw is director of the International Food and Nutrition Program at the Massachusetts Institute of Technology.

Food Policy
Butterworth Scientific Limited
P.O. Box 63
Westbury House, Bury Street
Guildford GU2 5BH
United Kingdom

In North America:
Butterworth, Journals Fulfillment Department
80 Montvale Avenue
Stoneham, MA 02180
Quarterly. Individuals $69, institutions $243.
ISSN 0306-9192

This international journal is designed for scholars and development practitioners who are concerned with the economics, planning, and politics of food, agriculture, and nutrition as a means to eliminate hunger. It began in 1975 in response to a need revealed by the 1972–1974 world food crisis for more expertise devoted to the world hunger problem by economists and political scientists. In addition to short essays, longer research reports, and book reviews, each issue contains announcements and reports of professional meetings, synopses of documents from food-related United Nations agencies, and news affecting food problems in Africa, Asia, Pacific island nations, the Caribbean, and Latin America.

Food Research Institute Studies
Food Research Institute
Stanford University
Stanford, CA 94304
Three issues per volume (published irregularly). $30.
ISSN 0193-9025

Lengthy research reports on food consumption, hunger, and malnutrition appear occasionally among the equally lengthy, detailed discussions of production and trade that are more typical of this scholarly journal for agricultural economists. The journal is indexed and abstracted in *Agrindex, PAIS,* and the *Journal of Economic Literature* (see "Bibliographies, Indexes, and Abstracts," above). The editor is Walter P. Falcon, director of the Food Research Institute. The institute was founded in 1925; publication of the journal began in 1930.

Human Ecology
Plenum Publishing Corporation
233 Spring Street
New York, NY 10013
Quarterly. Individuals $39, institutions $155.
ISSN 0300-7839

The complex and varied systems of interaction among people and their environments are the general subject here. Many research reports deal with local food systems in developing countries. Contributors include both academics and practitioners from fields as diverse as anthropology, geography, psychology, biology, sociology, and urban planning. The journal was begun in 1972.

Hunger Notes
World Hunger Education Service
P.O. Box 29056
Washington, DC 20017
Bimonthly. Individuals $18, institutions $45.
ISSN 0740-1116

Interrelationships are emphasized among economic, political, scientific, social, and environmental factors that affect the access of low-income people to food. Each issue treats a single topic in depth, in nontechnical terms for a broad audience. A networking department features publications and activities of a highly diverse spectrum of organizations and individuals—"establishment" and "anti-establishment," official and private, researchers, activists, students, and development practitioners.

ifda dossier
International Foundation for Development Alternatives (IFDA)
4 Place du Marche
1260 Nyon, Switzerland
Bimonthly. $32.

Agriculture, consumer issues, ecology, human economic and political rights, poverty, and women's issues are frequent topics in this unique forum. It was established in the mid-1970s for a global network of development advocates who stress the concerns of people at the grassroots rather than those of national or international elites. English is the language of general information (announcements, book reviews, indexes), but articles are published in English, French, or Spanish as received from the author. An index for 1988–1989 appears in the November/December 1989 issue by author and title, association, and subject.

IFPRI Abstract
International Food Policy Research Institute (IFPRI)
1776 Massachusetts Avenue, NW
Washington, DC 20036
Monthly. Free.

Each issue is a four-page summary of recent IFPRI research on some aspect of technological change, agricultural growth, overall economic growth, or social welfare as it relates to the world hunger problem. Directed by John Mellor, IFPRI is the sole institute of social and nutritional scientists within the multilateral Consultative Group on International Agricultural Research (CGIAR). The complete report summarized by each *IFPRI Abstract* can be ordered separately.

ILO Information
International Labour Office
Geneva, Switzerland

In North America:
ILO, Washington Branch
1828 L Street, NW

Washington, DC 20036
Five times a year. Free.

The ILO is one of the world's premier research centers on poverty-related development questions. This modest eight-page newsletter is a valuable source of current information. It carries short articles and news items concerning conditions of industrial and agricultural laborers around the world. It also monitors the roles of multinational or transnational enterprises in questions of employment and basic human needs.

Journal of Developing Areas (JDA)
Western Illinois University
900 West Adams Street
Macomb, IL 61455
Quarterly. Individuals $18, institutions $25.
ISSN 0022-037X

The objective of this journal is to promote a fuller understanding of the relationship between humans and the development process. The agrarian situation in Latin America (a key to hunger there) is a frequent topic. Articles directly about hunger or food are relatively infrequent. In addition to the mix of social sciences common in interdisciplinary journals, this journal includes work by contributors from the arts, literature, philosophy, law, and even military science. Publication began in 1963.

Journal of Developing Societies
E. J. Brill
POB 9000, 2300 PA
Leiden, The Netherlands
Semi-annual. Dutch Guilders 96.
ISSN 0169-796X

Both applied theory and applied research appear in this international journal, presented by scholars from the humanities as well as from the social sciences. The relevance of theory to immediate practical problems, for example, is illustrated by a recent article in which three different explanations of African famine are traced to three contrasting theories of economic development.

Journal of Development Studies
Frank Cass & Co., Ltd.
Gainsborough House
11 Gainsborough Road
London E11 1RS
United Kingdom

Quarterly. Individuals $65, institutions $130.
ISSN 0022-0388

Research and perspectives on poverty and progress, primarily in rural areas, are featured by this scholarly journal, which began in 1964. Disciplines represented include sociology, economics, political science, and social anthropology. Three of the four editors are affiliated with the Institute of Social Studies in The Hague, Netherlands.

Journal of Modern African Studies
Cambridge University Press
Journals Department
40 West 20th Street
New York, NY 10011
Quarterly. Individuals $49, institutions $108.
ISSN 0022-278X

The subtitle aptly identifies this as a "survey of politics, economics and related topics in contemporary Africa." Articles or book reviews dealing with food and hunger in Africa appear in every issue. The journal began in 1962 and is a good source for scholarly treatment of the African famines and the ongoing food crisis of the 1970s and 1980s.

Journal of Peasant Studies
Frank Cass & Co., Ltd.
Gainsborough House
11 Gainsborough Road
London E11 1RS
United Kingdom
Quarterly. Individuals $65, institutions $125.

The topics of this academic journal are the political, economic, and social issues affecting rural peoples mainly, but not only, in developing countries. Most of the theoretical and descriptive analyses here are presented from the perspective of current Marxian theory.

Land Reform, Land Settlements and Cooperatives
FAO, Human Resources
Institutions and Agrarian Reform Division
Via delle Terme di Caracalla
00100 Rome, Italy
Distributed by FAO Publications Division, Distribution
and Sales Section
Semi-annual. Free.

Articles, reports, book reviews, and legislative information on agrarian reform in developing countries have appeared here since 1963. A cumulative index from 1963–1988 is included in the combined issue No. 1/2, 1988 (published in 1989).

Land Use Policy
Butterworth Scientific, Ltd.
P.O. Box 63
Westbury House, Bury Street
Guildford GU2 5BH
United Kingdom

In North America:
Butterworth, Journals Fulfillment Department
80 Montvale Avenue
Stoneham, MA 02180
Quarterly. Individuals $80, institutions $168.
ISSN 0264-8377

The conservation and sustainability of food-producing resources, farmers, and farming systems are among the hunger-related topics in this international journal that began in 1984. Approximately half of the articles and book reviews deal with political, social, economic, and legal aspects of land use in developing countries.

Latin-American Perspectives
Sage Publications
2111 West Hilcrest Drive
Newberry Park, CA 91320
Quarterly. Individuals $30, institutions $85.
ISSN 0094-582X

Hunger, malnutrition, and agrarian poverty are conspicuously rare topics in scholarly journals that specialize in Latin America. When such topics appear, it is most likely to happen in this journal for "discussion and debate on the political economy of capitalism, imperialism and socialism in the Americas." The Marxist-oriented editors seek to include a diversity of political viewpoints.

Population and Development Review
Population Council
One Dag Hammarskjold Plaza
New York, NY 10017
Quarterly. $24.

The intent of this journal is to advance knowledge of the interrelationships between population and socioeconomic development. It also provides a forum for discussion of related public policy. The journal began in 1975. About half of the articles are on developing countries, often in relationship to conditions that affect hunger.

Progress in Human Geography
Edward Arnold
41 Bedford Square
London WC1B 3DQ
United Kingdom
Quarterly. Individuals $62, institutions $95.

On average, two or three hunger-related articles or book reviews appear in each issue of this international review of geographical work in the social sciences and humanities. It began in 1977, titled *Progress in Geography*.

Review of African Political Economy (ROAPE)
Regency House
75-77 St. Mary's Road
Sheffield S2 4AN
United Kingdom
Three times a year. Individuals $30, institutions $55.
ISSN 0305-6244

Direct observation from the authors' personal experiences combines with academic research in this journal. Hunger and famine are frequent topics, primarily viewed from a socialist perspective. The journal began in 1974 and is indexed in the *Alternative Press Index*.

Rural Africana
African Studies Center
Michigan State University
East Lansing, MI 48824-1035
Three times a year. $21.
ISSN 0085-5839

Each issue publishes current, multidisciplinary research on one specific question or area of research about rural Africa, often including food production and hunger. The journal began in 1967. The editor is Assefa Mehretu; associate editors are Michael Bratton, Carl K. Eicher, and Carl Liedholm.

SCN News
Secretariat, U.N. Administrative Committee for Coordination,
Subcommittee on Nutrition (ACC/SCN)
United Nations
New York, NY 10017
Semi-annual. Free.

This is a periodic review of developments in international nutrition compiled from information available to the ACC/SCN. It provides a valuable, practical perspective on problems, ideas, and projects of current interest to international nutritionists and program administrators attempting to alleviate or prevent hunger crises. Recent topics have included research findings on the effect of cash cropping on food consumption in Africa and strategies for managing disaster response.

Seeds
222 East Lake Drive
Decatur, GA 30030
Bimonthly. $16.

In 1982, *Seeds* was among the first winners of the Annual World Hunger Media awards for hunger journalism addressed to a popular audience. The magazine was initiated in 1978 by a Baptist congregation in Decatur, Georgia, but is now independent and unaffiliated. Short, lively articles, special departments, and illustrations promote understanding and action on the spiritual, political, and economic realities that lie at the roots of hunger. Ideals of biblical justice characterize the editorial perspective.

Why Magazine
World Hunger Year
261 West 35th Street
New York, NY 10001-1906
Quarterly. $18.

"Challenging hunger and poverty" is the motto of this lively magazine edited by Peter Mann. *Why* incorporated and replaced *Food Monitor Magazine* in spring of 1989. True to its name, *Why* raises important questions that are intelligently probed in short articles or interviews by leading spokespersons from varying points of view. *Food Monitor* was started in 1977 by World Hunger Year, singer Harry Chapin's organization, and the Institute for Food and Development Policy, led by Frances Moore Lappé and Joseph Collins.

The World Bank Economic Review
World Bank Publications
1818 H Street, NW
Washington, DC 20433
Three times a year. Individuals $25, institutions $45.
ISSN 0258-6770

Research sponsored by the World Bank on questions of economic development policy is reported here to a professional audience of economists and social scientists in government, business, international agencies, universities, and development research institutions. Topics related to food and hunger include such matters as the effects of land-ownership security on farmer behavior, economic incentives for farmers in Africa and Asia, and how to determine the economic impact of nutritional status. The journal began in 1987.

The World Bank Research Observer
World Bank Publications
1818 H Street, NW
Washington, DC 20433
Semi-annual. Free.
ISSN 0257-3032

Non-economists will find this publication useful for keeping informed about economic research currently in progress within the World Bank. Articles address events and trends in aspects of economics that the bank considers particularly relevant for development policy. Technical language is rigorously avoided. Advanced high school students and college students at any level of study in the social sciences should find this readable.

World Development
Pergamon Press
Maxwell House, Fairview Park
Elmsford, NY 10523
Monthly. Students $56, individuals $116, institutions $410.

Development, social institutions, and science and technology are the three main subject areas of this journal for an international, multi-disciplinary audience. Editorial policy defines development as "an attack on the chief evils in the world today: malnutrition, disease, illiteracy, slums and unemployment." Research papers, essays, and book reviews relating to hunger appear frequently. The editor of the unusually extensive book review department is Guy Gran. The journal was founded in 1973 by Paul Streeten, who chairs the editorial board. Streeten is director of the World Development Institute of Boston University. Despite similarity in names, journal and institute are not affiliated.

Monograph and Occasional Paper Series

Cornell International Nutrition Monograph Series
Cornell Program in International Nutrition
Division of Nutritional Sciences

Cornell University
Ithaca, NY 14863-6301

Twenty-one titles have appeared since 1974. Monographs are ordered individually by title and are $3 each. *Hunger and Society,* a special subseries consisting of Numbers 17, 18, and 19, appeared in 1988, edited by Michael Latham, Uwe Johnson, and others.

Land Tenure Center Papers
Land Tenure Center Research Papers
Land Tenure Center
1300 University Avenue
University of Wisconsin–Madison
Madison, WI 53706

Land Tenure Center (LTC) Research Papers tend to deal with agrarian issues in greater detail and on a smaller scale (e.g., the Central District of Botswana or Southern Haiti) than do monographs in the LTC Papers series, where discussion may include the whole of Africa or Latin America. There is no subscription for either series. Monographs are purchased individually according to details in the latest "Available Publications List."

Hearings Reports
Staff Reports
Select Committee on Hunger
U.S. Congress, House of Representatives
Washington, DC 20515

The Select Committee on Hunger serves as the principal fact-finder for Congress on current matters relating to hunger in developing countries or in the United States. The committee holds approximately ten hearings each year, mainly on international issues. Hearings Reports and the less frequent Staff Reports may be requested from the Select Committee (202-226-5470) or purchased from the U.S. Government Printing Office. No list of titles is available.

Occasional Papers
Reprint Series
Research Reports
Hunger Reports (annual beginning with 1988)
World Hunger Program
Box 1831
Brown University
Providence, RI 02912

Monographs are ordered individually from the World Hunger Program Publications List.

Worldwatch Papers
Worldwatch Institute
1776 Massachusetts Avenue, NW
Washington, DC 20036

The influence of trends in population and agriculture on the sustained adequacy of food-producing resources has been a frequent topic of this monthly series since 1975. Monographs may be ordered individually ($4 each) or received regularly through annual membership in Worldwatch Institute ($25).

Landmark Monographs

The books, reports, and essays in this section have had a particularly marked influence on the way large numbers of people perceive the problem of hunger or they have signaled a change in established wisdom about hunger. This selection, however, is only that: a selection. The list is indicative, not exhaustive.

Barnet, Richard J., and Ronald E. Muller. **Global Reach: The Power of Multinational Corporations.** New York: Simon and Schuster, 1974.

During debates on the world food crisis of 1972–1974, many voices from the unofficial public, especially Marxist intellectuals and Christian ethicists, accused multinational corporations of being either a primary cause of poverty and hunger in developing countries or at least an important part of the cause. Those views found strong support in this well-researched critique, although the work does not deal with hunger directly.

Berg, Alan, with Robert J. Muscat. **The Nutrition Factor: Its Role in National Development.** A study sponsored jointly by the Foundation for Child Development and the Brookings Institution. Washington, DC: Brookings Institution, 1973.

This was the first major work to translate the knowledge of health professionals, nutritionists, and relief workers about malnutrition and famine in developing countries into the language and concerns of those who make national economic policy. It is still a good place to start an examination of what national policy makers should know.

Borgstrom, Georg. **The Hungry Planet: The Modern World at the Edge of Famine.** New York: Macmillan, 1965. Second revised edition 1972, Colliers.

One of the most influential neo-Malthusian warnings that imprinted popular awareness in the 1960s, this book originated as a series of radio broadcasts. Borgstrom, noted professor of food science and geography at Michigan State University, warned not only of impending disaster from population growth but also of the strain upon planetary resources inflicted by modern technology and high-consumption Western societies.

Boserup, Ester. **Woman's Role in Economic Development.** London: George Allen and Unwin, 1970; New York: St. Martin's Press, 1970.

Women in development (WID), a new kind of development policy research with great significance for the world hunger problem, was launched by this pioneering work. This Danish economist highlighted the critical importance of women agriculturalists in Africa and the ways in which development innovations in Africa had handicapped women's ability to produce food or to succeed in their other economic roles.

Brown, Lester. **By Bread Alone.** New York: Praeger Publishers, 1974. Published for the Overseas Development Council.

Strains in the world's food supply, this agricultural economist warns, come from three main causes: increased population pressure, the consumption patterns of the affluent, and farming practices that deplete natural resources essential to produce food. All of Brown's many writings, dating from the early 1960s, raise the same warning: The human race is heading for disaster because of its excessive demand on natural resources. A change of course is urgent. This book is his most comprehensive discussion of the world food system, published at the height of the food crisis of 1972–1974.

Cornea, Giovanni Andrea, Richard Jolly, and Frances Stewart, eds. **Adjustment with a Human Face.** Vol. 1, **Protecting the Vulnerable and Promoting Growth.** Oxford and New York: Oxford University Press, 1987.

The Third World debt crisis is also a hunger crisis, as documented in these two volumes. Rising malnutrition and mortality rates among infants and children in many developing countries during the 1980s reversed three decades of development progress. The main reasons, UNICEF and others argue, stem from drastic adjustments in national policies that have been forced on debt-burdened countries by the World Bank and the International Monetary Fund as the price of assistance. Even before these volumes appeared, "adjustment with a human face" became universal shorthand for alternative economic adjustment policies, advocated forcefully by economist Richard Jolly and others at UNICEF, that challenge the conventional wisdom of the World Bank and IMF.

Council on Environmental Quality and the U.S. Department of State. **The Global 2000 Report to the President: Entering the Twenty-first Century.** 3 vols. Washington, DC: U.S. Government Printing Office, 1980. London: Penguin edition, Vol. 1, **Summary,** 1982.

Though technically flawed, this is the most ambitious effort of its kind yet undertaken by the U.S. government. The Global 2000 study projects the consequences of probable changes in the world's population, natural resources, and environment through the end of this century if current national and international policies continue. The conclusions point to alarming stresses on the earth's carrying capacity for the human population by the year 2000, including stresses on food supply. The study was undertaken in response to a directive issued by President Jimmy Carter on 23 May 1977 and was completed in 1980.

Food and Agriculture Organization of the United Nations (FAO). **Agriculture: Toward 2000.** Rome: FAO, 1981.

FAO's most ambitious review of the future of world agriculture describes three scenarios with the aid of computer modelling. One scenario projects trends of the status quo forward to the year 2000. A second scenario assumes modest improvements in trends since the early 1960s. A third scenario assumes more ambitious rates of agricultural growth. In addition to agricultural growth, the review examines the distribution of access to productive assets and the benefits of production.

Freire, Paulo. **Pedagogy of the Oppressed.** New York: Seabury Press, 1970. Translated by Myra Bergman Ramos from the original 1968 Portuguese manuscript.

This landmark remains a classic for those who view hunger primarily as a result of the oppression of the poor by powerful elites. The English translation of the exiled Brazilian educator's revolutionary treatise on pedagogical theory went through ten printings within only three years. It illuminates a methodology for assisting the oppressed poor in any society to achieve liberation nonviolently. Freire's theories derive from personal experience among Brazil's poor before he was forced into exile by the ruling oligarchy.

Gabel, Medard, with the World Game Laboratory. **Ho-Ping: Food for Everyone.** Garden City, NY: Anchor Press/Doubleday, 1979.

The World Game, a group simulation of problem-solving upon which this book is based, applies Buckminster Fuller's theories of design science to global problems. Research on world food systems began the process in 1971 and the first World Game Workshop was conducted in 1974. The World Game's reputation as a method of thinking creatively about world problems has grown rapidly, most recently among policy makers and development professionals. This book's significance is as an introduction to the principles that shape the World Game: global problems must be viewed globally because the sum of local solutions will never deal adequately with a global problem; *only* the whole big system works, because parts of a system cannot work in isolation; the synergies of global solutions can mitigate or eliminate local problems; and the present state of human knowledge is such that a nutritionally sound diet is available for everyone on earth today and can be maintained continuously for all generations to come if we use our resources as well as we know how.

George, Susan. **How the Other Half Dies: The Real Reasons for World Hunger.** Montclair, NJ: Allanheld, Osmun, 1977.

George's first major essay on world hunger, meticulously documented, went through three printings in its first year. It remains a classic in the "hunger is politics" school of thought. Since hunger is caused by the present mal-distribution of power over food-producing resources between rich and poor nations and between the elites and the majority of the people within nations, George argues, the solution lies in political action and social change.

Hardin, Garrett. **"The Tragedy of the Commons."** *Science* 162 (13 December 1968): 1243–1248.

This is the rather abstract essay that launched Hardin's path to fame as the advocate of "lifeboat ethics" during the world food crisis of 1972–1974. To many, the position taken by the noted genetic biologist represents extreme immorality in choosing how to respond to the hunger problem. To others, Hardin is a supreme realist. The tragedy assumed here is that, inevitably, any limited resource open to unrestricted use by all will be ruined for all because of abuse by the least conscientious and greediest of its users. Hardin's "commons" was a metaphor for planet earth endangered by unrestricted population growth. The metaphor later changed to a "lifeboat" and Hardin's position came to be known as "lifeboat ethics": lower birth-rate nations are in a lifeboat surrounded by overpopulated and hungry nations that are drowning in a sea of hunger. To save those in the lifeboat, Hardin argued, it was necessary to let most of those in the water drown. He believed that the alternative—feeding the hungry without restricting their right to reproduce—would doom everyone.

The Hunger Project. **Ending Hunger: An Idea Whose Time Has Come.** New York: Praeger Publishers, 1985.

This work is a landmark in the body of literature designed for popular education on the multiple factors that interrelate in the world hunger issue and on the diversity of views held by experts. Through spectacular photography, state-of-the-art graphic design, and expert public relations skills, this coffee-table book has gained entrance to hundreds of thousands of private homes in the United States and elsewhere. It also provides a wealth of substantive information, including footnotes and a complete index, for those who look beyond the pictures.

Independent Commission on International Development Issues. **North-South: A Program For Survival.** Cambridge, MA: M.I.T. Press, 1980.

The conclusions and recommendations of a voluntary, independent group of international leaders probing urgent global problems are reported here. The underlying problem common to all others, the commission finds, is the failure of the world economic system to deal with gross inequality. Hunger and poverty are prominent among the issues studied. The group of investigators is popularly called the Brandt Commission after its chairperson, Nobel laureate in peace and former West German chancellor Willy Brandt.

International Labour Office (ILO). **Employment, Growth and Basic Needs: A One-World Problem.** New York and London: Praeger Publishers, 1977. Published for the Overseas Development Council and the ILO. Introduction by James P. Grant.

The World Employment Conference of the ILO in 1976 advocated a "basic needs strategy" of development planning to correct the failure of conventional economic planning to eliminate hunger and other manifestations of poverty. To spread the conference's ideas more widely, this report was published with the help of the Overseas Development Council, a private organization in Washington, D.C. "Basic needs" has become a permanent concept in development terminology since the ILO conference.

Lappé, Frances Moore. **Diet for a Small Planet.** New York: Ballantine, 1971. Revised 1975.

This best-seller addressed a characteristic 1960s question: "How close are we to the limit of the earth's capacity to provide food for all humanity?" The answer: Not close at all, because the "incredible level of protein waste" built into the U.S. meat-centered diet leaves a large margin for change. The United States could feed many more people from the same natural resource base if Americans consumed protein directly from plants instead of indirectly through animals. At a time when the world hunger problem was commonly seen as a lack of enough food, this message fired the imagination of Americans glad to help the hungry by "eating farther down the food chain." More than a million copies of the book sold, with 12 printings alone between 1971 and 1974.

Lappé, Frances Moore, and Joseph Collins. **Food First: Beyond the Myth of Scarcity.** New York: Ballantine, 1977. Revised 1978.

Written for a popular audience, this challenge to conventional wisdom since World War II about hunger's causes and solutions is probably the most influential hunger book to appear since the 1974 World Food Conference. Hunger, *Food First* argues persuasively, is caused not by food shortages, weather, or overpopulation. Rather, hunger is caused by injustice that deprives the poor of power over productive resources. A few food and development specialists previously had put forward similar views in various reports, professional journals, or conferences, but with little effect. The wide distribution and enormous popularity of this book won greater attention to such interpretations than ever before. Many points of the argument made in this work have become the new conventional wisdom, although some remain controversial.

Library of Congress, Congressional Research Service. **Feeding the World's Population: Developments in the Decade following the World Food Conference of 1974.** Washington, DC: U.S. Government Printing Office, 1984.

This four-part report is the most comprehensive review of its kind, a major landmark in congressional knowledge of the world hunger problem. It describes the background and results of the World Food Conference, the world food situation in the decade following the conference, and trends in U.S. and multilateral foreign aid. Abstracts of 56 major studies and reports since 1974 are provided chronologically in Part 4. An appendix reprints the complete text of World Food Conference resolutions. The report was prepared for the Foreign Affairs Committee of the U.S. House of Representatives by the Foreign Affairs and National Defense Division of the Congressional Research Service.

McNamara, Robert. **"Address to the Board of Governors, Nairobi, Kenya, September 24, 1973."** Reprinted in *The McNamara Years: Major Policy Addresses of Robert S. McNamara 1968–1981,* edited by Robert McNamara and others. Washington, DC: World Bank, 1981.

The Nairobi address by World Bank President McNamara to the bank's board of governors contributed the terms *bottom 40 percent* and *absolute poverty* to the standard language of development. It is remembered as McNamara's most thorough description of the extent and nature of absolute poverty and perhaps the most catalytic discussion of these topics within the "official development community" up to that point. It is also one of his most eloquent pleas for increased development assistance as an act of moral conscience on the part of the citizens and governments of wealthy countries toward the hundreds of millions living in a condition of life "so limited as to prevent realization of the potential of the genes with which one is born; a condition of life so degrading as to insult human dignity—and yet a condition of life so common as to be the lot of some 40% of the peoples of the developing countries."

Malthus, Thomas Robert. **Essay on the Principle of Population as It Affects the Future Improvement of Society.** London, 1798; reissued in two volumes, Patricia James, ed. Cambridge: Cambridge University Press, 1990.

This is the original exposition of the now classic argument that famines due to overpopulation are inevitable. Malthus's views became conventional wisdom during the nineteenth century for British policy and also in other countries. Malthus reasoned that, since population grew geometrically while agricultural production increased only arithmetically (assumptions disproved later), a recurring imbalance was inevitable; the balance would be restored periodically, through tragic necessity, by a sharp rise in the death rate from famine, disease, or war. "Malthusian tragedy" has become a common figure of speech for famine from overpopulation.

Meadows, Donella H., et al. **The Limits to Growth: A Report for the Club of Rome's Project on the Predicament of Mankind.** New York: University Books, 1972.

The intent of the computer-modelling project reported here was to determine the impact for the next 100 years of global trends in rapid population growth, widespread malnutrition, depletion of nonrenewable resources, accelerating industrialization, and a deteriorating environment. The report's gloomy findings were widely publicized and exerted strong influence on the debate over potential world food production during the 1970s.

Mooney, Pat Roy. **Seeds of the Earth: A Private or Public Resource?** Ottawa: International Coalition for Development Action, 1980.

This small book, published by an NGO coalition, created a storm of controversy and put the seeds debate "on the map" worldwide and also on the agenda of the FAO. In great detail, Mooney documents the decline of genetic diversity in the world's food system brought about by the spread of modern agriculture, with its emphasis on genetic uniformity and hybrid varieties (which do not reproduce fertile seeds in nature). Mooney argues further that the IARCs aid and abet the alarming growth of power exercised over the present and future world food supply by multinational seed corporations through these corporations' patent monopolies on new seeds distributed through the market.

National Academy of Sciences (NAS), National Research Council. **World Food and Nutrition Study: The Potential Contributions of Research.** Washington, DC: National Academy of Sciences, 1977.

This scientific study, requested by President Gerald Ford following the 1974 World Food Conference, broke new ground among scientists by naming politics, rather than science and technology, as the key to ending hunger. The principal conclusion of the final report is often quoted: "given the political will here and abroad, it should be possible, by the turn of this century, to eliminate most of the hunger and malnutrition now associated with mass poverty."

Paddock, William, and Paul Paddock. **Famine—1975! America's Decision: Who Will Survive?** Boston: Little, Brown & Co., 1967. Reissued in 1976 under the title **Time of Famines: America and the World Food Crisis.**

This is the work that contributed the metaphor of *triage* to the ethical debate about how the United States should respond to world hunger. The Paddocks argued that aid should be given only to those nations most likely to benefit from it. Some nations, they argued, are "basket cases": too overpopulated, poor, or badly governed to be saved. In their view, aid resources were limited and should not be wasted on such countries.

Presidential Commission on World Hunger. **Overcoming World Hunger: The Challenge Ahead.** Washington, DC: Presidential Commission on World Hunger, 1980.

President Carter established this commission in 1978 in response to a congressional resolution introduced a year earlier and eventually co-sponsored by 265 members of the House of Representatives and 51 senators. The congressional process was catalyzed by World Hunger Year's founders, Harry Chapin (who served on the commission) and Bill Ayres, and promoted by an ad hoc coalition of many nongovernmental organizations. A "Dear Colleague" letter from the resolution's original sponsors (senators Patrick Leahy and Robert Dole and representatives Benjamin Gilman and Richard Nolan, all of whom served on the commission) described the commission's primary goals: "(1) to establish clearly the causes of domestic and international hunger and malnutrition and their interrelationships; (2) to identify and evaluate existing U.S. programs and policies . . . ; and (3) to present . . . specific . . . recommendations to significantly reduce hunger and malnutrition, and to outline specific steps for the development of a clearly defined and coordinated national food policy." The commission's principal recommendation is that "the U.S. government make the elimination of hunger the primary focus of its relationships with developing countries." With the dissenting and clarifying comments that were added by various commissioners, the commission's report demonstrates the main points at issue in the world hunger problem—the very points the commissioners could not resolve among themselves. An abridged edition of the final report received wide distribution and was the focus of organized study and discussion by church, civic, and campus groups.

Reutlinger, Shlomo, and Marcelo Selowsky. **Malnutrition and Poverty: Magnitude and Policy Options.** Baltimore, MD: Johns Hopkins University Press, 1976. Published for the World Bank.

The World Bank began examining nutrition in the context of its own programs in 1973. This monograph presents the conclusions of the first large research effort by the bank to determine the global dimension of malnutrition in low-income countries. Using income and calorie consumption data rather than food supply figures, the bank's estimate (840 million) added several hundred million more hungry people to the Food and Agriculture Organization's figure (435 million), which had been the accepted estimate up until then. Disagreement between the World Bank and FAO on the dimensions of the world hunger problem has continued ever since this report. The report also tried, for the first time ever, to estimate the economic aspects of various policies used by governments to reduce or prevent malnutrition.

Rostow, Walt Whitman. **The Stages of Economic Growth: A Non-Communist Manifesto.** Cambridge: Cambridge University Press, 1960.

The theory in this work by an economic historian, who was then on the faculty of the Massachusetts Institute of Technology, became the bible for the "trickle-down" development strategies hailed in the 1960s, the First United Nations Development Decade. The benefits of economic growth were predicted to "trickle down" from more progressive and prosperous groups in society to the poor. According to Rostow, modern economies evolved toward prosperity through five sequential stages: (1) the traditional society, (2) preconditions for "take-off," (3) "take-off," (4) the drive to maturity, and (5) the age of high mass-consumption. By the end of the First Development Decade, the growing gap between rich and poor and the deepening poverty in developing countries discredited "trickle-down" development. The stage was set for the great ferment of fresh debate and struggle for more equitable growth in the 1970s, which still continues.

Schumacher, E. F. **Small Is Beautiful: Economics as if People Mattered.** London: Blond & Briggs; New York: Harper & Row, 1973.

It was the second part of the title that Schumacher himself preferred: economics as if people mattered. Hunger, many were convinced by the time this volume appeared, could only be eliminated by economic strategies radically different from those in operation. Much as Rostow's theories had inspired conventional economists and planners in the 1960s, this collection of essays by the German-born British economist inspired radically different ideas in the 1970s. Schumacher takes a fresh look at the fundamental purpose of economic development, offering a new philosophical stance but not a coherent economic system. This landmark monograph also introduced "intermediate" ("appropriate") technology to the language of development.

Sen, Amartya. **Poverty and Famines: An Essay on Entitlement and Deprivation.** Oxford: Oxford University Press, 1981.

What causes starvation and famines? Not food shortages, this analysis concludes, but a loss of the famine victim's "entitlement" to food. This entitlement, Sen reasons, is based on an exchange of something for food, usually money but also labor or bartered goods. Starvation occurs even in the presence of an adequate food supply when the exchange value of what is offered for food falls too low. Many conditions can cause this to happen, but the cause is always more intricate than weather. Sen applies new ways of describing and measuring poverty to research on several of the worst famines of recent times. This study marks a watershed in conventional perspective on the nature of hunger crises and on appropriate governmental responses.

Simon, Arthur. **Bread for the World.** New York: Paulist Press; Grand Rapids, MI: Wm. B. Eerdmans, 1975. Revised 1984.

Political action by ever growing numbers of Americans seeking to end hunger is the goal of this explanation of the world hunger problem. The author is the director and one of the founders of the citizen advocacy organization by the same name. The book quickly became one of the most widely read treatments of the hunger problem for the U.S. public when it first appeared in 1975, a distinction it has never lost. Designed particularly for a religious, specifically Christian, audience, it won the national Religious Book Award for 1976. More than 300,000 copies have been published.

United Nations World Food Conference. **Assessment of the World Food Situation: Present and Future.** E/Conf.65/3. Rome: United Nations World Food Conference, 1974.

The Economic and Social Council of the United Nations (ECOSOC) prepared this report for the World Food Conference. It became the basic background document for the conference, setting out the nature and reality of the food problem and recommending action priorities. ECOSOC's data (mainly from the Food and Agriculture Organization) projected a growing "food gap" that would require developing countries to import 85 million metric tons of cereal per year by 1985 (compared with net imports of 16 million tons in the period 1969–1972). Only major changes in food production, distribution, and stockholding could prevent an even larger food gap. Developing countries especially would have to produce more food by fully developing their own potential—physical, technological, biological, and human.

United Nations World Food Council. **World Food Security for the 1980s: Report by the Executive Director.** WFC/1979/5. Rome: World Food Council, 26 April 1979.

The World Food Council was established by resolution of the 1974 World Food Conference expressly to promote food security for all nations, but security was narrowly defined in terms of national food stocks. Comprehension of food security changed greatly during the first few years of the World Food Council's work. In his tenure as the council's executive director, Maurice Williams, principal author of this document, contributed greatly to the acceptance of a broader and more pragmatic understanding of the issues involved in food security. The definition of food security in this report for the 1980 session of the World Food Council has become the accepted standard in international dialogue. It differs in important aspects from the definition assumed in the 1974 World Food Conference documents.

U.S. Department of Agriculture, Economic Research Service (USDA/ERS). **The World Food Situation and Prospects to 1985.** Foreign Agricultural Economic Report No. 98. Washington, DC: USDA, Economic Research Service, December 1974 (slightly revised March 1975).

For the decade 1974–1985, this was the major official U.S. document on the world food situation. Its first objective was to provide basic information in preparation for the 1974 World Food Conference. The second objective was to give the U.S. public a more factual perspective in the welter of conflicting and confusing views appearing on all sides. Working for more than a year, a large team of researchers in the

Department of Agriculture analyzed the major factors that influenced food production, consumption, and trade in the two decades prior to 1972. It then analyzed the problems of 1972–1974 and predicted—correctly, as it turned out—that the crisis would be temporary and not characteristic of longer trends. The study did not support apocalyptic views of the world food situation, although "substantial malnutrition will . . . persist among low-income groups in the less prosperous countries and special national and international programs will be necessary to help those most seriously threatened." The principal author was Harry Walters (on leave from the World Bank), assisted by L. Jay Atkinson, Linda Bernstein, Charles Hanrahan, and many others.

U.S. President's Science Advisory Committee. **The World Food Problem: A Report.** 3 vols. Washington, DC: The White House, May 1967.

President Lyndon B. Johnson requested this report at the height of the Bihar famine in India when public alarm about the population explosion was reaching a peak. "Food shortage" was the way the hunger problem was defined, and "technological progress" was where most of the solutions were sought. Cursory treatment was given to the questions of why people go hungry even when food is available or how socioeconomic inequity causes hunger even when natural resources are adequate. Social scientists other than agricultural economists are conspicuous by their absence from the discussion. The change in expert perception of the world hunger problem that occurred during the mid-1970s becomes striking when this culturally dated report is compared with the National Research Council's report for President Gerald Ford following the 1974 World Food Conference.

Wortman, Sterling, and Ralph W. Cummings, Jr. **To Feed This World: The Challenge and the Strategy.** Baltimore, MD: Johns Hopkins University Press, 1978.

The world food-poverty-population situation is indeed critical but not hopeless: The unfulfilled potential of small farmers throughout the developing world is the key, say these agricultural specialists from the Rockefeller Foundation. The greatest number of the world's hungry, ironically, live in rural areas capable of producing food. Many of them are farmers. If those millions of poor farm families are enabled to increase food production, the effects will reduce hunger and poverty everywhere in a vast global ripple effect. Only then will it be possible also to check population growth significantly. Empowerment of small farmers requires giving them access to technology appropriate to their actual situations, which already exists. It also requires greater economic and social justice in the countryside. These views were becoming widespread when this book appeared, but the authors' words carried special authority as a result of their many years of working on the cutting edge of agricultural research in developing countries and also with small farmers. Their message reached a very wide audience of both development specialists and the concerned public.

7

Nonprint Resources

THIS CHAPTER IS ORGANIZED IN TWO SECTIONS: computerized references and audiovisual resources for educational programs. The computerized references for research on the world hunger problem described here include databases available for online access, diskettes available for purchase by personal computer users, and a new compact disk service by OCLC (Online Computer Library Center), the worldwide network of cooperating libraries that has created an online bibliographic database of their combined library collections. The section on audiovisual resources will assist instructors and event planners in selecting and locating the right program for their particular purposes. It includes a list of audiovisual distributors with materials relevant to the world hunger problem, a bibliography of guides to audiovisual resources, and descriptions of 30 films, videocassettes, slideshows, and filmstrips on various aspects of the world hunger problem.

Computerized References

Online Databases

AGRICOLA
Agricultural OnLine Access
Producer: National Agricultural Library
              U.S. Department of Agriculture

10301 Baltimore Boulevard
Beltsville, MD 20705
Vendor: BRS
McLean, VA
(800) 289-4277

Dialog Information Services
Palo Alto, CA
(800) 334-2564

This bibliographical database on agriculture, food, nutrition, and related subjects is compiled from 6,500 journals worldwide, plus
monographs and government reports at the National Agricultural Library of the U.S. Department of Agriculture. It is updated monthly. The
database began in 1970 as CAIN; its name was changed to AGRICOLA
in 1976. It contains more than three million records and adds more
than 150,000 each year. Search aids include a list of subject headings,
user manuals, database documentation, and a thesaurus. Two subsets
of the database appear in print: (1) *National Agricultural Library Catalog,*
and (2) *Bibliography of Agriculture, Food and Nutrition Quarterly Index.*

AGRIS

International System for the Agricultural Sciences and Technology
Producer: AGRIS Coordinating Centre
Food and Agriculture Organization of the
United Nations (FAO)
Via delle Terme di Caracalla
00100 Rome, Italy
Vendor: Dialog Information Services
Palo Alto, CA
(800) 334-2564

This bibliographic database on agriculture, food, and related topics is
compiled through a cooperative system of more than 100 national and
multinational agricultural research and experimentation centers. It is
updated monthly. Coverage begins with 1975. The database contains
approximately 1.5 million records and is adding 110,000 per year. A
printed version is titled *Agrindex.*

CAB Abstracts

WAERSA (World Agricultural Economics and
Rural Sociology Abstracts)
RDA (Rural Development Abstracts)
Producer: Commonwealth Agricultural Bureaux (CAB)
United Kingdom

In North America contact:
CAB International

845 North Park Avenue
Tucson, AZ 85719

Vendor: BRS
McLean, VA
(800) 289-4277

Dialog Information Services
Palo Alto, CA
(800) 334-2564

The entire cumulative bibliographical database of the *CAB Abstracts,* going back to 1973, contains more than two million entries. *WAERSA* is the data subset that relates particularly to the world hunger problem. *WAERSA* monitors 1,080 journals and adds appoximately 7,500 entries each year. It is updated monthly. *RDA* is a data subset of *WAERSA.* It monitors 180 journals and many working papers from various research institutes around the world. *RDA* is updated quarterly and adds approximately 3,000 entries each year.

CIDS
Computerized Information Delivery Service
Producer: Office of Information
U.S. Department of Agriculture (USDA)
Washington, DC 20250
Vendor: Martin Marietta Data Systems
Computing Services
4795 Meadow Wood Lane
Chantilly, VA 22021
(703) 802-5136

This is a database of reports from all divisions of USDA. Economic Research Service data includes "Situation and Outlook" summaries on food aid needs, wheat and rice production, U.S. foreign agricultural trade, world agriculture, Chinese agriculture, and the agriculture of developing economies, as well as the full text and tables from the last three reports. The Foreign Agriculture Service provides reports on the world grain situation and outlook and also offers summaries from GEDES (Global Economic Data Exchange System), the daily economic reports prepared by agricultural attachés in U.S. embassies abroad.

Enviroline
Producer: EIC/Intelligence, Inc.
New York
Vendor: Dialog Information Services
Palo Alto, CA
(800) 334-2564

Topics in all areas of environmental concern are monitored in 3,500 journals for the entries in this bibliographical database. Approximately 7,000 entries are added annually. The database is updated ten times during the year.

OECD DAC Financial Flows to Developing Countries

Producer: I. P. Sharp Associates
2 First Canadian Place, Suite 1900
Toronto, Ontario M5X 1E3
Canada

Organization for Economic Cooperation and
Development (OECD)
2 rue André-Pascal
75775 Paris 16
France

Vendor: I. P. Sharp Associates
Toronto, Ontario

This is a statistical database of financial aid to developing countries (grants, loans on concessionary terms, and food aid) coming from national governments and multilateral agencies. Coverage begins with 1968 and is updated annually by the Development Assistance Committee (DAC) of the OECD. A printed version is published annually as *Development Cooperation* (popularly called "the DAC Report").

PAIS International

Producer: Public Affairs Information Service
New York

Vendor: BRS
McLean, VA
(800) 289-4277

DataStar (North American representative of
Radio Suisse)
Wayne, PA
(800) 221-7754

Dialog Information Services
(fees assume institutional subscribers such as
libraries rather than individuals)
Palo Alto, CA
(800) 334-2564

This international bibliographical index emphasizes current social, economic, and political issues and the making and evaluating of public policy. The citations combine those printed in the *PAIS Bulletin* and the

PAIS Foreign Language Index. The online database is more variously indexed and has additional notes similar to abstracts. Non-English entries begin with 1972; English-language entries begin with 1976. Citations include journal articles, government reports and documents, monographs and books, conference proceedings, newspaper articles, private agency reports, directories, and statistical reports.

Popline

Population Information Online

Producer: Four university programs compile this database in cooperation with the National Library of Medicine of the National Institutes of Health in the U.S. Department of Health and Human Services. The university programs are:

The Johns Hopkins University
Population Information Program
527 St. Paul Place
Baltimore, MD 21202

Columbia University
Library/Information Program
Center for Population and Family Health
60 Haven Avenue
New York, NY 10032

Princeton University
Office of Population Research
21 Prospect Avenue
Princeton, NJ 08540

University of North Carolina at Chapel Hill
Carolina Population Center
University Square 300A
Chapel Hill, NC 27514

Vendor: MEDLARS
National Library of Medicine
Lister Hill Center, Room 4N-404
8600 Rockville Pike
Bethesda, MD 20894
(800) 638-8480

For institutions and researchers with access to MEDLARS, manager of 30 databases for the National Library of Medicine, this database provides bibliographic citations and abstracts to the worldwide literature on population and family planning, demography, censuses, vital statistics, and related health, law, and policy issues.

Social Sciences Index

Producer: H. W. Wilson Co.
              950 University Avenue
              Bronx, NY 10452
Vendor: Wilsonline
              (fees assume institutional subscribers such as
              libraries rather than individuals)
              Bronx, NY
              (800) 367-6770

Since February 1984, this bibliographic database has indexed articles and book reviews in 307 English-language periodicals in the social sciences. The database is updated twice a week. Anthropology, economics, environmental sciences, geography, international relations, sociology, and women's studies are among the areas included.

Diskettes for Personal Computers

Floppy disks for use on PCs by individual researchers are available from two major centers of research on world food and development topics: the U.S. Department of Agriculture and the World Bank.

U.S. Department of Agriculture, Economic Research Service (ERS). **Africa Grain Supply & Utilization,** etc. (see below). ERS-NASS, P.O. Box 1608, Rockville, MD 20849-1608. Toll-free telephone: (800) 999-6779.

System specifications: Double-sided, double-density 5.25 DOS–compatible diskettes.

Most research reports by ERS are now produced in both print and nonprint forms. Listed below are some representative diskettes useful for world hunger research. A list of currently available diskettes will be sent from the order department on request.

> *Africa Grain Supply & Utilization.* October 1986. Four disks. $55. Catalog number 86002.
>
> *Asia/Near East Agricultural Trade.* February 1989. Three disks. $45. Catalog number 89012.
>
> *Chinese Agricultural Statistics.* October 1989. Five disks. $65. Catalog number 88001.
>
> From the series *World Agriculture Trends and Indicators* (updated semi-annually):
>
> *Caribbean.* June 1989. Two disks. $35. Catalog number 89024C.

Central America. June 1989. Two disks. $35. Catalog number 89024B.

East Asia & People's Republic of China. June 1989. Two disks. $35. Catalog number 89024K.

North Africa & Middle East. June 1989. Four disks. $55. Catalog number 89024H.

Oceania. June 1989. Two disks. $35. Catalog number 89024L.

South America. June 1989. Three disks. $45. Catalog number 89024D.

South Asia. June 1989. Two disks. $35. Catalog number 89024I.

Southeast Asia. June 1989. Two disks. $35. Catalog number 89024J.

Sub-Saharan Africa. June 1989. Eight disks. $95. Catalog number 89024G.

World Bank. **World Development Indicators 1989.** World Bank Publications, Order Fulfillment Operations, 1818 H Street, NW, Washington, DC 20433. Orders may be placed also by telephone: (201) 225-2165. Seven diskettes. $95. Catalog number IB1126.

System specifications: Double-sided, double-density 5.25 diskettes for PCs with MS-DOS release 2.0 or higher. Available in two formats: .WKS format for use with Lotus 1-2-3 (release 1a or higher) and .PRN format for use with software that cannot read a worksheet file.

The World Bank produces a new set of tables of world development indicators each year with the most comprehensive and current data available on social and economic development in 120 countries. These 32 tables of statistics are available in print as appendixes of the *World Development Report* issued that year and also on a corresponding set of diskettes.

OCLC Agriculture Series on Compact Disk

OCLC's compact disk bibliographic service is called Search CD450. Both system specifications and fee structure assume institutional purchasers such as libraries rather than individuals.

Three of the specialized bibliographic databases available on CD-ROM through this service are referred to collectively as the OCLC Agriculture Series. These are useful for world hunger bibliographic searches and are described individually below. They may be ordered from OCLC, 6565 Frantz Road, Dublin, OH 43017-0702, (614) 764-6000.

System specifications: Users must have either the IBM-PC XT or PC AT, a PC compatible with at least 640K RAM, or the OCLC M300XT or M310 Workstation; a hard disk drive or hard card; and a compact disk drive (by Philips, Hitachi, Sony, or Amdek).

AGRICOLA and CRIS Databases 1983 to Present. Three CD-ROM disks, updated quarterly. $695; OCLC member price $595. Product code #6350.

AGRICOLA is the U.S. Department of Agriculture (USDA) bibliographical database from the National Agricultural Library and its cooperating institutions. Coverage of topics is worldwide. CRIS, produced by USDA's Cooperative Research Service, cites abstracts and progress reports for current research pertaining only to the United States. Both USDA databases are combined in this CD-ROM series. Approximately 100,000 new records are added every year.

AGRICOLA Retrospective File 1979–1982. One CD-ROM disk. $350; OCLC member price $300. Product code #6352.

This single CD-ROM includes AGRICOLA entries for the four years prior to the combined AGRICOLA/CRIS CD-ROM database described above.

Agriculture Library. One CD-ROM disk, updated annually. $350; OCLC member price $300. Product code #6354.

The more than 300,000 entries in this bibliographical database are drawn from the OCLC Online Union Catalog, the world's largest online bibliographical reference. OCLC's Agriculture Library includes books, journals, theses, microforms, filmstrips, videocassettes, recordings, and more. Coverage emphasizes the twentieth century but goes back as far as the sixteenth century. Agricultural economics, natural resource management, and rural sociology are among the topics related to the world hunger problem.

Audiovisual Resources, Distributors, and Guides

This section is in three parts: Audiovisuals on World Hunger, Audiovisual Distributors, and Guides to Audiovisuals.

A great variety of films, videocassettes, filmstrips, and slideshows on topics related to world hunger are available from a large number of sources. Most such material is intended for general audiences with limited expertise. Those described here are only a representative sample. Each distributor listed has useful material and will provide a descriptive catalog of its collection on request.

The Church World Service (CWS) Audiovisual Library and the Mennonite Central Committee (MCC) Resource Library lend audiovisuals at no charge except the cost of shipping. Many of the following resources are included in these unusually large and diverse collections. That fact is indicated, however, only when an item is no longer available from its original distributor.

All university media centers have audiovisuals pertinent to the world hunger problem. Three with particularly noteworthy material are included in this list of distributors. All university media centers are covered by the *Educational Film & Video Locator;* this indispensable guide is included in the "Guides to Audiovisuals" section at the end of the chapter.

Audiovisuals on World Hunger

Addresses for distributors in the list of distributors that follows this section are not repeated here.

A World Hungry. A five-part series: (1) *You May Have Heard,* (2) *How Hunger Happens,* (3) *Plans for Justice,* (4) *Personal Responses,* and (5) *More Personal Responses.*
Type:	Filmstrips (5) with audiocassettes; VHS videocassette
Length:	Filmstrips, 10 min. each; videocassette, 51 min.
Date:	1976
Cost:	Purchase $154 (set of 5 filmstrips), $103 (video)
Source:	Franciscan Communications
	1229 S. Santee Street
	Los Angeles, CA 90015

This classic from the time of the world food crisis of 1972–1974 is still useful. C. D. Freudenberger, an agronomist and theologian with years of experience in Africa, describes major causes of hunger—political, environmental, economic, and social. He then suggests a variety of ways concerned Americans can help the hungry end their own hunger.

The Big Village
Type:	16mm color film
Length:	25 min.
Date:	c. 1982
Cost:	Purchase $395
Source:	Barr Films

This United Nations film by Mohebbur Rahman Khair, a producer-director from Bangladesh, is a visual essay on how people in developing nations see the world and on how they view those residents of the "Big Village" who live in the industrialized countries. The hunger problem is placed here in the context of rising levels of expectations among people who now know there are alternatives to hunger.

Bottle Babies

Type: 16mm color film
Length: 30 min.
Date: 1975
Cost: Rental $20
Source: American Baptist Films

Deaths from malnutrition soared among Third World infants in the 1960s and 1970s as more and more mothers in poor families switched from breast feeding to bottle feeding. Outspoken pediatricians and other observers blamed marketing strategies by infant formula manufacturers. The problem in Kenya is shown by German filmmaker Peter Krieg in this early film on the topic, which became a classic in Europe and North America. The film's influence helped to launch an international consumer campaign against infant formula manufacturers in which the Nestlé boycott eventually involved most major faith groups in the United States.

The Business of Hunger

Type: 16mm color film; VHS videocassette
Length: 28 min.
Date: 1985
Cost: Purchase $325 (film), $19.95 (video); rental $5 (video)
Source: West Glen Films or Maryknoll World Productions

This film has been adapted for Maryknoll World Productions from *Hungry for Profit* (see below). Comments from Archbishop Dom Helder Camara of Brazil and a bishop in the Philippines have been added. The topic is agribusiness expansion in developing countries. The argument is that the methods of agribusiness produce greater harm than good for the hungry of these countries. Examples are shown from the Philippines, the Sahel region of Africa, Brazil, and the Dominican Republic. An hour shorter than the original, this version is less informative and more polemical.

Consuming Hunger. A three-part series: *Getting the Story, Shaping the Image,* and *Selling the Feeling.*
Type: VHS videocassettes
Length: 29 min. each

Date: 1987
Cost: Purchase $50 (set of three), $19.95 each
Source: West Glen Films or Maryknoll World Productions

This extraordinary series by Maryknoll World Productions looks at U.S. popular understanding of hunger issues. What are the consequences when television is the principal instrument used by the public at large to respond to world events and problems? *Getting the Story* shows how the 1985 tragedy in Ethiopia evolved from just another famine to become the most moving news story of the decade. *Shaping the Image* asks why messages from media celebrities (as in Live Aid or Hands Across America) have more effect than messages from Africans or our own poor. *Selling the Feeling* examines the deliberate elimination of the political aspects of problems in the way such media events present these problems.

Edge of Survival
Type: 16mm color film
Length: 60 min.
Date: 1981
Cost: Rental free
Source: Mennonite Central Committee (no longer available
               from the original distributor, Wharton International
               Films of Madison, CT)

This film examines various agricultural development projects, asking how appropriate the technology is to the needs of the local people and what effect that technology will have on the land over the long run. Some projects successfully produce more food in ways that offer hope for people living on the edge of survival. The producer is Wharton International.

Exploding the Hunger Myths
Type: Slideshow with audiocassette; filmstrip with
               audiocassette; VHS videocassette
Length: 20 min.
Date: 1987
Cost: Purchase $100 (slideshow), $50 (filmstrip), $30 (video)
Source: Institute for Food and Development Policy
               145 Ninth Street
               San Francisco, CA 94103

This is an updated version of the thesis in the audiovisual program *Food First* (see below), with more attention paid to the politics of hunger in cases such as Central America and the Philippines. Viewers are encouraged to become politically active to change U.S. policies that prevent the hungry from ending their own poverty.

Famine and Chronic, Persistent Hunger: A Life and Death Distinction

Type:	VHS videocassette
Length:	11 min.
Date:	1989
Cost:	Free
Source:	The Hunger Project
	1388 Sutter Street
	San Francisco, CA 94109-5452

The message here is that chronic undernutrition accounts for 90 percent of hunger's death toll, while famine, despite its drama, accounts for only 10 percent. Therefore, actions to end hunger must concentrate on persistent, chronic undernutrition rather than on famine relief. Audiences whose information has come from television alone (see *Consuming Hunger,* above) need to hear what world hunger specialists have been saying for more than 20 years. Graphs, maps, photography, and an emotive soundtrack drive home the point repeatedly. A discussion guide and lesson plan for high school classes comes with the video.

Firewood: The Other Energy Crisis

Type:	16mm color film; VHS videocassette
Length:	15 min.
Date:	1984
Cost:	Purchase $225 (film), $175 (video)
Source:	Dick Young Productions
	118 Riverside Drive
	New York, NY 10025

Connections between deforestation and increased hunger are illustrated in South Asia, a story that also applies in other regions. Many people face the tragic dilemma that their need for one necessity, fuel for cooking and heating, is destroying the land that has to produce their food. The film was produced for the United Nations Environment Programme by Dick Young Productions.

Food First

Type:	Slideshow with audiocassette; filmstrip with audiocassette
Length:	30 min.
Date:	1980
Cost:	Purchase $80 (slideshow), $30 (filmstrip)
Source:	Institute for Food and Development Policy
	145 Ninth Street
	San Francisco, CA 94103

Like the book upon which it is based, this program dispels the myth of food scarcity. The main cause of hunger, it argues, is lack of control by the poor over food-producing resources.

The Forgotten Farmers: Women and Food Security

Type: VHS videocassette
Length: 28 min.
Date: 1985
Cost: Free
Source: FAO Radio and TV Section, Rome (also available from the MCC Resource Library)

The unrecognized importance of women as agricultural producers is the topic of this video by the Food and Agriculture Organization of the U.N. Filming was done in Africa, the Middle East, Southeast Asia, and Latin America. It is a good companion piece for *What Rights Has a Woman,* another FAO production (see below).

Fragile Harvest

Type: 16mm color film; VHS videocassette
Length: 50 min.
Date: 1986
Cost: Purchase $800 (film), $525 (video); rental $110 (film), $80 (video)
Source: Bullfrog Films (in the United States)
Kensington Communications (in Canada)
490 Adelaide Street West, Suite 304
Toronto, Ottawa M5V 1T2
Canada

Modern biotechnology is producing profound changes in the genetic structure of many foods, changes that are already being translated into marketable technology. Both the world's food supply and millions of small farmers in developing countries are going to be affected by these innovations, for better or worse. This prize-winning documentary features Pat Mooney, an internationally known specialist in the world hunger problem and seed research. It was produced by Kensington Communications for a Canadian Broadcasting Corporation science program, "The Nature of Things." A 30-minute version titled *Seeds* is also available especially for schools and nonprofit educational programs.

Guess Who's Coming to Breakfast

Type: Slideshow with audiocassette
Length: 20 min.
Date: 1976
Cost: Rental $15 for nonprofit organizations, $20 for schools and colleges
Source: American Friends Service Committee

Many controversial and interrelated messages are given in this worst-case scenario of multinational corporate control over agricultural resources and wages in a poor developing country and over the living conditions of workers' families—here, the corporation is Gulf & Western in the Dominican Republic. Connections between multinational investments and world hunger were much discussed in the 1970s as part of a larger debate regarding the effects of the international economic order on development progress. The problems have not vanished, although, for many reasons, the debate has waned. This vintage 1970s shocker poses more questions than it answers, even more so than its producers may have intended. In spite of that (or because of it), this is an effective educational tool within the context of a more thorough examination of the problems portrayed.

Hunger Hotline
Hunger Hotline Revisited: Global Food Crisis

Type:	Filmstrips with audiocassettes
Length:	*Hunger Hotline,* 12 min.; *Hunger Hotline Revisited,* 18 min.
Date:	1982; 1984
Cost:	Purchase $15 each
Source:	Church World Service

In both filmstrips, the naive host of a television talkshow interviews an expert on the world hunger problem. First, a church overseas assistance worker (white male), who has just returned from Asia, lays out the many interrelated factors behind hunger. In *Hunger Hotline Revisited,* a high school social studies teacher (black female), who has written a book, tells how she understands the hunger issue and how her students have become deeply involved. Factual content is sophisticated but sparse. The main agenda is to stimulate the viewer to seek more understanding and to become involved in action.

Hungry for Profit

Type:	16mm color film; VHS videocassette
Length:	86 min.
Date:	1985
Cost:	Purchase $1,195 (film), $695 (video); rental $120 (film), $75 (video)
Source:	Richter Productions
	330 West 42nd Street
	New York, NY 10036

This critical examination of the role of multinational agribusiness firms in developing countries packs a tremendous amount of information into every minute—too much, probably, for viewers who are not already well informed to absorb and process fairly. (Being able to read the script would help greatly.) Unlike *The Business of Hunger* (the shortened version—see above), *Hungry for Profit* does not end by condemning cash crops or production for export. Rather, it looks at examples in Kenya and Mexico where conventional agribusiness methods of production for export have been modified to benefit and protect small farmers, apparently with success. The viewer must wait for the second half of the show, however, to encounter the less stereotypically critical material.

Maragoli

Type:	16mm color film
Length:	58 min.
Date:	c. 1980
Cost:	Rental $32
Source:	University of California Extension Media Center

This film was produced as part of a doctoral thesis on the population problem in Kenya (which has one of the highest growth rates in the world) and its relationship to land distribution and rural development. Filmed interviews with local people by the Ph.D. candidate, a Kenyan, are combined with understated narration. The perspective of the development specialist is contrasted subtly but tellingly with the views of people involved in the problem, most of whom are becoming rapidly poorer and hungrier while a few grow more prosperous.

On the Edge of the Forest

Type:	16mm color film; VHS videocassette
Length:	32 min.
Date:	1978
Cost:	Purchase $450 (film), $115 (video); rental $50 (video)
Source:	Bullfrog Films

E. F. Schumacher talks directly to the viewer about the essential ecology of forests, topsoil, and all human existence in this award-winning film photographed in western Australia. The deeper message here is characteristic of the British economist considered by many to be one of the most important thinkers of the century: Economic behavior is justified and is truly sane only when it supports and respects human life. This is what makes Schumacher part of the debate on ending hunger.

The Politics of Food. A five-part series: (1) *A Question of Aid*, (2) *The Food Machine*, (3) *The Hunger Business*, (4) *The Avoidable Famine*, and (5) *Sharing the Land*.

Type:	VHS videocassettes
Length:	28 min. each
Date:	1987
Cost:	Purchase $950 (set of 5 videos), $195 each
Source:	Journal Films (in the United States)
	930 Pitner Avenue
	Evanston, IL 60202

CBC Enterprises (in Canada)
Educational Sales
Box 500 Station A
Toronto, Ontario M5W 1E6

Yorkshire Television in the United Kingdom produced this series to examine the cycle of poverty and famine and point to ways for poor nations to become self-sufficient. Part 1 contrasts hunger in Bangladesh with self-sufficiency in the Indian state of Kerala. Part 2 questions the relevance of North American agricultural technology as a solution for hunger. Part 3 questions the role of food aid. Part 4 uses Sudan as a case study of hunger growing worse because of inappropriate technology. Part 5 uses Brazil's experience to illustrate hunger made worse by inappropriate (trickle-down) economic development.

Roots of Rebellion: Land and Hunger in Central America
Type: Slideshow with audiocassette
Length: 12 min.
Date: 1986
Cost: Purchase $75 for institutions, $50 for individuals;
             rental $25 institutions only
Source: The Resource Center
             Box 4506
             Albuquerque, NM 87196

Clear and useful background information is provided on the historical relationship between land ownership, land use, the distribution of wealth, and the desperate poverty of rural populations in Central America. The logic falters when production of crops for export is named as the cause of hunger. More to the point are the issues of who decides what is grown and how it is used, who reaps the benefits, and why.

Sharing Global Resources
Type: Slideshow with audiocassette
Length: 35 min.
Date: c. 1977
Cost: Rental $15 for nonprofit organizations,
             $20 for schools and colleges
Source: American Friends Service Committee

This program, produced by NARMIC (National Action Research on the Military-Industrial Complex), is an exceptionally lucid, short description of obstacles to development progress for poor people and poor nations that are inherent in the present international economic order. Demands raised in the United Nations by developing countries calling for a "new international economic order" (NIEO) coincided with the food crisis of 1972–1974. These demands became part of the debate over how to end hunger. The problems remain, although the NIEO is now considered a dead issue politically.

What Rights Has a Woman

Type:	16mm color film; VHS videocassette
Length:	40 min.
Date:	1985
Cost:	Free loan for one month
Source:	World Food Programme (an FAO production)

The subtitle is "The Role of Women in Rural Development." Problems of rural women are examined in Africa, Asia, and Latin America. Although details differ from region to region, the universal observation is made that economic and social discrimination against women holds back development progress for both the women and their countries. This is a good companion piece for *The Forgotten Farmers* (see above).

When the Almsgiving Stops

Type:	Slideshow with audiocassette; filmstrip with audiocassette
Length:	22 min.
Date:	c. 1979
Cost:	Rental free
Source:	Mennonite Central Committee (no longer available from the original distributor, Key Light Productions of Oakland, CA)

The title is a literal translation of the Bengali term for famine. Bangladesh illustrates some common causes of hunger that occur needlessly in countries with rich agricultural potential. For example, the rights to productive resources typically are poorly distributed and the resources often are underdeveloped. Social, economic, and political reforms are essential to end hunger. Key Light Productions created this program for the Presidential Commission on World Hunger.

Audiovisual Distributors

American Baptist Films
Valley Forge, PA 19481

American Friends Service Committee (AFSC) Film Library
2161 Massachusetts Avenue
Cambridge, MA 02140

Specializes in peace and justice issues affecting developing countries.

Barr Films
P.O. Box 5667
Pasadena, CA 91107

Bullfrog Films
Oley, PA 19547

Emphasizes sustainability and social justice in topics about environment, agriculture, development and global issues, and other topics in science and social studies.

CBC Enterprises (Canadian Broadcasting Corporation)
Educational Sales
Box 500 Station A
Toronto, Ontario M5W 1E6
Canada

Church World Service (CWS)
Audio-Visual Library
P.O. Box 968
Elkhart, IN 46515

Free loan policy.

Development Education Center (DEC) Films
229 College Street
Toronto, Ontario M5T 1R4
Canada

EcuFilm
810 12th Avenue South
Nashville, TN 37203

Ecumenical distributor of audiovisuals for religious audiences.

Food and Agriculture Organization of the United Nations (FAO)
Radio and TV Section, Information Division
Via delle Terme di Caracalla
00100 Rome
Italy

Indiana University Audio-Visual Center
Bloomington, IN 47405

International Development Education Resource Association (IDERA)
2524 Cypress Street
Vancouver, British Columbia V6J 3N2
Canada

The *IDERA Film Catalog* costs $2.

International Fund for Agricultural Development (IFAD)
Information & Communications Division
107 Via del Serafico
00142 Rome
Italy
Tel. 011-39-6-54591
FAX 5043463

Maryknoll World Productions
Media Relations
Maryknoll, NY 10545

Specializes in videocassettes for global awareness with a social and economic justice emphasis.

Mennonite Central Committee (MCC)
Resource Library
12th Street
Akron, PA 17501-0500

MCC Canada
134 Plaza Drive
Winnipeg, Manitoba R3T 5K9
Canada

Both MCC offices have a free loan policy.

National Film Board of Canada
P.O. Box 6100
Montreal, Quebec H3C 3H5
Canada

1251 Avenue of the Americas, 16th Floor
New York, NY 10020

National Public Radio (NPR)
Cassette Publishing
2025 M Street, NW
Washington, DC 20036

Audiocassettes only.

Oxfam America
302 Columbus Avenue
Boston, MA 02116

Third World Newsreel
160 Fifth Avenue
New York, NY 10011

United Nations Children's Fund (UNICEF)
Division of Information and Public Affairs
Radio/TV/Film Unit
UNICEF House
3 United Nations Plaza
New York, NY 10017

United Nations Development Programme (UNDP)
Division of Information
United Nations, DC 1, Room 1928
New York, NY 10017

University of California
Extension Media Center
Berkeley, CA 94720

University of Illinois Film Center
1325 South Oak Street
Champaign, IL 61820

West Glen Films
1430 Broadway
New York, NY 10018

World Bank
Film and Video Unit
1818 H Street, NW
Washington, DC 20433

World Food Programme
Public Affairs and Information Branch
Via delle Terme di Caracalla
00100 Rome
Italy
Tel. 011-39-6/5797-6377

All WFP films are color 16mm films. They can be obtained for a free one-month loan by writing to Rome.

Guides to Audiovisuals

Africa Studies Center. **Africa on Film and Videotape 1960–1981.** East Lansing, MI: Africa Studies Center, 100 International Center, Michigan State University, East Lansing, MI 48824-1035. 1982. 551p. $17.95 (reduced price) plus postage ($2 in the United States).

Each item is described in detail and its appropriate audience is indicated. The 75-page index is organized by title, topic, region, country, and more. A revised, updated edition is in preparation.

Consortium of College and University Media Centers and R. R. Bowker. **Educational Film & Video Locator.** 4th ed. 2 vols. New York: R. R. Bowker, 1990. 3,260p. $166.25. ISBN 0-8352-2624-7.

This reference covers audiovisuals available for rent from the media collections of 46 colleges and universities. Items are indexed by subject, title, and audience level. Among the major subject areas useful for locating world hunger material are Africa, Asia, geography, home economics, and social sciences.

Facets Multimedia, Inc. **Human Rights Film Guide.** Chicago: Facets Multimedia, 1517 West Fullerton Avenue, Chicago, IL 60614. 1987. 100p. $7.50.

The right to food is one of the human rights topics included here. The 400 films and videos described in this guide are available in the United States for rent or free loan. Items are cross-indexed by subject, region, and country.

Hoeffel, Paul, ed. **Guide to Third World Movie Resources.** New York: Development Forum, P.O. Box 5850, GCPO, New York, NY 10163-5850. 1989. 15p. photocopy. Free.

The editor of *Development Forum* (the news journal sponsored by the United Nations) has created this helpful guide to films about development produced in both developing and industrialized nations.

Media Network. **Guide to Films on Apartheid and Southern Africa.** New York: Media Network, 121 Fulton Street, 5th Floor, New York, NY 10038. 12p. $3.

This is a directory of 40 recommended films on apartheid, anti-apartheid resistance, South Africa, Namibia, Angola, Mozambique, and Zimbabwe.

——. **Guide to Films on Central America.** New York: Media Network, 121 Fulton Street, 5th Floor, New York, NY 10038. 24p. $4.

Descriptions are given of 40 selected films, videocassettes, and slideshows on the culture and conflicts in Central America. This guide also lists low-cost film libraries and speakers' bureaus.

Glossary

absolute poverty A World Bank term used in the 1970s to mean a level of income too low to supply an adequate amount of any of life's material necessities.

ACC/SCN United Nations Administrative Committee on Coordination, Subcommittee on Nutrition. (ACC also has a Taskforce on Rural Development.)

ADF African Development Foundation, a U.S. official development agency channeling aid funds directly to community-based and grassroots development projects initiated and managed by local people.

adult literacy rate The percent of people 15 and over who can read and write. Male literacy rates tend to be much higher in developing countries than female literacy rates. It tells more about a country's level of development to disaggregate adult literacy rates into male literacy and female literacy. Female literacy correlates positively with lower rates of infant mortality, maternal fertility, and population growth.

agrarian reform Policies to increase rural economic and social equity by greatly improving the access of poor and disadvantaged groups to productive resources such as land, water, credit, improved seeds, fertilizer, training, roads, and market opportunities. Agrarian reform usually includes but is more comprehensive than land reform.

A.I.D. United States Agency for International Development, major official development assistance agency of the U.S. government. Internationally known as USAID. Counterpart agencies in DAC countries (see below) include CIDA (Canada), DANIDA (Denmark), NORAD (Norway), and others.

balance-of-payments A summary statement of all the economic transactions between one country and the rest of the world in a given period, usually one year. A negative balance means that a country paid out more than it received (for example, if imports had higher value than exports). If a negative balance continues too long, a country will face rising indebtedness and a foreign exchange crisis; it will cease to be able to import goods and services.

basal metabolism rate (BMR) Basal metabolism is the amount of internal energy required by any organism to keep itself alive. BMR is measured as the heat emanating through a person's skin while he/she is awake and at complete rest in a warm place "in a fasting state," usually 12 to 18 hours after eating. BMR is expressed in kilocalories per hour. The minimum dietary energy required to prevent undernutrition is expressed as a multiple of BMR (e.g., 1.2 BMR or 1.4 BMR).

basic human needs (BHN) A strategy for development progress that emphasizes the health and welfare of the poor, including adequate food and nutrition, safe and accessible water, fuel for cooking and heating, sound shelter, primary education, primary health care, and so on. The BHN perspective was popularized in the 1970s by the World Bank under Director Robert McNamara, the ILO, and other organizations to counteract the worsening poverty that accompanied the "trickle down" policies (see below) in vogue everywhere in the 1950s and 1960s. BHN places greater emphasis on investment in the development of human resources than on development of natural resources as the foundation of economic and social progress.

basic indicators Social and economic facts about a country expressed in statistics and assumed to indicate a country's level of development in relationship to other countries. GNP, IMR, adult literacy rate, and life expectancy are among the measurable conditions often used as basic indicators.

bilateral assistance Development assistance transacted between two governments (the donor country and the recipient country).

BOSTID Board on Science and Technology for International Development of the National Research Council, an independent, nongovernmental scientific organization in the United States.

Brandt Commission Popularly named after its chairman, Willy Brandt, former chancellor of the Federal Republic of Germany, this is officially the Independent Commission on International Development Issues, established in 1977 at the urging of Robert McNamara, then director of the World Bank.

Brundtland Commission World Commission on Environment and Development, established by the U.N. General Assembly in 1983 under Mrs. Gro Harlem Brundtland, who later became prime minister of Norway.

calorie A unit of measure of the energy value of food. A "large calorie," or kilocalorie, is the amount of heat needed to raise the temperature of one kilogram of water by one degree centigrade.

CARE (also written C.A.R.E.) Cooperative for American Relief Everywhere, Inc., a U.S. PVO (see below) with international affiliates; a major distributor of P.L. 480 project food aid. At CARE's founding immediately following World War II, the acronym stood for Cooperative for American Remittances to Europe.

cash cropping Raising crops for sale in the market rather than for family consumption; the opposite of subsistence farming. Cash cropping usually implies producing for export, but the term also can apply to producing for a domestic market.

Catholic Relief Services (CRS) A U.S. PVO (see below); major distributor of P.L. 480 project food aid and Catholic contributions for grassroots development overseas.

CCC U.S. Commodity Credit Corporation; provides loans for purchase of agricultural commodities on the U.S. market including funding to purchase P.L. 480 food aid.

cereal grains/coarse grains An international trade distinction: "cereal grains" are produced exclusively for human consumption (e.g., wheat and rice), while "coarse grains" are produced also for animal consumption (e.g., sorghum, oats, maize, millet). Botanically, all grains are cereals, and all are eaten by people somewhere in the world.

CGIAR Consultative Group on International Agricultural Research. Supports CIAT (Centro Internacional de Agricultura Tropical), CIMMYT (Centro Internacional de Mejoramiento de Maiz y Trigo, or International Center for Improvement of Maize and Wheat), CIP (Centro Internacional de la Papa, or International Potato Center), IBPGR (International Board for Plant Genetic Resources), ICARDA (International Center for Agricultural Research in the Dry Areas), ICRISAT (International Crops Research Institute for the Semi-Arid Tropics), IFPRI (International Food Policy Research Institute), IITA (International Institute of Tropical Agriculture), ILCA (International Livestock Center for Africa), ILRAD (International Laboratory for Research on Animal Diseases), IRRI (International Rice Research Institute), ISNAR (International Service for National Agricultural Research), and WARDA (West African Rice Development Association).

Church World Service (CWS) A U.S. PVO (see below) and the overseas development assistance agency of the National Council of Churches.

CILSS Comité Inter-Etats pour la Lutte contre la Sécheresse au Sahel (Interstate Committee for Drought Control in the Sahel), formed by the nations of Burkina Faso, Cape Verde, Chad, Gambia, Mali, Mauritania, Niger, and Senegal in 1973.

Club du Sahel   A collaborative association of the CILSS and the OECD for the purpose of achieving long-range food self-reliance in the Sahel region of Africa, formed in 1976.

concessional loans   Loans made on easier terms of credit than are available through normal commercial banks. Concessional terms usually include no or very little interest, a long time in which to repay, often a grace period of several years before repayment must begin, and sometimes agreement to accept repayment in the borrowing country's own currency rather than in U.S. or Canadian dollars, Japanese yen, British pounds, French francs, or West German marks.

debt service ratio   The percentage of a country's export earnings that must be used to repay old loans; an important measurement of the seriousness of a national government's foreign debt to banks, businesses, and governments of other countries.

developed countries   Countries in which industry provides the highest share of gross domestic product and in which national averages on basic indicators are high. *Developed countries, more developed countries, industrialized countries, high-income countries,* and *the North* are roughly interchangeable terms. (The term *First World* is no longer used for the OECD capitalist countries, nor is *Second World* used for the U.S.S.R. and other centrally planned industrial countries.)

developing countries   Countries with relatively low national averages on the basic indicators and relatively high proportions of gross domestic product derived from agriculture rather than industry and from export of raw materials rather than finished goods. Most developing countries have recently emerged from generations of foreign domination as colonies of European countries or the United States. *Developing countries, less developed countries, underdeveloped countries, Third World,* and *the South* are generally interchangeable terms. *Low-income countries* refers to only some of the developing countries. The World Bank classifies developing countries as "low-income countries," "lower middle-income countries," and "upper middle-income countries."

Development Assistance Committee (DAC)   Committee of donor country members of the OECD (there are currently 18 committee members). Its purposes are to secure an expansion of the total amount of financial resources made available to developing countries for nonmilitary economic and social development and to improve the effectiveness of such assistance.

dietary energy supply (DES)   The total food energy available for human consumption in a country's national food supplies, as estimated according to the food balance sheet (see below), stated in kilocalories (kcals).

donor country A country that makes grants or concessional loans to developing countries.

dwarf varieties Term applied to short-stalked HYV rice and wheat, varieties genetically developed by IRRI and CIMMYT to enable plants to utilize higher levels of fertilizer and produce higher yields of grain without the plants toppling over ("lodging") before harvest.

ECA U.N. Economic Commission for Africa.

ECLA U.N. Economic Commission for Latin America and the Caribbean.

ECOSOC Economic and Social Council of the United Nations, the major administrative division of the U.N. for policies and actions pertaining to human welfare.

effective demand Consumer demand supported by purchasing power; the effective demand for food is demand by definition of economic power in the marketplace, not by definition of nutritional need or the promptings of hunger.

ERS Economic Research Service, U.S. Department of Agriculture.

ESCAP U.N. Economic and Social Commission for Asia and the Pacific.

FAO Food and Agriculture Organization of the United Nations.

farming systems research (FSR) Research on the way a farm (rather than a single crop) functions in a particular ecological and social environment as a system. System variables include the interaction among various crops, interaction between crops and animals, and the interrelationship between various objectives served by the decisions of the farm household or farm operator.

FAS Foreign Agriculture Service, U.S. Department of Agriculture.

fertility rate The average number of children that each woman in a country would bear if she were to live to the end of her child-bearing years and bear children at each age in accordance with prevailing fertility rates in that country.

Food Aid Convention An agreement negotiated between food surplus countries first in 1971 and since periodically revised; stipulates minimum annual pledges for the quantity of food aid to be made available by the countries signing the convention and establishes other standards affecting food aid operations.

food balance sheets A method of estimating the total per capita food supply in a country by comparing the quantity of domestic food production that is left after exports and the amount to be used for purposes other than direct human consumption (such as feed for livestock, seeds to be planted for the next crop, methanol, alcohol, etc.). What remains is the food balance, from which it is possible to calculate per capita dietary energy supply (DES).

food-deficit countries Countries that must import grain to meet either the market demand or the nutritional requirement for food; only low-income food-deficit countries (below $1,040 per capita GNP by 1989 standards) are of concern, because of their difficulty in paying for imports.

Food First Alternate name for the Institute for Food and Development Policy; also the title of the institute's first major publication.

Food for Peace An alternative name for the P.L. 480 food aid program, a name that was popularized in the U.S. during the 1960s but is seldom used now except by USAID.

food for work A form of food aid in which food provided by a donor is distributed to very poor, unemployed people in exchange for their labor on a public project.

food security In current usage, food security means a condition in which all people at all times have access to enough food for an active and healthy life. At the 1974 World Food Conference, *food security* referred to whether or not sufficient wheat or rice was available to countries from trade, domestic agriculture, or food aid.

Food Security Wheat Reserve A U.S. government-owned grain reserve of 4 million tons of wheat established by Congress in 1980 to ensure a minimum quantity of wheat would be available for food aid regardless of the market price.

foreign aid An all-encompassing term for material and technical assistance provided on grant or concessional terms from one nation to others; it includes assistance for military and strategic objectives as well as for economic, social, and humanitarian purposes and is not, therefore, synonymous with the term *development assistance*.

G-77, Group of 77 U.N. term for the political caucus of developing countries that call themselves "the Non-Aligned Countries," meaning countries belonging to alliances of neither the United States nor the

USSR. The actual number of countries in the G-77 has nearly doubled but the original term is still used.

GIEWS Global Information and Early Warning System, food crisis–preventing project of the Food and Agriculture Organization of the U.N.

grain reserves Stocks of grain held intentionally by governments or a multilateral agency to be available as a buffer against food scarcity.

Green Revolution A term coined and popularized by news media in the late 1960s to describe the dramatic production success in Asia of HYV rice developed at IRRI; now the term is applied broadly to any scientifically developed method of agriculture intended to increase harvests of food staples in developing countries by utilizing HYV strains with optimal applications of fertilizer, water, insecticides, and methods of planting and cultivation.

gross domestic product (GDP) An expression of the total value of the output of goods and services produced by an economy in their final use. The value in U.S. dollars is obtained by converting from domestic currencies at the official exchange rate. GDP does not include income sent into a country by its citizens living abroad. The definitions used in analyzing GDP are established by the latest edition of the U.N. *System of National Accounts*.

gross national product (GNP) The dollar value of a country's final output of goods and services in a year, including income residents receive from abroad for labor and capital less similar payments made to nonresidents who contributed to the domestic economy. Reflects the value of a country's economic activity and the income of its residents; does *not* reflect the distribution of income and wealth among the residents.

high-income economies World Bank category for countries with per capita GNP of $6,000 or more. Six in this group are classified still as developing countries by the U.N. and by their own governments: Hong Kong, Israel, Kuwait, Saudi Arabia, Singapore, and United Arab Emirates.

high-yielding variety (HYV) A term applied primarily to rice and wheat varieties genetically developed at IRRI and CIMMYT to increase the yield per hectare of these crops in developing countries; the term can be applied also to new strains that similarly increase the yield of any staple food substantially, but so far success of such a magnitude has occurred only with rice and wheat.

The Hunger Project   A U.S. NGO (see below) based in San Francisco and New York with branches in other countries.

IAF   Inter-American Foundation, U.S. agency for official development aid for Latin America channeled directly to local organizations and communities.

IARC   Acronym for international agricultural research center, referring especially to centers in the CGIAR system.

IBRD   International Bank for Reconstruction and Development (official name of the World Bank).

IDA   International Development Association, administered by the World Bank to channel highly concessionary financing to the poorest countries, currently those with per capita GNP (in 1987 dollars) of $580 or less.

IDRC   International Development Research Centre, funded by the Canadian government.

IEFR   International Emergency Food Reserve of the U.N., administered by the World Food Programme.

IFAD   International Fund for Agricultural Development, a U.N. specialized agency created after the 1974 World Food Conference to assist only small farmers and the rural poor.

IFDP   Institute for Food and Development Policy, a U.S. NGO (see below) sometimes called Food First.

IFPRI   International Food Policy Research Institute, a U.S. think tank that became part of the CGIAR system.

ILO   Acronym for both the International Labour Office and its sponsor, the International Labour Organization, a U.N. specialized agency that, having been founded in 1919, predates the U.N. itself.

IMF Cereal Facility   A special credit program within the International Monetary Fund created in 1981 to help low-income food-deficit countries pay for essential food imports.

INCAP   Institute of Nutrition for Central America and Panama, a pioneer in research on child nutrition in developing countries.

infant mortality rate (IMR)   The annual number of deaths of infants under one year of age per 1,000 live births, a partial but sensitive indicator of general levels of health and nutrition in developing countries.

informal sector   Economic activity at the micro-enterprise level operating outside the economic mainstream, usually without government regulation. A major sector for employment of the poor.

INSTRAW Institute for Training and Research for the Advancement of Women, a U.N. specialized agency. Among other achievements, a catalyst for reforms to create gender-specific basic indicators (see above) in demographic research and the definitions in the U.N.'s *National System of Accounts.*

InterAction American Council for International Voluntary Action, an association of U.S. NGOs—primarily PVOs—concerned with economic and social development (see NGO and PVO, below).

IWC International Wheat Council, an independent multilateral organization of major wheat exporting and importing countries; provides framework for negotiating provisions relating to international wheat trade.

labor force in agriculture A demographic statistic showing the percentage of economically active people in a country who work in agriculture, forestry, hunting, and fishing above a given age (sometimes set as low as ten years).

land reform Governmental redistribution of access to agricultural land. Typically, land reform reduces the largest holdings, increases the size of farms for the smallest farmers, expands the number of landowners, and gives greater protection to tenant farmers. Land reform usually, but not always, sets an upper limit (ceiling) on the amount of land any one person may own.

least developed countries (LDCs) Sometimes referred to as less developed countries. U.N. term for developing countries with three characteristics: (1) per capita gross domestic product (GDP) under $500; (2) manufacturing share of total GDP 10 percent or less; (3) adult literacy rate 20 percent or less. Forty-two countries were so characterized in 1989: Haiti in the Western Hemisphere; Kiribati, Samoa, Tuvalu, and Vanuatu in Oceania; Bangladesh, Bhutan, Burma, Laos, Maldives, and Nepal in Asia; Afghanistan and Yemen in the Near East; Benin, Botswana, Burkina Faso, Burundi, Cape Verde, Central African Republic, Chad, Comoros, Djibouti, Equatorial Guinea, Ethiopia, Gambia, Guinea, Guinea-Bissau, Lesotho, Malawi, Mali, Mauritania, Mozambique, Niger, Rwanda, São Tome and Principe, Sierra Leone, Somalia, Sudan, Togo, Uganda, and Tanzania in sub-Saharan Africa.

life expectancy The number of years a newborn infant would be likely to live if patterns of mortality prevailing for all people in the country at the time of its birth were to stay the same throughout its life.

low birth weight Below 2,500 grams, usually a result of malnutrition of the mother during pregnancy. Low birth weight reduces an infant's chances of survival or normal health and growth.

low-income country   U.N. and UNCTAD category of developing countries with per capita GDP from $500 to $1,500 (based on 1980 data).

macroeconomics   Economic forces and analysis at the national and international levels.

malnutrition   Malnutrition occurs when a diet contains too little or too much of one or more essential nutrients: proteins; vitamins; minerals; and calories from fats, starches, and sugars (all three sources are considered nutritionally important). Clinical malnutrition refers to malnutrition that has gone on long enough to produce physical symptoms of hampered growth and development or ill health.

market economies   Countries that rely on voluntary exchanges of goods and services through the market as a primary method to regulate investments and production decisions, in contrast to centrally planned economies.

maternal-child health (MCH)   Health care programs for infants, young children, and pregnant or nursing mothers. Nutrition monitoring and special aids to nutrition (nutrition intervention) are important components of MCH.

MDB   Multilateral development bank, generic term for banks owned jointly by a group of governments for the purpose of making loans for economic and social development in developing countries—e.g., the World Bank, AfDB (African Development Bank), ADB (Asian Development Bank), CDB (Caribbean Development Bank), IDB (Inter-American Development Bank), and others.

microeconomics   Economic forces and analysis at the level of households and local communities.

micro-enterprise   Very small economic venture—e.g., farm producing little marketable surplus, cottage industry, street-vending, "backyard" manufacturing or repair shop—owned and managed by one entrepreneur employing fewer than five people.

middle-income countries   U.N. and UNCTAD category for developing countries with per capita GDP above $1,500 (based on 1980 data).

multilateral assistance   Development assistance channeled through international organizations.

NIEO   New international economic order, a collective term applied to a package of reforms in international economic practices that was proposed in the early 1970s by the G-77 to reduce existing inequities in the international economic system between developed and developing countries and to accelerate the national economic development progress of developing countries. The NIEO campaign focused on commodity pricing, the nature and quantity of capital flows to and from developing countries, technology transfer, and similar matters.

Non-Governmental Liaison Service (NGLS) An office within ECOSOC (with one branch in New York and another in Geneva) to further cooperation between the U.N. and NGOs (see below).

nongovernmental organization (NGO) Term originating in ECOSOC, now used worldwide for any independent, not-for-profit association formed for educational, scientific, or humanitarian purposes, especially to promote human welfare or the welfare of disadvantaged groups. NGO is a broader and more inclusive term than PVO (see PVO, below), but in the United States the two terms often are used interchangeably.

North Collective term for the industrialized countries, most of which are located at present in the Northern Hemisphere; synonym for the developed countries as a group.

nutritionally at risk, nutritionally vulnerable Synonymous terms applied to population groups whose health is particularly subject to damage from poor nutrition—infants, small children, pregnant and nursing mothers, the ill, and the elderly; sometimes adolescents are included in this category.

OECD Organization for Economic Cooperation and Development, an independent multilateral organization of industrial market economies based in Paris.

official development assistance (ODA) Term created by the DAC (see above) to refer to publicly financed capital provided to developing countries as grants or concessional loans with at least a 25 percent grant element compared with normal commercial loans; by definition, ODA must be used to promote economic and social development.

OPEC Organization of Petroleum Exporting Countries (all members of OPEC are developing countries).

Overseas Development Council (ODC) An independent think tank and NGO in the United States.

Oxfam British private, voluntary, development assistance agency that originated in the Oxford Famine Relief Committee of World War II. Oxfam-America is its counterpart in the United States.

paddy Rice before the husk has been removed. Also refers to an irrigated or flooded field in which rice is grown.

PAG Protein-Calorie Advisory Group for the U.N.; replaced in 1977 by the ACC/SCN (above).

physical quality of life index (PQLI) A concept developed by ODC in the late 1970s as an alternative to GNP for measuring development progress. PQLI uses adult literacy, life expectancy, and infant mortality to arrive at a relative scale from least developed to most developed countries (see also basic indicators, above).

P.L. 480 Shortened term for Public Law 83-480, the legislation originating with the 83rd Congress that established and, as amended, continues to regulate U.S. food aid programs; also called Food for Peace.

population density The number of people living within a specific area of land (usually stated as people per hectare).

population growth rate The increase in a country's population during a certain period of time (usually one year), expressed as a percentage of the population at the start of the period. Natural population increase is found by subtracting the number of deaths from the number of births. A national (in contrast to world) population growth rate reflects natural increase, immigration, and emigration.

primary commodities An economic term referring to raw materials for industrial processes and unprocessed products of agriculture, mining, lumbering, and fishing. The foreign trade of developing countries suffers from dependence on the export of primary commodities alone, usually a very limited range of primary commodities.

primary health care (PHC) Programs of preventive health at the community level, including nutrition monitoring of infants, nutrition education, family planning, sanitation, and immunization.

private voluntary organization (PVO) USAID term for independent, not-for-profit organizations formed for the purpose of providing relief or development assistance overseas. (PVOs are also NGOs, but not all NGOs are PVOs.)

project food aid Food aid provided as a grant for a particular project to aid a particular population, e.g., maternal and child feeding, food for the poorest of the poor paid as wages for public work, food for refugees, etc. All WFP food aid and aid under Title II of P.L. 480 is project food aid, whereas food sold to a government on concessional terms is nonproject food aid. The primary international user of project food aid is the WFP, and the major U.S. users are PVOs such as CARE and CRS.

protein-energy-malnutrition (PEM) A term for the most common form of serious malnutrition in children, in which both calories and protein are deficient in the diet.

Sahel A semi-arid region stretching across the continent of Africa immediately south of the Sahara Desert. The term is associated especially with five Sahelian countries stretching west of Sudan to the Atlantic Ocean—Chad, Niger, Mali, Burkina Faso, and Mauritania.

South Collective term for the developing countries, most of which are located in the Southern Hemisphere. Increasingly used in preference to *Third World* because of the lack of hierarchical connotation.

stunting Low height-for-age, less than 77 percent approximately of the median height-for-age indicated for a given population by the United States National Center for Health Statistics. If not genetic, stunting indicates chronic PEM (see above) during childhood.

Third World Collective U.N. term for all developing countries. The preferred U.N. term now is *the South.*

trickle-down Development strategy emphasizing investment in modern industry and capital-intensive infrastructure improvements as a means to promote rapid economic growth "at the top" of a society, among the elite, from which the benefits are expected to "trickle down" throughout the society as jobs, income, and improved living standards for all. Contrasts with development "from below," that is, investment in economic activity that directly reduces poverty and increases the self-reliance of the poor. Also contrasts with BHN (see above).

UNCTAD United Nations Conference on Trade and Development, a permanent agency formed in 1964 to accelerate economic development in developing countries through improved foreign trade relations, especially *vis a vis* developed countries.

under-five mortality rate Annual number of deaths of children under five years of age per 1,000 live births. A basic indicator of the level of nutrition and health in a developing country (see basic indicators, above).

undernutrition A serious form of malnutrition in which food energy (calories) is critically lacking from eating too little food of any kind and the body begins to waste away; in extreme form, undernutrition becomes starvation. Stunting, wasting, and weight-for-age are standard methods for diagnosing undernutrition.

UNDP United Nations Development Programme, the central U.N.

agency for marshalling and coordinating technical assistance for developing countries.

UNDRO   United Nations Disaster Relief Organization; coordinates relief efforts of all branches and agencies of the United Nations.

UNEP   United Nations Environment Programme.

UNFPA   United Nations Population Fund (formerly U.N. Fund for Population Activities).

UNHCR   United Nations High Commissioner for Refugees. This term applies to both the commissioner and the commissioner's office (as an agency).

UNICEF   United Nations Children's Fund (originally United Nations International Child Emergency Fund).

UNIFEM   United Nations Development Fund for Women (originally United Nations Voluntary Fund for Women).

UNPAAERD   U.N. Programme of Assistance for African Economic Recovery and Development, mandated by the General Assembly Special Session on the African Emergency in 1986.

USAID   International acronym for the U.S. Agency for International Development (see also A.I.D., above).

USDA   U.S. Department of Agriculture.

wasting   Low weight-for-height, specifically less than 77 percent of the median weight-for-height of a particular population as defined by the United States National Center for Health Statistics, a sign of acute, current undernourishment.

WCARRD   World Conference on Agrarian Reform and Rural Development, the last big U.N. conference of the 1970s, hosted by FAO in 1979.

weight-for-age   The standard criterion of adequate or inadequate consumption of calories and protein for infants and children too young to be diagnosed by weight-for-height. Mild or moderate undernutrition means between 60 percent and 80 percent of desirable weight-for-age; severe undernutrition is anything less than 60 percent.

WHES   World Hunger Education Service, a U.S. NGO.

WHO   World Health Organization, a U.N. specialized agency.

women in development (WID)   A term commonly used in the description of programs, policies, and research focused on the economic and social roles and status of women in developing countries.

World Food Council (WFC)   High-level agency of the U.N. established in 1975 to monitor and promote progress toward the prevention and elimination of hunger and food insecurity, specifically to monitor and coordinate national and international fulfillment of the recommendations of the World Food Conference of 1974.

World Food Programme (WFP)   Food aid agency of the U.N. and FAO.

World Hunger Year (WHY)   A U.S. NGO.

World Soil Charter   A framework for agricultural policy and planning adopted by the FAO Conference in 1981 and recommended to all national governments to protect the world's soils from further erosion and loss of fertility and to promote soil reclamation wherever possible.

Index